Fodor's

CITYGUIDE
WASHINGTON
DISTRICT OF COLUMBIA

2ND EDITION

FODOR'S TRAVEL PUBLICATIONS

NEW YORK • TORONTO • LONDON • SYDNEY • AUCKLAND

WWW.FODORS.COM

STREETFINDER

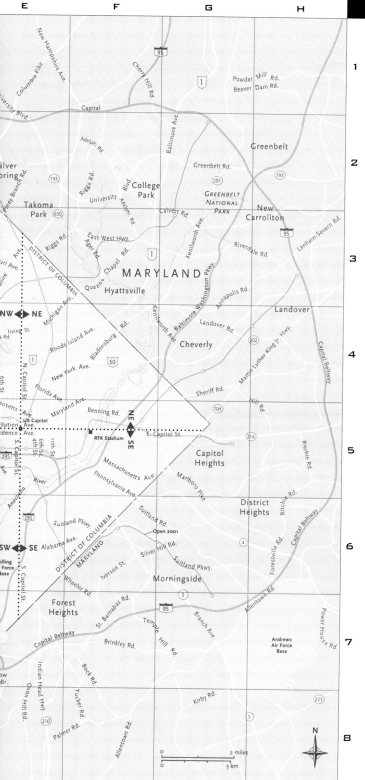

WASHINGTON, D.C., OVERVIEW

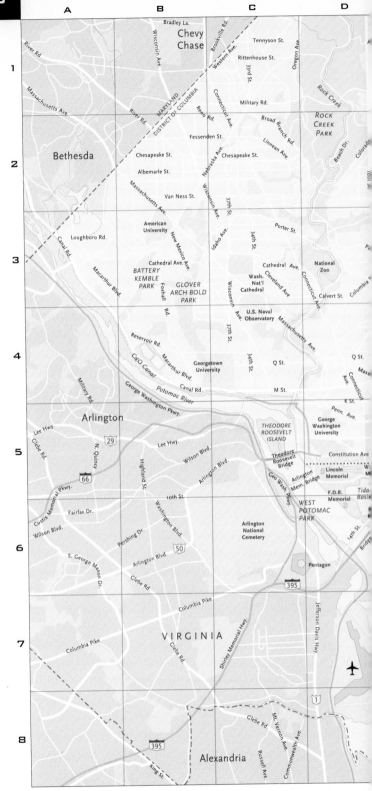

A B C D

1

2

3

4

5

6

7

8

Bradley La.

Chevy Chase

Brookville Rd.

Tennyson St.

Western Ave.

Rittenhouse St.

33rd St.

Oregon Ave.

Wisconsin Ave.

Rock Creek

River Rd.

Military Rd.

Reno Rd.

Connecticut Ave.

Massachusetts Ave.

MARYLAND

DISTRICT OF COLUMBIA

River Rd.

ROCK CREEK PARK

Broad Branch Rd.

Beach Dr.

Fessenden St.

Linnean Ave.

Colorado

Bethesda

Chesapeake St.

Nebraska Ave.

Chesapeake St.

Albemarle St.

Massachusetts Ave.

Van Ness St.

Wisconsin Ave.

37th St.

American University

New Mexico Ave.

Idaho Ave.

34th St.

Porter St.

Loughboro Rd.

Cathedral Ave.

BATTERY KEMBLE PARK

Foxhall Rd.

Cathedral Ave.

Cleveland Ave.

National Zoo

Macarthur Blvd.

GLOVER ARCH BOLD PARK

Wisconsin

Wash. Nat'l Cathedral

Connecticut Ave.

Canal Rd.

Calvert St.

Columbia

Reservoir Rd.

37th St.

U.S. Naval Observatory

Massachusetts Ave.

P

Macarthur Blvd.

C&O Canal

Georgetown University

34th St.

Q St.

Q St.

Mass

George Washington Pkwy.

Potomac River

Canal Rd.

M St.

Connecticut Ave.

Military Rd.

K St.

Penn. Ave.

Arlington

Lee Hwy.

Lee Hwy.

THEODORE ROOSEVELT ISLAND

George Washington University

Glebe Rd.

N Quincy

29

Wilson Blvd.

Theodore Roosevelt Bridge

Constitution Ave.

W

Highland St.

Arlington Blvd.

Geo Wash. Pkwy.

Arlington Mem. Bridge

Lincoln Memorial

66

Washington Blvd.

10th St.

F.D.R. Memorial

Tida Basi

Custis Memorial Pkwy.

Fairfax Dr.

WEST POTOMAC PARK

Wilson Blvd.

Pershing Dr.

50

Arlington National Cemetery

14th St.

S. George Mason Dr.

Arlington Blvd.

Bridg

Clebe Rd.

Columbia Pike

Pentagon

395

Columbia Pike

Glebe Rd.

VIRGINIA

Shirley Memorial Hwy.

Jefferson Davis Hwy.

Columbia Pike

1

395

Glebe Rd.

Mt. Vernon Ave.

King St.

Russell Rd.

Commonwealth Ave.

Alexandria

STREETFINDER

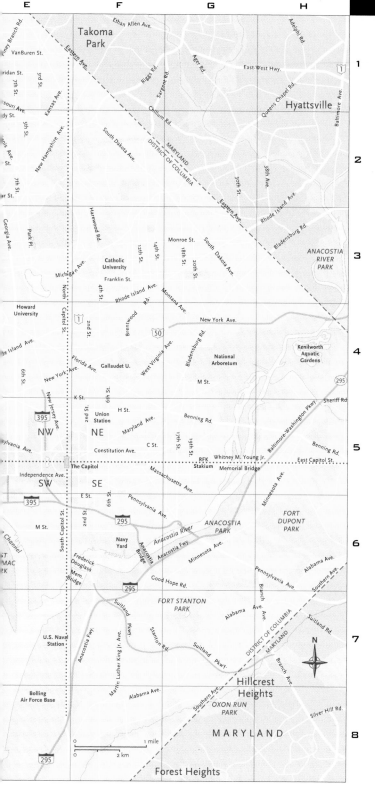

WASHINGTON, D.C.

	A	B	C	D

1

Brandywine St.
38th St.
Appleton St.
36th St.
Connecticut Ave.
Gates Rd.
31st St.
Brandywine St.
30th St.
Linnean Ave.
29th St.
Albemarle St.
Albemarle St.
Alton Pl.
Reno Rd.

Audubon Ter.
Yuma St.
Windom Pl.
SOAPSTONE VALLEY PARK
Windom Pl.

2

38th St.
37th St.
Warren St.
35th St.
UNIVERSITY of the DISTRICT of COLUMBIA
Connecticut Ave.
Veazey St.
Van Ness St.
Howard Univ Law School
Veazey St.
Van Ness St.

3

Upton St.
Tilden St.
HEARST REC. CENTER
Springland La.
Wisconsin Ave.
Sedgewick St.
Rodman St.
Rowland Pl.
Quebec St.
Upton St.
29th St.
Tilden St.
MELVIN HAZIN PARK

4

Quebec St.
Porter St.
35th St.
34th St.
Quebec St.
Porter St.
Porter St.
30th St.
Connecticut Ave.
29th St.
Quebec
Porter
Idaho Ave.
Ordway St.
Norton Pl.
36th St.
34th Pl.
Highland Pl.
Ashley Terr.
27th
Newark St.

5

N
38th St.
Macomb St.
35th St.
34th St.
33rd St.
Macomb St.
CLEVELAND PARK
Lowell St.
Woodley St.
31st St.

6

Washington Cathedral
Klingle Rd.
Klingle Rd.
Devonshire Pl.
Cortland Pl.
Cathedral Ave.
Cathedral Ave.
Garfield St.
33rd Pl.
Cleveland Ave.
31st St.
Garfield Terr.
29th St.
28th St.
Massachusetts Ave.
Wisconsin Ave.
35th Pl.
34th Pl.
34th St.
33rd St.
Wood

7

Fulton St.
36th Pl.
36th St.
35th Pl.
Fulton St.
31st St.
31st Pl.
Woodland Dr.
29th Pl.
Edmunds St.
Observatory Circle
Davis St.
Normanstone Terr.
Normanstone Dr.
29th St.
McGill Terr.

8

Calvert St.
GUY MASON RECREATION CENTER
Naval Observatory
NORMANSTONE PARKWAY
Edgevale Terr.
ock
Tunlaw Rd.
37th St.
Observatory La.
Massachusetts Ave.
30th St.
Benton Pl.
Observatory Pl.
Hall Pl.
W. Pl.

0 — 1200 feet
0 — 400 meters

STREETFINDER

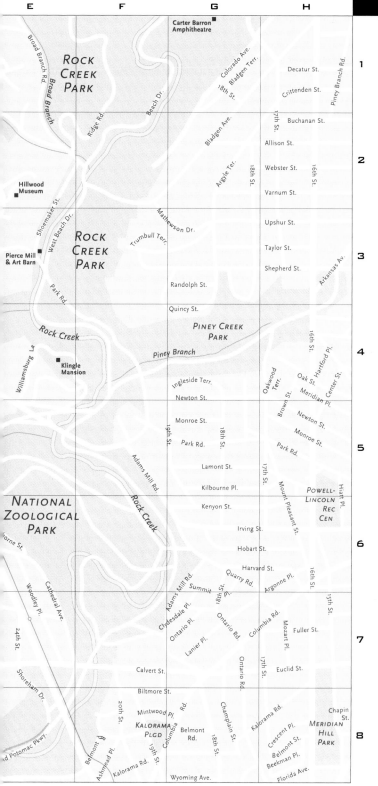

E F G H

1

Carter Barron
Amphitheatre

ROCK
CREEK
PARK

Broad Branch Rd.

Broad Branch

Ridge Rd.

Beach Dr.

Colorado Ave.

Bladgen Terr.

18th St.

Decatur St.

Crittenden St.

Piney Branch Rd.

2

Bladgen Ave.

Argyle Terr.

18th St.

17th St.

Buchanan St.

Allison St.

Webster St.

Varnum St.

16th St.

Hillwood
Museum

Shoemaker St.

West Beach Dr.

Mathewson Dr.

Trumbull Terr.

Upshur St.

Taylor St.

Shepherd St.

Arkansas Ave.

3

ROCK
CREEK
PARK

Pierce Mill
& Art Barn

Park Rd.

Randolph St.

Quincy St.

Rock Creek

PINEY CREEK
PARK

16th St.

4

Williamsburg La.

Klingle
Mansion

Piney Branch

Ingleside Terr.

Newton St.

Oakwood
Terr.

Brown St.

Oak St.

Hartford Pl.

Center St.

Meridian Pl.

Newton St.

Monroe St.

5

19th St.

Monroe St.

Park Rd.

18th St.

Lamont St.

Kilbourne Pl.

17th St.

Park Rd.

Adams Mill Rd.

Rock Creek

Kenyon St.

Mount Pleasant St.

POWELL-
LINCOLN
REC
CEN

Hiatt Pl.

6

NATIONAL
ZOOLOGICAL
PARK

...horne St.

Irving St.

Hobart St.

Harvard St.

Quarry Rd.

Argonne Pl.

16th St.

7

Woodley Pl.

Cathedral Ave.

24th St.

Shoreham Dr.

Adams Mill Rd.

Summit

Clydesdale Pl.

Ontario Pl.

Lanier Pl.

18th St.

Ontario Rd.

Columbia Rd.

Ontario Rd.

17th St.

15th St.

Mozart Pl.

Fuller St.

Euclid St.

Calvert St.

8

...d Potomac Pkwy.

Belmont Pl.

Ashmead Pl.

Kalorama Rd.

Biltmore St.

20th St.

Mintwood
Pl.

KALORAMA
PLGD

19th St.

Columbia Rd.

Belmont
Rd.

18th St.

Champlain St.

Wyoming Ave.

Kalorama Rd.

Crescent Pl.

Belmont St.

Beekman Pl.

Florida Ave.

Chapin
St.

MERIDIAN
HILL
PARK

ADAMS-MORGAN (NORTH), WOODLEY PARK, MOUNT PLEASANT

4

	A	B	C	D
1				

Emerson St.

Georgia Ave.

Illinois Ave.

Emerson St.

Decatur St.

14th St.

Sherman Circle

Decatur St.

Crittenden St.

Buchanan St.

13th St.

Iowa Ave.

9th St.

7th St.

Buchanan St.

Allison St.

Arkansas Ave.

Allison St.

Webster St.

Webster St.

4th St.

Varnum St.

Varnum St.

Grant Circle

Upshur St.

8th St.

5th St.

Illinois Ave.

N

Kansas Ave.

Georgia Ave.

Irving St.

New Hampshire Ave.

Quincy St.

Spring Rd.

Quebec Pl.

9th St.

Rock Creek Church Rd.

Perry Pl.

Quebec Pl.

Pershing Dr.

Parkwood Pl.

11th St.

10th St.

Princeton Pl.

Otis Pl.

Otis Pl.

Oak St.

Newton Pl.

Newton Pl.

Newton St.

Park Rd.

Park Rd.

Newton St.

Warder St.

Park Pl.

Newton St.

Monroe St.

Morton St.

29

New Hampshire Ave.

Kenyon St.

Irving St.

Kenyon St.

Kenyon St.

Irving St.

Irving St.

Columbia Rd.

Michigan Ave.

Columbia Rd.

13th St.

Hobart St.

Hobart St.

Harvard St.

14th St.

Harvard St.

Girard St.

McMillan Reservoir

Fairmont St.

Howard University

Euclid St.

12th St.

11th St.

Sherman Ave.

9th St.

Georgia Ave.

Clifton St.

Clifton St.

Howard Pl.

McMilla

Chapin St.

BANNEKER RECREATION CENTER

6th St.

College St.

4th St.

Belmont St.

Belmont St.

Barry Pl.

29

Belmont St.

Florida Ave.

12th Pl.

Bryant St.

0   1200 feet

0   400 meters

W St.

W St.

STREETFINDER

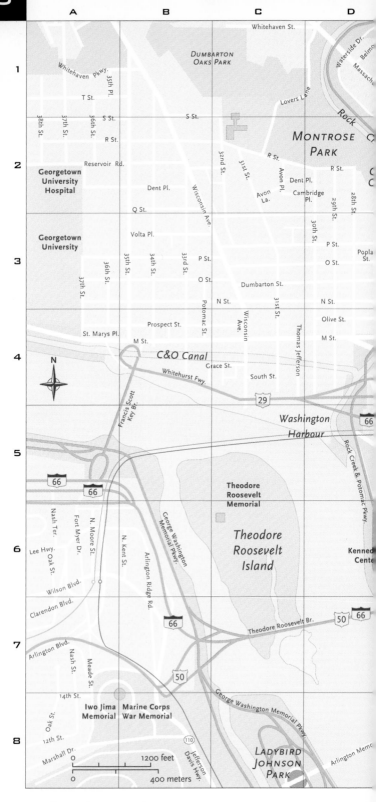

A   B   C   D

Whitehaven St.

DUMBARTON
OAKS PARK

1

Whitehaven Pkwy.   35th Pl.

Waterside Dr.

Belmo

Massache

T St.

Lovers Lane

S St.   S St.

32nd St.

R St.

Rock   *C*

38th St.   37th St.   36th St.

MONTROSE
PARK

R St.

31st St.

Avon Pl.

R St.

28th St.

29th St.

C

2

Reservoir Rd.

Georgetown
University
Hospital

Dent Pl.

Wisconsin Ave.

Dent Pl.
Avon
La.   Cambridge
Pl.

Q St.

30th St.

3

Georgetown
University

Volta Pl.

P St.

Popla
St.

O St.

36th St.

35th St.

34th St.

33rd St.

P St.

O St.

37th St.

Dumbarton St.

N St.

31st St.

N St.

Potomac St.

Prospect St.

Wisconsin
Ave.

Olive St.

St. Marys Pl.

M St.

Thomas Jefferson

M St.

4

C&O Canal

Grace St.

N

Francis Scott Key Br.

Whitehurst Fwy.

South St.

29

Washington
Harbour

66

5

66

66

Theodore
Roosevelt
Memorial

Rock Creek & Potomac Pkwy.

6

Nash Ter.

Fort Myer Dr.

N. Moore St.

N. Kent St.

George Washington Memorial Pkwy.

Arlington Ridge Rd.

Theodore
Roosevelt
Island

Kenne
Cente

Lee Hwy.

Oak St.

Wilson Blvd.

Clarendon Blvd.

50   66

7

Arlington Blvd.

Nash St.

Meade St.

66

Theodore Roosevelt Br.

50

50

14th St.

Oak St.

Iwo Jima
Memorial

Marine Corps
War Memorial

George Washington Memorial Pkwy.

8

12th St.

110

LADYBIRD
JOHNSON
PARK

Marshall Dr.

Jefferson
Davis Hwy.

Arlington Memo

0   1200 feet

0   400 meters

STREETFINDER

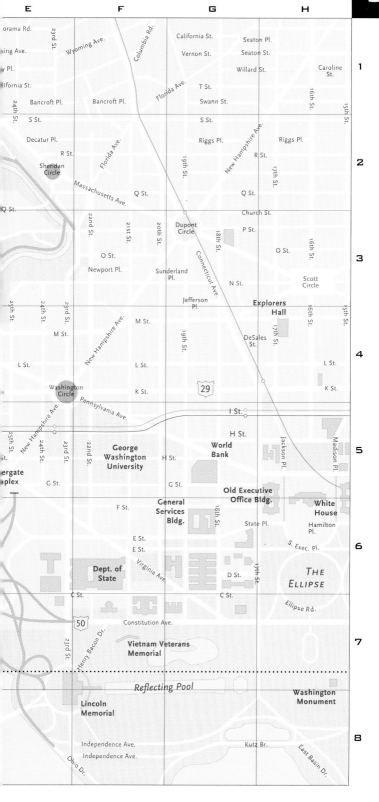

GEORGETOWN, DUPONT CIRCLE, FOGGY BOTTOM

DOWNTOWN, CAPITOL HILL

A   B   C   D

1

2

3

4

5

6

7

8

12th St. Expwy.
10th St.
9th St.
D St.
School St.
E St.
Southwest Fwy.
395
D St.
Virginia Ave.
7th St.
6th St.
4th St.
4th
Pl.
G St.
Maine Ave.
Water St.
Ohio Dr.
H St.
I St.
K St.
3rd St.
395
M St.
N St.
4th St.
J. Creek Pkwy.
EAST POTOMAC
PARK
Washington Channel
A St.
3rd Ave.
B St.
1st Ave.
2nd Ave.
4th Ave.
5th Ave.
Fort
McNair
Ohio Dr.
Ohio Dr.
Potomac
River
Hains
Point
Anaco
N
0   1200 feet
0   400 meters

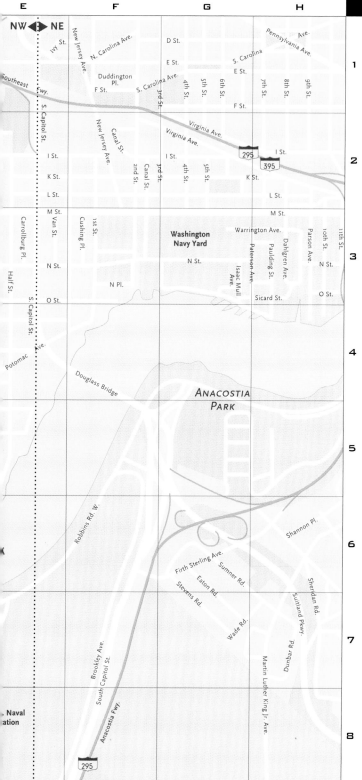

NW ⬥ NE

E   F   G   H

1

Ivy St.
New Jersey Ave.
N. Carolina Ave.
D St.
E St.
S. Carolina Ave.
E St.
Pennsylvania Ave.
Southeast
Fwy.
S. Capitol St.
Duddington Pl.
F St.
S. Carolina Ave.
3rd St.
4th St.
5th St.
6th St.
7th St.
8th St.
9th St.
F St.

2

S. Capitol St.
I St.
New Jersey Ave.
Canal St.
2nd St.
Canal St.
3rd St.
I St.
4th St.
5th St.
Virginia Ave.
Virginia Ave.
295
395
I St.
K St.
K St.
L St.
L St.

3

Carrollburg Pl.
Half St.
M Van St.
N St.
Cushing Pl.
1st St.
N Pl.
Washington Navy Yard
N St.
Warrington Ave.
Paterson Ave.
Isaac Mull Ave.
Sicard St.
Dahlgren Ave.
Paulding St.
M St.
Parson Ave.
10th St.
11th St.
N St.
O St.

4

S. Capitol St.
Potomac Ave.
Douglass Bridge

5

ANACOSTIA PARK

6

Robbins Rd. W.
Shannon Pl.
Firth Sterling Ave.
Sumner Rd.

7

Brookley Ave.
South Capitol St.
Eaton Rd.
Stevens Rd.
Wade Rd.
Sheridan Rd.
Suitland Pkwy.
Dunbar Rd.
Martin Luther King Jr. Ave.

8

Naval Station
Anacostia Fwy.
295

WATERFRONT, NAVY YARD, ANACOSTIA

A **B** **C** **D**

1

IVY HILL
CEMETERY

7

Timber Branch Pkwy.

Alexandria Ave.

Commonwealth Ave.

Newton St.

Wayne St.

Ramsey St.

Glendale Ave.

Adams St.

Spring St.

Braddock Rd.

Melrose St.

Kings Ct.

Summers
Dr.

Myrtle St.

Masonic View Ave.

Wayne St.

Janneys Lane

Junior St.

Johnston Pl.

Chapman St.

2

Skyhill Rd.

Taylor Run Pkwy.

Taylor Run Pkwy.

Putnam
Pl.

West View Terr.

Rucker Pl.

King St.

Masonic View Terr.

Oak St.

Russell Rd.

Walnut St.

Little St.

Lamond Pl.

Putnam St.

Braxton Pl.

Elm St.

Maple St.

Hilltop Terr.

Linden St.

Ave.

South View Terr.

Hillside Dr.

Rosemont

GEORGE
WASHINGTON
PARK

GEORGE
WASHINGTON
PARK

Upland Pl.

Park Rd.

Ridge La.

Cedar St.

Mount Ver

3

Taylor Run Pkwy.

Moncure Dr.

Hilton St.

Roberts La. N.

Carlisle Dr.

7

WASHINGTON
MASONIC
MEM.

George
Washington
Masonic
Nat. Mem.

Sunset Dr.

Bu

Longview Dr.

Duke St.

Alexandria Railroad Station

Dechai

Reinekers La.

Georges La.

Duke St.

4

Telegraph Rd.

Dove St.

236

Diagonal Rd.

Pershing Ave.

Stovall St.

Mill Rd.

Holland La.

5

Eisenhower Ave.

Hooffs Run Dr.

Capital Beltway

95

6

Cameron Run

7

Kings Hwy.

Huntington Ave.

1

8

241

Richmond Hwy.

Fort Hunt Rd.

E   F   G   H

le Ave.

Douglas St.

Payne St.   1st St.   Vernon St.   Powhatan St.   Portner Rd.   2nd St.   3rd St.

Braddock Pl.   1st St.   2nd St.   Royal St.   Fairfax St.

1

Madison St.   Montgomery St.   Pendleton Ave.

Wythe St.   Madison St.

Pendleton St.   Wythe St.   ORONOCO BAY PARK

2

oft Ct.   West St.   Payne St.   Fayette St.   Henry St.   Patrick St.   Alfred St.   Columbus St.   Washington St.   Pendleton St.

eyton St.   Princess St.

Queen St.   Oronoco St.   Tancil Ct.   Princess St.

Main Library ■   Brocketts Al.

Muirs Ct.   Quay St.   FOUNDERS PARK

Cameron St.   Queen St.

400   Thompsons Al.

3

King St.   Cameron St.

Emerson Al.   Ross Al.

ans Ct.   236   King St.   Ramsay Al.   Torpedo Factory Art Center ■

Swifts Al.   WATERFRONT PARK

Prince St.   Wales Al.

Strand St.

4

Duke St.

Wolfe St.

ne St.   Fayette St.   Henry St.   Old Town Rd.   Wilkes St.

Old Town Ct.

POMMANDER PARK

Gibbon

Franklin St.   Union St.   Potomac River

1   Washington St.   Franklin St.   Pommander Walk St.

5

Jefferson St.   Pommander Walk St.

Green St.   St. Asaph St.   Pitt St.   Royal St.   Fairfax St.   Lee St.   Potomac St.

Church St.   400   Green St.

Lee Ct.

6

Jones Point Rd.

Alfred St.   South St.   95   Woodrow Wilson Memorial Bridge

JONES POINT PARK   N

7

George Washington Memorial Pkwy

8

0 _____ 1200 feet

0 _____ 400 meters

ALEXANDRIA

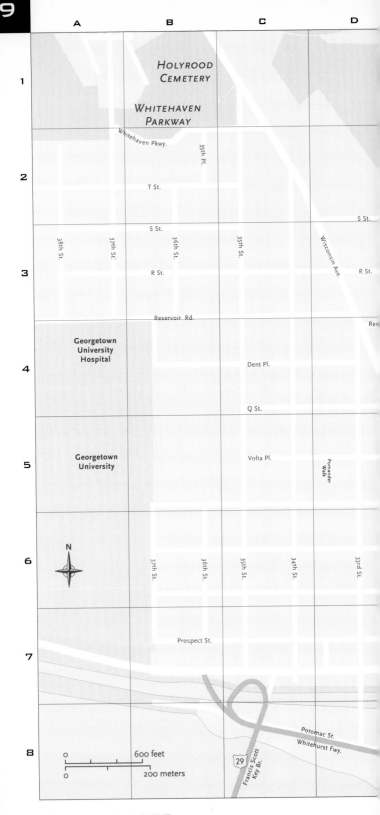

9

A   B   C   D

1

HOLYROOD CEMETERY

WHITEHAVEN PARKWAY

Whitehaven Pkwy.

35th Pl.

2

T St.

S St.

S St.

38th St.

37th St.

36th St.

35th St.

Wisconsin Ave.

3

R St.

R St.

Reservoir Rd.

Georgetown University Hospital

Dent Pl.

4

Q St.

Georgetown University

Volta Pl.

Pomander Walk

5

37th St.

36th St.

35th St.

34th St.

33rd St.

N

6

Prospect St.

7

Potomac St.

Whitehurst Fwy.

0   600 feet

0   200 meters

29

Francis Scott Key Br.

8

STREETFINDER

E   F   G   H

Whitehaven St.

MBARTON
AKS PARK

1

Waterside Dr.

Tracy Pl.

Massachusetts Ave.

2

Lovers Lane

Rock Creek & Potomac Pkwy.

MONTROSE
PARK

Rock Creek

3

OAK HILL
CEMETERY

R St.

31st St.

Avon Pl.

R St.

Dent Pl.

30th St.

29th St.

28th St.

4

Avon Ln.

Cambridge Pl.

Q St.

32nd St.

Orchard La.

Lane Keys W

5

P St.

Poplar St.

O St.

Dumbarton St.

Wisconsin Ave.

31st St.

30th St.

29th St.

28th St.

27th St.

6

N St.

Olive St.

7

M St.

Canal

ce St.

Cherry

Wisconsin Ave.

31st St.

Thomas Jefferson St.

30th St.

29th St.

8

South St.

West Al.

Copperthwaite
La.

E   F   G   H

I St.   I St.

Capital Children's Museum

H St.   H St.

G St.   G St.

1

2

3rd St.   4th St.   5th St.   6th St.   7th St.   8th St.   Pickford Pl.

Morris Pl.

F St.   F St.

Groff Ct.   Acker Pl.

3

E St.   E St.

Lexington Pl.

Massachusetts Ave.

Maryland Ave.

D St.   D St.

4

Art Bldg.

C St.   Stanton Square   C St.

Justice Ct.

Maryland Ave.

N

5

Constitution Ave.

Frederick Douglass Ct.

Massachusetts Ave.

Terrace Ct.   Millers Ct.   A St.

6

NE

SE

Folger Shakespeare Library

A St.   A St.

John Adams Bldg.

Library Ct.   4th St.   5th St.   6th St.   7th St.

North Carolina Ave.

7

Independence Ave.

8th St.

3rd St.   Seward Ave.

Eastern Market

Seward Square   C St.   C St.

8

0   600 feet

0   200 meters

Seward Ave.   Pennsylvania Ave.

Folger Square

CAPITOL HILL

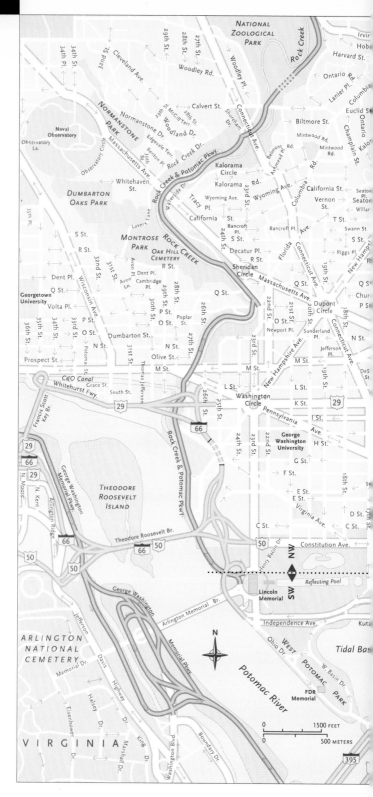

DRIVING AND PARKING

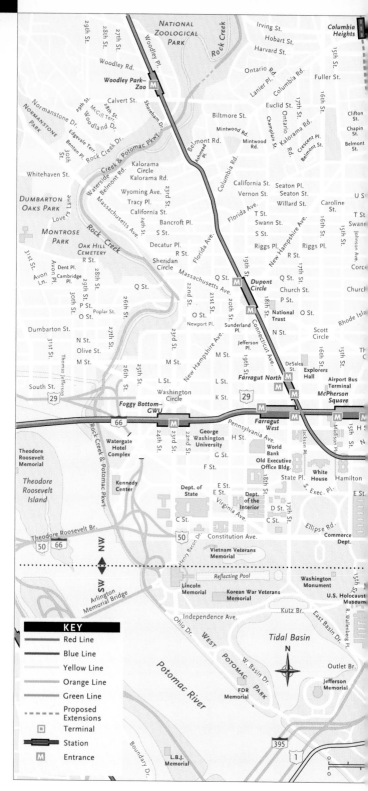

METRORAIL

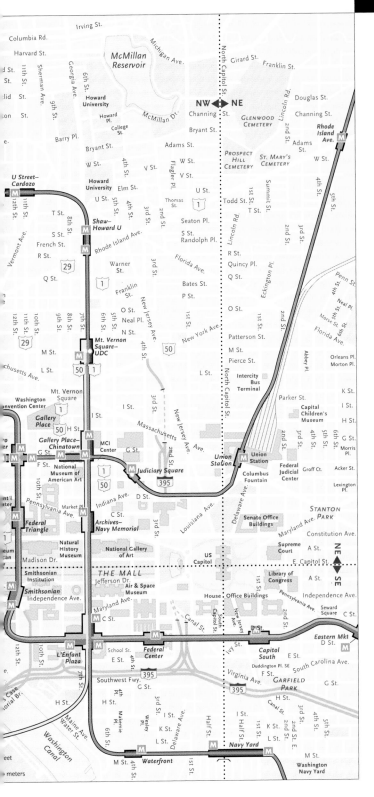

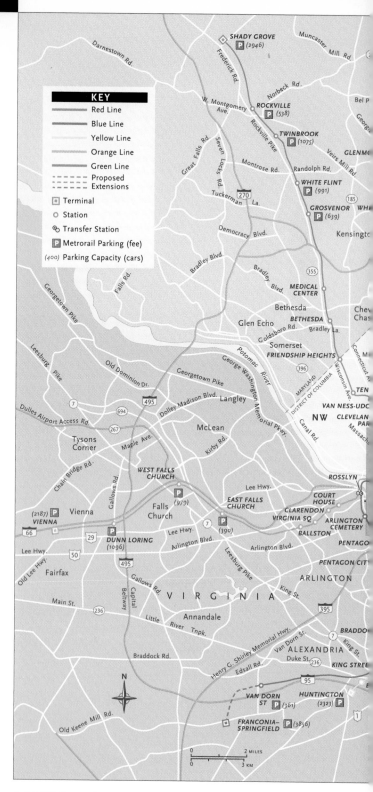

METRORAIL

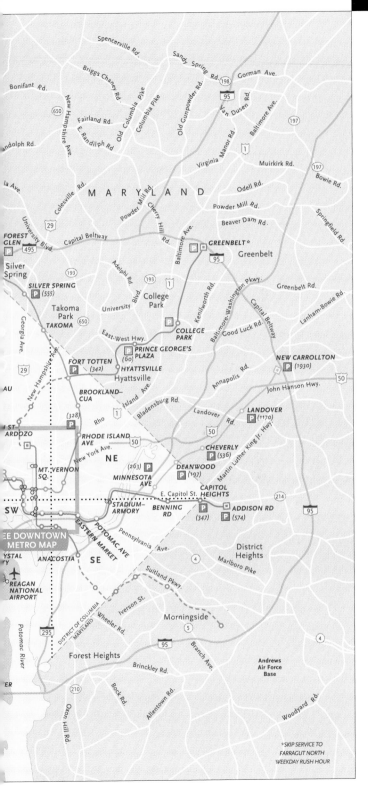

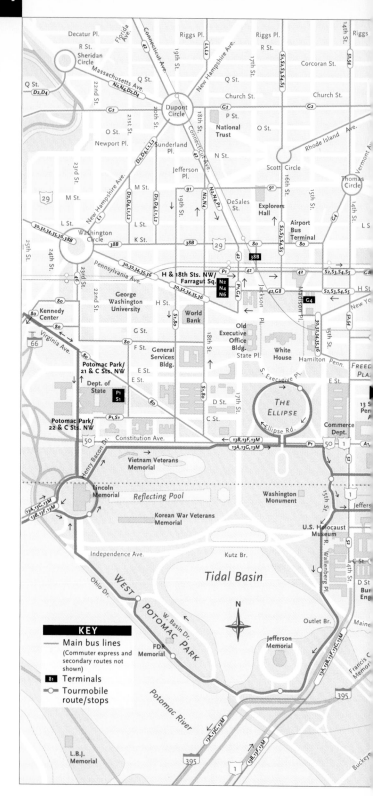

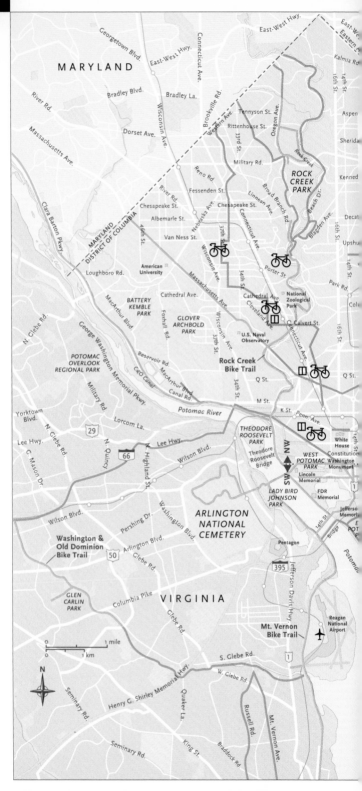

BIKING AND RECREATION

MARYLAND

Northwest Branch Bike Trail

Sligo Creek Bike Trail

University of Maryland

NW ◆ NE

NE ◆ SE

SW ◆ SE

MARYLAND

MARYLAND — DISTRICT OF COLUMBIA

DISTRICT OF COLUMBIA — MARYLAND

ANACOSTIA RIVER PARK

National Arboretum

Kenilworth Aquatic Gardens

Catholic University

Union Station

The Capitol

RFK Stadium

ANACOSTIA PARK

FORT DUPONT PARK

Navy Yard

Frederick Douglass Mem Bridge

FORT STANTON PARK

U.S. Naval Station

Bolling Air Force Base

OXON RUN PARK

OXON RUN PARK

KEY
— On-street paths
— Off-street paths
🚲 Bike lockers
▯ Metro bike racks

The Sourcebook
for Your
Hometown

MANY MAPS • WHERE & HOW

FIND IT ALL • NIGHT & DAY

ANTIQUES TO ZIPPERS

BARGAINS & BAUBLES

ELEGANT EDIBLES • ETHNIC EATS

STEAK HOUSES • BISTROS

DELIS • TRATTORIAS

CLASSICAL • JAZZ • COMEDY

THEATER • DANCE • CLUBS

COCKTAIL LOUNGES

COUNTRY & WESTERN • ROCK

COOL TOURS

HOUSECLEANING • CATERING

GET A LAWYER • GET A DENTIST

GET A NEW PET • GET A VET

MUSEUMS • GALLERIES

PARKS • GARDENS • POOLS

BASEBALL TO ROCK CLIMBING

FESTIVALS • EVENTS

DAY SPAS • DAY TRIPS

HOTELS • HOT LINES

GET A LAWYER • GET A DENTIST

PASSPORT PIX • TRAVEL INFO

HELICOPTER TOURS

DINERS • DELIS • PIZZERIAS

BRASSERIES • TAQUERÍAS

BOOTS • BOOKS • BUTTONS

BICYCLES • SKATES

SUITS • SHOES • HATS

RENT A TUX • RENT A COSTUME

BAKERIES • SPICE SHOPS

SOUP TO NUTS

Fodor's

CITYGUIDE
WASHINGTON
DISTRICT OF COLUMBIA

FODOR'S TRAVEL PUBLICATIONS
NEW YORK • TORONTO • LONDON • SYDNEY • AUCKLAND
WWW.FODORS.COM

FODOR'S CITYGUIDE WASHINGTON, DC

EDITOR
Deborah Kaufman

EDITORIAL CONTRIBUTORS
Holly Bass, Shane Christensen, Carol Cutler, Robin Dougherty, Leigh Durig, Lisa Guttman Greaves, Constance Hay, Donald Hay, Amy Karafin, John A. Kelly, Kathleen McCabe, Celeste McCall, Dave McKenna, Suzanne Whelton, CiCi Williamson

EDITORIAL PRODUCTION
Kristin Milavec

MAPS
David Lindroth, *cartographer;* Bob Blake and Rebecca Baer, *map editors*

DESIGN
Fabrizio La Rocca, *creative director;* Allison Saltzman, *text design;* Tigist Getachew, *art director;* Jolie Novak, *senior picture editor;* Melanie Marin, *photo editor*

PRODUCTION/MANUFACTURING
Robert B. Shields

COVER PHOTOGRAPH
James Lemass

COPYRIGHT

Copyright © 2001 by Fodors LLC

Fodor's is a registered trademark of Random House, Inc.

All rights reserved under International and Pan-American Copyright Conventions. Published in the United States by Fodor's Travel Publications, a unit of Fodors LLC, a subsidiary of Random House, Inc., and simultaneously in Canada by Random House of Canada Limited, Toronto. Distributed by Random House, Inc., New York.

No maps, illustrations, or other portions of this book may be reproduced in any form without written permission from the publisher.

Second Edition

ISBN 0–679–00785–7

ISSN 1526–3193

SPECIAL SALES

Fodor's Travel Publications are available at special discounts for bulk purchases for sales promotions or premiums. Special editions, including personalized covers, excerpts of existing guides, and corporate imprints, can be created in large quantities for special needs. For more information, contact your local bookseller or write to Special Markets, Fodor's Travel Publications, 280 Park Avenue, New York, NY 10017. Inquiries from Canada should be directed to your local Canadian bookseller or sent to Random House of Canada, Ltd., Marketing Department, 2775 Matheson Boulevard East, Mississauga, Ontario L4W 4P7. Inquiries from the United Kingdom should be sent to Fodor's Travel Publications, 20 Vauxhall Bridge Road, London SW1V 2SA, England.

PRINTED IN THE UNITED STATES OF AMERICA

10 9 8 7 6 5 4 3 2 1

CONTENTS

directories

METROPOLITAN LIFE

On a bad day in a big city, the little things that go with living shoulder-to-shoulder with a few million people wear us all down. But the special pleasures of urban life have a way of keeping us out of the suburbs—and thankful, even, for every second of stress. The field of daffodils in the park on a fine spring day. The perfect little black dress that you find for half price. The markets—so fabulously well stocked that you can cook any recipe without resorting to mail-order catalogs. The way you can sometimes turn a corner and discover a whole new world, so foreign you can hardly believe you're less than a mile from home. The never-ending wealth of possibilities and opportunities.

If you know where to find it all, the city cannot defeat you. With knowledge comes power. That's why Fodor's has prepared this book. It will put phone numbers at your fingertips. It'll take you to new places and remind you of those you've forgotten. It's the ultimate urban companion—and, we hope, your **new best friend in the city.**

It's the **citywise shopaholic** who always knows where to find something, no matter how obscure. We've made a concerted effort to bring hundreds of great shops to your attention, so that you'll never be at a loss, whether you need a perfect birthday present for a perfect friend or some obscure craft items to make Halloween costumes for your kids.

It's the **restaurant know-it-all** who's full of ideas for every occasion—you know, the one who would never send you to Café de la Snub, because she knows the food is boring, the wait staff is rude, and they always overbook. In this book we'll steer you around the corner, to a perfect little restaurant with five tables, a fireplace, and a chef on his way up.

It's a **hip barfly buddy** who can give you advice when you need a charming nook, not too noisy, to take a new friend after work. Among the dozens of bars and nightspots in this book, you're bound to find something that fits your mood.

It's **the sagest arts maven you know,** the one who always has the scoop on what's on that's worthwhile on any given night. In these pages, you'll find dozens of concert venues and arts organizations.

It's also the **city whiz** who knows how to get where you're going, wherever you are.

It's **the best map guide** on the shelves, and it puts **all the city in your briefcase** or on your bookshelf.

Stick with us. We'll lay out all the options for your leisure time—and gently nudge you away from the duds—so that you can enjoy the metropolitan living experience that makes Washington worthwhile.

YOUR GUIDES

No one person can know it all. To help get you on track around the city, we've hand-picked a stellar group of local experts to share their wisdom.

Holly Bass, who wrote our Arts, Entertainment, & Nightlife chapter, writes about the arts for *Washington City Paper* and the *Washington Post.* She recently received a fellowship from the National Arts Journalism Program in New York, where she will research hip-hop theater and performance art.

Shane Christensen, who helped expand our Restaurants chapter, has written extensively for Fodor's on destinations in the United States, South America, and Europe. He has updated *The Wall Street Journal's Guide to Business Travel in Washington, DC,* and has been the Washington bureau chief for ontheroad.com, a Web site for business travelers, for the past three years. A resident of the eclectic Adams-Morgan neighborhood, he is the thinnest restaurant critic you'll ever meet, but he never skips a chance to dine around the city.

Carol Cutler, an award-winning author of eight cookbooks and columnist for Copley News Service, helped expand the Restaurants chapter. She has been a restaurant critic as well as consultant to Time-Life Books, and her writing has appeared in *Travel & Leisure, Harper's Bazaar,* and other national publications. She and her journalist husband live in the Georgetown section of D.C., where they settled after 15 years abroad, 12 of them in Paris, where they pampered their palates while acquiring a culinary education. Since moving to Washington, they have had the pleasure of following the meteoric rise of restaurant quality, quantity, and diversity.

Shopping updater **Robin Dougherty** lives and shops in Washington, D.C. She reviews film, theater, and television for a variety of local and national publications, and she thinks there should be more movies about shopping.

Lisa Guttman Greaves savored the chance to rediscover the museums, monuments, gardens, and strolls of the city of her lifelong home as she updated the Places to Explore chapter. When not visiting favorite spots like the Library of Congress reading room, Lisa is at home on Capitol Hill with her artist husband or at her job as a trade association publications manager.

Constance and Donald Hay, who contributed to the Restaurants chapter, have lived around the world, but finally made their home in the Washington area for its international flavor. Their food and travel articles are based on a lifetime of travel and their respective professional backgrounds in food and photography.

A graduate of Washington's Georgetown University, **Kathy McCabe** began her career in television news and now works in Internet journalism. When Kathy isn't writing about shopping for Fodor's, she enjoys covering her other favorite sport, politics, for USATODAY.com.

Celeste McCall, a former food and travel writer and restaurant critic for the *Washington Times*, has spent most of her life in Washington, D.C. She has contributed to regional and national publications, including *Caribbean Travel & Life, Porthole, The Washington Post, Restaurant Digest,* and *Roll Call.* She is a member of Les Dames d'Escoffier, an organization of women in the restaurant and hospitality industries, and the Titanic Historical Society. When not traveling or writing, Celeste and her husband like to cook out in their backyard on Capitol Hill, where they dwell with their three cats: Leo, Eggplant, and Artichoke. Celeste updated the City Sources chapter.

D.C. residents **Dave McKenna,** who writes about pop culture and sports for the weekly *Washington City Paper* and other publications, and **Leigh Durig,** a researcher, updated the Parks, Gardens, & Sports chapter.

Suzanne Whelton, who covered Maryland and Tenleytown dining for the Restaurants chapter, is a fourth-generation Washingtonian who has lived in D.C., Maryland, and Virginia. Her passion for finding the best places to eat was cultivated 20 years ago in the cafés of Cleveland Park, Adams-Morgan, and Dupont Circle. To support her current habit of restaurant hopping, she edits comic strips for *The Washington Post* Writers Group.

CiCi Williamson has been a food and travel writer and syndicated newspaper columnist for more than two decades. She met and married her husband, **John A. Kelly,** in Annapolis, Maryland, and they now live in McLean, Virginia. Inveterate travelers, they have visited a whopping 100 countries on six continents, and all 50 U.S. states. But only the D.C. area is home, where John and CiCi have lived for 20 years. CiCi and John covered plenty of local terrain writing the original Places to Explore, Hotels, and City Sources chapters and adding Virginia eateries to the Restaurants chapter for the second edition.

It goes without saying that no establishment has paid to be included in this book. Each has been chosen by our contributors strictly on its merits.

HOW TO USE THIS BOOK

The first thing you need to know is that everything in this book is **arranged by category and alphabetically** within each category.

Now, before you go any farther, check out the **city maps** at the front of the book. Each map has a number, in a black box at the top of the page, and grid coordinates are along the top and side margins. On the text pages, listings are keyed to one of these maps. Look for the map number in a small black box preceding each establishment name, with the grid code following in italics; for establishments with more than one location, additional map numbers and grid codes appear at the end of the listing. To locate a museum that's identified in the text as **7** *e-6*, turn to Map 7 and locate the address within the e-6 square. To locate restaurants that are nearby, simply skim the text in the restaurant chapter for listings identified as being on Map 7.

Throughout the guide, as applicable, we name the neighborhood in which each sight, restaurant, shop, and other destination is located. We also give you the nearest Metro stop as well as, at the end of each listing, complete opening hours and admission fees for sights; days closed for shops; and credit cards accepted, price levels, reservations policy, days closed, and meals not served for restaurants.

At the end of the book, in addition to an **alphabetical index,** you'll find **directories of shops and restaurants by neighborhood.**

Chapter 7, City Sources, covers essential information for residents—everything from vet and lawyer referral services to caterers worth calling.

We've worked hard to make sure that all the information we give you is accurate at press time. Still, time brings changes, so always confirm information when it matters—especially if you're making a detour.

Feel free to drop us a line. Were the restaurants we recommended as described? Did you find a wonderful shop you'd like to share? If you have complaints, we'll look into them and revise our entries in the next edition when the facts warrant. So send us your feedback. Either e-mail us at editors@fodors.com (specifying *Fodor's CITYGUIDE Washington, DC* on the subject line), or write to the *Fodor's CITYGUIDE Washington, DC* editor at 280 Park Avenue, New York, New York 10017. We look forward to hearing from you.

Karen Cure
Editorial Director

chapter 1

RESTAURANTS

Washington has an unjustified reputation as a city uninterested in food. Wheeling and dealing, it was always said, are more important to any D.C. diner than the food on the plate. Although this idea didn't come from nowhere, it must be said that Washington has come into its culinary own in the last 20 years.

Of course the rising tide of food-consciousness in the nation at large has lifted all ships, and the rising tide of immigration in D.C. has resulted in scads of restaurants opened by refugees and newcomers from Vietnam, Thailand, Cambodia, El Salvador, Ethiopia, and elsewhere. These varied cuisines have been welcomed and enthusiastically patronized by a population that is well traveled. And even the French-trained chefs who have traditionally set the dining standard here are turning to New American, spicy Southwestern, or Spanish cuisine for inspiration. You can now kick back to African pop music while sampling moi-moi (black-eyed peas, tomatoes, and corned beef) or nklakla (tomato soup with goat); feast on feijoada (a rich Brazilian stew of black beans, pork, and smoked meats); or soothe your palate with an old-fashioned bouillabaisse. For a taste closer to home, attack spicy Carolina shrimp (peel 'em and eat with steaming white grits) or some of the finest marbled steaks and butter-soft roast beef this side of the Mississippi.

The hottest area for new restaurants in the last few years has been the old Downtown, its development spurred by the recent opening of the MCI Center and the cluster of theaters nearby. The restaurants in nearby Chinatown have been joined by a flood of new brew pubs, moderately priced ethnic eateries, and posh white-tablecloth establishments.

NO SMOKING

Restaurants in D.C. itself are required to designate 25% of their seats (not including those in the bar) as no-smoking, going up to 50% in restaurants built or substantially remodeled after 1988. In the city of Alexandria, 50% of a restaurant's seats must be no-smoking. In Arlington County, restaurants with more than 75 seats must set aside 25% as no-smoking, and in practice nearly all restaurants have some no-smoking seats. In Maryland smoking is permitted in a restaurant's bar and in separate, enclosed rooms designated smoking areas.

RESERVATIONS

Reservations are only crucial at the very hottest places, but it's always a good idea to call ahead if you're going to a popular place. For weekends it's safest to reserve several days in advance.

TIPPING

A tip of 15% is the norm, going up to 20% in fancier restaurants or for exceptional service.

PRICE CATEGORIES

CATEGORY	COST*
$$$$	over $35
$$$	$26–$35
$$	$15–$25
$	under $15

*per person for a three-course meal, excluding drinks, service, and sales tax (10% in D.C., 4.5%–9% in VA, 5% in MD)

restaurants by cuisine

AFGHAN

 a-1

KAZAN RESTAURANT

A popular dining spot in restaurant-sparse McLean, this attractive eatery shares a shopping strip with a large grocery store and a pharmacy. In addition to the requisite kebabs, the menu has interesting appetizers, roasted meats, stews, and fragrant vegetables. Specialties include lamb kapama (shanks) and fresh seafood. Entrées come with salad, rice, and pita bread. *6813 Redmond Dr., at Old Dominion, McLean, VA, 703/734–1960. AE, DC MC, V. Closed Sun. No lunch Sat. $–$$*

1 *b-3*

PANJSHIR

Both of these very good Afghan restaurants offer succulent kebabs of beef, lamb, and chicken as well as fragrant stews of meat, fruit, and vegetables served on impeccably cooked rice. Entrées come with a salad and hearty Afghan bread. For dessert, try the elephant ears—made of pastry, dusted with cardamom and pistachios. *924 W. Broad St., Falls Church, VA, 703/536–4566. AE, DC, MC, V. No lunch Sun. Metro: East Falls Church. $$*

224 Maple Ave. W, Vienna, VA, 703/281–4183. Metro: Vienna/Fairfax–GMU.

AFRICAN

3 *g-8*

BUKOM CAFÉ

You'll soon see the connection between West African and Caribbean cooking in this cheerful café. African pop music often plays in the background, and live music is sometimes scheduled. Main courses range from *egussi* (goat with melon seeds) to *kumasi* (chicken in peanut sauce) to vegetarian dishes such as *jollof* rice and fried plantains. *2442 18th St. NW, Adams-Morgan, 202/265–4600. AE, D, DC, MC, V. No lunch. Metro: Woodley Park–Zoo. $*

6 *a-1*

CAFÉ NEMA

The menu here combines Somali, North African, and Middle Eastern cuisines. Entrées are simple but flavorful. Grilled chicken, lamb, and beef kabobs and salmon steak are paired with fresh vegetables and an outstanding curried basmati-rice pilaf that has bits of caramelized onion, whole cloves, and raisins. The chef gives such appetizers as *sambousa* (flaky fried triangles of dough filled with curried vegetables or meat), hummus, and *baba ghanoush* (eggplant puree) a distinct touch. There's also a good selection of pastas, salads, and sandwiches. At $4, the generous, made-to-order falafel sandwich is one of the best bargains in the city. *1334 U St. NW, U Street, 202/667–3215. AE, D, DC, MC, V. Metro: U St.–Cardozo. $*

AMERICAN

10 *d-2*

AMERICA

Well designed to take advantage of the dramatic spaces in Union Station, this popular restaurant offers a large menu of homey American classics, including enormous sandwiches, salads, burgers, and other entrées, and desserts for the glutton. It's open daily until midnight. *Union Station, 50 Massachusetts Ave. NE, near 2nd St., Capitol Hill, 202/682–9555. AE, D, DC, MC, V. Metro: Union Station. $$*

10 *g-8*

BLUESTONE CAFÉ

Having arrived on the scene in the summer of 1999, Bluestone Café is making a name for itself with its eclectic New American menu. Dishes change frequently based on seasonally available local produce. As one patron put it, "You could throw a dart at the menu and the choice would be good." Past menus have included ricotta-filled ravoli with kumquats and tomatoes, and jumbo crab cake with local white corn. The former-post-office location captures the feel of the neighborhood with imaginative architectural use of wood and mosaic-tile accents. *327 7th St. SE, Capitol Hill, 202/547–9007. AE, D, DC, MC, V. Metro: Eastern Market. $$$$*

10 *b-4*

CAPITOL VIEW CLUB

A private club at lunchtime, although available to nonmembers paying a cover charge, this hotel restaurant opens to the public for dinner, offering one of the most dramatic views in Washington—the floodlighted dome of the U.S. Capitol. The American regional menu of grilled meats and seafood changes seasonally. Live piano music accompanies your meal and view between 7 and 11. *Hyatt Regency Washington, 400 New Jersey Ave. NW, between D and E Sts., 11th floor, Capitol Hill, 202/783–2582. AE, DC, MC, V. Metro: Union Station. $$$$*

1 *a-4*

FEDORA CAFÉ

California-Italian is a good way to describe the food at this spiffy restaurant, but the dishes stretch beyond innovative wood-burning-oven pizza and pastas. House specialties include potato-crusted salmon, spit-roasted duck, and seared beef tenderloin. Daily specials might be tender calf liver and onions in balsamic sauce or a Provençal chicken pie. The tile-floored, art-deco dining room is subtly divided so it's not just one big space. Young urban professionals gather in the sofa-filled lounge. *Tysons Corner, 8521 Leesburg Pike, McLean, VA, 703/556–0100. AE, D, DC, MC, V. Metro: Vienna/Fairfax–GMU. $$*

FOUR & TWENTY BLACKBIRDS

Although 90 minutes outside of D.C., this quaint, country gourmet outpost is worth the trip. The original creations and menu whims of owner-chef Heidi Morf utilize seasonal fresh produce and country meats. Expect dishes such as pork tenderloin with apples and prunes in a cognac sauce, halibut with red-onion confit, and fabulous vegetable creations such as wilted kale and scalloped sweet potatoes. Vegetarians can revel in a shepherd's pie of roasted root vegetables iced with mashed potatoes. For dessert, try the rustic apple pie with walnut ice cream or the chocolate bread pudding. A folk harpist plays on Friday and Saturday nights. Brunch is served on Sunday. *650 Zachary Taylor Hwy., Flint Hill, VA, 540/675–1111. AE, D, DC, MC, V. Closed Mon.– Tues. No lunch Wed.–Sat. No dinner Sun. $$$$*

3 *g-8*

LITTLE FOUNTAIN CAFÉ

This charming garden-level restaurant is one of Washington's best-kept secrets—a quiet setting on a frenzied row of ethnic restaurants, bars, and cafés. The dining room has 12 candlelighted tables, a trickling fountain, and an impressive wine rack (Wednesday night, all bottles are half price). The modern international menu is short but creative—the best dishes include grilled salmon on a bed of Belgian endive and radicchio, pan-seared venison with a pinot noir and cherry sauce, and breast of free-range chicken and morel mushrooms baked in pastry with a white wine brandy cream. *2339 18th St. NW, Adams-Morgan, 202/462–8100. AE, MC, V. No lunch. Metro: Woodley Park–Zoo. $$$*

10 *g-8*

MARKET LUNCH

On Saturdays, the lines start forming at 7:15 AM for the homey breakfast fare at this self-service café tucked into a corner of Eastern Market. Have your morning eggs with crab cakes or fish cakes, or skip them altogether and dive into the blueberry pancakes or French toast with strawberries or peaches. Old-fashioned white bread is baked fresh daily. Seating is limited, and they don't take reservations, but on nice days a lot of people order takeout and eat elsewhere in the market. *225 7th St. SE, off Pennsylvania Ave., Capitol Hill, 202/547–8444. No credit cards. Closed Mon. Lunch only on Sun. Metro: Eastern Market. $*

10 *d-4*

THE MONOCLE

If you want to peep at Washington celebrities—i.e., politicians—park yourself in this Washington institution, the nearest restaurant to the Senate side of the Capitol. The American home cooking is thoroughly reliable, if rarely adventurous. The crab cakes, served as either a platter or a sandwich, are a longtime specialty, and depending on the day of the week, you might encounter a great pot roast or a first-rate fish dish. Still, the real draw to this historic town house is the old-style Capitol Hill atmosphere, warmed by a fireplace in winter. Valet parking is complimentary with meals. *107 D St. NE, between 1st and 2nd Sts., Capitol Hill, 202/546–4488. AE, DC, MC, V. Closed weekends. Metro: Union Station. $$$*

5 *g-4*

SHOLL'S COLONIAL CAFETERIA

This 72-year-old Washington institution—open for breakfast, lunch, and early dinner—caters to a mixture of office workers, retirees, and students, all of whom are fiercely loyal to its dependable cooking and low prices. Your breakfast ham is sliced off a whole ham, your lunchtime turkey off a whole turkey. Sholl's is famous for its apple, blueberry, peach, and other fruit pies. *1990 K St. NW, entrance near I St., Downtown, 202/296–3065. No credit cards. No dinner Sun. Metro: Farragut West. $*

AMERICAN/CASUAL

3 *g-8*

BELMONT KITCHEN

The outdoor patio, tucked under lighted trees at the corner of 18th Street and Belmont Road, is the most inviting in

Adams-Morgan. The innovative Saturday and Sunday brunch menu entices with such delights as goat-cheese strudel on a bed of mixed greens with basil vinaigrette, or homemade brioche French toast with fresh fruit and a side of apple wood–smoked bacon. Although less crowded at dinner, Belmont Kitchen serves a decent selection of soups and salads, pizzas, pastas, and burgers. *2400 18th St. NW, Adams-Morgan, 202/667–1200. AE, DC, MC, V. Metro: Woodley Park–Zoo. $$*

6 a-1
BEN'S CHILI BOWL

This comfortable diner-style restaurant has been serving D.C. chili lovers since 1958. In the evening, it's filled with U Street hipsters and neighborhood regulars who love the chili dogs, chili half-smokes, chili burgers, and just plain chili. Ben's also serves a delicious, Southern-style breakfast Monday through Saturday, starting at 6 AM. *1213 U St. NW, U Street, 202/667–0909. No credit cards. Metro: U St.–Cardozo. $*

1 c-6
BISTRO BISTRO

The Shirlington location serves a varied menu of satisfying foods, including sandwiches, soups, salads, pizzas, pastas, meat, and fish. The basic hamburger gets a twist here; it can be made of lamb, beef, or turkey. The oyster stew has fresh shellfish in a creamy infusion of Swiss chard, onion, and pepper. Pasta is tossed with either house-smoked scallops, spinach, herbs, and shiitake mushrooms, or with crunchy, diced, Italian bacon in a little cream. Platters vary from grilled lamb to veal meat loaf to roast chicken accompanied by piles of vegetables and commendable breads. Drinks include numerous draft beers and an extensive list of by-the-glass wines. *4021 S. 28th St., Shirlington Village. Arlington, VA, 703/379–0300. AE, D, DC, MC, V. $$*

5 f-3
BRICKSKELLER

Beer lovers from across the country stop in at the Brickskeller to choose from among the hundreds of domestic and imported brews on its shelves. The burgers, sandwiches, and pizza are perfect accompaniments to the main attraction. It's open nightly until 2 AM— and 3 AM on Friday and Saturday (last

call is half an hour before closing). *1523 22nd St. NW, between P and Q Sts., Dupont Circle, 202/293–1885. AE, D, DC, MC, V. Metro: Dupont Circle. $*

1 d-7
BULLFEATHERS

More restaurant than bar, Bullfeathers nevertheless has a large separate bar offering a daily happy hour from 4:30 to 7, with some free nibbles and lots of mid-career types with whom to schmooze. Soups, salads, sandwiches, and heartier main dishes such as pasta, poultry, and fish make up the menu. It's well-prepared American food, but not cutting-edge innovative. *112 King St., Alexandria, VA, 703/836–8088. AE, D, MC, V. Metro: King St. $$*

5 f-3
C.F. FOLKS

The sandwiches and salads on the menu at this no-frills weekday diner are nothing special: order instead from the daily specials, which feature a different cuisine daily. On Monday, it's Cajun; on Tuesday, Mexican; on Wednesday, Indian and Italian; and on Thursday and Friday, seafood. The cooking is superb, and the

A BREATH OF FRESH AIR

On a sunny day or a sultry night, there's nothing like the great outdoors to go with your meal.

Belmont Kitchen (American/Casual)
This is one of the most inviting outdoor patios in Adams-Morgan.

Cactus Cantina (Tex-Mex)
Young professionals and families flock to the outdoor patio in warm weather.

Lauriol Plaza (Latin)
Dine on Latin American and Spanish cuisine on the rooftop deck or outdoor patio of this popular neighborhood spot.

Old Angler's Inn (Contemporary)
The nearby C&O Canal forms a lovely backdrop for outdoor dining in summer.

Xando (Cafés)
If you insist upon dining alfresco in cooler weather, head to this popular Dupont Circle café-coffeehouse, which has a year-round heated outdoor patio.

crowds know it. Note that no alcohol is served, and they don't take reservations or credit cards. *1225 19th St. NW, between M and N Sts., Dupont Circle, 202/293– 0162. Reservations not accepted. No credit cards. Closed weekends. No dinner. Metro: Dupont Circle. $$*

3 *a-5*

CAFÉ DELUXE

Café Deluxe may look like a Parisian bistro, but the menu is contemporary American, with the likes of grilled melt-in-your-mouth meat loaf with horserad-ish-flavored mashed potatoes, and grilled-tuna-steak sandwiches with french fries. Servings are ample, and prices are low. Go early, as this popular restaurant fills up quickly, even on week-nights, with neighborhood regulars. The spartan decor is kid-friendly (read: crayons are welcome), with white butcher paper covers over white table-cloths. Outdoor dining is available. *3228 Wisconsin Ave. NW, Cleveland Park, 202/686–2233. AE, MC, V. Metro: Cleveland Park or Tenleytown–AU. $$*

1 *c-2*

4910 Elm St., Bethesda, MD, 301/656–3131. Metro: Bethesda.

2 *b-1*

CHEESECAKE FACTORY

Both the menu and the portions are enormous at this southern California transplant, which became an instant hit in Washington. The 200-item menu ranges over Asian, Latin, and traditional American food, and the desserts, of course, include 38 varieties of cheese-cake. They don't take reservations, so the wait is often long, but they're open until 12:30 AM on Friday and Saturday. *Chevy Chase Pavilion, 5345 Wisconsin Ave. NW, between Jennifer St. and Western Ave., Upper Northwest, 202/364–0500. AE, D, DC, MC, V. Metro: Friendship Heights. $$*

1 *c-1*

White Flint Mall, 11301 Rockville Pike, Bethesda, MD, 301/770–0999. Metro: White Flint.

9 *e-7*

CLYDE'S OF GEORGETOWN

The flagship restaurant of this popular local chain draws a crowd of both locals and out-of-towners for pub food of unusually high quality. Summertime is a special treat here—Clyde's sends trucks to the country for local produce, which it

then incorporates in its daily specials. This branch is open until 2 AM on week-days and until 3 AM on Saturday. *George-town Park Mall, 3236 M St. NW, between Wisconsin Ave. and Potomac St., George-town, 202/333–9180. AE, MC, V. Metro: Foggy Bottom–GWU. $$*

1 *a-4*

CLYDE'S OF TYSONS CORNER

This large, popular Tysons Corner out-post of Clyde's serves dependable cook-ing in a sophisticated atmosphere of art-deco decor. Year-round the menu highlights seafood—halibut and wild Copper River salmon from Alaska, Maine lobster, Maryland crab cakes, and daily specials. Seasonal regional fare fills out the menu along with salads, soups, and burgers. Berry desserts are terrific in summer. Doors are open nightly until 2 AM. *8332 Leesburg Pike, Tysons Corner, Vienna, VA, 703/734–1900. AE, D, DC, MC, V. $–$$*

6 *c-6*

DISTRICT CHOPHOUSE & BREWERY

A handsomely restored old building summons up chophouses of yesteryear in size (huge), food (straight American), and portions (very generous). Industrial copper pipes overhead announce that this is a working brewery. Regulars enjoy the great on-site microbrews that go perfectly with the cooking. Some is even used in the cooking, like the oatmeal stout and black-strap molasses stout used to marinate the 16-ounce rib eye. Is that American or what? *509 7th St. NW, between E and F Sts., Downtown, 202/347–3434. AE, DC, MC, V. Metro: Archives–Navy Memorial. $$*

1 *d-7*

FIREHOOK BAKERY

Opened in Old Town Alexandria in 1992, Firehook has expanded to several loca-tions thanks to the baking skills of Gene Gathright, the head baker, and Kate Jansen, the pastry chef. All their breads depend on sourdough for leavening. In addition to the mainstay, authentic *pain au Levain* (French sourdough bread), an enticing assortment of breads—such as olive, rosemary, and walnut—is avail-able daily. These same breads are made into delicious sandwiches. Jansen's fab-ulous pastries, such as lemon tarts, pecan squares, and decadent chocolate cakes, make a fine ending for a light meal. You can eat in or take out. *214 N. Fayette St., Old Town Alexandria, VA, 703/519–8020. MC, V. Fayette St. location closed Sun. Metro: King St.* $

5 *g-3*

3411 Connecticut Ave. NW, Dupont Circle, 202/362–2253. Metro: Dupont Circle.

5 *g-4*

912 17th St. NW, Downtown, 202/429–2253. Metro: Farragut North.

5 *g-2*

1909 Q St. NW, Dupont Circle, 202/588–9296. Metro: Dupont Circle.

9 *e-7*

3241 M St. NW, Georgetown. Metro: Foggy Bottom–GWU.

9 *d-5*

GEORGETOWN CAFE

A 24-hour restaurant, this neighborhood café is a favorite of students and other locals for its pasta, pizzas, kebabs, gyros, and such home-style American favorites as roast beef, baked chicken, and mashed potatoes. *1623 Wisconsin Ave., Georgetown, 202/333–0215. Reservations not accepted. D, MC, V.* $

9 *b-7*

THE GUARDS

The Guards has been a hangout for generations of Georgetown University students. The food, although hardly cutting edge, remains dependable. It's a lively place for a burger and a beer, and stays open until 3 AM on weekends. Lighting is always dim, but at lunchtime the back room under the skylight is cheery. *2518 M St. NW, Georgetown, 202/965–2350. AE, D, DC, MC, V. Metro: Foggy Bottom–GWU or Rosslyn.* $

HARD TIMES CAFE AND HARD TIMES ROCKVILLE

Good chili is a subject of hot debate. To keep the fire burning, Hard Times Cafe offers three styles—Texas, Cincinnati, and vegetarian—and prepares each one as a three-way (with chili, spaghetti, and cheese), a four-way (those three plus onions), or a five-way (plus onions and beans). The terrific Hard Times Lager is made locally by the Virginia Brewing Company. *1117 Nelson St., near Rte. 28, Rockville, MD, 301/294–9720. Reservations not accepted. AE, MC, V. Metro: Rockville.* $

1 *g-2*

College Park Marketplace, 4738 Cherry Hill Rd., College Park, MD, 301/474–8880.

8 *f-4*

1404 King St., at West St., Alexandria, VA, 703/683–5340. Metro: King St.

1 *c-5*

3028 Wilson Blvd., Arlington, VA, 703/528–2233. Metro: Clarendon.

10 *f-8*

THE HAWK AND DOVE

Good burgers, salads, and omelets attract a mix of residents and congressional staffers to this popular Capitol Hill spot. It's open nightly until 2 AM. The three gas fireplaces are a bonus in winter; an outdoor patio is great for warmer weather. *329 Pennsylvania Ave. SE, between 3rd and 4th Sts., Capitol Hill, 202/543–3300. AE, D, DC, MC, V. Metro: Capitol South or Eastern Market.* $$

9 *e-7*

HOUSTON'S

The best time to come here is the middle of the afternoon, as that's about the only time you can avoid a wait. Houston's is an extraordinarily well-run restaurant with good burgers, hearty salads, and other solid American favorites like ribs and chili. *1065 Wisconsin Ave. NW, between M St. and C&O Canal, Georgetown, 202/338–7760. Reservations not accepted. AE, MC, V. Metro: Foggy Bottom–GWU.* $$

1 *c-2*

7715 Woodmont Ave., Bethesda, MD, 301/656–9755. Metro: Bethesda.

1 *c-1*

12256 Rockville Pike (near Montrose Rd.), Rockville, MD, 301/468–3535. Metro: White Flint.

9 *e-7*

J. PAUL'S

Another popular Georgetown pub, J. Paul's is busiest on weekends, when clubgoers crowd in for the raw bar, hickory-smoked burgers and ribs, and sweet-potato chips. It's open nightly until 11:30; on weekends that stretches to 2:30 AM, with the kitchen hanging in there until midnight. *3218 M St. NW, between Potomac St. and Wisconsin Ave., Georgetown, 202/333–3450. AE, DC, MC, V. Metro: Foggy Bottom–GWU.* $$

5 *g-2*

KRAMER BOOKS & AFTERWORDS: A CAFE

This popular bookstore–café is a favorite neighborhood breakfast spot and late-night intellectual gathering place on weekends, when it's open around the clock. There's a simple menu, with soups, salads, and sandwiches, but many people just drop in for cappuccino and dessert. There's live music (rock, soul, blues) Wednesday through Saturday from 8 PM to midnight. *1517 Connecticut Ave. NW, between Dupont Circle and Q St., Dupont Circle, 202/387–1462. Reservations not accepted. AE, D, MC, V. Metro: Dupont Circle. $$*

3 *g-8*

MILLIE & AL'S

Here's a beloved neighborhood joint that feels like a country bar—not a trendy nightspot. The menu is Italian and the pizza is good (although not as good as the jukebox). There's a DJ on Friday and Saturday nights, when people move to modern dance music in the upstairs bar and dance floor. Millie & Al's stays open until 3 AM weekends, and Wednesday nights all draft beers are $1. *2440 18th St. NW, Adams-Morgan, 202/ 387–8131. MC, V. Closed Sun. No lunch. Metro: Woodley Park–Zoo. $*

8 *f-4*

MURPHY'S

Irish pubs rise or fall with their beer. With your trusty pint of Guinness at this Old Town tavern, you can also enjoy good fish-and-chips, Irish stew, and burgers. There's live Irish music nightly, and a fireplace makes the room especially cozy in winter. Murphy's is open until 2 AM on weekends. *713 King St., between Washington and Columbus Sts., Alexandria, VA, 703/548–1717. AE, DC, MC, V. Metro: King St. $$*

6 *a-6*

OLD EBBITT GRILL

Always crowded and always noisy, the Old Ebbitt is Washington's most popular bar. The carefully prepared pub food includes Buffalo wings, burgers, Reubens, and a more ambitious selection of fresh pastas and fish specials. The popular raw bar serves a rotating selection of farm-raised oysters from certified waters. The Corner Bar, the newest expansion, has spacious booths,

an impressively long bar for casual dining, and a view of the Treasury Building. It's open nightly until 1 AM. *675 15th St. NW, between F and G Sts., Downtown, 202/347–4800. AE, D, DC, MC, V. Metro: Metro Center. $$*

1 *d-7*

POTOWMACK LANDING

The view from this casual restaurant pleases the psyche. Located on the Potomac River just south of National Airport, the site is home to a private boat marina, so it's unusual not to see sailboats skimming over the water nearby. The food and ambience are casual: sandwiches and burgers at lunchtime; dressier dishes for dinner. You can hear live jazz at the popular Sunday brunch buffet. *1 Marina Dr., off the George Washington Pkwy., Alexandria, VA, 703/548–0001. AE, D, DC, MC, V. Metro: National Airport. $$*

5 *f-2*

TIMBERLAKE'S

This friendly neighborhood pub has surprisingly good food. The burgers, sandwiches, and salads are staples, but Monday nights feature a lobster special, and on Tuesday it's prime rib. Timberlake's is also popular for its à la carte champagne brunch, served Saturday and Sunday from 10:30 to 3:30. *1726 Connecticut Ave. NW, between R and S Sts., Dupont Circle, 202/483– 2266. AE, D, DC, MC, V. Metro: Dupont Circle. $$*

BARBECUE

O'BRIEN'S PIT BARBECUE

Homesick Texans crowd this no-frills barbecue joint for its ribs and brisket. The chili is good, too. Live entertainment adds kick on Wednesday and Saturday nights. *387 E. Gude Dr., Rockville, MD, 301/340–8596. Reservations not accepted. AE, D, DC, MC, V. Metro: Shady Grove. $$*

46006 Regal Plaza, Sterling, VA, 703/ 450–8490.

5 *c-4*

OLD GLORY

Old Glory is smoky, somewhat grungy, and wildly popular with a young crowd. This is stick-to-the-ribs food, with plenty of heavy dipping sauces, batter-fried items, dripping sandwiches, and barbecue in several regional flavors. Come with a big appetite and join in the loud fun. *3139 M St., near Wisconsin Ave., Georgetown, 202/337–3406. AE, DC, MC, V. $$*

1 *c-5*
RED HOT & BLUE

This local chain is about Tennessee-style barbecue. The ribs come "wet" (with sauce) or "dry" (simply smoked). The delicious pulled-meat sandwiches and reasonable prices lure hungry throngs. *1600 Wilson Blvd., Arlington, VA, 703/276–7427. Reservations not accepted. AE, MC, V. Metro: Rosslyn. $$*

Takeout only: 3014 Wilson Blvd., Arlington, VA, 703/243–1510. Metro: Clarendon. $$

5 *b-1*
ROCKLANDS

Let your nose guide you to this small barbecue joint; just follow the piquant aroma created by the old-fashioned way of smoking—slowly, very slowly, over red oak, hickory, and charcoal. The result is addictively tender meat. Choose from pork spareribs, beef ribs, chicken, fish, and more, and munch on ballpark peanuts while you wait. Flavorful greens, potato salad, corn pudding, and corn bread shot with jalepeños make excellent sides. There's not much seating at Rocklands, which does a lot of carryout business. The Arlington location is a popular hangout for Gen Xers. *2418 Wisconsin Ave. NW, near Calvert St., Glover Park, 202/333–2558. AE, DC, MC, V. $*

1 *c-5*
4000 N. Fairfax Dr., Arlington, VA, 703/528–2126. AE, D, DC, MC, V. Metro: Ballston.

BRAZILIAN

6 *c-5*
COCO LOCO

The popular bar scene at this downtown destination is fueled by tapas appetizers of endless variety that are generally washed down with wine or beer. Serious meat-eaters should go for the Brazilian-style *churrasqueria*—a series of grilled meats that are brought to your table and sliced right onto your plate. On Friday and Saturday nights, half the restaurant becomes an upscale nightclub. *810 7th St. NW, Downtown, 202/289–2626. AE, MC, V. Closed Sun. No lunch Sat. Metro: Gallery Pl.–Chinatown. $$*

3 *g-8*
GRILL FROM IPANEMA

Start your evening with one of the 4,000 tart *caipirinhas* (Brazil's potent national cocktail of fresh lime, sugar, crushed ice, and cachaça, a spirit akin to rum) served here each month, then progress to one of the two house specialties, the traditional *feijoada*—a stew of black beans, pork, and smoked meat—or *moqueca*, a seafood stew. Appetizers include fried yucca with spicy sausages and, for intrepid palates, fried alligator. The Sunday champagne brunch is a neighborhood favorite. *1858 Columbia Rd. NW, Adams-Morgan, 202/986–0757. AE, D, DC, MC, V. No lunch weekdays. Metro: Woodley Park–Zoo. $$*

3 *g-8*
TOM BRAZIL

A Brazilian restaurant and club more for entertainment than gourmet dining, Tom Brazil is extremely popular with Washington's Brazilian and Latin communities. The downstairs restaurant (with an outdoor patio) mixes Brazilian, Argentine, and Uruguayan dishes, with an emphasis on beef. The upstairs club hosts Brazilian music and dancing on Friday and Saturday nights, and other Latin rhythms during the week. *1832 Columbia Rd. NW, Adams-Morgan, 202/232–4151. AE, MC, V. Closed Mon. Metro: Woodley Park–Zoo. $$*

2 *b-2*
VIDA LOCA

Savor the myriad flavors of Brazil at D.C.'s newest South American café, Vida Loca. To experience the full spectrum, start with *frango à passarinho* (chicken marinated in basil, garlic, and white wine, and lightly fried) or *sopa de feijao* (a spicy rendition of traditional black bean soup). Move on to *camarao baiana* (shrimp cooked in a zesty blend of coconut milk, tomatoes, cilantro, onions, and bell peppers) for the main course. The dark dining room seems to be illuminated only by the glow of neon art on the walls, but the covered deck outside offers a brighter view on the menu. The café sits on noisy Wisconsin Avenue, but Brazilian music (live Thursday through Saturday nights) drowns out the hum of traffic. *4615 Wisconsin Ave. NW, Tenleytown, 202/537–3200. AE, D, MC, V. Metro: Tenleytown–AU. $$$*

BURMESE

6 c-5

BURMA

Burma, now officially called Myanmar, is bordered by India, Thailand, and China, and its cuisine picks up flavors from each. Curry and tamarind share pride of place with lemon, cilantro, and soy seasonings. Batter-fried eggplant and squash are paired with complex, peppery sauces. Green tea leaf and other salads, despite their odd-sounding names and ingredients, leave the tongue with a pleasant tingle. Such entrées as mango pork and tamarind fish are equally satisfying. *740 6th St. NW, 2nd floor, Downtown, 202/638–1280. AE, D, DC, MC, V. No lunch weekends. Metro: Gallery Pl.–Chinatown. $*

CAFÉS

5 c-4

PEACOCK CAFÉ

With its abundant selection of vegetarian dishes and a great full-service juice bar, Peakcock is a local favorite for its straightforward preparation of very fresh products. When's the last time you got a jolt of energy from a glass of wheat-grass juice? Wednesday from 6 to 9 PM has proven a popular drop-in time for flights of six wines at the bar. The owners and help are super friendly. *3251 Prospect St. NW, near Potomac St., Georgetown, 202/625–1402. AE, MC, V. $$*

1 c-2

TASTEE DINER

The Tastees are perhaps the most popular haven for round-the-clock comfort food. Grilled cheese sandwiches, french fries, eggs, pancakes, homemade pies, and an endless flow of coffee are standbys in these 24-hour diners. The location in Silver Spring serves beer and wine and offers patio seating in warmer weather. *7731 Woodmont Ave., Bethesda, MD, 301/652–3970. MC, V. Metro: Bethesda. $*

1 e-2

8601 Cameron St., Silver Spring, MD, 301/589–8171. AE, D, MC, V. Metro: Silver Spring.

118 Washington Blvd., Laurel, MD, 301/725–1503. AE, MC, V.

3 g-8

TRYST

Adams-Morgan was in deep need of a comfortable café where students and would-be philosophers could switch on a laptop computer, linger over a newspaper, or ponder political shifts in Washington. Tryst—a down-to-earth gathering spot with sofas, chairs, and big wood tables great for working or conversing—stepped in to fill that role. The café menu offers surprisingly good food: soups, salads, and sandwiches (including vegetarian choices), as well as appetizers such as bread and brie or roasted pepper and feta dip. Breakfast items are served all day, as are, of course, coffee, espresso, and a variety of premium teas. *2459 18th St. NW, Adams-Morgan, 202/232–5500. MC, V. Metro: Woodley Park–Zoo. $*

5 f-2

XANDO

This popular Dupont Circle hangout is a coffeehouse by day and a crowded liquor bar and café by night. Everyone living in Dupont Circle seems to drop by on a regular schedule. The menu includes grilled Xandwiches, quesadillas, wraps and salads, and desserts. Most people, however, come for the lattes and mochas, iced coffees, or frozen smoothies. The heated outdoor patio is open year-round. *1647 20th St. NW, Dupont Circle, 202/332–6364. AE, MC, V. Metro: Dupont Circle. $*

CAJUN/CREOLE

3 g-7

BARDIA'S NEW ORLEANS CAFÉ

It's not quite New Orleans, but Bardia's friendly staff and good food have earned this restaurant a loyal clientele. The seafood is always a hit, whether batter-fried, blackened, or sautéed (try the traditional crawfish étouffée or the Cajun linguine with seafood sauce). The po'boy sandwiches (hefty French-bread subs) served with Cajun fries are also safe bets. Breakfast, which is served all day, includes traditional eggs Benedict or a New Orleans–style egg dish with fried oysters, crabmeat, and hollandaise. The beignets (puffs of fried dough sprinkled with powdered sugar) are made to order and served hot. *2412 18th St. NW, Adams-Morgan, 202/234–0420. Reserva-*

tions not accepted. AE, MC, V. Metro: Woodley Park–Zoo. $$

1 *d-7*

WAREHOUSE BAR & GRILL

Caricatures of entertainers and other famous people line the walls and stairwell of this perennially popular eatery. Its Cajun-style offerings are subtle and creative. You won't feel like you're in New Orleans here—more like a pale-yellow-tablecloth, fine Virginia seafood restaurant—but if you come for Sunday brunch, the Cajun comes out to play. Acadian peppered shrimp and eggs *Hussarde* (eggs Benedict made with grilled tomato and red wine gravy) are the real thing. Crawfish-and-shrimp étouffée, the fish of the day, and fried-chicken salad are good choices. Share an ample Creole bread pudding for dessert. *214 King St., Alexandria, VA, 703-683–6868. AE, D, DC, MC, V. Metro: King St. $$*

CARIBBEAN

7 *h-1*

BANANA CAFÉ & PIANO BAR

The only thing missing for a true Caribbean dining experience is an ocean breeze. Soft island colors and original artwork by owner Jorge Zamorano and other local artists set the stage for the menu of Cuban, Puerto Rican, and Mexican favorites. Try yucca filled with chorizo, carrots, and olives and served with cilantro sauce; codfish fritters; or any of several tapas to start, accompanied by a margarita or Mangorita. If you still have room for dessert, finish the meal with banana bread pudding or seasonal flans, such as pumpkin. Specialty drinks are half price during happy hour at the upstairs piano bar. *500 8th St. SE, Capitol Hill, 202/543–5906. AE, D, DC, MC, V. Metro: Eastern Market. $$$*

CHINESE

1 *c-6*

CHARLIE CHIANG'S

Pale-pink fabrics, brass, and mirrors give a light, modern look to this restaurant serving cuisine from Taiwan and several regions of mainland China. There's even an excellent sushi bar near the front entrance. Specialties include crab wontons, crispy hot beef, Singapore-style angel-hair noodles with curry sauce, Taiwanese noodles with brown sauce, and steamed whole fish. The entire menu is coded for low-cholesterol and low-fat choices, and the Revolution Diet items are served without salt, sugar, cornstarch, or MSG. *4060 S. 28th St., Shirlington Village, Arlington, VA, 703/671–4900. AE, DC, MC, V. $*

5 *f-2*

CITY LIGHTS OF CHINA

The owners of this busy Dupont Circle restaurant make frequent attempts to turn the tables—that is, don't be surprised if you're asked to leave after about an hour and a half. The flip side is that service is fast. Try the lamb in a tangy peppery sauce, shark's-fin soup, or jumbo shrimp, baked in their shells and then quickly stir-fried with ginger and spices. The dim sum is another classic. *1731 Connecticut Ave. NW, Dupont Circle, 202/265–6688. AE, D, DC, MC, V. Metro: Dupont Circle. $$*

1 *b-5*

FORTUNE CHINESE SEAFOOD RESTAURANT

This huge Chinese restaurant dressed in lavender with crystal chandeliers seats at least 400 people in a freestanding building adjacent to Seven Corners Mall. Live sea creatures swim in tanks along the entry hall. Lunchtime dim sum—with about 70 different items—is served from rolling carts between 11 and 3. For weekend dim sum brunches, you'll probably have to wait for a table. The extensive dinner menu has seven pages alone of exotic sea creatures such as sea cucumber and conch. Whole fish, numerous poultry and meat dishes, and vegetable choices are all there, too. *6249 Seven Corners Center, facing Arlington Blvd., Falls Church, VA, 703/538– 3333. AE, D, MC, V. Metro: East Falls Church. $$*

6 *c-5*

FULL KEE

Both Asian and non-Asian crowds return to Full Kee for the meal-size soups garnished with roast meats. Look on the last page of the menu for a list of the dishes favored by the Chinese clientele. Friday and Saturday they're open until 3 AM. *509 H St. NW, Chinatown, 202/371–2233. No credit cards. Metro: Gallery Pl.–Chinatown. $$*

6 c-5

HUNAN CHINATOWN

More attractive than the run of Chinatown restaurants, and with more attentive service, Hunan Chinatown serves better-than-average versions of familiar dishes. Try the fried dumplings, the tea-smoked duck, the Szechuan eggplant, or the Hunan-style crispy whole fish. *624 H St. NW, between 6th and 7th Sts., Chinatown, 202/783–5858. AE, D, DC, MC, V. Metro: Gallery Pl.–Chinatown.* $$

1 a-4

HUNAN LION

Gold lions flank the entrance to this excellent restaurant located on the first floor of a large office building within sight of Tysons Corner. The extensive menu has several interesting dishes not usually seen at neighborhood Chinese take-out spots. Specialties include crispy whole fish Hunan-style, shrimp with black bean sauce, Peking duck, and General Tso's chicken. In between courses, the waiter brings a complimentary palate-cleansing sorbet. The restaurant is formally decorated with folding lacquer screens, frosted mirrors, and a tropical-fish aquarium. *2070 Chain Bridge Rd., Vienna, VA, 703/734–9828. AE, D, DC, MC, V. Closed Mon. Metro: Vienna.* $–$$

1 a-4

HUNAN LION II

Hunan Lion's nearby more casual sister, Hunan Lion II, draws members of the local Chinese community with dim sum on weekends. Several good choices from the regular menu include Taiwan sausages with Chinese leeks; crunchy seaweed with garlic dressing; and Szechuan-style tofu. *Galleria at Tysons II, 2001 International Dr., McLean, VA, 703/583–1938. AE, D, DC, MC, V.* $

5 f-4

MEIWAH

Tinkling Bells pork or chicken comes on a sizzling platter; flounder duet is presented in the shape of a boat. Located well outside Chinatown, Meiwah doesn't look like its brethren. The spacious two-level interior features a pair of 19th-century bronze doors that connote Canton and can close off part of the dining room for private parties. *1200 New Hampshire Ave. NW, at M St., Downtown, 202/833–2888. AE, DC, MC, V. Metro: Foggy Bottom–GWU.* $$

6 c-5

MR. YUNG'S

The cooking at this traditional Cantonese restaurant is always authentic and sometimes exotic. Standouts include whole fried shrimp steamed in a lotus leaf and soup with shredded roast duck, noodles, and snow cabbage. Dim sum is served from rolling carts at lunchtime. *740 6th St. NW, between G and H Sts., Chinatown, 202/628–1098. AE, D, DC, MC, V. Metro: Gallery Pl.–Chinatown.* $

6 c-5

NEW BIG WONG

When new owners took over Big Wong, they added "New" to the name, expanded the range of Chinese cuisine offered, and turned up the heat in the spicing. But this basement restaurant still offers inexpensive traditional Cantonese cooking. Dim sum is served for lunch daily from 11 to 3:30; weekend lunches are particularly popular with families. Beer is the only alcohol served. *610 H St. NW, at 6th St., Chinatown, 202/628–0490. AE, MC, V. Metro: Gallery Pl.–Chinatown.* $

1 b-6

PEKING GOURMET INN

A favorite of former president George Bush, the Peking Gourmet Inn has covered its walls with photos of the celebrities who have dined here. The specialty of the house is Peking duck, but don't miss the leek dumplings, the farm-grown garlic sprouts, or the black-pepper shrimp. There's often a wait if you don't have a reservation, but efficient service keeps turnover brisk. *6029 Leesburg Pike, Falls Church, VA, 703/671–8088. AE, D, DC, MC, V. Metro: East Falls Church.* $$

6 c-5

TONY CHENG'S MONGOLIAN RESTAURANT

There are only two choices in this attractive Chinatown eatery: Mongolian barbecue and Mongolian hot pot, both with a do-it-yourself dimension. If you choose the barbecue, you assemble your own mixture of meats and vegetables and hand them over to the grill person to be cooked. For the hot pot, you cook your own meat and vegetables in boiling broth, then drink the resulting soup. Both options are delicious and popular. *619 H St. NW, between 6th and 7th Sts.,*

Chinatown, 202/842–8669. AE, MC, V. Metro: Gallery Pl.–Chinatown. $$

6 *c-5*

TONY CHENG'S SEAFOOD RESTAURANT

Upstairs from the Mongolian restaurant is the same owner's Hong Kong–style seafood house, with salt-water tanks housing live fish, eels, and lobsters. Try the shrimp wrapped in lotus leaves, the delicious grouper with Chinese greens and garlic sauce, or the chopped chicken in ginger sauce. Dim sum is served from a menu on weekdays, from rolling carts on weekends. *619 H St. NW, between 6th and 7th Sts., Chinatown, 202/842–8669. AE, MC, V. Metro: Gallery Pl.–Chinatown. $$*

3 *d-4*

YENCHING PALACE

This old-timer is known locally as the site of the secret meeting between U.S. and Soviet negotiators that successfully resolved the 1962 Cuban missile crisis. The kitchen specializes in the cuisine of China's northern provinces. The menu won't broaden your culinary horizons, but the cooking is even and the chilis are hot. Parking is free. *3524 Connecticut Ave. NW, near Porter St., Cleveland Park, 202/362–8200. AE, D, DC, MC, V. Metro: Cleveland Park. $$*

CONTEMPORARY

1 *c-1*

ADDIE'S

You could drive right past this old bungalow opposite the White Flint Mall on Rockville Pike and not know that you're passing one of the most exceptional restaurants in the region. It's such an odd, unassuming locale for this incredible culinary oasis. Inventive first-course offerings include Southern-style cornmeal-coated oysters and grilled mozzarella wrapped in prosciutto. Don't miss the sushi-style grilled yellowfin tuna, orange-crusted halibut, or Angus rib eye in a cabernet *demi-glace* (brown sauce). Addie's three small dining rooms are cheerfully decorated with antiquated household appliances, whimsical clocks, and artwork. *11120 Rockville Pike, Rockville, MD, 301/881–0081. AE, DC, MC, V. Metro: White Flint. $$$$*

2 *f-5*

BIS

A second restaurant from Vidalia chef Jeffrey Buben (*see Southern, below*), the high-style Bis is a contemporary American-French bistro. Appetizers include a ragout of snails with artichokes and potatoes; traditional onion soup; and a lovely *galette* (round, flat cake) of goat cheese, potato, and ragout of rabbit. Entrées run to grilled meats and updated bistro fare, such as sweetbreads, duck confit, and veal stew. *Hotel George, 15 E St. NW, between New Jersey Ave. and N. Capitol St., Capitol Hill, 202/661–2700. AE, D, DC, MC, V. Metro: Union Station. $$$$*

6 *a-6*

BUTTERFIELD 9

With a tip of the hat to the ladies who shopped here at what was once the popular Garfinkel's department store, Butterfield 9 puts on an elegant face in the manner of the 1950s. The name of the restaurant—a nod to the film *Butterfield 8*, starring Elizabeth Taylor—reflects owner Amarjeet Singh's admiration for vintage glamour movies. The black-and-white glamour-puss photos that line the walls are not old movie stills, but contemporary re-creations. The restaurant has several levels that recall the interiors of the great liners that once crisscrossed the Atlantic. Chef Martin Saylor, after returning to the city where he first starred at the Lafayette restaurant in the Hay-Adams Hotel, is in command of the kitchen. His creative dishes, such as foie gras herb pancake with mango truffle relish, and grilled bison with cabernet *jus*, match the setting—sleek, dramatic, and very tasteful. *600 14th St. NW, at F St., Downtown, 202/289–8810. AE, DC, MC, V. Metro: Metro Center. $$$$*

1 *c-2*

CAFE BETHESDA

This small and attractive restaurant has an equally small and attractive menu. Specials change frequently, but favorites on the regular menu include grilled yellowfin tuna with Mediterranean relish and duck breast with ginger-cassis sauce. The cappuccino crème is a memorable dessert. *5027 Wilson La., Bethesda, MD, 301/657–3383. AE, D, MC, V. No lunch weekends. $$$*

1 c-6

CARLYLE GRAND CAFE

Possibly the best restaurant in the Shirlington Village complex of eateries and movie theaters, the Carlyle Grand offers chef Bill Jackson's imaginative, generous interpretation of modern American cooking. Start with lobster pot stickers, lazily flopped over the plate; then move on to such entrées as sea scallops "steak" wrapped in smoked ham with mustard crumbs, or crab cakes. Peach crème brûlée is the most popular dessert. *4000 S. 28th St., Shirlington Village, Arlington, VA, 703/931–0777. AE, DC, MC, V. $$*

3 g-8

CASHION'S EAT PLACE

Ann Cashion's popular Adams-Morgan restaurant is usually jammed with regulars, who feast on Cashion's up-to-date home-style cooking. Meat and fish are often local and seasonal, and are always skillfully prepared. The side dishes—the likes of garlicky mashed potatoes or buttery potatoes Anna—sometimes upstage the main course. The à la carte Sunday brunch is excellent. *1819 Columbia Rd. NW, between Biltmore and Mintwood Sts., Adams-Morgan, 202/797–1819. MC, V. Closed Sun. No lunch Tues.–Sat. Metro: Woodley Park–Zoo. $$$*

3 g-8

CITIES

Every year, this trendy Adams-Morgan restaurant recasts its menu and its photographic collection to honor a different city; honorees have ranged from Venice to Istanbul to Mexico City. The food is better than you might expect of such a scene-conscious venue. The bar is lively, and the crowd is young and stylish; fittingly, the place is open nightly until 2 AM, Friday and Saturday until 3 AM. The once-private upstairs club (Privée) is now open to the public on weekend nights. *2424 18th St. NW, at Columbia Rd., Adams-Morgan, 202/328–2100. AE, D, DC, MC, V. No lunch. Metro: Woodley Park–Zoo. $$$*

5 d-4

CITRONELLE

Having relocated to Washington from Los Angeles, California-French chef Michel Richard quickly proclaimed Citronelle, in the Latham Hotel, his flagship restaurant and had it entirely remodeled, with a glass-front kitchen and a wall that changes color every 59 seconds. It's an expensive show, but Richard's artistry is worth the price of admission. His working tools are largely seafood, foie gras, rabbit, exotic mushrooms, truffles, and pedigree poultry; his flavoring combinations are daring and masterful. Witty appetizer specials might include an impressive "tart" of thinly sliced grilled scallops or "beignets" of foie gras coated with *kataife* (a grain product that resembles shredded wheat) and deep-fried. Main-course loin of venison might come with chestnuts, mushrooms, and wine sauce. Breast of squab is served with an ethereal truffle sauce. A showcase wine cellar is filled with top-notch bottles. *Latham Hotel, 3000 M St. NW, Georgetown, 202/625–2150. AE, DC, MC, V. Metro: Foggy Bottom–GWU. $$$$*

6 b-4

COEUR DE LION

This elegant hotel restaurant now has a chef to match the setting. Fred Lewis' menu may read trendy, but it is soundly based on combinations that complement each other. Dishes include Shenandoah angry trout with potato-salmon hash and smoky chipotle-pepper jus, and rack of lamb with a balsamic orange demi-glace. Afternoon tea is served in the Wilkes Room, an English-style parlor off the lobby. The brick-wall atrium dining room has a romantic cast that makes it perfect for quiet, special occasions. A pianist plays jazz Sunday through Thursday, and a full jazz trio shows up on Friday and Saturday. *Henley Park Hotel, 926 Massachusetts Ave. NW, at 10th St., Downtown, 202/414–0500. AE, D, DC, MC, V. Metro: Metro Center. $$$*

6 a-4

DC COAST

Chef Jeff Tunks celebrates seafood from the East, West, and Gulf coasts at this high-style restaurant with an active bar scene. He has a sure touch with a variety of culinary palettes: classic mid-Atlantic seafood and both New Orleans– and Asian-inspired dishes. The fried oysters and crab cakes are among the best in town, and you'd be insane to miss the gilded chocolate-hazelnut pyramid for dessert. The acoustics are a major challenge here; ask for the intimate mezzanine tables, which are more romantic and calm. *1401 K St. NW, at 14th St., Downtown, 202/216– 5988. AE, D, DC,*

MC, V. Closed Sun. No lunch Sat. Metro: McPherson Sq. $$$

8 *f-4*
ELYSIUM

One of your best bets for a civilized meal in very civilized Old Town, the dining room at the Morrison House hotel is worth seeking out. Chef Yomi Faniyi prepares prix-fixe three-, four-, or five-course dinners that change nightly. Previous dinners have included lobster in phyllo crisp, Dover sole meunièr, and duck confit. The wine list has a good selection of American and European bottles. *116 S. Alfred St., Alexandria, VA, 703/838–8000. Reservations essential. AE, DC, MC, V. No dinner Sun.–Mon. Metro: King St. $$$$*

5 *g-5*
EQUINOX

The unconventional name Equinox reflects owner-chef Todd Gray's credo. As seasons change, so do his ingredients and the dishes he prepares. His plates have no irrelevant garnishes just for the sake of appearance; every morsel counts. Seared Maine scallops, moistened with truffled vinaigrette, come with sweet peas. Period. Only crispy fried onions accompany the grilled Angus T-bone and its cabernet sauce. You get the idea. Gray was executive chef at one of Washington's finest Italian restaurants, Galileo, for seven years, so pay attention to the Italian listings on the menu. The sleek interior design echoes what's going on in the kitchen. *818 Connecticut Ave. NW, at I St., Downtown, 202/331–8118. Reservations essential. AE, DC, MC, V. Metro: Farragut West. $$$*

3 *g-8*
FELIX

Chef David Scribner's skillful New American cooking draws an older crowd at dinner and a fashionable urban crew after 10 PM, when live blues and jazz are played nightly. Start with the tomato and brie *bruschetta* (toasted bread); then move on to the Chilean sea bass or thyme- crusted lamb chops with basil mashed potatoes. Food is placed vertically on plates, creating unique and colorful presentations. If you come on a Friday, you'll find an unlikely treat—challah bread, matzo ball soup, and brisket, just like Scribner's mother used to make. Wednesday is Sinatra Night, when dancers move to the sounds of swing. *2406 18th St. NW, Adams-Morgan, 202/*

483–3549. AE, MC, V. No lunch Mon.–Sat. Metro: Woodley Park–Zoo. $$$

INN AT LITTLE WASHINGTON

It may be a 90-minute drive from downtown D.C., but Washingtonians claim Virginia's luxurious Inn at Little Washington as their own. It's decorated as a fantasy of an English country house, and the beautifully choreographed service makes the evening flow seamlessly. After a first course of tiny canapés, you have an excellent soup: perhaps chilled fruit or creamy leek. Trout smoked over apple wood might come next—or medallions of veal with Virginia country ham and wild mushrooms, or roast venison with black currants and tart greens. Desserts, which you can savor in the garden in warm weather, are fanciful and elegant. None of this comes cheap; prix-fixe dinner without wine costs $98 Monday through Thursday, $108 on Sunday and Friday, and $128 on Saturday. *Middle and Main Sts., Washington, VA, 540/675–3800. Reservations essential. MC, V. Closed Tues., except in May and Oct. No lunch. $$$$*

5 *f-2*
JOCKEY CLUB

Despite a series of hotel management changes in recent years, the distinguished Jockey Club (in the Westin Fairfax) continues to attract political, entertainment, and society figures. The red-check tablecloths, country-hunt decor, and fireplace in the cocktail lounge make a fitting setting for the old-fashioned but delicious luxury cooking, which includes Dover sole, rack of lamb, and possibly the best crab cakes in the city. With 40 years under its belt, this is one of Washington's longest-running dining rooms. *Westin Fairfax Hotel, 2100 Massachusetts Ave. NW, at 21st St., Dupont Circle, 202/835–2100. AE, D, DC, MC, V. Metro: Dupont Circle. $$$$*

6 *a-6*
M&S GRILL

Brought to you by the owners of the very successful McCormick & Schmick's, this busy American grill reflects owner Bill McCormick's wish to pattern a restaurant after the legendary eateries of the late 1800s. The classics are all here: clam chowder, jumbo lump crab in cakes or cocktail, macaroni and cheddar, and grilled steaks and chops. Those with trendier palates may prefer the likes of fried calamari, grilled tuna, or fettuccine with rock shrimp and bay scallops. *600 13th St. NW, at F St., Downtown, 202/347–1500. AE, DC, MC, V. Metro: Metro Center. $$*

6 *c-6*

MALONEY & PORCELLI

If the name sounds like a law firm, that's because this restaurant was indeed christened after two New York lawyers who work for the owner. Chef David Burke's menu features crab cakes, thin pizzas, paella, garlicky roast chicken, and a great crackling pork shank with firecracker applesauce (applesauce with jalapeño peppers). Steak lovers have a choice of several very beefy cuts. Portions are generous. The restaurant's clean contemporary design is accented by turn-of-the-20th-century paintings and antiques, including a giant eagle, huge clocks, and a bronze relief of President William McKinley. *601 Pennsylvania Ave. NW, entrance on Indiana Ave., Downtown, 202/478–7274. AE, DC, MC, V. Metro: Archives–Navy Memorial. $$$$*

6 *c-6*

THE MARK

This cheery place expands the choices in this rapidly changing quarter of the city. Chef Alison Swope, who previously worked in a Southwestern restaurant in Old Town Alexandria, brought with her chili flavors and heat, but here they are subdued and used sparingly. Most of the menu is straight, modern American cuisine, with interesting spins on some of the combinations. Swope's gravlax is cured with gin, brown sugar, juniper berries, and, unexpectedly, cilantro. Pan-seared pork tenderloin is paired with a smoked-tomato and poblano-chili salsa. Monday evening, bottles of wine and champagne are half price with the purchase of an entrée. The inviting dining room is full of curves, hot colors, and trendy dangling spotlights. *401 7th St. NW, at D St., Downtown, 202/783–3133. AE, DC, MC, V. Metro: Archives–Navy Memorial. $$$*

5 *d-4*

MENDOCINO GRILLE & WINE BAR

The stated inspiration for this trendy spot is "the wine country of California, with its rolling vistas, fine restaurants, and wonderful wines." Mendocino delivers on all counts: the cooking is California-light, the wine list first-rate. And fieldstone walls suggest a hint of the countryside. There is a token wine rack in the back room (the big guns are elsewhere). *2917 M St. NW, Georgetown, 202/333–2912. AE, D, DC, MC, V. Metro: Foggy Bottom–GWU. $$$*

6 *b-4*

MORRISON-CLARK INN

A lovely restaurant in a hotel made by combining two 19th-century town houses, Morrison-Clark has been a hit since it opened its doors in 1987. Executive Chef Robert Beaudry carries on a tradition of modern American regional cuisine with an unexpected kick from touches of country ham, chipotle (smoked chili), or cilantro sauce. *1015 L St. NW, between Massachusetts Ave. and 11th St., Downtown, 202/898–1200. AE, DC, MC, V. No lunch Sat. Metro: Metro Center. $$$*

3 *e-6*

MRS. SIMPSON'S

After having been closed for more than a year, Mrs. Simpson's is back in business with more charm than ever. Named for Wallis Warfield Simpson, who became the Duchess of Windsor after King Edward VIII abdicated the British throne, this restaurant proudly displays memorabilia from Mrs. Simpson and the king, with a player piano adding to the romantic ambience. The skilled chef offers French-inspired American cuisine that is as healthy as it is delicious, and there's a light-fare menu for those watching calories. The rack of lamb Provençale, seared and with no fat, is delicious. A three-course pretheater menu is offered from 5:30 to 7. *2915 Connecticut Ave. NW, at Cathedral Ave., Woodley Park, 202/332–8700. AE, D, DC, MC, V. Closed Mon. No lunch weekdays. Metro: Woodley Park–Zoo. $$$*

5 *c-4*

NATHAN'S

Nathan's has anchored this heart-of-Georgetown corner for more than 30 years. Its loyal following includes many D.C. power brokers. Having recovered from a few stumbles, this snappy meeting place is once again riding high and turning out food that deserves praise. The menu, with such dishes as lobster fettuccine, has an Italian slant, but several lighter choices broaden the appeal.

3150 M St. NW, at Wisconsin Ave., George-
town, 202/338–2000. AE, DC, MC, V. $$$

3 e-7
NEW HEIGHTS

The lovely dining room, with large win-
dows overlooking nearby Rock Creek
Park, has been a neighborhood favorite
for years. Chef R. J. Copper's brief but
creative menu blends traditional Euro-
pean techniques with modern American
cooking. Try the endive salad sprinkled
with Roquefort followed by rare yellowfin
tuna or clove-dusted venison. New
Heights is also a Democratic stronghold
and has served many party officials over
the years. Sunday brunch is a particular
treat. 2317 Calvert St. NW, on Connecticut
Ave., 2nd floor, Woodley Park, 202/234–
4110. AE, D, DC, MC, V. No lunch Mon.–
Sat. Metro: Woodley Park–Zoo. $$$$

5 f-2
NORA

Chef-owner Nora Pouillon is something
of a pioneer in insisting that fresh,
organically raised meat and produce are
not only better for you but taste better,
too. Her cooking—like the quilt-deco-
rated dining room in which it's served—
is sophisticated and attractive. Hers was
the first certified organic restaurant in
the country, with fresh, organic products
making up nearly 100% of the menu.
Although dishes change seasonally,
you'll always find what's fresh and best:
soft-shell crabs as soon as they're avail-
able; lovely greens; wonderful, heirloom
tomato varieties; old-fashioned fruit
pies. 2132 Florida Ave. NW, at R St.,
Dupont Circle, 202/462–5143. D, MC, V.
Closed Sun. No lunch. Metro: Dupont Cir-
cle. $$$$

6 a-6
OCCIDENTAL GRILL

Recent refurbishing of this century-old
Washington institution has lightened
and brightened its look. Photos of politi-
cal figures, past and present, who have
dined here line the walls. Chef Patric
Bazin has snapped up the menu with
items such as bay cod with wild-mush-
room crust, Carolina shrimp with warm
potato-lobster salad, and a variety of
duck preparations. Rest assured, the
grilled meat still ranks high. 1475 Penn-
sylvania Ave. NW, at 14th St., Downtown,
202/783– 1475. AE, DC, MC, V. Metro:
Metro Center. $$$

1 b-3
OLD ANGLER'S INN

A summer dinner or Sunday brunch at
the Old Angler's Inn is one of the most
pleasant outdoor dining experiences in
Washington. The C&O Canal is just
across the road; the woods begin at the
edge of the deck; and the stars are
bright overhead. The large fireplace in
the lounge is the draw in winter. The
modern American menu changes seasonally. Recent hits from the appetizer
menu have included seared jumbo sea
scallops with yucca and beet jus, and
deep-fried goat cheese with a potato
crust. Main courses often feature game:
seared loin of venison with Savoy cab-
bage and onions; seared Muscovy duck
breast with shallot jus. Leave room for
the lemon tart with blueberries. 10801
MacArthur Blvd., 1 mi past Clara Barton
Pkwy., Potomac, MD, 301/365–2425. AE,
DC, MC, V. Closed Mon. $$$$

5 h-4
OLIVES

Celebrity chef-owner Todd English
opened his first Olives in Boston. He's
since branched out and has arrived in
the capital with a splash with this popular bi-level showcase restaurant in a
bland office building. The upper level is
dominated by a huge open kitchen with
a wood-burning oven that's the source
of the enticing aroma you sniff as you
enter. The food is often more complicated than successful, so it's best to
stay with the simple preparations. Sample dishes include wood-grilled beef tenderloin and barbecued Tuscan meat loaf
on Israeli couscous. Seating upstairs is
tight and uncomfortable. Downstairs is
more comfortable and quieter, but is
much more somber and dim, even on
bright sunny days. This is a good spot
for people-watching; Redskins owner
Dan Snyder is a regular. 1600 K St. NW,
Downtown, 202/452–1866. AE, DC, MC,
V. Metro: Farragut North. $$$$

5 h-5
OVAL ROOM

The name refers to the Oval Office—
just across Lafayette Square at 1600
Pennsylvania Avenue—and this modern
American restaurant has become a
favorite lunch spot with the Executive
Branch, politicians, lobbyists, and journalists. Despite its intimate size, the
Oval Room allows for privacy while dining. The bar is a popular hangout after

work. *800 Connecticut Ave. NW, at H St., Downtown, 202/822–6000. AE, D, DC, MC, V. Closed Sun. No lunch Sat. Metro: Farragut North or Farragut West. $$$*

6 *a-6*

PALOMINO

This two-story restaurant bills itself as a Mediterranean bistro despite the fact that $5 million went into the decorating—some bistro. The splashy look incorporates everything from faux Matisse and Leger paintings to American art glass. The menu is just as wide-ranging. Pick your dish and country: meat loaf, paella, rigatoni, grilled chicken breast with apricot and cilantro sauce (from where?), and grilled New York strip. The upper level has a popular bar and lighter snack food at slightly lower prices. *Ronald Reagan Bldg., 1300 Pennsylvania Ave., Downtown, 202/842–9800. AE, DC, MC, V. No smoking. Metro: Metro Center or Archives–Navy Memorial. $$$*

3 *g-8*

PEYOTE CAFÉ/ ROXANNE RESTAURANT/ ON THE ROOFTOP

These connected Adams-Morgan restaurants attract a young crowd, including students, with a menu of Mexican and traditional Southern food. Dine on the rooftop deck in good weather, when many folks come to nibble on appetizers and drink frozen margaritas. *2319 18th St. NW, Adams-Morgan, 202/462–8330. AE, DC, MC, V. No lunch Mon.–Sat., except Sat. in summer. Metro: Woodley Park–Zoo. $$*

6 *a-1*

POLLY'S CAFE

This cozy U Street café is at its best on cold nights, when you can scarf down a burger and knock back a beer in front of the fireplace. Stick to the better-than-average bar food. At about $8, Polly's hearty brunch is also a good value. *1342 U St. NW, U Street, 202/265–8385. MC, V. No lunch weekdays. Metro: U St.–Cardozo. $$*

5 *f-4*

PRIME RIB

Consistency is the hallmark of a good restaurant, and the Prime Rib has built its reputation by serving consistently excellent prime rib, steaks, and fish in a luxurious setting that recalls Miami

Beach in the '50s. It's popular with lobbyists, sharp people who like to dress up, and the rest of the expense-account crowd. A jacket and tie are required. *2020 K St. NW, between 20th and 21st Sts., Downtown, 202/466–8811. AE, DC, MC, V. Closed Sun. No lunch Sat. Metro: Farragut North. $$$$*

5 *g-4*

RELISH

The latest addition to the capital's office canyon, Relish refers to its food as "Progressive American Cuisine," which translates into a mix of Italian, Japanese, and steak house fare, along with good old-fashioned American standbys such as meat loaf sandwich with mashed potatoes and gravy. The dining room is spacious and handsome, and a courtyard entrance distances the restaurant from the midday bustle. *1800 M St. NW, entrance on 18th St., Downtown, 202/785–1177. AE, DC, MC, V. Closed Sun. Metro: Dupont Circle. $$*

1 *c-2*

ROCK BOTTOM

This brew house seems to have been decorated by a Colorado native who was a fan of Frank Lloyd Wright. The mission-style decor is tastefully accented with paintings, pottery, and plants straight from Boulder. The eclectic menu runs the gamut, but the best bet is to make a meal of the bountiful appetizers. Titan Toothpicks (fried tortillas stuffed with smoked chicken, jack cheese, and Southwest seasonings) and fried calamari dipped in beer batter and toasted sesame seeds are two of the more innovative items. Beer lovers can experience all five of Rock Bottom's homemade brews—just ask for the beer sampler. After dining, try your hand at one of four pool tables upstairs, or request a tour of the in-house brewery. *7900 Norfolk Ave., Bethesda, MD, 301/652–1311. AE, MC, V. Metro: Bethesda. $$*

5 *d-6*

ROOF TERRACE

The view is the main attraction at this Kennedy Center dining room, and it's naturally handy for a pre-performance lunch or dinner. The prices are high, but the staff appreciates that you need to be out before the curtain goes up. Sunday brunch, an elaborate buffet laid out in the kitchen, is probably the best meal here. *Kennedy Center, 2700 F St. NW, at*

Virginia Ave., Foggy Bottom, 202/416–8555. AE, DC, MC, V. Lunch on matinee days only. Metro: Foggy Bottom–GWU, with shuttle to Kennedy Center. $$$$

6 c-4
RUPPERTS

Possibly the hippest restaurant in D.C.—with a sea of black-clad diners to prove it—Rupperts is ensconced in a rather dicey area north of downtown that is fast changing thanks to the nearby MCI Center and the plot of land that will eventually be turned into a new convention center. Chef John Cochran makes a point of finding the freshest regional ingredients and changing his menu daily. Look for vegetable soups made entirely without cream, game birds, seasonal mushrooms, and such Southern delicacies as greens and grits. The decor is spare but achingly stylish, like the centerpieces—a single small but perfect vegetable or fruit. 1017 7th St. NW, Downtown, 202/783–0699. AE, MC, V. Closed Sun.–Tues. No lunch Fri.–Wed. Metro: Mt. Vernon Sq.–UDC. $$$

9 g-7
SEASONS

If you're in the mood to splurge, this sophisticated dining room at the Four Seasons Hotel is just the place. Since the restaurant opened two decades ago, Chef Doug McNeil has presided over one of Washington's best-regarded kitchens. The cuisine has received many awards for lightened classic dishes as well as alternative cuisine, which offers dishes lower in calories, cholesterol, sodium, and fat—healthful, but not dreary on the palate. Service is correct without being stuffy, and the food is beautifully prepared and presented. Piano music creates the background from 4 PM on. Four Seasons Hotel, 2800 Pennsylvania Ave. NW, Georgetown, 202/342–0444. AE, DC, MC, V. Metro: Foggy Bottom–GWU. $$$$

9 g-8
SEQUOIA

This enormous, two-story, glass-walled restaurant is more noted for its riverside location than its food, but the view makes it perfect for a springtime drink after work or a Sunday brunch on the deck. It's open nightly until midnight, weekends until 1 AM. 3000 K St. NW, between Thomas Jefferson and 30th Sts., Washington Harbour, Georgetown, 202/

944–4200. AE, D, DC, MC, V. Metro: Foggy Bottom–GWU. $$

6 c-6
701

A pioneer on this 7th Street corridor, 701 brought Continental sophistication to an area where none had existed before. Now it has company but still shines for its dramatic decor and on-target contemporary cuisine with roots based in Italy, France, Asia, and the Americas. Want just a small, luxurious bite? Sit at the Caviar Lounge bar for either those eponymous briny pearls or tapas. If you're attending a performance at the nearby Shakespeare Theatre, this is a convenient, upper-crust choice. Music is provided nightly by a piano-and-bass duo. 701 Pennsylvania Ave. NW, Downtown, 202/393–0701. AE, DC, MC, V. No lunch weekends. Metro: Archives–Navy Memorial. $$$

9 b-7
1789

Perhaps Washington's overall first choice for celebrating milestone birthdays and anniversaries, 1789 is a model of consistency. There are dining rooms on each of the three floors, but the first-floor colonial-style John Carroll room is the one to ask for. Chef Ris Lacoste was named 1999 Chef of the Year by the Restaurant Association of Metropolitan Washington. One bite and you'll know why. Soups, such as the rich black bean soup with unsweetened chocolate or the seafood stew, are flavorful. Rack of lamb and fillet of beef are specialties, and seared tuna stands out among the excellent seafood dishes. Nearby Georgetown University students usually hang out in the subterranean pub, the Tombs, but when parents come to town, they slick up and dine upstairs. 1226 36th St. NW, at Prospect St., Georgetown, 202/965–1789. AE, DC, MC, V. No lunch. $$$

5 g-3
TABARD INN

Make your way through the maze of overstuffed sofas and chairs in the hotel parlor, and you'll find a distinguished modern American restaurant. Chef David Craig made his reputation as a seafood cook, and here at the Tabard he continues to pair simply, perfectly cooked fish or meat with interesting combinations of grains and greens. Much of the produce is from the inn's own farm. The pretty courtyard is open in good weather. *1739 N St. NW, between 17th and 18th Sts., Dupont Circle, 202/ 833–2668. AE, DC, MC, V. Metro: Dupont Circle. $$$$*

5 *d-4*

TAHOGA

A restaurant that has had its kitchen ups and downs is way up again. Decor is minimalist, as is the pared-down menu. Instead of dozens of choices, you have around 10 carefully crafted "beginnings" and a like number of "mains." Try the cornmeal-crusted, roasted catfish with black bean hush puppies or the shoft-shell-crab po'boy. Noise carries on the first level; it's quieter upstairs. In nice weather the romantic courtyard is the perfect setting for alfresco dining. *2518 M St. NW, Georgetown, 202/338–5380. AE, DC, MC, V. Metro: Foggy Bottom– GWU. $$*

5 *h-4*

TIMOTHY DEAN'S RESTAURANT AND BAR

Gone are the gilt-framed paintings, massive bouquets, and heavy leather chairs; in fact the millions of dollars that went into doing up the now-closed Lespinasse, which used to reside here, have been swept away. The new incarnation is stripped down and bright with lemony-yellow walls and contemporary chairs. Chef Timothy Dean was brought in from the kitchen at Palladin in New York. But he's no stranger to Washington: he was sous-chef to Jean-Louis Palladin at the superb Jean-Louis in the Watergate hotel. His menu features premium products cooked in simple ways to maximize their true flavors. Temptations abound: whether fish, fowl, or meat, choices will be difficult. One dish worth trying is the grilled lobster served with an array of wood-grilled root vegetables. Saturday lunch is served in the bar only, not in the restaurant. *St. Regis Hotel, 16th and K Sts. NW, Downtown, 202/879–6900. AE, DC, MC, V. Metro: Farragut North. $$$$*

3 *g-8*

TOM TOM

Pizza, tapas, salads, grilled meat, fish— Tom Tom has every menu trend, and every fashion trend as well. On warm nights the rooftop patio is packed, as young professionals down cocktails and nibble on the restaurant's unique fried plantains and calamari appetizers. Hip, artsy crowds wait almost an hour for tables on weekends. Desserts are a highlight, including the sinful *boca negra*—a baked chocolate truffle topped with cinnamon whipped cream. *2333 18th St. NW, Adams- Morgan, 202/588– 1300. AE, D, DC, MC, V. Closed Tues. No lunch. Metro: Woodley Park–Zoo. $$*

10 *e-4*

TWO QUAIL

The maze of rooms and the estate-sale decor give Two Quail an unusual personality for a Capitol Hill restaurant. The seasonal menu has both rich fare—pork chops stuffed with apricot and sausage, chicken *cordon bleu* (chicken stuffed with ham and sautéed), game meats, filet mignon—and lighter seafood pastas and meal-size salads. Service can be leisurely. *320 Massachusetts Ave. NE, Capitol Hill, 202/543–8030. AE, D, DC, MC, V. No lunch Sat. Metro: Union Station. $$$*

6 *a-1*

UTOPIA

Most people go to Utopia not so much for the food as to be seen, and to listen to the excellent jazz, blues, or Brazilian bands. But the food—a mix of flavors from New Orleans, Italy, and the Mediterranean—is lighthearted and fun. The lamb couscous, seafood bisque, and pasta dishes such as the Chef's Advice (a combination of shrimp, chicken, andouille sausage, and sweet peppers) are sure hits. *1418 U St. NW, U Street, 202/483–7669. AE, D, DC, MC, V. Metro: U St.–Cardozo. $$*

5 *e-4*

WEST END CAFE

This attractive, sophisticated place is open a bit later on weekends than the run of Washington restaurants—they serve until midnight Friday and Saturday. The spirited New American menu features fresh seasonal ingredients: choice items may include grilled salmon fillet with spinach risotto or tuna loin with sunflower seeds, *soba* noodles, and beurre blanc. Piano music adds a bit of romance on Friday and Saturday evenings. *1 Washington Circle Hotel NW, between New Hampshire Ave. and 23rd St., Foggy Bottom, 202/293–5390. AE, D, DC, MC, V. Metro: Foggy Bottom–GWU. $$$*

6 *a-6*

THE WILLARD ROOM

Stepping into the Willard Room, with its stately Edwardian decor, is like taking a quick trip to old Europe. There's lots of space between tables, which is very important since it's big-money, big-power dining here. Chef Gerard Mandani does not cook to the setting, however; his food is inspired contemporary American, plus some French, plus some English—as in Yorkshire pudding, but this time the biscuit is filled with Peekytoe crabmeat. Service is intensely correct and discreet. This is definitely a big-occasion spot. *Willard Hotel, 1401 Pennsylvania Ave. NW, Downtown, 202/637–7440. AE, DC, MC, V. Metro: Metro Center. $$$$*

DELICATESSENS

2 *h-2*

FRANKLIN'S GENERAL STORE AND DELICATESSEN

Step back to a simpler time, when penny candy actually cost a penny and your favorite toy was a Slinky. You'll feel like a kid again when you walk through the door of this 1940s-style general store that sells everything from toys (don't miss the rubber chickens and paper dolls) to gourmet foods, including a huge selection of hot sauces, microbrews, and imported wines. Once you tear yourself away from all the delights in the store, head to the deli section, which offers about 40 creative sandwiches, homemade chili, and sumptuous Cajun-spiced fries. Franklin's is the perfect place to take kids of all ages for a special outing. *5121 Baltimore Ave., Hyattsville, MD, 301/927–2740. AE, D, MC, V. $*

2 *b-2*

KRUPIN'S

Purists may be disappointed, but Krupin's is Washington's best imitation of a New York deli. The smoked salmon, sturgeon, and whitefish are imported from Brooklyn. (The deli meats come from Baltimore.) Don't miss the rich, old-fashioned chicken soup. As for the combined schtick of brothers Mel and Morty Krupin, you couldn't miss it if you tried. *4620 Wisconsin Ave. NW, Tenleytown, 202/686–1989. AE, MC, V. Metro: Tenleytown–AU. $$*

ETHIOPIAN

3 *g-8*

MESKEREM

Washington has more Ethiopian restaurants than anywhere else in the country, but Meskerem stands out for its bright, attractively decorated dining room and its balcony, where you can dine Ethiopian-style—seated on the floor on leather cushions, with large woven baskets for tables. Each entrée is served on a large piece of *injera*, a large yeast pancake; you eat family-style, and scoop up mouthful-size portions of the hearty dishes with extra bread. Among Meskerem's specialties are stews made with spicy berbere chili sauce; *kitfo*, a buttery beef dish served raw, like steak tartare, or very rare; and a tangy, green-chili vinaigrette potato salad. Live Ethiopian music and dancing take place Friday and Saturday nights. *2434 18th St. NW, at Columbia Rd., Adams-Morgan, 202/462–4100. AE, DC, MC, V. Metro: Woodley Park–Zoo. $$*

3 *g-8*

RED SEA

Red Sea is a lively and casual place where both native Ethiopians and Adams-Morgan denizens feel comfortable eating spicy Ethiopian stews. There's often a wait, particularly on weekends, when there's live Ethiopian music. *2463 18th St. NW, at Kalorama Rd., Adams-Morgan, 202/483–5000. AE, D, DC, MC, V. Metro: Woodley Park–Zoo. $$*

5 *d-4*

ZED'S ETHIOPIAN CUISINE

The move from the other end of M Street gave Zed's a zippy new look and increased popularity. It remains the best of Washington's many Ethiopian restaurants. The menu is much like that at the others, but there are a few Zed specialties: short ribs of beef with rosemary, and cubed beef stewed with collard greens. *1201 28th St. NW, at M St., Georgetown, 202/333–4710. AE, D, DC, MC, V. Metro: Foggy Bottom–GWU. $$*

FRENCH

9 *e-6*

AU PIED DE COCHON

This longtime late-night hangout—it never closes—has weathered some administrative chaos, but its popularity is undiminished. Stick to omelets, frîtes, and grilled meats. *1335 Wisconsin Ave. NW, between Dumbarton and N Sts., Georgetown, 202/333–2333. AE, MC, V. $$*

BAILIWICK INN

Whether you're dining indoors or outdoors (in season), you'll have several choices from the five-course prix-fixe-only dinner menus, which change every two weeks. Chef Jeff Prather specializes in classic French cuisine with a New American twist and often uses exotic mushrooms, venison, quail, duck, sea bass, and tuna. Two popular main dishes are pistachio-crusted rack of lamb with Madeira sauce, and sea bass prepared with a honey-thyme glaze and served with saffron potatoes. Desserts include Melting Chocolate Cake, light French apple tarts, and chocolate mousse in a brandy gingersnap cup. Before dinner, hors d'oeuvres and wine are served in two parlors with working fireplaces. A lovely high tea is held Thursdays at 3:30 and Sundays at 3. The 1812 historic hotel that houses the Bailiwick is said to be where the first Confederate soldier died—out in the front yard. *Fairfax City Inn, 4023 Chain Bridge Rd., Fairfax, VA, 703/691–2266. Reservations essential. AE, MC, V. Closed Monday. No lunch Tues., Thurs., and weekends. $$$$*

5 f-2
BISTRO DU COIN

This energetic bistro has a light-filled dining room bustling with lively conversations and table celebrations. In a town known for pretentious French dining, Bistro du Coin comes as a welcome surprise—it's casual, friendly, and a great value given the high quality of food. Start with a warm leek salad with smoked duck, or try a *tartine* with smoked salmon, onions, and capers. Next, order the *moules marinieres* (steamed mussels served with flaming hot fries) or the *casserole de lapin aux spatzle* (rabbit stew in a cream sauce with carrots, onions, mushrooms, and spaetzle. There is an excellent selection of French wines to accompany your meal. *1738 Connecticut Ave. NW, Dupont Circle, 202/234–6969. AE, MC, V. No lunch Mon. Metro: Dupont Circle. $$*

5 c-4
BISTRO FRANÇAIS

After 25 years in operation, Bistro Français remains pure Parisian, with nostalgic posters, a hanging wine press, and real bistro buzz. Here you'll find hearty bistro fare at old-fashioned prices. Daily specials might include roast pigeon, duck confit with white beans, or roast pork with potatoes au gratin. The $11.95 fixed-price lunch and $17.95 early and late-night dinner specials are bargain options. It's open Sunday through Thursday until 3 AM, Friday and Saturday until 4. *3128 M St. NW, between 31st St. and Wisconsin Ave., Georgetown, 202/338– 3830. AE, DC, MC, V. Metro: Foggy Bottom–GWU or Dupont Circle. $$*

5 b-2
BISTROT LEPIC

Chef Bruno Fortin presides over this small, charming Georgetown bistro, which has become a favorite with the locals. The menu changes seasonally and includes many bistro classics: veal cheeks, boned pigs' feet, cassoulet in winter. A recently opened private salon, dubbed "Rue Lepic," has a bar and a sitting area and can pamper up to 10 guests for a prix-fixe dinner. *1736 Wisconsin Ave. NW, Georgetown, 202/333–0111. AE, DC, MC, V. Closed Mon. $$$*

6 a-5
GERARD'S PLACE

Perhaps Washington's most serious French restaurant these days, Gerard's Place is the creation of acclaimed chef Gerard Pangaud, whose cooking combines traditional techniques with modern tastes. The menu, which changes daily, might include Gerard's signature poached lobster with a sauce of ginger, lime, and sauternes; venison with pumpkin, dried fruit, and beetroot puree; or seared tuna with black olives and roasted red peppers. Desserts— such as the chocolate tear, a flourless chocolate cake shaped like a teardrop and veined with raspberry—are exquisite. *915 15th St. NW, Downtown, 202/737– 4445. AE, DC, MC, V. Closed Sun. No lunch Sat. Metro: McPherson Sq. $$$$*

1 d-6
THE GRILL, RITZ-CARLTON AT PENTAGON CITY

This wood-paneled restaurant, with its spacious, clubby room of muted greens and taupes, horse paintings, and fresh flowers at every table, is a handsome spot for special-occasion dining. The food is innovative, and the table settings and service are impeccable. Start your meal with caviar-topped *amuse bouche* (appetizers). Main dishes, from delicate fish to hearty rack of lamb, are well cooked, and the desserts are attractive as well as delicious. The extravagant Sunday champagne brunch (seatings are at noon and 1:30) features five all-inclusive stations: a raw bar, hot and cold meats and egg dishes, seafood, fruits and breads, and desserts. *The Fashion Centre at Pentagon City, 1250 S. Hayes St., Arlington, VA, 703/415–5000 or 703/412–2760. AE, D, DC, MC, V. Metro: Pentagon City. $$$$*

8 *g-4*

LA BERGERIE

This elegant Old Town restaurant, dressed in paisley and chandeliers, is run by brothers Jean and Bernard Campagne and specializes in the food of the Basque region in southern France. Try such robust dishes as duck confit and Basque *piperade* (stew) of vegetables, but don't neglect the specials, which showcase some of brother Jean's most imaginative cooking. Main-course selections usually include fish in classic sauces, coq au vin, duck, venison, and lamb. Dessert soufflés and the apple tart must be ordered when you pick your entrée. *218 N. Lee St., between Queen and Cameron Sts., 2nd floor, Alexandria, VA, 703/683–1007. AE, D, DC, MC, V. Closed Sun. Metro: King St. (about 20 blocks away). $$*

10 *e-4*

LA BRASSERIE

At its best in the spring and fall, when you can dine in its front garden, this pleasant Capitol Hill gathering place occupies two floors of adjoining town houses. The basically French menu changes seasonally, but poached salmon and breast of duck are always available. The small, selective wine list is also in flux. The crème brûlée, served cold or hot with fruit, is superb. *239 Massachusetts Ave. NE, between 2nd and 3rd Sts., Capitol Hill, 202/546–9154. AE, D, MC, V. Metro: Union Station. $$$*

5 *d-4*

LA CHAUMIÈRE

A favorite of Georgetown's old guard, La Chaumière (which means "the thatched cottage") has the rustic charm of a French country inn, especially in winter, when its central stone fireplace warms the room. Fish stew, mussels, and scallops are always available, and specials invariably include a number of grilled fishes. Indeed, many locals plan their meals around La Chaumière's rotating specials, particularly Wednesday's couscous and Thursday's tasty cassoulet. *2813 M St. NW, at 28th St., Georgetown, 202/338–1784. AE, DC, MC, V. Closed Sun. No lunch Sat. Metro: Foggy Bottom–GWU. $$*

10 *b-3*

LA COLLINE

Its location in a sterile office block doesn't inspire confidence, but chef Robert Gréault's kitchen turns out some of the best traditional French cooking in Washington. The seasonal menu emphasizes market-fresh vegetables and seafood, with items that range from simple grilled preparations to fricassees and gratins with imaginative sauces. Choices usually include duck with orange or cassis sauce and veal with chanterelle mushrooms. *400 N. Capitol St. NW, between D and E Sts., Capitol Hill, 202/737–0400. AE, DC, MC, V. Closed Sun. No lunch Sat. Metro: Union Station. $$$*

3 *g-8*

LA FOURCHETTE

Another long-running show in a transient neighborhood, La Fourchette has won a loyal clientele by offering sumptuous bistro food at reasonable prices—in fact, this is the least expensive French cuisine you'll find in the District. Most of the menu is made up of daily specials, but you can usually count on finding bouillabaisse and rabbit on the list. Other entrées might include chicken in beurre blanc or sweetbreads in a mushroom cream sauce. La Fourchette looks just as a bistro should, with an exposed-brick wall, a tin ceiling, bentwood chairs, and quasi–postimpressionist murals. An inviting outdoor patio is open in warm weather. *2429 18th St. NW, between Belmont St. and Columbia Rd., Adams-Morgan, 202/332–3077. AE, DC, MC, V. Closed Aug. No lunch weekends. Metro: Woodley Park–Zoo. $$*

L'AUBERGE CHEZ FRANÇOIS

When François Haeringer moved his downtown restaurant into the Virginia countryside, his devoted clientele followed him. L'Auberge remains one of Washington's favorite places for special-occasion dining. Both the cooking and the decor are Alsatian; a huge fireplace dominates the main dining room, German knickknacks line the walls, and red-coated waiters guide you courteously through your meal. The price of an entrée includes a first course and dessert. Sausage and foie gras served on sauerkraut, salmon in a pastry crust for two, and medallions of beef and veal are a few of the outstanding and generously portioned choices. For dessert, try a soufflé or the delicious plum tart. You must reserve ahead several weeks in advance. 332 Springvale Rd., between Beach Mill and Walker Rds., Great Falls, VA, 703/759–3800. Reservations essential. AE, DC, MC, V. Closed Mon. No lunch. $$$

3 d-5
LAVANDOU
This recently expanded Cleveland Park restaurant serves the flavorful, aromatic cooking of Provence. The menu features hearty soups and an emphasis on fresh fish and grilled meats, all robustly seasoned and enhanced by a sunny, south-of-France decor. 3321 Connecticut Ave. NW, Cleveland Park, 202/966–3003. AE, DC, MC, V. No lunch weekends. Metro: Cleveland Park. $$

8 e-4
LE GAULOIS
The authentic cuisine bourgeoise at this attractive Old Town restaurant decorated in minimalist woods is often delivered with an uncomfortable dash of authentic hauteur. The best time to eat here is in the winter, when classics such as pot-au-feu, cassoulet, confit of duck, beef brains in vinaigrette, and bouillabaisse can dissolve the evening chill. There are many daily specials. 1106 King St., between Patrick and Henry Sts., Alexandria, VA, 703/739–9494. AE, DC, MC, V. Closed Sun. Metro: King St. $$

1 d-7
LE REFUGE
The menu at this local Alexandria favorite is firmly planted in the 1950s—and there's nothing wrong with that. This is where you can find longtime French favorites: onion soup, bouillabaisse, beef Wellington, salmon in puff pastry, leg of lamb, cassoulet, and poultry in mustard cream. The excellent main dishes and vegetables are why patrons keep coming back year after year to this charming little restaurant on

the city's main thoroughfare. Pink tablecloths and flowers enliven the small establishment, where you'll fast become friends with the diners at the oh-so-close next table. Don't forget to end with an excellent French-style dessert. Pre-theater early dinner specials are available Tuesday through Thursday. 127 N. Washington St., Alexandria, VA, 703/548–4661. AE, D, MC, V. Closed Sun. Metro: King St. $

7 b-2
LE RIVAGE
Enjoy a panoramic view of the harbor while dining in a romantic atmosphere created by the soft glow of oil lamps and the waterside location. Chef Jean-Marc Drimille has prepared classical and imaginative French dishes at Le Rivage since 1985. In his compact kitchen, Drimille creates everything from house-smoked salmon to sorbets and cookies. Regulars know they can depend on the consistent quality of the fare and the professionalism of the staff. A pretheater, fixed-price menu is available before 6:30 PM for the convenience of those headed to the nearby Arena Stage. Dining is available on an outdoor terrace during the warmer months. 1000 Water St. SW, Waterfront, 202/488–8111. AE, D, DC, MC, V. No lunch Sat. or Sun. Metro: L'Enfant Plaza. $$$

6 b-6
LES HALLES
Les Halles is about as close as you can come to a Parisian bistro without going to France. Start your meal with the terrific salad of frisée with bacon and blue cheese, then order a slab of Aberdeen Angus beef—the onglet (hangar steak) is particularly flavorful—accompanied by the best french fries in town. 1201 Pennsylvania Ave. NW, Downtown, 202/347–6848. AE, DC, MC, V. Metro: Metro Center. $$$

5 e-4
MARCEL'S
Marcel's became an instant power scene the minute it opened, thanks to owner-chef Robert Wiedmaier's loyal following. His French-Belgian roots are reflected in subtle ways: savory tarts, snail ragouts, and emphatic flavors with right-on combinations. Fresh seafood is accompanied by artfully selected garnishes and sauces. The dense, almost-sweet onion tart is cooked slowly and then spiked

with sharp Belgian ham. The wine list has a strong selection of California and French labels; the prices are not bashful. Noise carries in the dining space, although this is not a problem in the outdoor café. Smoking is only allowed in the bar. *2401 Pennsylvania Ave., Georgetown, 202/296–1166. AE, DC, MC, V. Metro: Foggy Bottom–GWU. $$$$*

5 *a-1*

SAVEUR

Step in from the outside bustle to calm and a breath of Provence. Bouquets of dried flowers planted on the pale walls enhance the feeling, as does a menu that recalls the great bistros of France. The gutsy bouillabaisse is deservedly popular. Other specialties include duck country pâté and Black Angus beef fillets with bone marrow and a reduction of cabernet. At $18, Sunday brunch is a bargain. *2218 Wisconsin Ave. NW, below Calvert St., Glover Park, 202/333- -5885. AE, DC, MC, V. $$$*

5 *c-4*

SENSES

Shhh. That's what you first notice about the restaurant that *Bon Appetit* pronounced one of the best new spots in the area just months after it opened. While Georgetown buzzes, Senses stands alone on a quiet side street with almost no traffic. The building is small and white, the dining room is small and white, and soft classical music soothes in the background. Two chefs combine talents, one attending to the French-inspired dishes, the other to the irresistible carry-out pastries. The result is always something special breakfast, brunch, lunch, or dinner. Try the Moroccan-style chicken *tagine* with preserved lemons, or the quiche of the day. *3206 Grace St. NW, between K St. and the C&O Canal, Georgetown, 202/342–9083. AE, MC, V. Metro: Foggy Bottom–GWU. $$$*

GERMAN

10 *e-4*

CAFÉ BERLIN

Chef Thomas Bach of Café Berlin prepares traditional dishes—and a few international favorites—with a light touch. Sauerbraten, schnitzels, and *kassler rippchen* (smoked pork loin) with sauerkraut are favorites. Seasonal specialties, such as *spargel* (white asparagus), and Oktoberfest are celebrated. Seated outside with a goblet of *Berliner weisse* (light wheat beer flavored with a shot of raspberry or woodruff syrup), it's easy to pretend you're on the Kurfurstendamm. *322 Massachusetts Ave. NE, Capitol Hill, 202/543–7656. AE, D, DC, MC, V. Metro: Union Station. $$$*

3 *a-8*

OLD EUROPE RESTAURANT & RATHSKELLER

In business for more than half a century now, Old Europe remains the place in D.C. for hearty German cooking: schnitzel, sauerbraten, liver dumplings, and game in season. European pastries are made on the premises. The restaurant's Asparagus Festival is as sure a harbinger of spring as the first daffodils, and that's not even to mention the May Wine Festival and the winter Game Festival. Wash it all down with liters of German beer or a bottle of good Rhine wine, and enjoy the live entertainment. *2434 Wisconsin Ave. NW, Glover Park, 202/333–7600. AE, DC, MC, V. No lunch Sun. $$$*

GREEK

1 *c-5*

AEGEAN TAVERNA

Outside, you can dine on Greek food under a front canopy of climbing vines. Inside, the walls bear brightly colored Aegean artifacts, and there's live Greek music on Friday and Saturday nights. You can't go wrong ordering the Greek sampler plate of moussaka, *pastitsio* (layered casserole of pasta and meat, topped with cream sauce), spanakopita, and stuffed grape leaves, but the lamb dishes are also excellent, and the deep-fried calamari appetizer is tender with a crispy coating. The "taverna" part of the name is fulfilled with an extensive selection of drinks, including ouzo, retsina, *metaxa* (sweet Greek brandy), beers, and a long list of Greek wines. *2950 Clarendon Blvd., Arlington, VA, 703/841–9494. MC, V. No lunch Sat. Metro: Clarendon. $*

AMPHORA RESTAURANT

The impressive menu, anchored by Greek dishes such as pastitsio and moussaka, has a range of options, with everything from soups and sandwiches to surf and turf. Such variety, along with the convenience of 24-hour service, has kept Amphora a popular neighborhood restaurant for decades. Indulge in an array of homemade pies, tortes, and other assorted pastries on the dessert list. *377 Maple Ave. W, Vienna, VA, 703/938–7877. AE, D, DC, MC, V. Metro: Vienna. $$*

8 f-4
TAVERNA CRETEKOU

White walls, tile floors, waiters who sing and dance, outdoor garden dining—you can almost imagine that you're in Greece rather than button-down Old Town. Broiled squid stuffed with shrimp is a terrific main course, as are octopus in wine sauce, roasted lamb, and trout stuffed with spinach, mushrooms, and feta. There's live Greek music on Thursday night. *818 King St., between Alfred and Columbus Sts., Alexandria, VA, 703/548–8688. AE, MC, V. Closed Mon. Metro: King St. $$*

10 e-8
TAVERNA THE GREEK ISLANDS

Stick to the basics and you'll have a good Greek meal at this Capitol Hill restaurant. Lamb is always tasty, particularly the *exohiko*, the house specialty of lamb, olives, and cheese wrapped in phyllo pastry. Chase your food with retsina, served by the glass or the bottle. *305 Pennsylvania Ave. SE, between 3rd and 4th Sts., Capitol Hill, 202/547–8360. AE, D, DC, MC, V. Closed Sun. Metro: Capitol South. $$*

5 f-2
ZORBA'S CAFÉ

Order at the counter of this casual Greek café and take your meal to one of the blue-and-white-checkered tables inside or out. Zorba's serves delectable pita-bread sandwiches, shish kebab and souvlaki plates, and spanakopita. A number of Greek-style pizzas also decorate the menu. *1612 20th St. NW, between Hillyer St. and Connecticut Ave., Dupont Circle, 202/387– 8555. AE, DC, MC, V. Metro: Dupont Circle. $$*

ICE CREAM

3 a-8
MAX'S BEST ICE CREAM

Max and Marsha Keshani have created more than 200 flavors of homemade ice cream since 1993. Tastes range from the unexpected melon flavors, such as cantaloupe or watermelon, to the unique ginger-snap ice cream punched up with fresh ginger root. Mozambique ice cream is perfectly spiced with nutmeg, cinnamon, and a hint of cloves. Fragrant waffle cones and several desserts such as apple pie are made on the premises. Photos of satisfied customers—smiling children—deck the walls in confirmation of the popularity and friendliness of this

---

FOR THE KIDS

Your kids don't care for foie gras and escargot? Got ants in their pants? Here are a few places that have menus or attractions that'll keep them entertained and allow you to have a relatively sane meal.

America (American)
Stop here after you hop off the Amtrak train or while visiting Union Station's shops and movie theaters.

Café Deluxe (American/Casual)
There's a children's menu, and kids can draw on the paper-covered tables.

Cheesecake Factory (American/Casual)
Kids are bound to find something they like on this huge menu, and the atmosphere is always lively and loud.

Franklin's General Store and Delicatessen (Delicatessens)
Browse an old-fashioned general store with toys galore before hitting the great deli.

Ledo (Pizza)
A family restaurant that's also a favorite spot for Little League and soccer coaches, who take their teams here for victory celebrations.

Max's Ice Cream (Ice Cream)
Photo collages of thousands of smiling children watch over this melt-in-your-mouth business.

Pizzeria Paradiso (Pizza)
If you're packing a couple of hungry kids under your arms, head to this popular Dupont Circle joint, where pizza, salads, and desserts will please every member of the family.

Tastee Diner (Cafés)
Perfect for connoisseurs of hot dogs, grilled cheese, fries, and milkshakes.

Washington institution. *2416 Wisconsin Ave. NW, Glover Park, 202/333–3111. No credit cards. $*

INDIAN

9 *d-7*

ADITI

D.C. has gotten a crop of new Indian restaurants in the last few years, but this elegant favorite, with its burgundy carpets and chairs and pastel walls with brass sconces, still turns out some of the best Indian food around. A $13.95 special buys you a sampling of several dishes. House specialties include lamb vindaloo, okra curry, tandoori meat and fish, and excellent breads. *3299 M St. NW, near 32nd St., Georgetown, 202/625–6825. AE, D, DC, MC, V. Metro: Foggy Bottom–GWU. $$*

5 *h-5*

BOMBAY CLUB

The beautiful Bombay Club strikes a Raj pose and is the most attractive Indian restaurant in Washington. The bar, which serves hot hors d'oeuvres during cocktail hour, is furnished with rattan chairs and paneled with dark wood; the dining room, with potted palms and a bright-blue ceiling above white plaster moldings, is elegant and decorous. The menu includes unusual seafood specialties and a large number of vegetarian dishes, but the real standouts are the breads and the seafood appetizers. There's live piano music during dinner and Sunday brunch. *815 Connecticut Ave. NW, between H and I Sts., Downtown, 202/659–3727. AE, DC, MC, V. No lunch Sat. Metro: Farragut West. $$*

5 *f-4*

BOMBAY PALACE

Part of an international chain of upscale Indian restaurants, the Bombay Palace offers attentive service and a luxurious setting, with tablecloths, modern appointments, and immaculate pink walls. The prix-fixe lunch is a bargain, as is the weekend brunch; but the à la carte menu has the most delicious specialties, such as lamb or chicken pilaf, tandoori prawns, lamb vindaloo, and exciting vegetarian curries. The weekend brunch is also a great deal. *2020 K St. NW, between 20th and 21st Sts., Downtown, 202/331–4200. AE, DC, MC, V. Metro: Farragut West. $$*

5 *a-1*

HERITAGE INDIA

It's another world up the two flights to this restaurant from frenetic Wisconsin Avenue. This newest addition to choices for fine Indian cuisine is a calm oasis in a hard-edged neighborhood. From the door pulls to the wall hangings, all is beautiful and serene. As the refined Indian cooking will testify, Heritage is not an ordinary curry stop. The tandoori oven turns out wonderfully smoky meats and fish, and vegetarian options abound. *2400 Wisconsin Ave. NW, near Calvert St., Glover Park, 202/333–3120. AE, DC, MC, V. $$*

5 *g-1*

HIMALAYAN GRILL

This unique restaurant actually combines Indian, Nepalese, and Tibetan cooking, advertising that it is the only *"momo"* place in town (momos are delicious Tibetan dumplings). Gracious servers will help you create a well-balanced meal if you don't have anything particular in mind; some suggestions include the shrimp curry platter and the *palak paneer* (homemade pieces of cheese and ground spinach with potatoes and fresh spices). The $6.96 all-you-can-eat lunch special is a great bargain; be sure to order nan bread and a *lassi* (a thick plain-yogurt drink served sweet or salty) to go with your meal. *1805 18th St. NW, between S and T Sts., Dupont Circle, 202/986–5124. AE, D, DC, MC, V. Metro: Dupont Circle. $*

1 *h-2*

MAHARAJA

Authentic Indian music fills the small, dark dining room, where diners can watch as Maharaja's chef prepares breads such as nan and *keema partha* (whole-wheat bread stuffed with ground lamb) in the tandoor oven. Nibble on *papadum* (crisp lentil-flour wafers) dipped in coriander chutney before choosing from signature dishes such as tandoori chicken or palak paneer. Treat yourself to a creamy mango lassi; it will coat your stomach and ease the way for the more adventurous beef vindaloo and spicy mixed vegetable curry. This is an extremely popular lunchtime spot for the employees of neighboring NASA-Goddard Space Flight Center. *8825 Greenbelt Rd., Greenbelt, MD, 301/552–1600. AE, D, MC, V. No lunch Mon. $*

IRISH

3 d-5

IRELAND'S FOUR PROVINCES

This merry Irish pub and restaurant is well-known for its slow Guinness pours and its nightly live music, but few people realize that the Irish fare is good (if fairly plain) and reasonably priced. Favorites include traditional Irish stew, shepherd's pie, and fish-and-chips; the pot roast served with homemade mashed potatoes is another hit. Four Provinces also has the best Saint Patrick's Day party in the city. *3412 Connecticut Ave. NW, Cleveland Park, 202/244–0860. AE, MC, V. Metro: Cleveland Park. $$*

ITALIAN

6 c-4

A.V. RISTORANTE ITALIANO

You'll think you've stepped back into the '50s when you walk into this popular, eccentric restaurant, and in fact little has changed here since then. The white pizza is a classic; the rest of the hearty Italian fare is dependable, and gets even better when you accompany it with one of the hearty and affordable Italian wines. The fireplace is popular in winter, the large (60-seat) garden in summer. *607 New York Ave. NW, at 6th St., Downtown, 202/737–0550. AE, DC, MC, V. Closed Sun. Metro: Gallery Pl.–Chinatown. $$*

5 b-4

CAFE MILANO

Washington's beautiful people have made a home in this Georgetown restaurant, decorated with a Milanese-fashion motif. The food is of very high quality, uncomplicated but beautifully prepared—fresh pastas with flavorful sauces, good pizzas, seasonal composed salads, and the elegant lobster with linguine—and is best enjoyed during the quieter, luncheon hours. The bar is lively late at night. *3251 Prospect St. NW, Georgetown, 202/333–6183. AE, DC, MC, V. $$$$*

6 a-1

COPPI'S

Casual and popular, Coppi's is cleverly decorated with bicycling posters and related racing gear. The wood oven–baked pizzas are the main attraction; when it appears as a special, you must order the pizza *spinaci e pancetta* (with spinach and unsmoked bacon). *1414 U St. NW, between 14th and 15th Sts., U Street, 202/319–7773. AE, D, MC, V. No lunch. Metro: U St.–Cardozo. $$*

3 d-4

COPPI'S VIGORELLI

Chef Elizabeth Bright specializes in the food of Liguria, creating far more than just pizzas in her wood-burning ovens. Start with a rustic soup, look for rabbit or seafood as a main course, and finish your meal with the calzone full of Nutella. Then walk across the street to the Uptown Theatre for a movie. *3421 Connecticut Ave. NW, Cleveland Park, 202/244–6437. AE, D, MC, V. No lunch in summer. Metro: Cleveland Park. $$*

1 a-4

DA DOMENICO RISTORANTE

This Tysons Corner classic is a large eatery that manages to appear cozy, thanks to curtained booths and secluded spaces. The Genoese owner vouches for the ravioli *alla Genovese*—homemade pasta stuffed with spinach, sausage, Parmesan cheese, eggs, and basil. Standouts are the immense veal chop, which usually appears as a daily special, and the assortment of cutlets and seafood dishes. Its location near a conglomeration of high-tech companies makes this place popular for power tête-à-têtes. *Tysons Corner Center, 1992 Chain Bridge Rd., McLean, VA, 703/790–9000. Closed Sunday. AE, D, MC, V. $$*

1 d-7

ECCO CAFÉ

Although an Italian restaurant popular for its inventive pizzas, Ecco Café has a hint of a Parisian bistro in it. The excellent bouillabaisse proves it, with a flavorful broth that begs to be sopped up with the excellent breads. At your table is a basket stocked with rosemary focaccia, snappy-thin breadsticks, and tasty sun-dried-tomato muffins. The pastas are excellent and come mixed with a variety of fragrant vegetables, shellfish, and chicken. Chocolate desserts are hard to pass up. The four dining rooms are eclectically styled with neon, stained glass, lace curtains, etched glass, and flowered oilcloth. *220 North Lee St., Alexandria, VA, 703/684–0321. AE, D, MC, V. Metro: King St. $*

5 f-2
ETRUSCO

Formerly Sostanza, this attractive trattoria by chef Francesco Ricchi focuses on Tuscan cuisine. Many recipes delicately blend ingredients such as olive oil, wine, sage, and garlic to create rich, flavorful dishes. The pastas and sausages are homemade, and the fish and vegetables are perfectly fresh. Try the semolina and ricotta pasta with artichoke, sausage, and tomato sauce followed by braised veal shank with saffron capellini. The refined dining room, which has candle-lighted tables under a beautiful canopied ceiling, is one of the most romantic dinner spots in the neighborhood. All of the wines are Italian. *1606 20th St. NW, Dupont Circle, 202/667–0047. AE, MC, V. No lunch. Metro: Dupont Circle. $$$*

5 c-4
FILOMENA RISTORANTE

You can watch Italian women making pasta in the sidewalk-level pasta room, then continue the "Mamma mia" experience by descending to the crowded, friendly dining room for some great lasagna, seafood pasta, or linguine *cardinale*, with lobster meat and rosé wine. *1063 Wisconsin Ave. NW, between K and M Sts., Georgetown, 202/338–8800. AE, MC, V. Metro: Foggy Bottom–GWU or Rosslyn. $$*

2 d-3
FIO'S

Tucked away in the recesses of the mammoth Woodner apartment complex, Fio's has a loyal following that loves the unexpected location, friendly service, and inexpensive, home-style southern Italian cooking. Daily specials of roast duck, rabbit, and veal supplement the regular pizzas, pastas, and vegetable dishes. *3636 16th St. NW, Adams-Morgan, 202/667–3040. AE, DC, MC, V. Closed Mon. No lunch. Metro: Dupont Circle. $$*

5 f-4
GALILEO

Without a doubt the most sophisticated Italian restaurant in town, this flagship of Washington chef-entrepreneur Roberto Donna gets both consistently high marks for its cooking and frequent complaints about long waits for previously reserved tables. Fortunately, the former is usually worth the latter. Prepa-

rations are generally simple. Don't miss the remarkably light pastas, which can be split as a first course for two. The veal chop might be served with mushroom-and-rosemary sauce, the beef with black-olive sauce and polenta. The $65 five-course prix-fixe menu is a good value. *1110 21st St. NW, between L and M Sts., Downtown, 202/293–7191. AE, DC, MC, V. No lunch weekends. Metro: Farragut North or Foggy Bottom–GWU. $$$$*

8 f-4
GERANIO

This welcoming Old Town restaurant makes you remember why you loved Italian cooking as a child. Preparations are simple; the mozzarella in *carrozza* (fried) is delicious. Lobster with linguine, a frequent special, is fresh and satisfying. A fireplace warms the room in winter. *722 King St., between Washington and Columbus Sts., Alexandria, VA, 703/548–0088. AE, MC, V. No lunch weekends. Metro: King St. $$*

3 g-8
I MATTI

This crowded trattoria from Roberto Donna, owner of the far more swish Galileo, serves a varied and fairly sophisticated menu to a largely neighborhood crowd. If you stop in for lunch or a light snack, try one of the thin, crisp-crust pizzas or a pasta dish, perhaps the Pasta Pillows stuffed with veal and potatoes. Meat and fish dishes—which might include rabbit, salmon, or *bollito misto* (a mixture of meat, capon, and sausage cooked in a flavorful broth)—are pricier but well worth it. Service is often perfunctory, particularly on weekend evenings. *2436 18th St. NW, Adams-Morgan, 202/462–8844. AE, D, DC, MC, V. Metro: Woodley Park–Zoo. $$*

5 g-3
I RICCHI

The earthy Tuscan menu at this attractive, pricey trattoria features hearty soups and roast meats from the wood-burning grill. The spring-summer menu includes such offerings as rolled pork and rabbit roasted in wine and fresh herbs, and skewered shrimp; fall and winter bring grilled lamb chops, thick *ribollita* (Tuscan soup with chunks of bread), and sautéed beef fillet. The house-made breads alone are worth the trip. *1220 19th St. NW, between M and N*

Sts., Dupont Circle, 202/835–0459. AE, DC, MC, V. Closed Sun. No lunch Sat. Metro: Dupont Circle. $$$

5 *h-3*

IL RADICCHIO

If you want to try Roberto Donna's famed cuisine without breaking the bank, this is his least expensive Italian restaurant. The main draw at these "spaghetterias" is all the spaghetti you can eat, with your choice of 21 different sauces—the best is the "il radicchio" (which means red lettuce), a rich sauce with sausage, red wine, and tomatoes. Other options include pizza, spit-roast chicken, and enormous *panini* (Italian sandwich). Unfortunately, the food quality is not consistent. *1509 17th St. NW, between P and Q Sts., Dupont Circle, 202/986–2627. AE, DC, MC, V. No lunch Sun. Metro: Dupont Circle. $$*

6 *g-8*

223 Pennsylvania Ave. SE, between 2nd and 3rd Sts., Capitol Hill, 202/547–5114. Metro: Capitol South.

5 *f-2*

LA TOMATE

The owners of this popular neighborhood Italian eatery have transformed a previously neglected corner near Dupont Circle into an attractive garden-dining space. La Tomate is notable for its dependable pastas, traditional veal preparations, and friendly, if occasionally harried, service. Large, colorful ingredients—including ruby-red tomatoes and asparagus the size of saplings—make up the bulk of dishes: try the *crostini pomodor e basilico* (fresh tomatoes, basil, garlic, and olive oil on toast) followed by a 10-ounce veal chop with plum sauce or smoked rainbow trout. Live piano music is played Wednesday through Saturday after 7 PM. *1701 Connecticut Ave. NW, at R St., Dupont Circle, 202/667–5505. AE, DC, MC, V. Metro: Dupont Circle. $$*

5 *f-4*

LABORATORIO DEL GALILEO DA ROBERTA DONNA

There's good reason chef Roberto Donna's name is on this innovative new venture: if he's not cooking, it's closed. This glittering glass-enclosed kitchen-dining room within the main Galileo restaurant is sleekly contemporary and seats only 28. For private parties a few more delighted guests can be squeezed in. There is a stage-set aura to the room, and celebrants dress accordingly. There's no menu; you eat what Donna cooks from what he found in the markets that morning. Past dishes have included risotto flavored with vegetables, mushrooms, or truffles; roasted veal or lamb; and even suckling pig. Festivities begin with a glass of bubbly *prosecco* as you enter the inner sanctum. Ten courses follow, all mercifully small and served on an array of stunning rectangular plates. Dinner here is a memorable and expensive event, with a prix-fixe cost of about $100. *1110 21st St. NW, between L and M Sts., Downtown, 202/331–0880. Reservations essential. AE, DC, MC, V. No lunch. Metro: Farragut North or Foggy Bottom–GWU. $$$$*

6 *b-5*

LUIGINO

Luigino's decor is both traditional and stylish—a winning combination that works just as well in the kitchen. Start with a half-order of remarkably light pasta, perhaps linguine with a ragout of venison or "pinched ravioli" filled with chicken and veal. The entrée menu might feature suckling pig or a stew of baby goat and artichoke. *1100 New York Ave. NW, Downtown, 202/371–0595. AE, DC, MC, V. No lunch weekends. Metro: Metro Center. $$$*

1 *a-4*

MAGGIANO'S LITTLE ITALY

The American-style Italian food at this family restaurant is hearty, with lots of sauce, and comes in absolutely humongous servings. One section is a light, airy bakery with a self-service café offering bread-based victuals, pasta, and salads; the main dining rooms are dressed in mahogany and brass with lots of Italian family decor. You might want to ask for a doggy bag even before the mountains of food come; you're sure to need it. Dinners are served family-style for four or more, but some half portions for two are available. Lunch is strictly single portions. *Galleria at Tysons II, 2001 International Dr., McLean, VA, 703/356–9000. AE, D, DC, MC, V. $$*

2 *b-4*

5333 Wisconsin Ave. NW, Upper Northwest, 202/966–5500. Metro: Friendship Heights.

1 *c-1*

MAMMA LUCIA

Just when you think you've had enough shopping on the Pike, a small café serving provincial Italian cuisine pops up to replenish you for more. In addition to New York–style pizza and hearty pasta dishes such as baked ziti and lasagna, Mamma Lucia also offers delights such as shrimp Montese, pasta with shrimp and crab in a rosé-cream sauce, or the classic chicken marsala. Casual counter service is offered during lunch and waiter service at dinner. *Federal Plaza, 12274-M Rockville Pike, Rockville, MD, 301/770–4894. AE, MC, V. $$*

5 *f-3*

OBELISK

Chef Peter Pastan's small and tidy Dupont Circle dining room is usually booked solid with return customers, drawn back by the simple and elegant food. The entire menu consists of a five-course fixed-price dinner, which changes daily. The pastas are lovely; main courses run the gamut of meat, fish, and poultry. To end it all, you can choose either dessert or cheese. *2029 P St. NW, between 20th and 21st Sts., Dupont Circle, 202/872–1180. DC, MC, V. Closed Sun.–Mon. No lunch. Metro: Dupont Circle. $$$*

5 *f-2*

ODEON CAFE

The best tables in the Odeon are by the front windows, which have exciting views of the passing street life and are often open on pleasant evenings. Start with fried calamari or carpaccio, or a half-portion of pasta. Great entrées include the tricolor pasta with Alfredo sauce and the tortellini *a la panna* (four-cheese cream sauce). *1714 Connecticut Ave. NW, Dupont Circle, 202/328–6228. AE, DC, MC, V. Metro: Dupont Circle. $$*

5 *f-4*

OSTERIA GOLDONI

Chef Fabrizio Aielli's Venetian-style restaurant specializes in seafood. You'll dine well on his daily specials, which include the likes of risotto with scampi and artichokes, simply grilled whole fish, and fish cooked in parchment accompanied by creamy polenta. Aielli serves a selection of light dishes throughout the afternoon. *1120 20th St. NW, between L and M Sts., Downtown, 202/293–1521. AE, D, DC, MC, V. No lunch weekends. Metro: Foggy Bottom– GWU or Farragut North. $$$*

5 *e-4*

PANEVINO

Attractive, comfortable, and friendly, Panevino has the feel of a real neighborhood restaurant, where good food is served at reasonable prices. Comfortable wicker chairs surround sleek marbleized tables, and white latticework enhances the outdoor mood. The large antipasti buffet is a big draw. Although the menu emphasizes the Italian theme, don't expect gutsy food. This is more operetta than opera, and all the more engaging for that. *Embassy Suites Hotel, 1250 23rd St. NW, near M St., Downtown, 202/223–0747. AE, DC, MC, V. Metro: Foggy Bottom–GWU. $$*

5 *c-3*

PAOLO'S

This sleek California-Italian restaurant is a popular hangout with the young and fashionable. Homemade bread sticks get meals off to a crunchy start. Star appetizers include the Beggar's Purse stuffed with wild mushrooms, spinach, and Taleggio cheese, and the grilled sea scallops. Two of you can then split a pizza from the wood-burning oven, with toppings that range from roasted vegetables to grilled chicken to lobster. Grilled meats and a variety of pasta entrées (some low-fat) are also available. The Georgetown location is noisy. *1303 Wisconsin Ave. NW, at N St., Georgetown, 202/333–7353. AE, DC, MC, V. Metro: Foggy Bottom–GWU. $$*

11898 Market St., Reston, VA, 703/318–8920.

3 *g-8*

PASTA MIA

Homey and inexpensive, Pasta Mia is best known for its low prices: appetizers and entrées all cost a palatable $7–$9. Large bowls of steaming pasta are served with a generous layer of fresh-grated Parmesan. Best-sellers include fusilli with broccoli and whole cloves of roasted garlic; rich spinach fettuccine; and spicy penne *arrabiata* (served in marinara sauce). For dessert, tiramisu is served elegantly with espresso-soaked ladyfingers. *1790 Columbia Rd. NW, Adams- Morgan, 202/328–9114. MC, V. Closed Sun. No lunch. Metro: Woodley Park–Zoo. $*

5 *f-5*

PRIMI PIATTI

A pretty room that opens onto the sidewalk, with outdoor seating in good weather, this ambitious Italian trattoria serves fashionable Italian fare, such as risottos, polenta, carpaccio, pizza from a wood-burning oven, Tuscan-style grilled and roasted dishes, and of course, tiramisu for dessert. The Virginia location is less crowded, and the cooking is more consistent. *2013 I St. NW, between 20th and 21st Sts., Foggy Bottom, 202/223–3600. AE, DC, MC, V. Closed Sun. No lunch Sat. Metro: Foggy Bottom–GWU or Farragut West. $$$*

8045 Leesburg Pike, Vienna, VA, 703/893–0300.

5 *g-3*

SESTO SENSO

It's often seen as a nightspot for the young and chic crowd that throngs its bar late in the evening, but Sesto Senso has one of the best Italian kitchens in D.C. The list of daily specials often features appealing, homey dishes from the chef's Neapolitan childhood, such as beef cooked to melting tenderness in red wine and served with creamy polenta. Don't overlook the regular menu, though, for the best fried calamari in town, good pasta dishes, and well-prepared fish and veal. *1214 18th St. NW, Dupont Circle, 202/785–9525. AE, DC, MC, V. Closed Sun. No lunch weekends. Metro: Dupont Circle. $$$*

5 *g-4*

TEATRO GOLDONI

Fabrizio Aielli opened this dramatic restaurant around the corner from his much admired Osteria Goldoni. Both restaurants take their name from Carlo Goldoni, an 18th-century Venetian playwright and passionate gastronome, and both salute Venetian cuisine. Aielli prepares a wealth of seafood, delicate pasta dishes, and the expected poultry and meat offerings. Some dishes are a bit too complicated, but for the most part it's a sure hand in the kitchen. The dining room is a fantasy of colors and shapes, with Venetian masks, multicolor Murano-glass chandeliers, and theatrical screens. *1909 K St. NW, Downtown, 202/955–9494. AE, DC, MC, V. Metro: Farragut North or Farragut West. $$$$*

1 *c-7*

TEMPO

Aside from the high ceilings, there are few indications that you're dining in a renovated gas station. The food is predominantly northern Italian in style—the carpaccio is excellent—with hints of French, Southwestern, and California cuisine as eclectic undercurrents. You might want to start with the smooth and peppery crab soup. Seafood, the house specialty, dominates the menu, and both the sea scallops, decorated with fresh ginger and spring onions, and the mahimahi with cilantro and lime juice are tangy. Consider ending the meal with one of the homemade desserts, which include an excellent tiramisu. *4231 King St., Alexandria, VA, 703/370–7900. AE, D, DC, MC, V. Metro: King St. $$$*

JAPANESE

5 *f-3*

CAFÉ JAPONE

Ignore the tacky neon lights reminiscent of a 1970s strip club, and keep an open mind when listening to your cacophonous karaoke neighbors—Café Japone is an odd amalgam of black tables, red carpet, video screens, and wall mirrors. Not your typical Japanese restaurant, the café is nevertheless an entertaining treat; a place for sushi and song, shrimp boats and sake, *sumo nabe* and *shabu shabu* (beef cooked in boiling water and soup stock). The food is good, the service is better, and the karaoke (after 9 PM) makes Café Japone great fun for drink-related revelry. *2032 P St. NW, between 20th and 21st Sts., Dupont Circle, 202/466–2172. AE, DC, MC, V. No lunch. Metro: Dupont Circle. $$*

9 *d-3*

JAPAN INN

This handsome Japanese restaurant is popular for very good grilled beef, chicken, or shrimp, prepared at a communal table-cum-grill by chefs who wield their knives and spatulas like jugglers. *1715 Wisconsin Ave. NW, Georgetown, 202/337–3400. AE, MC, V. No lunch weekends. $$$*

5 *g-5*

KAZ SUSHI BISTRO

The restaurant's highlight is the sushi bar–stage where chef-owner Kaz Okochi reigns. Every dish is prepared up here, and since each item is hand rolled or cooked to order, you'll need to be patient: the food is worth it. The name "Sushi Bistro" may seem strange, but it announces Chef Kaz's approach of combining classic Japanese cuisine with some French contributions, such as foie gras. The experience is new and exhilarating. *1915 I St. NW, Downtown, 202/530–5500. AE, DC, MC, V. Metro: Foggy Bottom–GWU. $$$*

3 *g-8*

PERRY'S

One of the trendier spots on the D.C. night scene, Perry's caters to a champagne glass–clinking crowd that gazes at the stars from its rooftop deck in warm weather. The menu is American with an Asian flair; the sushi is popular. The Sunday drag brunch, in which men dressed as women serenade the diners, is another big draw. Perry's is open nightly until midnight, weekends until 1 AM. There is a $12-per-person minimum on the outdoor deck. *1811 Columbia Rd. NW, near 18th St., Adams-Morgan, 202/234–6218. AE, DC, MC, V. No lunch weekdays. Metro: Woodley Park–Zoo. $$$*

5 *f-3*

SAKANA

There are flashier Japanese restaurants in this neighborhood, but none surpasses the modest, attractive Sakana in authenticity or freshness. The sushi bar is tiny, but the fish and vegetable dishes are superb. If you don't like raw fish, try the very good sushi rolls, tempura, or *yosenabe*, a one-pot meal of noodles and seafood. *2026 P St. NW, between 20th and 21st Sts., Dupont Circle, 202/887–0900. AE, DC, MC, V. Closed Sun. No lunch Sat. Metro: Dupont Circle. $$*

3 *a-8*

SUSHI-KO

At the city's best Japanese restaurant, daily specials are always innovative: sesame oil–seasoned trout is layered with crisp wonton crackers, and a sushi special might be salmon topped with a touch of mango sauce and a tiny sprig of dill. And you won't find these whimsical desserts—green-tea ice cream or sake sorbet—at the local Baskin-Robbins. *2309 Wisconsin Ave. NW, Georgetown, 202/333–4187. AE, MC, V. No lunch Sat.–Mon. $$$*

5 *h-3*

SUSHI TARO

Beautifully decked out with wood panels and screens, this restaurant–cum–sushi bar is favored by visiting Japanese tourists and businessmen. The daily sushi specials are listed on a handwritten board behind the bar. The tempura is beautifully crisp, and the one-dish meals, such as yosenabe, are filling and delicious. Service is fast and friendly. *1503 17th St. NW, at P St., Dupont Circle, 202/462–8999. AE, D, DC, MC, V. Metro: Dupont Circle. $$$*

3 *e-7*

TONO

This sushi restaurant on the corner of Connecticut and Calvert serves the least expensive Japanese food you'll find in the District, including shrimp tempura, beef *negimaki* (grilled, thinly sliced beef wrapped around scallions with teriyaki sauce), and duck with shiitake mushrooms. Lunch is served quick and cheap, whereas dinner is a slightly more leisurely affair. There is also a wide selection of sushi and sashimi platters. *2605 Connecticut Ave. NW, Woodley Park, 202/332–7300. AE, MC, V. Metro: Woodley Park–Zoo. $$*

KOREAN

1 *b-7*

HEE BEEN

The main attraction at this fine Korean-Japanese restaurant is Korean barbecue, and that's probably what your server will assume you want. Beef, short ribs, chicken, *bulgogi* (spicy marinated pork), and several exotic meats are cooked at a grill on your table, and the server will show you how to wrap your portion in a lettuce leaf with some rice and condiments to make a bite-size package. The noodle dishes are also delicious. *6231 Little River Turnpike, Alexandria, VA, 703/941–3737. AE, D, MC, V. $$*

LATIN

6 *c-6*

CAFÉ ATLÁNTICO

Two chefs work in tandem to turn out Latin cuisine with a modern spin. The guacamole is whipped up tableside by your server, and chefs Christy Velie and

Katsuya Fukushima send out specialties such as Ecuadorian seared scallops, bacon-wrapped roasted pheasant breast with pheasant-leg confit, and accompaniments that include a tour de force—seared watermelon. The two-story café is bedecked with vibrant colors. Service is friendly and helpful. *405 8th St. NW, between D and E Sts., Downtown, 202/393–0812. No lunch Sun. Metro: Archives–Navy Memorial. $$$*

5 *f-3*

GABRIEL

Gabriel chef Greggory Hill breathes new life into classic Latin American and Spanish dishes to create a "neuvo Latino" menu; *pupusas* (Salvadoran meat patties), for example, are filled with chorizo and grilled scallops. You may prefer to order à la carte, but the extensive lunch and happy-hour tapas buffets are sure winners—the best are the spicy plantain and black bean empanadas with chipotle cream and the stuffed pimentos with goat cheese and olives. The Argentine beef tenderloin, the paella valenciana, and the seared sea scallops are all highly recommended. A chef's tasting menu for $45 lets you sample three courses. Tables are well-spaced, although Latin music and the dining room's acoustics keep the noise level fairly high. *2121 P St. NW, Dupont Circle, 202/956–6690. AE, D, DC, MC, V. No lunch Sat. Metro: Dupont Circle. $$*

5 *g-2*

LAURIOL PLAZA

In summer, both sides of this recently relocated restaurant fill with contented neighborhood diners eating chips and salsa, drinking margaritas, and enjoying the Latin American and Spanish food in the open air. Good choices include ceviche, paella, and Cuban-style pork. It's not the place for a quiet meal; the extremely crowded dining room can get noisy, and you may have to wait for a table. There's a popular rooftop deck and an outdoor patio open in favorable weather. *1835 18th St. NW, at S St., Adams-Morgan, 202/387–0035. Reservations not accepted. AE, DC, MC, V. Metro: Dupont Circle. $$*

3 *g-8*

RUMBA CAFE

Rumba Cafe takes you out of Washington and plants you firmly in a South American pueblo. It's a relaxed place for sampling Latin cuisine, sipping a rum-based cocktail, or smoking a Dominican cigar. The specialized menu highlights foods from Latin America, including Venezuelan corncakes, Argentine steaks, and Chilean fish. Live music is performed Wednesday through Saturday after 10:30 PM. *2443 18th St. NW, Adams-Morgan, 202/588–5501. AE, MC, V. Metro: Woodley Park–Zoo. $$*

MEXICAN

3 *e-7*

ACAPULCO

Although the staff is hardly Latin and it's doubtful that the chef has ever crossed the border, Acapulco nevertheless serves tasty food that has a good deal to do with Mexico (remember that authentic Mexican food is an unlikely find in Washington). Sip margaritas on the outdoor patio, nibble on a taco salad, or go for the full monty with a giant combination platter of shrimp, fish, and calamari served with rice, guacamole, and *pico de gallo* (relish of bell peppers, onions, jalepeño peppers, and spices). Tacos, burritos, and enchiladas all appear on the menu, and everything is very reasonably priced. *2623 Connecticut Ave. NW, Woodley Park, 202/986– 0131. AE, D, DC, MC, V. Metro: Woodley Park–Zoo. $$*

ANITA'S

Anita's specializes in New Mexico–style Mexican food—cooked with the artful use of chili peppers. In addition to the standard tacos and burritos, there are more intricate creations such as *carne adobada* (slices of pork marinated for 24 hours with red chilis). Prices are reasonable; for example, the restaurant's signature breakfast burrito has been sold at $1.30 ever since 1974, when the first Anita's opened. *521 Maple Ave. E, Vienna, VA, 703/255–1001. AE, D, DC, MC, V. Metro: Vienna. $*

1 *c-2*

CHIPOTLE MEXICAN GRILL

Customers place their orders and follow along the line to watch their 20-ounce custom-made burritos or tacos being assembled. The menu is simple, but the foods are fresh, flavorful, fast, and filling, not to mention inexpensive. Margaritas and Mexican beer are also on the menu. Cantina moderna decor combines disparate materials, such as corrugated metal and birch, to create unique designs. Takeout is available. *7600 Old Georgetown Rd., Bethesda, MD, 301/907–9077. MC, V. Metro: Bethesda. $*

11830 Rockville Pike, #178, Mid-Pike Plaza, Rockville, MD, 301/881–2600. Metro: Rockville.

564 N. Frederick Ave., near the Fairgrounds, Gaithersburg, MD, 301/632–1228.

10 *e-7*

LA LOMITA DOS

The decor is predictable: sombreros, serapes, and piñatas. But that doesn't keep neighborhood folks and those from across town from quickly filling the small restaurant. Many come for the tender and juicy *puerco asado* (roast pork) topped with onions and accompanied by rice, beans, and a bit of salad or one of the many shrimp concoctions. Margaritas come by the pitcher or half-pitcher. The portions are hearty and reasonably priced. There's also a children's menu. The 1339 Pennsylvania Avenue address, known as La Lomita, has a homey Mexican-cantina atmosphere and outdoor dining. *308 Pennsylvania Ave. SE, Capitol Hill, 202/544–0616. AE, D, MC, V. Metro: Capitol South. $*

2 *f-6*

1339 Pennsylvania Ave. SE, Capitol Hill, 202/546–3109. Metro: Potomac Ave. $

3 *g-7*

MIXTEC

Mixtec is a rarity—a homey Mexican restaurant in a city where Latin dining is dominated by the foods of El Salvador—and its menu may surprise those accustomed to American versions of our southern neighbor's cuisine. Don't expect tortilla chips as a preliminary nibble; they're largely a north-of-the-border phenomenon. What you'll get is a trio of delicious salsas to season the array of authentic dishes. The tacos *al carbon* are simple and perfect; unlike their fast-food counterparts, topped with lettuce and cheese, these tacos consist only of grilled beef or pork in fresh corn tortillas, nicely accompanied by grilled spring onions. Fajitas, enchiladas, and seafood are cooked in the regional styles of Veracruz, Mazatlán, and Acapulco, which the menu handily explains. The *licuados* (homemade fruit drinks) are refreshing complements to the sometimes spicy dishes. *1792 Columbia Rd. NW, between 17th and 18th Sts.,* *Adams-Morgan, 202/332–1011. Reservations not accepted. MC, V. Metro: Woodley Park–Zoo. $$*

1 *d-7*

SANTA FE CAFÉ

This straightforward eatery is painted in the color of foods: lime green, tangerine, chili pepper. Both green and red salsas are served with tortilla chips, and they're made from authentic New Mexico ingredients. It's best to stick to the peasant food here: *posole* (soup with pork or chicken, chili, and cilantro), fajitas, quesadillas, *chiles rellenos* (cheese-stuffed green chilis dipped in batter and fried), and enchiladas. The tart, delicious margaritas are not made from a mix but with freshly squeezed limes. *1500 Wilson Blvd., Arlington, VA, 703/276–0361. No credit cards. Closed Sun. No dinner Mon. No lunch Sat. Metro: Rosslyn. $*

MIDDLE EASTERN

5 *g-3*

BACCHUS

If you're in the mood for something light, try a meal of *mezze*, the Middle Eastern version of tapas, at Bacchus: combine the stuffed grape leaves, the phyllo turnovers stuffed with spinach, the grilled sausages, and the hummus topped with ground lamb. If you want something more substantial, try one of the pilafs or the minced beef kebabs. *1827 Jefferson Pl. NW, between M and N Sts., Dupont Circle, 202/785–0734. AE, D, DC, MC, V. Closed Sun. No lunch Sat. Metro: Dupont Circle. $$*

1 *c-2*

7945 Norfolk Ave., at Del Ray Ave., Bethesda, MD, 301/657–1722. AE, MC, V. No lunch weekends. $$

2 *b-2*

CAFÉ OLÉ

This casual, trendy Tenleytown haunt is a great place to dine before or after a movie. Sandwiches are inventive and delicious—try the Marrakech panini, grilled chicken with vegetables and hummus. The best of the wraps is the lamb tagine, filled with a delicious Moroccan stew. There's a selection of about 30 mezze at dinnertime, including a combination platter for two or more. Live Mediterranean music enhances the experience on weekend evenings. Café

Olé has full service evenings and weekends, counter service weekdays at lunch. *4000 Wisconsin Ave. NW, Tenleytown, 202/244–1330. AE, D, MC, V. Metro: Tenleytown–AU. $$*

5 *g-4*

LE TARBOUCHE

The name of the restaurant means "fez," and that pot-shape hat is the decorating leitmotiv used throughout in a very slick manner. Don't expect brass trays and the like: the decor is as contemporary as you can get to match the modernized Lebanese cuisine. Chef Bader Ali hails from Lebanon and has worked with famed French chefs here. His style of cooking is an ethereal blend of the two cuisines. A meal can be made of the extensive list of mezze, but then you would miss the chef's signature dish, falafel-crusted sea bass. *1801 K St. NW, Downtown, 202/331–5551. AE, DC, MC, V. Metro: Farragut North or Farragut West. $$$*

3 *e-7*

LEBANESE TAVERNA

Middle Eastern hospitality pervades this elegantly appointed restaurant. Begin with an order of Arabic bread, baked in a wood-burning oven, or one of the small fried pies—filled with spinach, cheese, or meat—called *fatayer*. They're buttery, but surprisingly light. Main courses feature your choice of lamb, beef, chicken, or seafood, each one grilled as a kebab, slow-roasted, or smothered with a garlicky yogurt sauce. The roast chicken wrapped in crackling-thin Lebanese bread is a treat. A group can make a meal of the mezze platters, a mixture of appetizers and shawarma meats. A glass of *arak*, a strong, anise-flavored liquor, makes an excellent digestive. *2641 Connecticut Ave. NW, Woodley Park, 202/265–8681. AE, D, DC, MC, V. No lunch Sun. Metro: Woodley Park–Zoo. $$$*

1 *b-5*

5900 Washington Blvd., Arlington, VA, 703/241–8681. Metro: East Falls Church.

3 *f-7*

MAMA AYESHA'S

This family-run neighborhood hangout has hosted journalists and politicians since the early '60s. Such staples as chicken and lamb kebabs can be had for less than $10, baskets of complimentary pita bread are served hot, and the crisp falafels are some of the best in town. The lamb shanks, long-cooked and fork tender, are one of the most popular dishes. *1967 Calvert St. NW, Adams-Morgan, 202/232–5431. AE, DC, MC, V. Metro: Woodley Park–Zoo. $$*

3 *e-7*

MEDATERRA

This colorful Mediterranean restaurant matches foods from across the North African coast to produce a casual but exotic dining experience. Lamb creations show up in a roasted lamb sandwich, a roasted lamb and goat-cheese salad, and an ambitiously named Lamb Kabob Extraordinaire. The grilled salmon, topped with a raisin puree over rice, is also recommended. There's an outdoor patio open in warm weather. Service is perfunctory. *2614 Connecticut Ave. NW, Woodley Park, 202/797–0400. DC, MC, V. No lunch Sun. Metro: Woodley Park–Zoo. $$*

1 *c-5*

PASHA CAFÉ

Many of the meals at this friendly restaurant are specific to Egypt, the homeland of the family in charge. The list of mezze, or appetizers, goes on for pages. The kebabs and lamb dishes are all excellent, but for something uniquely Egyptian try the *kosa bel zabadi*, a pureed zucchini dip that's a tart cousin to hummus, or the *moulkia*, a spinach-like vegetable stewed in broth, mixed with coriander and garlic, and served with your choice of boiled lamb or grilled chicken. *3815 Lee Hwy., Arlington, VA, 703/528–2126. AE, D, DC, MC, V. No lunch Sun. $$*

5 *h-2*

SKEWERS/CAFÉ LUNA

As the name implies, kebabs are the focus at Skewers. The two most popular variations are lamb with eggplant and chicken with roasted peppers, but vegetable kebabs and skewers of filet mignon and shrimp are equally tasty. All are served with almond-flaked rice or pasta. The appetizer selection is huge, with nearly 20 options. If the restaurant is too crowded, head downstairs for cheap eats (shrimp and avocado salad, mozzarella-and-tomato sandwiches, vegetable lasagna, pizza, and salads) at Café Luna, a neighborhood gathering place. *1633 P St. NW, Dupont Circle, 202/387–7400 Skewers; 202/387–4005 Café Luna. AE, D, DC, MC, V. Metro: Dupont Circle. $$*

MOROCCAN

6 *c-4*

MARRAKESH

A happy surprise is Marrakesh, a bit of Morocco in a part of the city better known for auto-supply shops. The neighborhood may be a little dicey after dark, but the ample and delicious food makes it worth the trip. The menu is a fixed-price ($24) feast shared by everyone at your table and eaten without silverware (use flatbread, which comes with each meal, as a scoop). Appetizers consist of a platter of three salads followed by *b'stella*, a chicken version of Morocco's traditional pigeon pie. For the first main course, choose from several chicken preparations, then move on to a beef or lamb dish. Wind down with vegetable couscous, fresh fruit, mint tea, and pastries. Belly dancers perform nightly. Alcoholic drinks can really drive up the tab. *617 New York Ave. NW, Downtown, 202/393–9393. Reservations essential. No credit cards. No lunch, except for large groups with advance reservations. Metro: Gallery Pl.–Chinatown. $$$*

PAN-ASIAN

5 *g-4*

OODLES NOODLES

Packed from the day they opened and with long lines waiting for tables and takeout, these attractive Pan-Asian noodle houses offer some terrific Asian cooking. You'll find Chinese, Japanese, Thai, Indonesian, Malaysian, and Vietnamese dishes. The quality of each is remarkably high, and it's served on a plate appropriate to the country's cuisine. Try the Thai drunken noodles, the Chinese clay-pot noodles, or the Vietnamese rice noodles with grilled chicken. *1120 19th St. NW, Dupont Circle, 202/293–3138. AE, DC, MC, V. Closed Sun. Metro: Farragut North. $*

1 *c-2*

4907 Cordell Ave., Bethesda, MD, 301/986–8833. No lunch Sun. Metro: Bethesda. $$

5 *f-3*

PAN-ASIAN NOODLES & GRILL

For a casual and affordable meal, drop into this brightly lighted Dupont Circle restaurant or its downtown sibling. Appetizers, including the Singapore Nuggets (crabmeat and minced chicken wrapped with bean curdskin), are very good; for the main course, try the meal-size drunken noodles (steamed flat rice noodles) or Cozy Noodles (cold noodles with shredded chicken and vegetables). Also tasty are the grilled chicken and the *satays* (marinated cubes of meat grilled on skewers). In the way of alcohol, only beer and wine are served. *2020 P St. NW, Dupont Circle, 202/872–8889. AE, MC, V. No lunch Sun. Metro: Dupont Circle. $$*

6 *a-4*

1018 Vermont Ave. NW, between K and L Sts., Downtown, 202/783–8899. No lunch Sun. Metro: McPherson Sq.

3 *d-5*

SPICES

Despite its casual atmosphere, Spices manages to attract a large crowd committed to serious Pan-Asian cooking. What is remarkable about this restaurant is that it manages to do an excellent job preparing each of the region-specific dishes, whether it's Chinese, Japanese, or Vietnamese. The small sushi bar serves commendable sushi, and other dishes like ginger chicken and garlic shrimp are widely ordered. Spices is especially popular with families. *3333A Connecticut Ave. NW, Cleveland Park, 202/686–3833. AE, DC, MC, V. No lunch Sun. Metro: Cleveland Park. $$*

6 *b-6*

TENPENH

A blockbuster of a restaurant, TenPenh is the second creation of the team that brought DC Coast to town, which hit like a hurricane and continues to roar. Chef Jeff Tunks delves into the fascinating flavors of Southeast Asia to create refreshingly eclectic dishes and startling new sauces. Some bring perspiration to the brow, but gentle choices prevail. Meats are grilled as you expect; exotica comes in the garnishes. Plump steamed mussels are enhanced by a creamy, vivid-yellow curry; briny raw oysters are served with crushed ice flavored with pickled ginger and sake. Desserts are a palate-tingling revelation: creamy coconut sorbet is sparked with lemongrass; five-spice chocolate cake is scented with star anise, cinnamon, clove, fennel, and Szechuan pepper. The decor fuses contemporary American styling with Asian accents, including Asian antiques. *10th St. and Pennsylvania Ave. NW, Down-*

town, 202/393–4500. AE, DC, MC, V. Metro: Archives–Navy Memorial. $$$

PIZZA

2 *b-2*

ARMAND'S CHICAGO PIZZERIA

Despite the name, Armand's is a Washington institution, featuring deep-dish pizza served up in a couple of tin-ceilinged dining rooms decorated with TV sets and neon beer signs. The pizzas are, well, thick, with arguably too much cheese and too much dough; some of the newer, California-style models, like veggie and Thai chicken, are more interesting. There's a $4.95 pizza and salad buffet at lunchtime, and they serve until midnight on weekends. *4231 Wisconsin Ave. NW, on Veazy St., Tenleytown, 202/686–9450. AE, D, DC, MC, V. Metro: Tenleytown–AU. $*

3 *a-8*

FACCIA LUNA

Aromas from the wood-burning oven in the open kitchen tempt the palate as you study the menu from your booth, separated from other tables by unusual redbrick dividers with glass tiles. Faccia Luna (which translates as "the face of the moon") features both red and white pizza styles, available in four different sizes, with a whopping list of toppings. It's a sure bet that kids and adults will find a light-crusted pizza everyone can enjoy. Fresh handmade pastas and enormous sub sandwiches are also available for eat-in alfresco dining or takeout. *2400 Wisconsin Ave. NW, Glover Park, 202/337–3132. AE, MC, V. $*

1 *d-7*

823 S. Washington St., Alexandria, VA, 703/838–5998. Metro: King St.

2 *b-5*

2909 Wilson Blvd., Arlington, VA, 703/276–3099. Metro: Clarendon.

1 *d-7*

GENEROUS GEORGE'S

This place of good cheer is for families and children of all ages. The dining rooms are full of toys and artifacts to entertain even the most rambunctious child or sulky teen. The pizzas are cheap and, like George, generous. The Positive Pineapple Pleasure pizza (pineapple slices, cheese, onion, and extra cheese) has been on the menu for years. George's yeasty crust is what makes every pizza special. Also offered are creative pastas and generous-size drinks. Less successful are the sandwiches and starters. On Tuesday nights there's live entertainment. *3006 Duke St., Alexandria, VA, 703/370–4303. AE, MC, V. Metro: King St. or Eisenhower. $*

1 *b-7*

7031 Little River Turnpike, Annandale, VA, 703/941–9600.

1 *a-7*

6131 Backlick Rd., Springfield, VA, 703/451–7111.

LEDO

Patrons have been waiting in long queues at this landmark for almost 50 years for the pizza, which some believe to be the best in the region. The recipes for the sweet, tangy tomato sauce that graces Ledo's famous square pizza and favorites such as toasted ravioli and eggplant parmigiana are well-guarded secrets. Sensational homemade soups—such as minestrone and hearty potato (with cheese, chives, onions, and crispy bacon)—are often and sadly overlooked by pizza lovers. The wait for a table is particularly long after a University of Maryland football or basketball game, but fans know it's worth a little patience. The dining room is often crowded and loud. *2420 University Blvd., Adelphi, MD, 301/422–8622. Reservations not accepted. MC, V. $*

5 *f-3*

PIZZERIA PARADISO

If you show up at this small, whimsically decorated pizza parlor at anything like a normal mealtime, expect to wait. The menu is strictly basic: pizzas, panini, salads, and desserts. Your first time here, try one of the set pizza combinations: the Atomica with spicy Italian salami, the Genovese with potatoes and pesto, or the four-cheese variety. The Siciliano is a fabulous vegetarian pizza with two cheeses. Most people are too happy with these to explore further. The sandwiches are assembled with homemade focaccia. Intensely flavored gelato, in such flavors as coffee and hazelnut, is a house specialty. *2029 P St. NW, Dupont Circle, 202/223–1245. Reservations not accepted. DC, MC, V. Metro: Dupont Circle. $*

9 *e-7*

PIZZERIA UNO

This offspring of the famous Chicago parlor makes the best deep-dish pie in Washington. Try the delicious four-cheese model, or, if you're feeling adventurous, order the works: the crisp crust is not overwhelmed by it. It's open Monday through Wednesday until midnight, Thursday until 1, and Friday and Saturday until 2. *3211 M St. NW, at Wisconsin Ave., Georgetown, 202/965–6333. AE, MC, V. Metro: Foggy Bottom–GWU. $*

5 *c-4*

PROSPECTS

This small pizzeria, an offspring of the popular Peacock Café down the street, has none of the kitschy decor of so many similar establishments. What you will find is a nice selection of fresh salads and individually baked pizzas that come piping hot out of the brick oven. Choose from a large array of exceptional toppings for your pie: fresh arugula, fennel, roasted garlic, truffle oil, and much more. Takeout is available. *3202 Prospect St. NW, near Wisconsin Ave., Georgetown, 202/298–6800. AE, MC, V. Closed Mon. $$*

3 *d-5*

VACE

People from the neighborhood are addicted to this take-out pizzeria and Italian deli. It's a hole-in-the-wall store where people line up to buy the gourmet pizzas, submarine sandwiches, and homemade pastas, including tortellini, ravioli, lasagna, and gnocchi. You can also buy packaged olives and oils imported from Italy. Note that there's no place to sit down, so you'll have to take your picnic elsewhere. *3315 Connecticut Ave. NW, Cleveland Park, 202/363–1999. AE, MC, V. No dinner Sun. Metro: Cleveland Park. $*

SEAFOOD

3 *d-5*

ARDEO

One of the newer spots in Cleveland Park, Ardeo has been packed as the positive buzz passes by word of mouth. Animated paintings adorn the walls of this bistrolike restaurant, which is perfect for celebratory meals and lively conversations. The menu, which changes weekly, offers a number of meat and pasta choices, but the real draw is seafood—wonderfully fresh and always carefully presented. A three-course, pretheater menu is offered from 5:30 to 6:45. Service is excellent. *3311 Connecticut Ave. NW, Cleveland Park, 202/244–6750. AE, DC, MC, V. No lunch. Metro: Cleveland Park. $$$*

1 *c-2*

BLACK'S BAR AND KITCHEN

Don't be fooled by the down-home atmosphere; this is a class act. Gulf coast seafood abounds on owner-chef Jeff Black's menu. For starters, try sharing Campeche (shrimp and lump crabmeat tossed with avocado, cilantro, and tomato). The Vermilion Bay seafood stew is an exceptional interpretation of bouillabaisse. Landlubbers needn't despair: the garlic and herb grilled chicken and the molasses and black pepper–cured duck are prepared with the same innovative flare as the seafood. Dining on the deck out front can lend a pleasant perspective on the hustle and bustle of Bethesda. *7750 Woodmont Ave., Bethesda, MD, 301/652–6278. AE, MC, V. Metro: Bethesda. $$$$*

8 *f-5*

BLUE POINT GRILL

This seafood satellite of the Sutton Place Gourmet market is one of the most comfortable and attractive restau-

FIREPLACES

On a chilly winter night, let the food warm your insides while the fire warms your outside.

The Hawk and Dove (American/Casual)
Discuss hot political topics on cold nights before any one of three fireplaces here.

Monocle (American)
Politicians are people, too—you may even see some of them trying to keep warm in front of the fire here as proof.

Polly's Cafe (Contemporary)
Chase away the chills with a beer and a burger in front of the fire in this cozy café.

Tabard Inn (Contemporary)
Perfectly cooked fish and meat taste even better in front of a warm fire.

rants in Alexandria. It's hard to get past the raw bar, with its seasonal variety of fresh oysters and clams, but press on and you'll encounter fine, simply prepared seafood dishes and daily specials such as sea scallops with balsamic vinaigrette or pepper-crusted tuna with white beans. *600 Franklin St., Alexandria, VA, 703/739–0404. AE, D, MC, V. $$$*

1 *f-3*

CALVERT HOUSE INN

Finding the perfect crab cake can be an obsession for those living near the Chesapeake Bay. A contender for this esteemed title would have to be the one served at the Calvert House Inn, near the University of Maryland. There are no fillers found in this cake—just pure, lump crabmeat straight from the bay, blended with a medley of spices. Five varieties of fresh fish are offered daily and can be fried, broiled, or nicely blackened in Cajun seasonings. The stuffed shrimp and seafood pasta dishes are other winners. Service in the bright, Federal-style dining room is always pleasant and efficient. *6211 Baltimore Ave., Riverdale, MD, 301/864–5220. AE, MC, V, D, DC. $$$*

1 *e-2*

CRISFIELD

Given an ambience that's no more elegant than that of a neighborhood barbershop, Crisfield's relatively high prices might seem absurd. But you get your money's worth: an eyeful of old Maryland arrested in time and some of the best no-nonsense seafood in the area. The general rule here is "The simpler, the better." The house clam chowder—creamy, chunky, and served with a bottomless bowl of oyster crackers—is rendered with down-home care. Crab cakes are good, but gummier than the lightly bound lump crabmeat served in more ambitious restaurants. *8012 Georgia Ave., between East–West Hwy. and Railroad St., Silver Spring, MD, 301/589–1306. AE, MC, V. Closed Mon. Metro: Silver Spring. $$$*

7 *b-2*

HOGATE'S

The tour buses outside don't mean the same thing as trucks beside a roadside diner. This cavernous seafood restaurant is notable only for its view, an attractive Potomac marina. The Mariner's Platter is a palatable choice. A jazz trio adds flavor to the Sunday brunch. *800 Water St.*

SW, between 9th St. and Maine Ave., Waterfront, 202/484–6300. AE, D, DC, MC, V. Metro: L'Enfant Plaza. $$

1 *h-3*

JERRY'S SEAFOOD

This nautically decorated restaurant is usually filled to capacity with devoted patrons who are willing to pay downtown prices for home-style fare in the suburbs. Jerry's Seafood is home of the Crab Bomb—a succulent, fluffy soufflé of lump crabmeat and spices. This dish is so popular it's also served to fans at the nearby FedEx Field during Redskins games. Jerry's beer-battered fried shrimp and stuffed soft-shell crabs deserve the same respect paid to the crab bomb. Don't pass up the homemade coleslaw or sweet stewed tomatoes side dishes. *9364 Lanham–Severn Rd., Seabrook, MD, 301/577–0333. Closed Sun. and Mon. No reservations. $$$$*

5 *f-5*

KINKEAD'S

Chef Robert Kinkead and company turn out an eclectic menu of mostly seafood dishes, inspired both by Kinkead's New England roots and by the foods of Asia and Latin America. Seasonal specialties include main-course soups and seafood stews, such as Scandinavian salmon stew. For the diet-conscious, the menu has simple grilled fish with cucumber relish on the side. Save room for dessert—the chocolate *dacquoise* (layer cake) is a knockout. *2000 Pennsylvania Ave. NW, Foggy Bottom, 202/296–7700. AE, DC, MC, V. Metro: Foggy Bottom–GWU. $$$$*

5 *f-4*

LEGAL SEA FOODS

Here's the first Washington branch of this beloved Boston seafood house. The fish is of first-rate quality, but it's occasionally prepared in a less-than-dignified manner. The best choices are Northeastern specialties—chowder, clams, scrod, and lobster—and the oysters are splendid. Midday, have a shrimp or lobster roll, one of the best lunches in town. *2020 K St. NW, Downtown, 202/496–1111. AE, MC, V. Metro: Farragut North or Farragut West. $$$*

5 *h-4*

MCCORMICK & SCHMICK'S

If at about 5 PM you wander into McCormick & Schmick's downtown, you may think you've inadvertently crashed a private cocktail party: the bar scene here, helped by reduced happy-hour prices on many items from the menu, is one of the liveliest in town. The seafood is always fresh, and sometimes very good; the problem with this Pacific Northwest chain is consistency. Stick to simple preparations. The new Tysons Corner location has handsome mahogany paneling, forest-green carpeting, and stained-glass lighting fixtures. *1652 K St. NW, between 16th and 17th Sts., Downtown, 202/861–2233. AE, D, DC, MC, V. No lunch weekends. Metro: Farragut North or Farragut West. $$$*

8484 Westpark Dr., at Leesburg Pike, Tysons Corner, McLean, VA, 703/848–8000. AE, D, DC, MC, V. Metro: Vienna.

11920 Democracy Dr., at Liberty St., Reston, VA, 703/481–6600. AE, D, MC, V.

5 *f-3*
PESCE
It's small, it's casual, it's usually packed, and it turns out some of the best Italian-style seafood in D.C. Pesce's menu is written on a chalkboard and changed daily according to what's available; choices include appetizers, a couple of soups, and the chef's imaginatively prepared seafood. Don't come here for an evening of quiet conversation; the din can be deafening. *2016 P St. NW, Dupont Circle, 202/466–3474. AE, D, DC, MC, V. No lunch Sun. Metro: Dupont Circle. $$$*

7 *b-2*
PHILLIPS FLAGSHIP
If you're pressed for time and must dine at one of the seafood restaurants overlooking the Capital Yacht Club marina—because you have tickets to, say, a performance at nearby Arena Stage—Phillips is your best bet. There's a sushi bar and seafood buffet Monday through Saturday, a party room with its own deck, and, all told, space for 1,400 people. The restaurant is distinguished by the quality of its raw materials, such as local fish and crab, which it acquires from a network of dealers built up over many years. *900 Water St. SW, Downtown, 202/488–8515. AE, D, DC, MC, V. Metro: L'Enfant Plaza. $$*

9 *f-7*
SEA CATCH
It takes a while to find Sea Catch, one of Georgetown's best-kept secrets; the

entrance is well away from the street in the cluster of galleries that make up the Canal Square complex. The first thing you see is the stunning, white Carrara marble raw bar, a good clue to what you should order. Try also the steamed shellfish combo, one of the kitchen's best dishes, served as a main course at lunch and as an appetizer at dinner, it's a mound of steamed oysters, clams, shrimp, and mussels in a broth of white wine and herbs. The pleasures don't stop there: the Louisiana-born chef also makes a terrific seafood gumbo. Romantic outdoor dining is available in season on the terrace overlooking the C&O Canal. *Canal Square, 1054 31st St. NW, at M St., Georgetown, 202/337–8855. AE, DC, MC, V. Closed Sun. $$$*

9 *f-8*
TONY & JOE'S SEAFOOD PLACE
The location is more exciting than the food, but Tony & Joe's remains popular for riverside dining; it's at its best when you get one of the umbrella-shaded tables outdoors on a nice day. Start with the cream-of-crab soup. The blackened fish and seafood pastas are dependable entrées. Doors stay open until midnight on weekends. *3000 K St. NW, between 30th and 31st Sts., Washington Harbour, Georgetown, 202/944–4545. AE, MC, V. Metro: Foggy Bottom–GWU. $$$*

8 *g-4*
THE WHARF
Housed in a former warehouse uphill from Alexandria's waterfront, this narrow, two-story restaurant has some original wood beams and brick walls. Seafood occupies the place of honor on the menu. Daily fish specials share billing with the restaurant's specialty, Crab Imperial, and crab cakes, stuffed flounder, rockfish, lobster and shrimp, and an excellent prime rib. Desserts favor Southern venues, with key lime pie and chocolate bourbon pecan pie. *119 King St., Alexandria, VA, 703/836–2834. AE, D, DC, MC, V. No dinner Sun. Metro: King St. $*

SOUTHERN

10 *d-2*
B. SMITH'S
This beautiful restaurant with a stylish, diverse clientele occupies the grand

spaces of what was once Union Station's Presidential reception room. The menu is Southern-inspired. The signature entrée, Swamp Thing, may not sound pretty, but this mix of mustard-seasoned shrimp and crawfish with collard greens is delicious. Desserts are comforting classics, slightly dressed up: bananas Foster, warm bread pudding, and sweet-potato pecan pie. *Union Station, 50 Massachusetts Ave. NE, Capitol Hill, 202/289–6188. AE, D, DC, MC, V. Metro: Union Station. $$$*

4 b-8
FLORIDA AVENUE GRILL

The hearty, Southern-style breakfast at this popular diner is a Washington institution. Your eggs come with grits, homemade biscuits, and salmon cakes. At lunch or dinner, try the ham hocks, Southern fried chicken, corn bread, and, for dessert, bread pudding. Note that alcohol is not served. *1100 Florida Ave. NW, at 11th St., Shaw District, 202/265–1586. Reservations not accepted. AE, D, DC, MC, V. Closed Sun.–Mon. Metro: U St.–Cardozo. $*

6 a-5
GEORGIA BROWN'S

The airy, curving dining room has white honeycomb windows and an unusual ceiling ornamentation of bronze ribbons. An elegant "New South" eatery and a favorite hangout of local politicians, Georgia Brown's serves Carolina-style shrimp (served with the head on, and steaming grits on the side); medallions of beef tenderloin with a bourbon-pecan sauce; thick, rich crab soup; and such specials as grilled salmon and smoked-bacon green beans. Fried green tomatoes are a frequent side dish. For dessert, try the sweet-potato cheesecake. *950 15th St. NW, Downtown, 202/393–4499. AE, DC, MC, V. No lunch Sat. Metro: McPherson Sq. $$$*

2 f-6
HEART & SOUL

Traditional Southern favorites are served here with a Caribbean-creole flair. You can order your catfish blackened or corn-fried, and enjoy chicken wings cooked with barbecue sauce or Jamaican spices. It's easy to make a meal out of the delicious sides: mashed potatoes, red beans and rice, candied sweet potatoes, collard greens, black-eyed peas. The service, although

friendly, can be very slow. *801 Pennsylvania Ave. SE, Capitol Hill, 202/546–8801. AE, MC, V. Metro: Eastern Market. $$*

5 g-4
VIDALIA

This distinguished regional-American restaurant takes its name from a type of onion native to Vidalia, Georgia. Onions are indeed a specialty here in season—you'll get onion marmalade to go with your bread, and can order a whole baked onion as an appetizer—but they're just the beginning. Inspired by the food of both the South and the Chesapeake Bay area, chef Jeffrey Buben's version of New American cuisine revolves around the best seasonal fruits, vegetables, and seafood he can find. Don't miss the roasted onion soup with spoon bread, the shrimp on yellow grits, or the sensational lemon-chess pie. *1990 M St. NW, Dupont Circle, 202/659–1990. AE, D, DC, MC, V. No lunch weekends. Metro: Dupont Circle. $$$*

SOUTHWESTERN

1 c-2
COTTONWOOD CAFE

The food at this stylish café is an innovative blend of flavors from Texas, Santa Fe, and other parts of the Southwest. The blue-cornmeal calamari appetizer is a must. Entrées are generous: try the Fire and Spice linguine, with andouille sausage and shrimp; *barbacoa*, grilled chicken and shrimp marinated in barbecue sauce with baked banana; or classic grilled fajitas. *4844 Cordell Ave., Bethesda, MD, 301/656–4844. AE, MC, V. No lunch Sun. Metro: Bethesda. $$$*

SPANISH

ANDALUCÍA

These two fine Spanish restaurants are now under separate ownership, but they share a pastry chef and the menus are almost identical. The food, of course, is from southern Spain, where seafood features prominently: try the *zarzuela*, a traditional seafood stew. Veal chops, either grilled with rosemary or sautéed with a dry sherry sauce, are hefty and cooked to order; duck is served in a brandy sauce with mushrooms. The Rockville location has classical Spanish guitarists and flamenco dancing on

Thursday night. *12300 Wilkins Ave., Rockville, MD, 301/770–1880. AE, D, DC, MC, V. Closed Mon. No lunch weekends. Metro: Twinbrook. $$$*

1 *c-2*

4931 Elm St., Bethesda, MD, 301/907–0052. Metro: Bethesda.

6 *a-6*

CATALAN

Chef Yannick Cam manages to squeeze two different culinary experiences under one roof in Catalan, his Spanish-focused restaurant. Zesty tapas are served in the quirky, colorful front bar room. These are not Spanish-style little tidbits, but small plates of beautifully executed main courses. Prices are very reasonable. The back room is Provençal in mood, and the food served here is very French. Prices are substantially higher. You'll dine well in either language. *1319 F St. NW, near 14th St., Downtown, 202/628–2299. AE, DC, MC, V. Metro: Metro Center. $$$*

6 *c-6*

JALEO

Much-applauded executive chef Jose Andrés has given new zest to one of the city's most spirited menus. There are entrées on the menu at this lively Spanish bistro, but—as in Spain—most people make a meal from the long list of hot and cold tapas. Highlights on the tapas menu are *gambas al ajillo* (sautéed garlic shrimp), fried potatoes with spicy tomato sauce, and *pinchitos* (skewers of grilled chorizo) with garlic-mashed potatoes. For dessert, dive into the crisp, buttery apple Charlotte or the chocolate-hazelnut tart. You may have to wait for a table, but service is quick. Tables can only be reserved for dining between 5 and 6:30. *480 7th St. NW, Downtown, 202/628–7949. AE, D, MC, V. Metro: Gallery Pl.–Chinatown. $$*

5 *g-5*

TABERNA DEL ALABARDERO

An atmosphere of old-fashioned formality, a skilled staff, and sophisticated Spanish cooking make this restaurant one of Washington's finest, and some say it's the best Spanish restaurant in the country. Start with such tapas as *piquillo* peppers stuffed with *bacalao* (salted cod), or roasted leg of duck wrapped in phyllo pastry. Proceed to a hefty bowl of gazpacho or white garlic soup, then venture forth to authentic paella and elegant Spanish country dishes. Ask the sommelier to recommend a good Spanish wine for your meal. Warm pineapple tart makes a light finale for the rich fare. The plush old-world decor and handsome bar create a romantic mood, and the crowd is well-heeled and cosmopolitan. *1776 I St. NW, at 18th St., Downtown, 202/429–2200. AE, DC, MC, V. Closed Sun. No lunch Sat. Metro: Farragut West. $$$*

STEAK

6 *b-5*

BOBBY VAN'S

All hints of previous restaurants (Italian and Mediterranean) have been swept away to be replaced by steak house standards: tons of wood, faux-leather chairs and banquettes, large wine displays (mostly magnums up front), and statues of steers. The meat is brought from New York several times a week and aged on the premises. Some cuts are beefy, others less so, but all are huge, as are the vegetable side orders. *809 15th St. NW, between H and I Sts., Downtown, 202/589–0060. AE, DC, MC, V. Metro: Metro Center. $$$$*

6 *c-6*

CAPITAL GRILLE

Since it opened in 1994, Capital Grille has been a hit, especially with Hill types and the lobbyists who follow them. Fans proclaim the beef and lobster the best in town; lamb chops are right up there, too. The wine list is serious and extensive. Service is considerate and friendly without being chummy, unless you're a regular. Not much of the restaurant is visible from the street, but the window of dry, aging beef will tell you this is it. *601 Pennsylvania Ave. NW, Downtown, 202/737–6200. AE, DC, MC, V. Metro: Archives–Navy Memorial. $$$$*

5 *c-3*

DAILY GRILL

Just as with most steak houses, there are plenty of other choices on the menu in addition to the filet mignon with bordelaise sauce and New York pepper steak: big salads, a variety of chicken offerings, pasta, and seafood. The difference in this offshoot of a California chain is that the food is cooked to formula. Still, prices are reasonable, and the bar scene is a huge draw. There's a good selection of hand-crafted bourbon and single-malt Scotch. Free two-hour valet parking is available. *Georgetown Inn, 1310 Wisconsin Ave. NW, at N St., Georgetown, 202/337–4900. AE, DC, MC, V. $$*

9 *e-7*

MORTON'S OF CHICAGO

The Georgetown branch of Morton's of Chicago materialized as a haunt for politicians and lobbyists during Chicagoan Dan Rostenkowski's reign as chairman of the House Ways and Mean Committee. It's still an expensive (read: expense-account) place, but its claim to serve the country's best beef might just be true. In the classic steak house tradition, the emphasis is on quantity as well as quality: the New York strip and porterhouse steaks, two of the most popular, are well over a pound each. And for those with truly epic appetites (or two who want to share), there's a 3-pound porterhouse on offer. The menu also includes lamb, veal, chicken, lobster, and grilled fish. *3251 Prospect St. NW, near Wisconsin Ave., Georgetown, 202/342–6258. No lunch. AE, DC, MC, V. Metro: Foggy Bottom–GWU. $$$$*

5 *g-4*

1050 Connecticut Ave. NW, Downtown, 202/955–5997. No lunch weekends. Metro: Farragut North.

1 *a-4*

8075 Leesburg Pike, Tysons Corner, Vienna, VA, 703/883–0800. No lunch weekends. $$$

5 *g-4*

THE PALM

Sometimes jokingly called Washington's Sistine Chapel, the Palm covers its walls with caricatures of celebrities who have dined here, and is still a favorite lunchtime hangout of power brokers. The main attractions are gargantuan steaks and Nova Scotia lobsters, several kinds of potatoes, and New York cheesecake. But one of the Palm's best-kept secrets is that it's also a terrific old-fashioned Italian restaurant: try the veal marsala or, on Thursday, the terrific shrimp in marinara sauce. *1225 19th St. NW, Downtown, 202/293–9091. AE, DC, MC, V. Closed Sun. No lunch Sat. Metro: Dupont Circle. $$$*

5 *g-4*

SAM & HARRY'S

Possibly D.C.'s most attractive steak house—and certainly the one with the best wine cellar—Sam and Harry's is understated, genteel, and packed at both lunch and dinner. The real draws are such prime meats as porterhouse and New York strip steaks served on the bone. Those who've sworn off beef may want to try the daily seafood specials, which include Maine lobster and fresh fish plates. End the meal with warm pecan pie laced with melted chocolate, or a Turtle Cake full of chocolate and caramel, big enough for two. *1200 19th St. NW, between M and N Sts., Dupont Circle, 202/296–4333. AE, D, DC, MC, V. Closed Sun. No lunch Sat. Metro: Dupont Circle. $$$$*

1 *a-4*

Tysons Corner, 8240 Leesburg Pike, McLean, VA, 703/448–0088. Metro: Vienna. $$$

TEA

5 *c-4*

CHING CHING CHA

Step away from the bustle of Georgetown into the serene aura of Ching Ching Cha. Owner Hollie Wong spent nearly two years studying Chinese teas and tea houses in China, Taiwan, and Hong Kong before introducing Washington to this new experience. The tearoom is a work of art in itself, with carefully selected tables, chairs, tea canisters, and teapots. Choose from almost 40 different teas, and the pot will be brewed at your table; a lesson in proper brewing is a bonus. A small menu offers small bites such as dumplings or five-spice peanuts. For $10 you can have a small full meal winningly presented in a sectioned *bento* box. Oh, and the name: Ching Ching is Chinese for Hollie, and *cha* is tea, of course. *1063 Wisconsin Ave., between M St. and the C&O Canal, Georgetown, 202/333–8288. AE, DC, MC, V. Metro: Foggy Bottom–GWU. $*

5 *f-2*

TEAISM

Located along Dupont Circle's tree-lined art gallery street, Teaism is a unique find: a small restaurant with a selection of more than 50 fine teas and a unique menu of delicious Japanese, Indian, and Thai foods. You can mix small dishes—

tandoori kebabs, tea-cured salmon, Indian flatbreads, salads, and various chutneys—to make creative snacks or full meals. Japanese bento boxes—which contain a salad, entrée, rice, and cookies—are meals in themselves; another unique favorite is the *ochazuke*, green tea poured over seasoned rice. Of course, you can always just enjoy a hot drink with a ginger scone. *2009 R St. NW, between Connecticut Ave. and 21st St., Dupont Circle, 202/667-3827. Reservations not accepted. AE, MC, V. Metro: Dupont Circle.* $

6 *c-6*

400 8th St. NW, at D St., Downtown, 202/638-6010. Metro: Gallery Pl.–Chinatown or Archives–Navy Memorial.

TEX-MEX

3 *a-8*

AUSTIN GRILL

This fine, local Tex-Mex chain is decorated in a Texas-funk style and serves some of the best Texas chili and margaritas in town. House specialties include quesadillas with fresh jumbo lump crab or Portobello mushrooms with beef, "Austin special" enchiladas with three sauces, and grilled, chili-rubbed shrimp and scallops. As a special treat, order a Swirlie, a frozen margarita with lime and strawberry flavors. Most locations are open until midnight on weekends. *2404 Wisconsin Ave. NW, at Calvert St., Glover Park, 202/337-8080. AE, D, DC, MC, V. Metro: Tenleytown–AU.* $$

6 *c-6*

750 E St. NW, Downtown, 202/393-3776. Metro: Gallery Pl.–Chinatown or Archives–Navy Memorial.

1 *c-2*

7278 Woodmont, at Elm St., Bethesda, MD, 301/656-1366. Metro: Bethesda.

8 *f-4*

801 King St., at N. Columbus St., Old Town, Alexandria, VA, 703/684-8969. Metro: King St.

8430A Old Keene Mill Rd., at Rolling Rd., West Springfield, VA, 703/644-3111.

3 *a-5*

CACTUS CANTINA

This cavernous Cleveland Park restaurant is perennially packed with locals, who come for the beef quesadillas, the mesquite-grilled shrimp and quail, the great pork tamale, and the à la carte chiles rellenos. Evenings here are a festive escape to south of the border, with Washingtonians toasting margaritas and Tecate beers to the sound of mariachi soundtracks. The outdoor patio, open in summer, is extremely popular with young professionals and families. *3300 Wisconsin Ave. NW, Cleveland Park, 202/686-7222. AE, D, DC, MC, V. Metro: Cleveland Park.* $$

2 *b-2*

GUAPO'S

Festively decorated with colorful lights, piñatas, and artwork, this lively neighborhood restaurant with a large outdoor patio is often filled with American University students looking for cheap eats and a good margarita. Bountiful plates of burritos, enchiladas, tacos, and fajitas are standard fare here, but the kitchen's best efforts are found on the Chef's Recommendations menu. The *costillas barbacoa* (mesquite-grilled pork ribs) is a nice departure from predictable Tex-Mex fare. *4515 Wisconsin Ave. NW, Tenleytown, 202/686-3588. AE, MC, V. Metro: Tenleytown–AU.* $$

1 *c-2*

8130 Wisconsin Ave., Bethesda, MD, 301/656-0888. Metro: Bethesda.

6 *a-6*

RED SAGE

No D.C. restaurant of the last decade enjoyed more ballyhoo around its opening than the Red Sage. The multimillion-dollar interior is a pseudo-adobe warren of dining rooms, with lizards and barbed wire the unlikely themes. The upstairs chili bar works well for a fairly inexpensive lunch; downstairs is much more pricey. The food is cowboy-chic—steaks, game, and grilled meat and fish, often served with mouth-searing chili rubs or sauces. *605 14th St. NW, at F St., Downtown, 202/638-4444. AE, DC, MC, V. Metro: Metro Center.* $$$$

1 *c-2*

RIO GRANDE CAFÉ

Quail, goat, and other upscale Tex-Mex fare make it worth braving Rio Grande's crowds. Crates of Mexican beer stacked against the walls add atmosphere, as does a perpetual-motion tortilla machine. Big portions make this a good spot for families. A young bar crowd likes to knock back the potent combination of frozen sangria and frozen margarita swirled in a frosted soda glass. *4919 Fairmont Ave., Bethesda, MD, 301/656–2981. AE, D, DC, MC, V. Metro: Bethesda. $$*

1 *c-5*

4301 N. Fairfax Dr., Arlington, VA, 703/528-3131. Metro: Ballston–MU.

1827 Library St., Reston Town Center, Reston, VA, 703/904-0703.

THAI

5 *b-4*

BANGKOK BISTRO

Contemporary Thai food is served in a stylish setting on a relatively quiet Georgetown street. Soups are delicately seasoned, and the popular crispy duck comes with crunchy noodles. A standout is the signature Shrimp in Paradise—grilled giant prawn topped with crabmeat, in a pool of chili-garlic sauce. Service always aims to please. *3251 Prospect St. NW, near 33rd St., Georgetown, 202/337–2424. AE, DC, MC, V. $*

3 *a-8*

BUSARA

Neon-lighted blue ceilings, smart primary-color wall art, and lacquered tables provide visual accompaniment for imaginative Thai cuisine. Whether it's green-papaya salad, naked shrimp with sake sauce, or *larb gai* (minced chicken in spicy lime juice), the presentation will highlight the dish, reminding you that you eat with both your eyes and your taste buds. There's garden seating in season. *2340 Wisconsin Ave. NW, Glover Park, 202/337–2340. AE, D, DC, MC, V. $$*

1 *b-6*

DUANGRAT'S

Duangrat's is simply the area's finest Thai restaurant, with more breadth and depth than any other. The elegant, pale-peach dining rooms are filled with Thai paintings and sculptures, and waitresses swish by in long gauzy gowns. Seafood is very good here—Thai fish stew, soft-shell crabs with chili sauce, lobster with black bean sauce. Roast pork with a soy plum sauce is excellent. Classic Thai dance is performed upstairs every Friday and Saturday night. *5878 Leesburg Pike, at Glen Forest Rd., Bailey's Crossroads, VA, 703/820–5775. AE, DC, MC, V. $$*

3 *e-7*

JANDARA

A festive Thai restaurant within easy walking distance of Adams-Morgan, Jandara resembles a lunar platform with an artificial celestial sky. The colorful dining room has meteors showering across its walls, space lights dangling from the heavens, and purple fabric seats that appear straight out of an episode of "The Jetsons." Once you're back to earth, consider the *ka phao* (chicken, beef, pork, or seafood sautéed with ground pepper, garlic, and fresh basil) or the less spicy *phad Thai* (rice noodles stir-fried with shrimp, bean sprouts, and sliced dry bean curd). *2606 Connecticut Ave. NW, Woodley Park, 202/387–8876. AE, DC, MC, V. Metro: Woodley Park–Zoo. $$*

2 *b-2*

4237 Wisconsin Ave. NW, Tenleytown, 202/237–1570. Metro: Tenleytown–AU.

5 *f-3*

SALA THAI

This small, good-value subterranean eatery has friendly service and a largely neighborhood following. Among the subtly seasoned offerings are *panang goong* (chicken or shrimp in curry-peanut sauce), chicken sautéed with ginger and pineapple, and flounder with a choice of four sauces. The Wild Chic—grilled chicken breast sautéed with asparagus in red curry sauce—is also good. *2016 P St. NW, Dupont Circle, 202/872–1144. AE, D, DC, MC, V. Metro: Dupont Circle. $$*

5 *g-4*

STAR OF SIAM

The Adams-Morgan branch of Star of Siam has a small, extremely casual section upstairs for those who want to dine Thai-style, on cushions at low tables; but both locations serve the same tasty food. Choice items include the Thai curries, which come red, green, or yellow, depending on the seasonings; deep-fried whole fish with chili sauce; and spicy rice noodles with beef and basil. *1136 19th St. NW, between L and M Sts., Downtown, 202/785–2838. AE, D, DC, MC, V. No lunch Sun. Metro: Farragut West. $$*

3 *g-8*

2446 18th St. NW, Adams-Morgan, 202/986–4133. No lunch weekdays. Metro: Woodley Park– Zoo.

TURKISH

10 g-8

ANATOLIA

An unexpectedly comfortable, intimate restaurant behind a Capitol Hill storefront, Anatolia is run by a hospitable husband-and-wife team. Start with warm pita and one or more of the excellent appetizer spreads, sweet roasted eggplant, or peppery hummus. There's a standard array of kebabs, but the *adana* kebab, a grilled homemade lamb sausage specific to Turkey, is delicious. Dessert is a classic: baklava and a cup of espresso-like Turkish coffee. *633 Pennsylvania Ave. SE, Capitol Hill, 202/544-4753. AE, D, MC, V. Closed Sun. No lunch Sat. Metro: Eastern Market. $$*

NIZAM'S

Doner kebab or gyros—layers of roasted lamb cooked on a vertical spit—is one of the glories of Turkish cooking, and a Tuesday and weekend special at this attractive suburban restaurant. Alternatively, try the kebabs of swordfish and shrimp; baked lamb topped with *kasseri* cheese; braised lamb shank with tomato sauce and yogurt; or delicious baked moussaka. Polish it all off with baklava and Turkish coffee. *523 Maple Ave. W, Vienna, VA, 703/938-8948. AE, D, MC, V. Closed Mon. No lunch Sat. or Sun. $$*

VEGETARIAN & MACROBIOTIC

6 a-1

FOOD FOR THOUGHT

This longtime alternative hangout has relocated to the Black Cat Club, where it now serves food in the Red Room bar. The focus is on vegetarian food, but they work with chicken and fish, too. Creations include vegan nachos, vegetarian chili over brown rice, and a few meat and chicken dishes. It's open nightly from 8 to 11. *1831 14th St. NW, at T St., U Street, 202/797-1095. No credit cards. No lunch. Metro: U St.–Cardozo. $*

VIETNAMESE

1 c-5

CAFÉ DALAT

In the heart of Arlington's "Little Saigon," Café Dalat offers inexpensive Vietnamese fare in a far-from-fancy but clean and pleasant setting. The service is known for an efficiency that nears the speed of light. The sugarcane shrimp could inspire a trip to Southeast Asia, and *da ram gung* is a sinus-clearing dish of simmered chicken and ginger. All the appetizers are winners, in particular the crispy spring rolls and the tangy Vietnamese shrimp salad in lemon vinaigrette. *3143 Wilson Blvd., Arlington, VA, 703/276-0935. MC, V. Metro: Clarendon. $*

8 f-4

EAST WIND RESTAURANT

A favorite of Old Towners, especially at lunchtime, this eatery presents its food beautifully. The usual Vietnamese soups share the extensive menu with such top-billed main dishes as *bo dun* (broiled beef tenderloin marinated in wine, honey, and spices); marinated shrimp and scallops charbroiled on skewers; and rice noodles with chunks of spiced beef, chicken, scallops, and shrimp. Peanut sauce complements the fresh garden rolls. *809 King St., Alexandria, VA, 703/836-1515. AE, D, MC, V. No lunch weekends. Metro: King St. $*

1 c-5

LITTLE VIET GARDEN

The Christmas lights never come down at this popular Clarendon joint. Loyalists swear by the crisp spring rolls and noodle-and-herb-filled summer rolls; tasty soups of beef broth and glass noodles; Saigon pancake stuffed with chicken, shrimp, bean sprouts, and green onion; and beef tips and potato stir-fried with onion in a smoky sauce. In the warmer months, reserve a table on the outdoor terrace, bordered by a white fence lined with flower boxes. *3012 Wilson Blvd., Arlington, VA, 703/522-9686. AE, D, DC, MC, V. Metro: Clarendon. $$*

9 f-7

MISS SAIGON

Perhaps the best Vietnamese restaurant in D.C., Miss Saigon pays careful attention to both seasoning and presentation. Begin with crisp egg rolls or chilled spring rolls, then proceed to exquisite salads of shredded green papaya topped with shrimp or beef. Daily specials feature the freshest seafood prepared in exciting ways. "Caramel"-cooked meats are standouts, as are the grilled meats. Prices are moderate, especially for lunch, but you may have to order several dishes to fill up. *3057 M St. NW, Georgetown,*

202/333–5545. AE, MC, V. No lunch weekends. Metro: Foggy Bottom–GWU. $$

2 b-5
PHO 75

A steaming bowl of *pho* at one of these bare-bones restaurants is one of the true bargains in D.C. dining. The Vietnamese eat this beef soup for breakfast or lunch. You can order it with a number of exotic meats, such as bible tripe (a cut of cow's stomach) and soft tendon, but your best bet on a first visit is eye of round and brisket. Pho starts with a bowl of hot broth and rice noodles; the beef is added at the last minute and cooked by the broth. A plate of fresh bean sprouts, mint leaves, lemon, and green chilis comes with every order so that you can spice your feast-in-a-bowl as you wish. Both the large and the small bowls are remarkable bargains. The restaurants close early—usually around 8—so plan to go for lunch or an early dinner. 1721 Wilson Blvd., Arlington, VA, 703/525-7355. No credit cards. Metro: Rosslyn. $

1 a-5
3103 Graham Rd., Suite B, Falls Church, VA, 703/204–1490.

1 e-2
1510 University Blvd., East Langley Park, MD, 301/434–7844.

1 e-2
PHO 99

This inexpensive little gem sits across the street from the Asian Village Market, so the dining room is often filled with Asian expats who know the best places to savor the foods of their homeland. In addition to the extensive pho options—most made with brisket, flank, or eye-round steak—the menu also offers a huge selection of seafood, vermicelli, and rice dishes. Most impressive are the *goi cuon* (rice paper–wrapped shrimp and pork served with peanut sauce) appetizer and main dishes such as grilled shrimp with lemongrass or caramelized pork in a clay pot. 2065 University Blvd. E, Suite E, Hyattsville, MD, 301/445–1431. MC, V. $

1 c-5
QUEEN BEE

The grande dame of Vietnamese restaurants in the Washington area, Queen Bee is a study in organized chaos. The spring rolls are terrific, as are the Hanoi-style grilled pork, the Queen Bee seafood on crispy noodles, the Saigon pancake, and the whole fried fish served with a spicy sauce on the side. French amber beer, in large bottles, is the thing to drink. 3181 Wilson Blvd., at Washington Blvd., Arlington, VA, 703/527-3444. AE, DC, MC, V. Metro: Clarendon. $$

3 e-7
SAIGON GOURMET

Ensconced in a somewhat affluent neighborhood, the relatively pricey Saigon Gourmet is dependable for its ultracrisp *cha-gio* (spring rolls), savory pho, seafood soups, and delicately seasoned and richly sauced entrées. Shrimp Saigon mixes prawns and pork in a peppery marinade, and another Saigon dish—grilled pork with rice crepes—is a Vietnamese variation on the Chinese moo shu. 2635 Connecticut Ave. NW, Woodley Park, 202/265–1360. AE, D, DC, MC, V. Metro: Woodley Park–Zoo. $$

chapter 2

SHOPPING

I t's hard to define where shopping begins and ends in Washington, D.C. Not only are the retail options vast, but the Washington area never really ends. Some clannish politicos may not much care what's "outside the Beltway," but shoppers certainly do. Most of the large malls and better shopping centers hover on the edge of the District's borders, still easily accessible by Metro. Shops in suburban Maryland and Virginia are not really suburban in the classic sense, and may in fact be easier for D.C. dwellers to get to than many places in the city itself.

Inside the District proper, you'll find distinct shopping areas, each with its own specialty—from Georgetown's upscale shops and antiques dealers to Adams-Morgan's eclectic, world-beat flavor. Washington's international population exerts influence well beyond Embassy Row: ethnic shops offer handmade artifacts, exotic culinary creations, and one-of-a-kind clothing. European expatriates' demand for Italian and French fashions has played a significant role in the proliferation of designer boutiques along Wisconsin Avenue. And you'll find ethnic food and spices from almost every part of the globe. Shopping around here is an adventure, and heaven knows it's more fun than politics.

shopping areas

DEPARTMENT STORES

1 *c-1*

BLOOMINGDALE'S
Bloomie's goes up and down, but on the whole it satisfies those who demand quality and originality. Both designer and casual clothing for men, women, and children are reliably upscale, and Bloomie's own label is one of the most attractive store lines around. Housewares and gifts are as fine as ever. *White Flint Mall, 11301 Rockville Pike, North Bethesda, MD, 301/984–4600. Metro: White Flint.*

1 *a-4*

Tysons Corner Center, 1961 Chain Bridge Rd., McLean, VA, 703/556–4600.

6 *b-5*

HECHT'S
This spacious downtown department store is the last of its kind, following the demise of such former local favorites as Garfinkel's and Woodward & Lothrop. Hecht's remains a classic department store, with clothing, fragrances, and accessories for everyone in the family—both trendy and classic—and strong selections of cosmetics, lingerie, and housewares. *12th and G Sts. NW, Downtown, 202/628–6661. Metro: Metro Center.*

1 *c-2*

Montgomery Mall, 7125 Democracy Blvd., Bethesda, MD, 301/469–6800. Metro: Medical Center.

1 *c-5*

Ballston Common Mall, 701 N. Glebe Rd., Arlington, VA, 703/524–5100. Metro: Ballston–MU.

1 *a-4*

Tysons Corner Center, 1961 Chain Bridge Rd., McLean, VA, 703/893–4900.

1 *c-3*

5400 Wisconsin Ave., Chevy Chase, MD, 301/654–7600. Metro: Friendship Heights.

2 *b-1*

LORD & TAYLOR
This expansive store, just behind the Mazza Gallerie in Upper Northwest, has maintained a pleasantly old-time aura. The look remains classically American, covering designer and casual clothing and accessories for men, women, and children. *5255 Western Ave. NW, Upper Northwest, 202/362–9600. Metro: Friendship Heights.*

1 *c-1*

White Flint Mall, 11301 Rockville Pike, North Bethesda, MD, 301/770–9000. Metro: White Flint.

1 *a-4*

MACY'S
Although the Pentagon City store is closest to downtown, this Macy's is the oldest and toniest in the D.C. area. If you're willing to brave the Tysons Corner traffic, you'll find a great selection of designer labels, housewares and gifts, and charming service. *Tysons Corner Cen-*

ter, 1961 Chain Bridge Rd., McLean, VA, 703/556-0000.

1 d-6

The Fashion Centre at Pentagon City, 1000 S. Hayes St., Arlington, VA, 703/418-4488. Metro: Pentagon City.

1 b-8

Springfield Mall, Springfield, VA, 703/719-6100. Metro: Franconia–Springfield.

2 b-1

NEIMAN MARCUS

Shoppers with a hankering for the best come to this luxury chain. Everything is deluxe here, including couture fashions, designer jewelry, furs, crystal, and silver; and the personal-shopping service is most attentive. The prices match the quality. *Mazza Gallerie, 5300 Wisconsin Ave. NW, Upper Northwest, 202/966-9700. Metro: Friendship Heights.*

1 a-4

Tysons Corner Center, 1961 Chain Bridge Rd., McLean, VA, 703/761-1600.

1 b-8

Springfield Mall, Springfield, VA, 703/971-3040. Metro: Franconia–Springfield.

1 d-6

NORDSTROM

Nordstrom is one of the most successful department stores in the area. You constantly hear it referred to with superlatives: "the best place to get children's clothes," "the best place to find shoes," "the best service in Washington." Personal service is indeed emphasized here, and it truly makes shopping a pleasure. Nordstrom has a great selection for the whole family, and fabulous sales. *The Fashion Centre at Pentagon City, 1000 S. Hayes St., Arlington, VA, 703/415-1121. Metro: Pentagon City.*

1 a-4

Tysons Corner Center, 1961 Chain Bridge Rd., McLean, VA, 703/761-0700.

1 c-2

Montgomery Mall, 7125 Democracy Blvd., Bethesda, MD, 301/365-8848. Metro: Medical Center.

2 b-1

SAKS FIFTH AVENUE

Although technically in the suburbs, this Saks is a Washington institution, providing a wide selection of European and American couture clothing, furs, lingerie, jewelry, and shoes. Just over the District line on upper Wisconsin Avenue, the store also has a personal-shopping service, a deluxe hair salon, and the only Giorgio Armani boutique in the Washington area, with both Collezione and Boronuovo (the "black label"). *5555 Wisconsin Ave., Chevy Chase, MD, 301/657-9000. Metro: Friendship Heights.*

1 a-4

Tysons Corner Center, 1961 Chain Bridge Rd., McLean, VA, 703/761-0700.

MALLS & SHOPPING CENTERS

2 b-1

CHEVY CHASE PAVILION

A more contemporary version of Mazza Galerie (and just across the street), the Chevy Chase Pavilion features such stores as Joan and David, Pottery Barn, Country Road, Steilmann European Selection, and that classic women's standby, Talbots. *5335 Wisconsin Ave. NW, Upper Northwest, 202/686-5335. Metro: Friendship Heights.*

1 d-6

THE FASHION CENTRE AT PENTAGON CITY

Across the Potomac River from Washington and easily accessible by Metro, this four-story shopping mall was once the height of chic for suburbanites as well as Washingtonians. Today it offers an amazing number and selection of the nation's most popular mainstream stores, including Gap, Gap Kids, Nordstrom, Macy's, RadioShack, Circuit City, Britches, The Limited, The Nature Company, and the Disney Store. *1000 S. Hayes St., Arlington, VA, 703/415-2400. Metro: Pentagon City.*

9 e-7

GEORGETOWN PARK

At the center of the Georgetown shopping district, Georgetown Park is a beautiful, three-level shopping mall full of prominent high-quality shops—Ann Taylor, Polo, J. Crew. There's also a wide variety of smaller stores, offering various deluxe items and accessories. *3222 M St. NW, Georgetown, 202/298-5577. Metro: Foggy Bottom–GWU.*

2 b-1

MAZZA GALLERIE

This four-level shopping mall is filled with glamorous shops, including the largest Neiman Marcus in the area, Pampillonia Jewelers, Kron Chocolates, Williams-Sonoma, and more. Take heart: you can at least fuel your spree cheaply with refreshment at the adjacent McDonald's. Or, you can window-shop and save your money for a movie at the mall's multiplex. *5300 Wisconsin Ave. NW, Upper Northwest, 202/966–6114. Metro: Friendship Heights.*

6 b-6
OLD POST OFFICE PAVILION

This handsome shopping center is situated in a historic 19th-century building. In addition to a dozen food vendors, there are 17 shops, most of them small businesses featuring collectibles, leather, and gifts, as well as a newsstand and a ticket outlet. The observation deck in the building's clock tower affords excellent views of the city. *1100 Pennsylvania Ave., Downtown, 202/289–4224. Metro: Federal Triangle.*

POTOMAC MILLS MALL

Make tracks for this behemoth, a half-hour drive from D.C., when you want serious bargains (or just an adventure—Virginia bills this suburban outlet mall as a tourist attraction in itself). There's an Ikea outlet, an Eddie Bauer outlet, a Britches Basement, a Laura Ashley outlet, a Benetton outlet, a Nordstrom Rack, a Sears outlet, a Linens 'n Things, and about 150 other great places to stretch your dollar. Diehards love it. *2700 Potomac Mills Circle, Woodbridge, VA, 800/826–4557.*

6 a-6
THE SHOPS AT NATIONAL PLACE

The shops take up three levels, one of which is devoted to food courts. Many of the stores, such as Claire's Boutique, are geared toward teens, but some, such as Filene's Basement and Foot Locker, work for all ages. *529 14th St. NW, Downtown, 202/662–1250. Metro: Metro Center.*

1 a-4
TYSONS CORNER CENTER AND THE GALLERIA AT TYSONS II

Originally just one mall at Tysons Corner, this development has grown into two separate and enormous shopping centers anchored by Bloomingdale's, Saks Fifth Avenue, Neiman Marcus, Macy's, and countless independent shops. Together, they comprise 363 retailers in all. *Tysons Corner Center, 1961 Chain Bridge Rd., McLean, VA, 703/893–9400; Galleria at Tysons II, 2001 International Dr., McLean, VA, 703/827–7700.*

10 d-2
UNION STATION

This beautiful shopping center in a Beaux Arts–style structure is one of D.C.'s treasures. Union Station is now both a working train station and a trilevel mall, with a food court and a cineplex on the bottom level and specialty shops up above. A highlight is the Great Train Store, which sells train memorabilia and toy trains from all over the world, some costing very little and others approaching the cost of a real train (*see* Collectibles *in* Toys & Games, *below*). Union Station itself stages nice seasonal attractions, such as a carved-pumpkin festival at Halloween and a no-holds-barred display at Christmastime. *50 Massachusetts Ave. NE, Capitol Hill, 202/371–9441. Metro: Union Station.*

5 e-5
WATERGATE MALL

From Richard Nixon to Monica Lewinsky, the Watergate Apartments and Hotel complex has seen its share of intrigue. The place *is* worth a visit, if only to window-shop at the upscale boutiques of Yves St. Laurent, Gucci, Vera Wang Bridal, and Valentino. If you come here in a buying mood, you'll need bucks to back it. If that won't happen, satisfy the urge to splurge with one of the Watergate Pastry's decadent creations. *600 New Hampshire Ave. NW, Foggy Bottom, no central phone. Metro: Foggy Bottom–GWU.*

1 c-1
WHITE FLINT MALL

Upscale shops in this enormous suburban-Maryland mall include Bloomingdale's, the Coach Store, Lord & Taylor, Eddie Bauer, and the Sharper Image. A free shuttle bus whisks you here from the Metro stop. *11301 Rockville Pike, North Bethesda, MD, 301/231–7467. Metro: White Flint.*

SHOPPING NEIGHBORHOODS

washington, d.c.

ADAMS-MORGAN

Unarguably Washington's most ethnically diverse neighborhood, Adams-Morgan has enough shopping to form a full day's excursion. Walk around Calvert Street, Columbia Road, and 18th Street NW to explore and collect lovely items from just about every nation on the planet. When you're tired, stop for a Jamaican brunch, a Salvadoran lunch, or an African dinner.

CAPITOL HILL

The area surrounding the United States Congress, in Northeast and Southeast Washington, is known as Capitol Hill, or simply The Hill. It's a charming neighborhood, with streets both large and small lined with Federal and Victorian town houses, neighborhood grocery stores, chic shops selling everything from art books to handwoven rugs, and restaurants with sidewalk cafés.

CHINATOWN

Chinatown is recognizable by its enormous colorful arch at the intersection of 7th and G streets. Interspersed with modern office buildings and small Baptist churches, Chinatown is an attractive combination of restaurants, shops selling produce and products from all over Asia, and stores and galleries with lovely East Asian porcelain and furniture. Chinatown isn't as large or notable as it once was, but you'll still hear many different languages here and see a number of nations represented in the shops and restaurants.

CLEVELAND PARK

This registered historic district in Northwest Washington is a lovely residential area with good restaurants and a cluster of shops around the Cleveland Park Metro stop, on Connecticut Avenue, selling pottery, gift items, and gastronomic delights. The centerpiece is the magnificent Washington National Cathedral, on Wisconsin Avenue, which towers over the whole area.

DUPONT CIRCLE

You can tell by the number of magnificent homes around here that Dupont Circle was once one of the District's deluxe residential neighborhoods. It can no longer make that claim, but it has a new rubric: D.C.'s bohemian district, as well as the center of the local gay community. Branching off from the central Dupont Circle fountain are novelty gift shops offering everything from gags to gay-and-lesbian-pride T-shirts to cheap presidential memorabilia; lots of bookstores and cafés; jewelry shops; and boutiques.

FOGGY BOTTOM

Tree-lined Foggy Bottom is full of charming small town houses and apartment buildings, but not shops. The two exceptions to this are the Kennedy Center, Washington's temple to the performing arts, where you can buy arts-related souvenirs; and the Watergate Mall.

GEORGETOWN

For years, Georgetown has been D.C.'s premiere place to shop, dine, club-hop, and, of course, live. The mix of affluent homeowners, transient college students, and tourists makes for interesting street traffic and the occasional civic skirmish—should Georgetown University students be allowed to vote for neighborhood commissioners? Should suburban shoppers be allowed to park on residential streets? This NIMBY-ish neighborhood lobbied strongly against building a Metro in Georgetown, so as a result the nearest station (Foggy Bottom—GWU) is a 15-to 20-minute walk away. On M Street, the main shopping drag, and Wisconsin Avenue you'll find both luxury items and mainstream chain stores. The charming residential area hides smaller, mom-and-pop specialty shops selling antiques, gardening supplies, and gourmet items.

U STREET—THE NEW U

Browse all sorts of funky things in this newly chic area of Northwest D.C., bordering Adams-Morgan. Various decorative shops carry vintage clothing, antique furniture, and contemporary "antiques," and ethnic stores purvey African clothing and objets d'art.

UPPER NORTHWEST

This vast area contains diverse retail distractions and is accessible from a number of different Metro stops. You can stroll Wisconsin Avenue or Connecticut Avenue for miles, popping into specialty clothing shops, bookstores, or jewelry stores, or upscale shopping malls like the Mazza Gallerie or the Chevy Chase Pavilion.

WOODLEY PARK

Right on the edge of Adams-Morgan, Dupont Circle, and Upper Northwest, Woodley Park is a lovely collection of stores, town houses, hotels, restaurants, and office buildings. On Connecticut Avenue you'll find a cluster of antiques stores, consignment shops, and ethnic restaurants with sidewalk seating.

maryland

BETHESDA

Wisconsin Avenue extends from the Potomac River into suburban Maryland. Once it arrives in Chevy Chase and Bethesda, it's lined with some of the best shops in the Washington metropolitan area. The Red-line Metro will take you here, but the best way to take advantage of this sprawling area is by car.

CHEVY CHASE

This upper-crust area straddles the state line where Northwest Washington meets one of the more exclusive parts of suburban Maryland. The center of the shopping district is Wisconsin Avenue, home to some of the swankest shops this side of Fifth Avenue. It's expensive, with the likes of Saks Fifth Avenue and Tiffany's, but the wares are certainly worth a peek.

COLLEGE PARK

With the vast University of Maryland at its center, this busy suburb is filled with shops geared toward the school and its students. Numerous shopping malls round them out.

TAKOMA PARK

In the summer, this charming village hosts a weekend farmers' market that's known throughout the Washington area for its excellent produce, much of it organic. Takoma Park is a tight-knit community, but it doesn't take long to strike up a rapport with local farmers, who will make an effort to keep regulars informed on the arrival of hard-to-find seasonal items. Annual street festivals feature good live music and artisans selling high-quality candles, cloth dolls, paintings, and other art. The quaint village shops are open year-round.

virginia

ALEXANDRIA

There's really no place more beautiful in the Washington area than Old Town Alexandria, founded 250 years ago as a seaport by Scottish immigrants. Despite the suburban sprawl around it, Old Town remains a delightful collection of 18th-century houses and streets with all the trappings of a small market town. (Two of Alexandria's better-known byways are all-but-impassable streets of large chunks of stone laid during the American Revolution by Prussian prisoners of war.) The streets are lined with charming shops, art galleries, cozy cafés, and trendy eateries, and the riverside parks invite you to sun, picnic, or just absorb the sights and sounds. A special attraction is the Torpedo Factory Art Center, next to the Potomac River, at 105 North Union Street, where local artists create and sell paintings, sculptures, and other artwork.

ARLINGTON

A vast county best known for the National Cemetery, where America's war heroes are buried, Arlington has several retail clusters, most of them malls, like the upscale Fashion Centre at Pentagon City and, just across the street, the shopping center housing the Price Club, Linens 'n Things, Marshalls, and Borders Books & Music.

FAIRFAX

This delightful Virginia town, a 30-minute drive from Washington, is at the heart of wealthy Fairfax County. The central village is charming, having maintained many of its buildings from past centuries; don't miss the enchanting antiques shops, stores selling all manner of local crafts, and an array of fine restaurants. There is also a bustling farmers' market on Saturday mornings, with abundant local produce. Shop for more modern items outside the village itself.

ROSSLYN

It used to be that only those who worked in Rosslyn's many office buildings shopped in this section of Arlington, but ever since the arrival of the twin towers—USA Today and Gannett News—shopping in Rosslyn has developed to cater successfully to area professionals, Washingtonians at large, and tourists, and will continue to do so after the newspaper giants move out to the suburbs in late 2000. Just across the Key Bridge from Georgetown, this cluster of glass-and-metal high-rises near the popular Newseum is worth a visit.

specialty shops

ANTIQUES

10 g-7

ANTIQUES ON THE HILL

Arrayed from the floor to the roof of this quirky store is an extraordinary jumble of knicknacks, odds and ends, and general bric-a-brac. You won't find clear-out sales here—one person's junk is another person's treasure, right?—but the sheer volume and variety make this a fun, interesting, and relatively inexpensive way to add to your collection. *701 N. Carolina Ave. SE, Capitol Hill, 202/543-1819. Closed Mon. Metro: Eastern Market.*

3 g-8

CHENONCEAU ANTIQUES

Chenonceau's two stories are full of fine 18th- and 19th-century pieces, mostly American and all obviously selected by someone with exquisite taste. Mixed in are some unusual and slightly more contemporary items, such as 19th-century paisley scarves and 1920s glass lamps. *2314 18th St. NW, Woodley Park, 202/667-1651. Closed weekdays. Metro: Woodley Park–Zoo.*

5 g-2

CHERISHABLES ANTIQUES, INC.

This charming shop sells mostly 18th- and 19th-century American furniture and decorative arts, along with handmade Christmas ornaments year-round. *1608 20th St. NW, Dupont Circle, 202/785-4087. Metro: Dupont Circle.*

9 g-7

GEORGETOWN ANTIQUES CENTER

Two different shops in one Victorian town house, the Georgetown Antiques Center is made up of the Cherub Gallery, specializing in Art Nouveau and Art Deco articles, and Michael Getz, specializing in fireplace equipment and silverware. *2918 M St. NW, Georgetown, 202/337-2224 (Cherub Gallery), 202/338-3811 (Michael Getz). Closed Sun. in summer. Metro: Foggy Bottom–GWU.*

5 d-4

G. K. S. BUSH & ACANTHUS ANTIQUES

G. K. S. Bush features formal 18th- and early 19th-century American furniture, and Acanthus sells paintings, prints, and decorative accessories from the same period. They offer expert appraisals. *2828 Pennsylvania Ave. NW, Foggy Bottom, 202/965-4173. Closed Mon. Metro: Foggy Bottom–GWU.*

2 d-4

GOOD WOOD

This friendly shop sells vintage and antique wood furniture, including great 19th-century American pieces, as well as stained glass and other decorative items. *1428 U St. NW, U Street, 202/986-3640. Metro: U St.–Cardozo.*

5 d-4

JUSTINE MEHLMAN ANTIQUES

Mehlman's oustanding collection of antique jewelry and decorative arts focuses on the Arts and Crafts period, which includes such top designers as Tiffany, Cartier, and Lalique. *2824 Pennsylvania Ave. NW, Georgetown, 202/337-0613. Closed Sun. in summer. Metro: Foggy Bottom–GWU.*

9 g-5

KELSEY'S KUPBOARD

Local estates provide this shop with its various antiques and collectibles, including lamps, mirrors, desks, chests, tables, chairs, beds, and smaller items in classic styles. *3003 P St. NW, Georgetown, 202/298-8237. Closed Mon. Metro: Foggy Bottom–GWU.*

5 f-3

MARSTON LUCE

Known all over the Washington area for items of both beauty and originality, Marston Luce carries American folk art, handmade quilts, and home and garden furnishings as well as some lovely American antiques and accessories and a number of pieces from Europe. *1314 21st St. NW, Dupont Circle, 202/775-9460. Closed Sun. Metro: Dupont Circle.*

2 d-4

MILLENNIUM

This store calls its wares "20th-century antiques" (read: Bakelite and Lava lamps) and has an eclectic selection of housewares, clothing, records, books, furniture, and accessories at reasonable, sometimes bargain-basement, prices. Browsing here is like entering a time capsule for the '60s, '50s, and '40s. *1528 U St. NW, U Street, 202/483–1218. Closed Mon.– Wed. Metro: U St.–Cardozo.*

9 *d-3*

MILLER & ARNEY ANTIQUES

With formal displays of beautiful 18th-century English, French, and American antiques, this Georgetown shop is more like a gallery than a store. The 19th-century pieces are equally fine, and it's all complemented by beautiful antique Asian porcelain. *1737 Wisconsin Ave. NW, Georgetown, 202/338–2369. Closed Sun. Metro: Foggy Bottom–GWU.*

3 *g-7*

MISS PIXIE'S

Two levels of well-chosen collectibles include gorgeous parasols and umbrellas, antique home furnishings, glass and silverware, vintage clothing, and hardwood bedframes. Low prices keep shoppers' attention. *1819 Adams Mill Rd. NW, Adams-Morgan, 202/232–8171. Closed Mon.–Wed. Metro: Woodley Park–Zoo.*

9 *f-6*

OLD PRINT GALLERY

The capital's largest collection of old prints and maps—including Washingtoniana—is housed in this Georgetown gallery. *1220 31st St. NW, Georgetown, 202/965–1818. Metro: Foggy Bottom–GWU.*

9 *d-4*

ROOMS WITH A VIEW

Browse here for 18th-, 19th-, and 20th-century furniture with an emphasis on early, paint-decorated country pieces. Accoutrements include folk art, textiles, pottery, and architectural ornamentation. *1661 Wisconsin Ave. NW, Georgetown, 202/625–0610. Metro: Foggy Bottom–GWU.*

9 *e-6*

SUSQUEHANNA

With three rooms upstairs, four rooms downstairs, and a garden full of cast-iron birdbaths, Susquehanna is the largest antiques shop in Georgetown. Paintings cover every inch of wall space, although the shop specializes in American and English furniture. *3216 O St. NW, Georgetown, 202/333–1511. Metro: Foggy Bottom–GWU.*

9 *f-8*

VEERHOFF GALLERIES

Established in 1871, this venerable shop has plenty of experience selling beautiful antique prints and maps, and provides superb custom framing. *1054 31st St. NW, Georgetown, 202/338–6456. Closed Sun. and Mon. Metro: Foggy Bottom–GWU.*

antiques centers & flea markets

10 *g-8*

EASTERN MARKET

Just a few blocks from the Metro stop of the same name, this famous indoor and outdoor market has some of the finest produce in the area, in addition to the creations of artists and artisans. The weekend flea market presents nostalgia by the crateful, and vendors are willing to negotiate prices. *7th St. and North Carolina Ave. SE, Capitol Hill, 703/534–7612. Metro: Eastern Market.*

9 *c-2*

GEORGETOWN FLEA MARKET

Beginning each year on the first Sunday in March, and continuing until the last Sunday in December, this market has anywhere from 60 to 100 vendors on a given day. The flea market has a well-deserved reputation as an antiquers' heaven, which, unfortunately, tends to cause the prices to be higher than at other flea markets in the area. If you go first thing in the morning, though, you can still find some wonderful bargains. *Parking yard for Family Rosario Adult Education Center, Wisconsin Ave. between S and T Sts. NW, Georgetown. Metro: Foggy Bottom–GWU.*

1 *e-2*

SILVER SPRING FLEA MARKET

This suburban flea market has only been in existence for a few years and is still growing in size and reputation. Some three dozen vendors offer jewelry, antiques, collectibles, and clothes each Friday, Saturday, and Sunday year-round. *101 Ripley St., Silver Spring, MD, 301/588–0055. Metro: Silver Spring.*

auction houses

6 c-6

ADAM A. WESCHLER & SONS

Weschler's weekly auction has been held every Tuesday at 9:30 AM since 1890. Wares include jewelry, coins, watches, 20th-century art, museum-quality Asian pieces, and Continental and American furniture. You can inspect the goods between 9 and 5 the day before the auction. *905 E St. NW, Downtown, 202/628–1281. Metro: Metro Center.*

1 c-1

G. SLOAN & COMPANY, INC.

Auctions are held at this suburban Maryland auction house throughout the year, usually on Saturday. Every Thursday at 10 AM there's an "attic auction," with viewing two hours prior, as well as the previous Wednesday evening. You can read about what's being auctioned (mainly household items) in Sloan's periodic catalogs. *4920 Wyaconda Rd., Rockville, MD, 301/468–4911. Metro: White Flint.*

LAWS AUCTION HOUSE

Laws is too far outside Washington to be accessible by Metro, but die-hard auction lovers will want to take a drive here. People come from as far as North Carolina for the big Sunday auctions; smaller auctions are held Friday through Monday. Viewing begins two hours before each auction. Six times a year Laws holds major auctions of artworks and furniture by catalog, with written descriptions of each item up for bid. *7209 Centreville Rd., Manassas, VA, 703/361–3148.*

ART SUPPLIES

1 b-4

COLOR WHEEL

Located in the Langley Shopping Center, this comprehensive, family-owned store has served area artists for more than 30 years, with a focus on excellent service and a wide selection of paper, paints, easels, and other supplies. Discounts are available to students, senior citizens, and members of local art leagues. *1374 Chain Bridge Rd., McLean, VA, 703/356–8477.*

1 d-7

PEARL ART & CRAFT SUPPLIES

This 20-store national chain offers significant discounts on general art supplies and carries hard-to-find items such as extra-large canvases and airbrush supplies. The huge Virginia location fills a former Safeway grocery store. *5695 Telegraph Rd., Alexandria, VA, 703/960–3900. Metro: Huntington.*

1 c-1

12266 Rockville Pike, Rockville, MD, 301/816–2900. Metro: Twinbrook.

2 c-3

SULLIVAN'S ART SUPPLIES

This old-fashioned shop is charmingly cluttered with paint sets, brushes, glues, poster board, carving kits, and pen nibs, as well as easels and inks. A visit to the adjoining toy store is a must. *3412 Wisconsin Ave. NW, Upper Northwest, 202/362–1343. Metro: Cleveland Park.*

6 b-5

UTRECHT ART & DRAFTING SUPPLIES

This downtown art-supply shop provides aspiring artists with all the basics—paints, charcoals, watercolors, paper, and canvases—at reasonable prices. *1250 I St. NW, Downtown, 202/898–0555. Metro: Metro Center.*

BEADS

1 c-1

ACCENTS BEAD SHOP

This shop is known for having the area's largest selection of beads, with countless styles—making it easy for jewelry makers to create distinctive items. *12083 Neville St., Rockville, MD, 301/881–2003. Closed Sun.–Wed. Metro: White Flint.*

1 e-2

ATLANTIC GEMS

Primarily a purveyor of jewelry supplies for serious artisans, this shop also carries a choice selection of ceramic and glass beads, crystals, and bindings, as well as gemstones. *1310 Apple Ave., Silver Spring, MD, 301/565–8094. Closed Sun. Metro: Silver Spring.*

5 *g-2*

BEADAZZLED

It *is* a dazzling array of ready-to-string beads and jewelry. Books explain the craft's history, various beading techniques, and how to create your wearable treasures. *1507 Connecticut Ave. NW, Dupont Circle, 202/265–2323. Metro: Dupont Circle.*

1 *e-3*

S & A BEADS

Beads and handmade jewelry from around the world give this shop an international flavor. You can also find amber and candles. *6929 Laurel Ave., Takoma Park, MD, 301/891–2323. Metro: Takoma.*

BEAUTY

fragrances & skin products

10 *d-2*

THE BODY SHOP

This hugely successful English chain, which believes you can never have too many boysenberry-scented soaps, now has cheery shops worldwide with toiletries for men and women. The fragrant, all-natural products come in biodegradable or recyclable packaging, do not pollute the water, and have not been tested on animals. *Union Station, 50 Massachusetts Ave. NE, Capitol Hill, 202/898–7826. Metro: Union Station.*

9 *e-7*

3207 M St. NW, Georgetown, 202/298–7353. Metro: Foggy Bottom–GWU.

1 *d-6*

The Fashion Centre at Pentagon City, 1000 S. Hayes St., Arlington, VA, 703/415–2166. Metro: Pentagon City.

9 *e-7*

CASWELL-MASSEY

This company has been in business since 1752, when it blended cologne for George and Martha Washington in Newport, Rhode Island. The lovely Georgetown store sells a large selection of soaps, creams, bath oils, herbal treatments, and fragrances for both him and her. *Georgetown Park Mall, 3222 M St. NW, Georgetown, 202/965–3224. Metro: Foggy Bottom–GWU.*

9 *e-7*

CRABTREE & EVELYN

England's famed all-natural toiletries and comestibles are beautifully packaged and presented for a touch of luxury. Just stepping into one of these stores can reduce your stress level. *Georgetown Park Mall, 3222 M St. NW, Georgetown, 202/342–1934. Metro: Foggy Bottom–GWU.*

10 *d-2*

Union Station, 50 Massachusetts Ave. NE, Capitol Hill, 202/289–0670. Metro: Union Station.

1 *d-6*

The Fashion Centre at Pentagon City, 1000 S. Hayes St., Arlington, VA, 703/415–2232. Metro: Pentagon City.

1 *a-4*

Tysons Corner Center, 1961 Chain Bridge Rd., McLean, VA, 703/356–0577.

9 *g-7*

EFX

Perfume junkies take note: if smelly stuff and pretty packaging delight you, this shop will make you giddy with joy. Browse and sniff soaps, aromatherapeutic oils, fragrant lotions, and nail polish (OK, don't sniff the polish) in colors from electric blue to deep burgundy; all the top brands of fragrant toiletries are represented, including Kiehl's. Beauty treatments such as facials, tinting, massage, aromatherapy, reflexology, waxing, and full-body spa treatments are also available at the Georgetown location. *3059 M St. NW, Georgetown, 202/965–1300. Metro: Foggy Bottom–GWU.*

5 *f-2*

1745 Connecticut Ave. NW, Dupont Circle, 202/462–1300. Metro: Dupont Circle.

9 *e-7*

GARDEN BOTANIKA

Derived from and inspired by plants, these easy-to-afford cosmetics and aromatic bath products come in a multitude of shades and scents. The products are not tested on animals. *Georgetown Park Mall, 3222 M St. NW, Georgetown, 202/338–5113. Metro: Foggy Bottom–GWU.*

1 *d-7*

The Fashion Centre at Pentagon City, 1000 S. Hayes St., Arlington, VA, 703/413–6600. Metro: Pentagon City.

5 *g-5*

PATRIZIA PARFUMERIE

Not only does this tiny shop purvey an amazing selection of women's and men's fragrances, but owner and operator Patrizia Ienzi will do the impossible: search the world for your favorite discontinued fragrance. *International Square, 1850 K St. NW, Downtown, 202/452–1298. Closed weekends. Metro: Farragut West.*

9 *e-7*

SEPHORA

Sephora carries a delicious collection of domestic and international makeup products, as well as the easy-on-the-purse-strings store brand, which is packaged in irresistible bottles and boxes. You can also pick up inexpensive nail tools and barrettes here. *3065 M St. NW, Georgetown, 202/338–5644. Metro: Foggy Bottom–GWU.*

hair care

5 *g-4*

ANDRE CHREKY SALON

Housed in an elegantly renovated, four-story Victorian town house, this salon offers an array of services—hair, nails, facials, waxing, massage, and makeup. Adjacent whirlpool pedicure chairs make it possible for two friends to be pampered simultaneously. While you splurge on a treatment, enjoy complimentary espresso and pastries (mornings) or wine and live piano music (evenings). *1604 K St. NW, Downtown, 202/393–2225. Metro: Farragut North.*

5 *g-4*

CHRISTOPHE

Straight from Beverly Hills, he of the $200-presidential-haircut-on-the-LAX-tarmac fame now cuts hair in Washington—and cuts it superbly. He charges $250 for the first cut; thereafter, cuts are a bargain at $175. A further bevy of Christophe-trained stylists can coif you for only $60. *1125 18th St. NW, Downtown, 202/785–2222. Metro: Farragut West.*

2 *b-2*

PR & PARTNERS

This salon, lauded by *Washingtonian* magazine for its deluxe services, specializes in hair color, design, and repairs for hair accidents that happen at home, but you can also get an excellent, unpretentious haircut for a reasonable price. *4000 Wisconsin Ave. NW, Upper Northwest, 202/966–7780. Metro: Tenleytown–AU.*

9 *g-8*

ROCHE SALON

This fashionable salon showcases owner and head coiffeur Dennis Roche, one of the best-known hairdressers in D.C., whose handiwork has been published in *Vogue* and *Harper's Bazaar. 3050 K St. NW, Georgetown, 202/775–0775. Metro: Foggy Bottom–GWU.*

5 *g-2*

S/P/ALON

Check in here for a cut or coloring fresh off the catwalks, or at least off the fashion-conscious streets of nearby Dupont Circle. *1605 17th St. NW, Dupont Circle, 202/462–9000. Metro: Dupont Circle.*

9 *f-7*

URY ELODIE & ASSOCIATES

This salon offers some of the best haircuts and makeovers in town. You can also get a massage to die for; just ask for Yolanda. *3109 M St. NW, Georgetown, 202/342–0944. Metro: Foggy Bottom–GWU.*

5 *e-5*

WATERGATE SALON

The Watergate is a sedate and quite popular alternative to the trendier salons in town, particularly if you're looking for a conservative cut and don't mind paying top dollar. *2532 Virginia Ave. NW, Foggy Bottom, 202/333–3488. Metro: Foggy Bottom–GWU.*

BICYCLES

9 *c-7*

BICYCLE PRO SHOP

This store is popular with bike messengers and professional racers for its extensive selection of locks, shocks, and brand-name bicycles. *3403 M St. NW, Georgetown, 202/337–0311. Metro: Foggy Bottom–GWU.*

1 *c-5*

BIG WHEEL BIKES

Calling itself "America's Bicycle Superstore," Big Wheel Bikes sells a wide range of top-name bicycles, equipment, and clothing, and has a repair shop to boot. *3119 Lee Hwy., Arlington, VA, 703/522–1110. Metro: Clarendon.*

5 *b-3*

1034 33rd St. NW, Georgetown, 202/337–0254. Metro: Foggy Bottom–GWU. Call for other locations.

3 *g-7*

CITY BIKES

This shop's closest neighbor is Ben & Jerry's, and the colorful mural between the two stores has become a neighborhood landmark: the famous cows riding oversize bikes. City Bikes sells all kinds of bicycles and accessories, rents bikes short-term, and guarantees its repairs. The air pump outside the shop is available free of charge at all times. *2501 Champlain St. NW, Adams-Morgan, 202/265–1564. Metro: Columbia Heights.*

BOOKS

general

9 *g-7*

BARNES & NOBLE

The Washington outlet of this massive chain has three floors of nonstop books. The café serves a nice selection of sweets, tea, and coffee, and the long coffee bar with floor-to-ceiling windows allows you to watch the constant foot traffic on M Street as you sip your cappuccino. *3040 M St. NW, Georgetown, 202/965–9880. Metro: Foggy Bottom–GWU.*

1 *c-3*

4801 Bethesda Ave., Bethesda, MD, 301/986–1761. Metro: Bethesda.

1 *b-5*

6260 Seven Corners Center, Falls Church, VA, 703/536–0774.

1 *d-7*

3651 Jefferson Davis Hwy., Alexandria, VA, 703/299–9124.

1 *c-1*

12089 Rockville Pike, Rockville, MD, 301/881–0237. Metro: White Flint.

5 *g-4*

BORDERS BOOKS & MUSIC

This vast chain store has a large and diverse selection of both books and music. Most locations have coffee bars, and several offer free films and jazz performances. *1800 L St. NW, Downtown, 202/466–4999. Metro: Farragut North.*

1 *d-6*

The Fashion Centre at Pentagon City, 1000 S. Hayes St., Arlington, VA, 703/418–0166. Metro: Pentagon City.

1 *c-1*

White Flint Mall, 11301 Rockville Pike, MD, 301/816–1067. Metro: White Flint.

2 *b-1*

5333 Wisconsin Ave. NW, Upper Northwest, 202/686–8270. Metro: Friendship Heights.

1 *c-6*

Crossroads Center, 5871 Crossroads Center Way, Baileys Crossroads, Falls Church, VA, 703/998–0404. Call for other locations.

6 *a-4*

CHAPTERS

Considered a "literary" bookstore, Chapters sells serious contemporary fiction, classics, and poetry in its inviting downtown shop. Browsing is encouraged; benches and reading tables allow book lovers to flip through potential buys comfortably. The store hosts a limited but impressive array of author appearances. *1512 K St. NW, Downtown, 202/347–5495. Metro: Farragut North.*

5 *g-2*

KRAMERBOOKS & AFTERWORDS

If you love books (or just like to hit on people who do), this fascinating combination bookstore–coffee bar–indoor-outdoor café with live folk music is key. The large and faithful clientele knows what it's doing. Smack in the middle of arty Dupont Circle, this complex buzzes all day—and all night on weekends. If you're sensitive to cigarette smoke you should avoid the rear of the store, near the café. *1517 Connecticut Ave. NW, Dupont Circle, 202/387–1400. Metro: Dupont Circle.*

6 *b-6*

OLSSONS BOOKS & RECORDS

A favorite meeting place for the literary set and a comfortable place to browse, Olssons has a large and diverse selection of books augmented by equally impressive musical holdings. *1200 F St. NW, Downtown, 202/347–3686. Metro: Metro Center.*

9 *e-7*

1239 Wisconsin Ave. NW, Georgetown, 202/338–9544. Metro: Foggy Bottom–GWU.

5 *g-3*

1307 19th St. NW, Dupont Circle, 202/785–1133. Metro: Dupont Circle.

6 *c-6*

418 7th St. NW, Downtown, 202/638–7610. Metro: Archives–Navy Memorial.

2 *c-2*

POLITICS AND PROSE

As the name indicates, this apt store features works on political matters, as well as topical novels and literary nonfiction. What the name doesn't indicate is the store's neighborly feel. A small nook shows off the excellent children's collection, complete with oversize floor puzzles and other games to keep the young 'uns occupied while their folks make selections. There are author readings almost nightly, and you can relax with your favorite tome in the popular coffee bar. *5015 Connecticut Ave. NW, Upper Northwest, 202/364–1919. Metro: Van Ness–DC.*

antiquarian

9 *f-7*

BOOKED UP

Don't miss this cozy Georgetown shop if you enjoy a fine selection of rare first editions and used and out-of-print books in good condition. *1204 31st St. NW, Georgetown, 202/965–3244. Metro: Foggy Bottom–GWU.*

10 *g-4*

CAPITOL HILL BOOKS

When you've finished antiquing and food shopping at the Eastern Market, pop into this lovely store to browse through a wonderful collection of out-of-print history books and modern first editions. *657 C St. SE, Capitol Hill, 202/544–1621. Metro: Eastern Market.*

3 *g-8*

IDLE TIME BOOKS

Idle Time has a decent selection of used and out-of-print books in good condition. *2410 18th St. NW, Adams-Morgan, 202/232–4774. Metro: Woodley Park–Zoo.*

5 *f-3*

SECOND STORY BOOKS

Faithful customers and newcomers alike spend hours with this impressive collection of used books and records. The real bonus: it's open until 10 PM seven days a week. *2000 P St. NW, Dupont Circle, 202/659–8884. Metro: Dupont Circle.*

discount

5 *g-3*

CROWN BOOKS

This giant is known throughout the Washington area for its large selection of popular hardcovers, paperbacks, and magazines at discounts of up to 40%. *11 Dupont Circle NW, Dupont Circle, 202/319–1374. Metro: Dupont Circle. Call for other locations.*

special-interest

10 *g-4*

BIRD-IN-HAND BOOKSTORE

Specializing in books on art and design, this Capitol Hill shop also carries exhibition catalogs. *323 7th St. SE, Capitol Hill, 202/543–0744. Closed Sun. and Mon. Metro: Eastern Market.*

5 *f-2*

MYSTERY BOOKS

Mystery lovers will be in paradise here with the area's largest collection of detective, crime, suspense, and spy fiction. You can even order crime novel–filled gift baskets for delivery all over the United States. *1715 Connecticut Ave. NW, Dupont Circle, 202/483–1600. Metro: Dupont Circle.*

2 *d-4*

SISTERSPACE AND BOOKS

This unique store focuses on books by, for, and about African-American women. The fine selection of literary titles is enhanced by books on health, personal development, and spiritual growth. Several writing workshops and book clubs meet here, and the store occasionally hosts author readings and book-signing events. *1515 U St. NW, U Street, 202/332–3433. Metro: U St.–Cardozo.*

2 *b-2*

TRAVEL BOOKS & LANGUAGE CENTER

Outdoor magazine aptly named this store the Library of Congress of Travel

Bookstores. More than 75,000 travel guides—plus globes, language tapes and books, cookbooks, and maps—line the walls of this inimitable resource for happy wanderers. Armchair travelers are also welcome here, as are those in search of quick language lessons. The store holds regular book signings and talks by travel experts, and the staff knows the ins and outs of national, international, and historic journeys ranging from the Orient Express to the Underground Railroad. *4437 Wisconsin Ave. NW, Upper Northwest, 202/237–1322. Metro: Tenleytown–AU.*

10 *e-7*
TROVER BOOKS
Trover has the latest political volumes and newspapers from all over the country. It's a great place for celebrity sightings in the form of (surprise!) political figures dropping in to sign their books. Where else but Capitol Hill? *221 Pennsylvania Ave. SE, Capitol Hill, 202/547–2665. Metro: Capitol South.*

5 *g-3*
VERTIGO BOOKS
Vertigo Books carries works on international politics, world literature, and African-American studies, and hosts frequent author readings. *7346 Baltimore Ave., College Park, MD, 301/779–9300. Metro: College Park–U of MD.*

3 *g-8*
YAWA
This compelling shop stocks a large collection of African and African-American fiction, nonfiction, magazines, and children's books, supplemented by ethnic jewelry, crafts, and greeting cards. *2206 18th St. NW, Adams-Morgan, 202/483–6805. Metro: Dupont Circle.*

CANDLES

9 *e-7*
CANDLES IN THE PARK
Be prepared to pay Georgetown prices in this shop, which sells candles, both graceful and playful, for all occasions. *Georgetown Park Mall, 3222 M St. NW, Georgetown, 202/338–3049. Metro: Foggy Bottom–GWU.*

1 *c-2*
ILLUMINATIONS
Possibly the best-smelling store in any mall, this purveyor of wax and wicks offers candles of all sizes, colors, and purposes, plus the equipment to care for them. The romantic atmosphere—provided by candlelight, of course—is free. *Montgomery Mall, 7125 Democracy Blvd., Bethesda, MD, 301/365–8848. Metro: Medical Center.*

1 *a-4*
Tysons Corner Center, 1961 Chain Bridge Rd., McLean, VA, 703/893–0647.

CHARITABLE CAUSES

9 *g-7*
THE JUNIOR LEAGUE SHOP
Many D.C. doyennes donate used designer duds to this nationally known charity consignment organization, which no longer has its own shop. Instead, the Junior League holds sales at different locations around town. Check the newspaper listings for upcoming sales. The children's clothes are in excellent condition. *3066 M St. NW, Georgetown, 202/337–6120. Metro: Foggy Bottom–GWU.*

9 *e-6*
OPPORTUNITY SHOP OF THE CHRIST CHURCH SOCIETY
This Georgetown thrift shop sells secondhand clothing and quality household goods. You can also find quite good antiques, crystal, and silver at moderate prices. *1427 Wisconsin Ave. NW, Georgetown, 202/333–6635. Metro: Foggy Bottom–GWU.*

9 *f-6*
WOMEN OF CHRIST CHURCH RUMMAGE SALE
Open on Wednesday only, this consignment shop offers real bargains on items that are generally in good condition. *3116 O St. NW, Georgetown, 202/333–6677. Metro: Foggy Bottom–GWU.*

CLOTHING FOR CHILDREN

9 *e-7*
GAP KIDS
Within skipping distance of the adult Gap, this store sells miniature versions of the ubiquitous chain's classic, bright, casual clothing. *1267 Wisconsin Ave. NW,*

Georgetown, 202/333–2411. Metro: Foggy Bottom–GWU.

5 *g-5*
2000 Pennsylvania Ave. NW, Downtown, 202/429–8711. Metro: Foggy Bottom–GWU.

1 *d-6*
The Fashion Centre at Pentagon City, 1000 S. Hayes St., Arlington, VA, 703/415–2400. Metro: Pentagon City. Call for other locations.

2 *b-1*
JEANNE'S SHOES
This exclusive children's shoe shop carries everything but Stride-Rite, and specializes in European-made shoes and orthopedic shoes in a variety of sizes for both boys and girls. *5110 Ridgefield Rd., Bethesda, MD, 301/654–3877. Metro: Friendship Heights.*

5 *g-3*
KID'S CLOSET
Quality contemporary children's clothing, shoes, and toys will fill your little ones' closets after you shop here. *1226 Connecticut Ave. NW, Dupont Circle, 202/429–9247. Metro: Dupont Circle.*

2 *c-1*
RAMER'S
Ramer's is an official Stride-Rite dealer, with both classic and sporty styles for boys and girls. *3810 Northampton St. NW, Upper Northwest, 202/244–2288. Metro: Friendship Heights.*

2 *b-2*
TRES JOLIE
Come here first if your only requirement is beauty: Tres Jolie has exquisite baby and children's clothes, including christening dresses, flower-girl dresses, and ring-bearer suits. *5232 44th St. NW, Upper Northwest, 202/237–8970. Metro: Tenleytown–AU.*

8 *g-4*
WHY NOT?
Shopping is actually fun here: you'll find soft cottons in bright colors, and fanciful, twirly dresses for young girls. Most of the clothes are designed by smaller independent firms, and there are some imports from France. Toys, books, and games are also on offer. *200 King St., Old Town Alexandria, VA, 703/548–4420. Metro: King St.*

CLOTHING FOR MEN/GENERAL

classic & casual

5 *h-4*
BRITCHES
Britches, with its stylish and classic menswear of the highest quality, has become a Washington institution. In addition to the store's private label, you'll find clothes by St. Andrew and Hickey Freeman. Fibers are all natural, and prices can be high. *1776 K St. NW, Downtown, 202/347–8994. Metro: Farragut North.*

9 *e-7*
1247 Wisconsin Ave. NW, Georgetown, 202/338–3330. Metro: Foggy Bottom–GWU.

1 *d-6*
The Fashion Centre at Pentagon City, 1000 S. Hayes St., Arlington, VA, 703/415–3500. Metro: Pentagon City.

1 *a-4*
Tysons Corner Center, 1961 Chain Bridge Rd., McLean, VA, 703/893–2083.

5 *g-4*
BROOKS BROTHERS
No one has been clothing American men longer; this store has been issuing its discreet "Brooks Brothers, Makers" label since 1818. Men with classic tastes—gray-wool sack suits, navy blazers, seersucker, repp ties, chinos, dignified formal wear, and, of course, the original, glorious, 5-trillion thread count cotton dress shirt—can always take comfort here. *1201 Connecticut Ave. NW, Downtown, 202/659–4650. Metro: Farragut North.*

5 *h-4*
BURBERRY
British to the core, Burberry sells the English country-weekend look in clothing, scarves, umbrellas, luggage, and, of course, trench coats, most of which are lined with the signature Burberry plaid. *1155 Connecticut Ave. NW, Downtown, 202/463–3000. Metro: Farragut North.*

1 *c-2*
JOHN B. ADLER
A longtime Washington clothier, John B. Adler offers the Ivy League look in casual wear, suits, sport coats, and formal wear at reasonable prices. *5272 River Rd., Bethesda, MD, 301/656–6044.*

5 *g-4*

JOSEPH A. BANKS

Good-quality classic men's suits and sport coats—both corporate and casual—go for excellent prices here. *1200 19th St. NW, Downtown, 202/466–2282. Closed Sun. Metro: Dupont Circle.*

5 *g-4*

J. PRESS

Founded in New Haven in 1902 as a custom shop for Yalies, J. Press sells traditional clothing of the highest quality, with a particularly good selection of Shetland and Irish wool sport coats. *1801 L St. NW, Downtown, 202/857–0120. Metro: Farragut North.*

9 *e-7*

POLO/RALPH LAUREN

This American designer made his name selling classic men's clothing, from the eponymous Polo shirts and wool sweaters to blue jeans and dress slacks. *Georgetown Park Mall, 3222 M St. NW, Georgetown, 202/965–0904. Metro: Foggy Bottom–GWU.*

contemporary

9 *e-7*

ABERCROMBIE & FITCH

This chain, which is largely geared toward a young crowd, carries sportswear and some casual-day-at-the-office possibilities. *Georgetown Park Mall, 3222 M St. NW, Georgetown, 202/965–6500. Metro: Foggy Bottom–GWU.*

9 *e-7*

ARMANI EXCHANGE

This is a great place to get a well-made suit with a little bit of LA or New York attitude. *1254 Wisconsin Ave., Georgetown, 202/965–9820. Metro: Foggy Bottom–GWU.*

1 *c-2*

Montgomery Mall, 7125 Democracy Blvd., Bethesda, MD, 301/469–6888. Metro: Medical Center.

9 *e-7*

BANANA REPUBLIC

Banana Republic stocks sportswear and suits for men who don't want to look like they work at the Pentagon, the Justice Department, or other places where bow ties and button-down shirts are de rigueur. Clothes have a cool, crisp look.

Georgetown Park Mall, 3222 M St. NW, Georgetown, 202/333–2554. Metro: Foggy Bottom–GWU.

2 *b-1*

5420 Wisconsin Ave., Chevy Chase, MD, 301/907–7740. Metro: Friendship Heights.

6 *a-6*

601 13th St, Downtown, 202/638–2724. Metro: Metro Center.

9 *e-7*

BENETTON

This chain's controversial ad campaigns may be more recognizable than their merchandise, but that doesn't mean you should pass up a chance to browse through their jazzy menswear section. The underwear collection, in Day-Glo hues of blue, yellow, and red, is reason enough to stop by. *1200 Wisconsin Ave. NW, Georgetown, 202/625–0443. Metro: Foggy Bottom–GWU.*

1 *a-4*

Tysons Corner Center, 1961 Chain Bridge Rd., McLean, VA, 703/448–6603.

5 *g-3*

1350 Connecticut Ave. NW, Dupont Circle, 202/659–1222. Metro: Dupont Circle.

1 *c-2*

Montgomery Mall, 7125 Democracy Blvd., Bethesda, MD, 301/365–3490. Metro: Medical Center.

5 *g-5*

THE GAP

The ubiquitous Gap is one-stop shopping for casual must-have basics like jeans, khakis, T-shirts, and oxford shirts. *2000 Pennsylvania Ave. NW, Downtown, 202/429–6862. Metro: Farragut West.*

5 *g-4*

1120 Connecticut Ave. NW, Downtown, 202/719–6100. Metro: Farragut North.

9 *e-7*

1258 Wisconsin Ave. NW, Georgetown, 202/333–2657. Metro: Foggy Bottom–GWU.

1 *a-4*

Tysons Corner Center, 1961 Chain Bridge Rd., McLean, VA, 703/893–0647.

1 *b-8*

Springfield Mall, Springfield, VA, 703/971–4665. Metro: Franconia–Springfield. Call for other locations.

1 *c-2*

GUESS?

When it's time to shed the pinstripe suit, head to Guess? for European-style blue jeans, aloha shirts, beachwear, and club wear. In D.C. proper, Guess? clothes are available at Hecht's department store. *Montgomery Mall, 7125 Democracy Blvd., Bethesda, MD, 301/ 365–3490. Metro: Medical Center.*

1 *a-4*

Tysons Corner Center, 1961 Chain Bridge Rd., McLean, VA, 703/448–6603.

9 *e-7*

PATAGONIA

West Coast–based Patagonia features outdoorsy clothes for urban explorers of all ages. Specializing in environmentally correct wear, they also sell clothing made from recycled materials. *1048 Wisconsin Ave. NW, Georgetown, 202/333–1776. Metro: Foggy Bottom–GWU.*

9 *e-7*

URBAN OUTFITTERS

This store, a favorite of college students, is the place to get a shirt and some sunglasses to match your lava lamp. Street fashions are quickly snatched up and thrown into dozens of combinations. *3111 M St. NW, Georgetown, 202/342–1012. Metro: Foggy Bottom–GWU.*

custom

5 *g-4*

BROOKS BROTHERS

Brooks is revered for custom-made clothing as well as ready-to-wear items. *1201 Connecticut Ave. NW, Downtown, 202/659–4650. Metro: Farragut North.*

9 *d-3*

FIELD ENGLISH CUSTOM TAILORS

William Field and son will be happy to custom-tailor your next authentic red hunting jacket—or, if your travels are more urban, cut a pattern by hand and sew a suit to fit your proportions exactly. This family-owned shop has been meeting customers' needs since 1970. *1742 Wisconsin Ave. NW, Georgetown, 202/333–2222. Metro: Foggy Bottom–GWU.*

3 *g-8*

LEGACY CUSTOM CLOTHING

In addition to stylish, contemporary ties and accessories, Legacy produces made-to-measure business suits and casual clothes. Their expertise in fashioning suits for big and tall men has led to a faithful clientele of professional athletes, such as NBA star Patrick Ewing and Dallas Cowboy Scott Galbraith, in addition to the usual mix of businessmen and professionals. Sales are by appointment only. *1930 18th St. NW, Suite 2B, Adams-Morgan, 202/332–7416. Metro: Dupont Circle.*

discount & off-price

EDDIE BAUER OUTLET

Eddie's comfy sportswear fills this emporium to the gills. If you're in the mood for a bargain, make the trip. *Potomac Mills Mall, 2700 Potomac Mills Circle, Woodbridge, VA, 703/490–3855.*

2 *b-1*

FILENE'S BASEMENT

To fully appreciate the bargains at Filene's Basement, you need to go window shopping at Neiman Marcus first and then head straight here. In addition to deep discounts on men's clothing by designers like Hugo Boss and Christian Dior, Filene's offers great deals on shoes, accessories, and leather goods. *Mazza Gallerie, 5300 Wisconsin Ave. NW, Upper Northwest, 202/966–0208. Metro: Friendship Heights.*

1 *c-1*

SYMS

This vast discount store sells trend-conscious men's clothing at bargain-basement prices. *11840 Rockville Pike, North Bethesda, MD, 301/984–3335. Metro: Bethesda.*

1 *c-1*

1900 Chapman Ave., Rockville, MD, 301/ 984–3335. Metro: Twinbrook.

1 *b-5*

1000 E. Broad St., Falls Church, VA, 703/ 241–8500. Metro: East Falls Church.

TODAY'S MAN

Count on Today's Man for well-tailored, well-priced suits under a variety of private labels. *5714 Columbia Pike, Falls Church, VA, 703/845–1307.*

1 *c-1*

5520 Randolph Rd., Rockville, MD, 301/
770–9660. Metro: White Flint.

11264 James Swart Circle, Fairfax, VA,
703/385–5670.

resale, vintage, surplus

10 *g-8*

A MAN FOR ALL SEASONS

Poke around this consignment shop for
stylish and well-priced suits, dress
shirts, casual wear, ties, and shoes. 321
7th St. SE, Capitol Hill, 202/544–4432.
Closed Mon. Metro: Eastern Market.

2 *f-1*

POLLY SUE'S VINTAGE SHOP

Pick up a couple of Hawaiian shirts or a
guayabera at this shop, which sells well-
preserved items from yesteryear and
from last week. 6915 Laurel Ave., Takoma
Park, MD, 301/270–5511. Metro: Takoma.

unusual sizes

10 *h-1*

GEORGE'S PLACE, LTD.

Large and tall men will find an extensive
collection of comfortable and stylish
clothing here. 1001 H St. NE, Capitol
Hill, 202/397–4113. Metro: Union Station.

5 *g-4*

ROCHESTER BIG AND TALL CLOTHING

This downtown shop carries men's suits
and casual wear in large and tall sizes.
1101 Connecticut Ave. NW, Downtown,
202/466–3200. Closed Sun. Metro: Farragut North.

CLOTHING FOR MEN/SPECIALTIES

formalwear

9 *e-7*

BRITCHES

Britches has a reputation for stocking the
finest men's formalwear in D.C., so stop
here for everything from cummerbunds
to cuff links. 3213 M St. NW, Georgetown,
202/338–5300. Metro: Foggy Bottom–
GWU.

5 *g-4*

SCOGNA FORMAL WEAR

Thanks to this store's convenient downtown location, you can practically pick
up a tux on the way to an evening function. The selection is excellent, and the
prices are quite reasonable, too. 1908 L
St. NW, Downtown, 202/296–4555.
Metro: Farragut North or Farragut West.

1 *c-1*

SYMS

Syms may not have been your first
thought, but buying a tuxedo at this discount store can be a real bargain. 11840
Rockville Pike, North Bethesda, MD, 301/
984–3335. Metro: Bethesda.

1 *c-1*

1900 Chapman Ave., Rockville, MD, 301/
984–3335. Metro: Twinbrook.

1000 E. Broad St., Falls Church, VA, 703/
241–8500. Metro: East Falls Church.

hats

9 *e-7*

HATS IN THE BELFRY

This Georgetown hat shop stocks just
about any kind of hat you and the
woman in your life might want at good
prices. 1237 Wisconsin Ave. NW, Georgetown, 202/342–2006. Metro: Foggy Bottom–GWU.

shirts

1 *d-6*

MARSHALLS

The doughty discounter sells bargain-
price shirts by Perry Ellis, Tommy Hil-
figer, and others. Pentagon Center, 1201
S. Hayes St., Arlington, VA, 703/413–
1668. Metro: Pentagon City.

9 *e-7*

POLO/RALPH LAUREN

Polo/Ralph Lauren is known for high-
brow duds of all kinds, but puts a partic-
ular emphasis on finely crafted shirts.
Georgetown Park Mall, 3222 M St. NW,
Georgetown, 202/965–0904. Metro:
Foggy Bottom–GWU.

2 *b-1*

T.J. MAXX

This is a great place to look for designer
shirts at cutthroat prices. 5252 Wisconsin

Ave. NW, Upper Northwest, 202/237–7616. Metro: Friendship Heights.

shoes & boots

5 *g-4*

CHURCH'S

This legendary British men's shoe store hawks its handmade products in this elegant shop. Church's shoes are known for their comfort and durability. *1820 L St. NW, Downtown, 202/296–3366. Metro: Farragut North.*

9 *e-6*

PRINCE & PRINCESS

This retailer carries a full line of men's shoes and boots, including Timberland and Sebago. *1400 Wisconsin Ave. NW, Georgetown, 202/337–4211. Metro: Foggy Bottom–GWU.*

2 *f-5*

SHOE CITY

At this discount store, you'll find an extensive selection of athletic shoes from the likes of Nike, Reebok, and New Balance as well as matching sweatshirts and jackets. *717 H St. NE, Northeast, 202/543–1833. Metro: Eastern Market.*

CLOTHING FOR WOMEN/GENERAL

classic and casual

5 *c-3*

ARMANI EXCHANGE

You've come to the right place if you're looking to dress like Jodie Foster, Alec Baldwin, or any number of celebrities who like the cool neat lines of this popular sportswear label. *1254 Wisconsin Ave. NW, Georgetown, 202/965–9820. Metro: Foggy Bottom–GWU.*

1 *c-2*

Montgomery Mall, 7125 Democracy Blvd., Bethesda, MD, 301/469–6888. Metro: Medical Center.

5 *g-4*

THE GAP

Jeans, khakis, whatever: Gap is the store where *everyone* shops for casual basics like blue jeans (boy cut, straight leg, sandblasted, boot cut), chinos, all-purpose T-shirts, ribbed tanks, and more. No promises, but this location is the closest to the White House. *2000 Pennsylvania Ave. NW, Downtown, 202/429–6862. Metro: Farragut West.*

5 *g-4*

1120 Connecticut Ave. NW, Downtown, 202/719–6100. Metro: Farragut North.

9 *e-7*

1258 Wisconsin Ave. NW, Georgetown, 202/333–2657. Metro: Foggy Bottom–GWU.

1 *a-4*

Tysons Corner Center, 1961 Chain Bridge Rd., McLean, VA, 703/893–0647.

1 *b-8*

Springfield Mall, Springfield, VA, 703/971–4665. Metro: Franconia–Springfield. Call for other locations.

10 *d-2*

JONES NEW YORK

Jones New York carries business clothes and casual wear for women who want to look hip without appearing to have just stepped off the college campus. *Union Station, 50 Massachusetts Ave. NE, Capitol Hill, 202/371–0618. Metro: Union Station.*

9 *e-7*

THE LIMITED

Never a standout but always there when you need it, The Limited sells trendy but reasonably discreet clothes for the relatively young. Even if you outgrow the clothes, it's worth coming here for the accessories, which are consistently attractive and very reasonably priced. *Georgetown Park Mall, 3222 M St. NW, 202/342–5150. Metro: Foggy Bottom–GWU.*

2 *b-1*

Chevy Chase Pavilion, 5335 Wisconsin Ave. NW, Upper Northwest, 202/686–7513. Metro: Friendship Heights.

1 *d-6*

The Fashion Centre at Pentagon City, 1000 S. Hayes St., Arlington, VA, 703/418–4973. Metro: Pentagon City.

1 *a-4*

Tysons Corner Center, 1961 Chain Bridge Rd., McLean, VA, 703/893–0647.

1 *b-8*

Springfield Mall, Springfield, VA, 703/719–6100. Metro: Franconia–Springfield. Call for other locations.

9 e-7

UP AGAINST THE WALL

This shop provides hip and inexpensive sportswear and separates for a young clientele with a hip-hop/club-kid bent. The Adams-Morgan store has a large clearance section and a concentration of older items. On weekends a live DJ spins beat-heavy tracks at the Georgetown location. *3219 M St. NW, Georgetown, 202/337–9316. Metro: Foggy Bottom–GWU.*

3 h-7

1749 Columbia Rd., Adams-Morgan, 202/328–8627. Metro: Dupont Circle or Woodley Park–Zoo.

conservative

5 g-4

BROOKS BROTHERS

The excellent women's clothes in this menswear bastion are often variations on old-boy standards. Women can snag loafers, double-breasted navy wool blazers, and men's-style, French-cuff, cotton button-down shirts. *1201 Connecticut Ave. NW, Downtown, 202/659–4650. Metro: Farragut North.*

5 h-4

BURBERRY

The stalwart British store fashions supremely classic women's clothing in tweeds and signature plaids. The specialty, of course, is rain gear. *1155 Connecticut Ave. NW, Downtown, 202/463–3000. Metro: Farragut North.*

10 g-7

FORECAST

If you favor a classic, contemporary look in clothing, Forecast should be in your future. It sells silk sweaters and wool blends in solid, muted tones that won't quickly fall out of fashion. *218 7th St. SE, 202/547–7337. Closed Mon. Metro: Eastern Market.*

1 c-3

JOHN B. ADLER

A longtime Washington clothier, John B. Adler offers the Ivy League look, from headbands to pearls; in fact, you can pick up every component necessary to create a complete casual or formal outfit. *5272 River Rd., Suite 520, Bethesda, MD, 301/656–6044.*

5 h-4

TALBOTS

Many Washington career women won't buy their business clothes anywhere else. You can count on Talbots for the most conservative clothes in town (and that's saying something). *1122 Connecticut Ave. NW, Downtown, 202/887–6973. Metro: Farragut North.*

2 b-1

Chevy Chase Pavilion, 5335 Wisconsin Ave. NW, Upper Northwest, 202/966–2205. Metro: Friendship Heights.

9 e-7

Georgetown Park Mall, 3222 M St. NW, Georgetown, 202/338–3510. Metro: Foggy Bottom–GWU.

contemporary

2 f-1

AMANO

Not to be confused with the gift shop A Mano, this laid-back boutique sells sophisticated and funky clothing that you can wear to work or relax in at home. Accessories include cloth briefcases, cartoon-character lunch boxes, silk scarves, hats, shoes, and tie-dye socks. *7030 Carroll Ave., Takoma Park, MD, 301/270–1140. Metro: Takoma.*

5 g-4

ANN TAYLOR

The national chain sells sophisticated, trend-conscious fashions and shoes to match. You can put together a very presentable boardroom outfit in one trip here, from crisp white blouse to hose. A tidy skirt suit runs about $300, and utilitarian bodysuits are around $50. The tailored look infuses the casual clothes, too. *1720 K St. NW, Downtown, 202/466–3544. Metro: Farragut West.*

9 e-7

Georgetown Park Mall, 3222 M St. NW, Georgetown, 202/338–5290. Metro: Foggy Bottom–GWU.

2 b-1

Mazza Gallerie, 5300 Wisconsin Ave. NW, Upper Northwest, 202/244–1940. Metro: Friendship Heights.

10 d-2

Union Station, 50 Massachusetts Ave. NE, Capitol Hill, 202/371–8010. Metro: Union Station.

2 *f-1*
ARISE
Primarily a purveyor of Asian artifacts, antiques, and furniture, Arise also carries a wonderful array of vibrant cotton and silk leisure clothing under its own label. Those who strive to express themselves through what they wear will consider this store a key find in a city where it's all too easy to dress like everyone else. Everyday prices are reasonable, but the sales are fantastic. *6925 Willow St. NW, Takoma Park, MD, 202/291–0770. Metro: Takoma.*

9 *e-7*
BANANA REPUBLIC
This popular chain's chic duds in basic black and, from time to time, other colors will help keep you from becoming a government drone during the week or help you reclaim your personality on the weekends. You can depend on Banana Republic for lightweight wool trousers, filmy scarves, and slim suits. *Georgetown Park Mall, 3222 M St. NW, Georgetown, 202/333–2554. Metro: Foggy Bottom–GWU.*

2 *b-1*
5420 Wisconsin Ave., Chevy Chase, MD, 301/907–7740. Metro: Friendship Heights.

6 *a-6*
601 13th St, Downtown, 202/638–2724. Metro: Metro Center.

9 *e-7*
BETSEY JOHNSON
Betsey Johnson's fanciful contemporary fashions are popular among the young and restless, and her D.C. boutique won't disappoint. Look here for updated versions of the slip dress Johnson helped make famous, plus club wear and play gear. *1219 Wisconsin Ave. NW, Georgetown, 202/338–4090. Metro: Foggy Bottom–GWU.*

5 *g-4*
BETSY FISHER
You can find one-of-a-kind accessories, duds, and jewelry in this appealing downtown store, which caters to women of all ages. *1224 Connecticut Ave. NW, Downtown, 202/785–1975. Metro: Farragut North.*

9 *e-6*
COMMANDER SALAMANDER
This outpost of alternative culture specializes in punk, fetish, and rave gear, from Doc Marten boots and leather pants to green hair dye and body glitter. Be prepared for the music—it's as loud as the clothes. *1420 Wisconsin Ave. NW, Georgetown, 202/337–2265. Metro: Foggy Bottom–GWU.*

5 *g-5*
EARL ALLEN
Sartorially ambitious women will find at Earl Allen classic but distinctive dresses and sportswear, wearable art, and one-of-a-kind items. *1825 I St. NW, Downtown, 202/466–3437. Metro: Farragut West.*

1 *c-1*
GUESS?
The up-to-the-minute European label, hard to find in this conservative city, sells trendy play clothes and playful accessories for the young and fashion conscious. In D.C. proper, the Guess? line is available at Hecht's department store. *Montgomery Mall, 7125 Democracy Blvd., Bethesda, MD, 301/365–3490. Metro: Medical Center.*

1 *a-4*
Tysons Corner Center, 1961 Chain Bridge Rd., McLean, VA, 703/448–6603.

8 *g-4*
NUEVO MUNDO
Nuevo Mundo's contemporary selection travels and wears well. Styles range from Nicole Miller's whimsical prints to Michelle St. John's all-cotton threads to jackets hand-painted by artists. Most of the designers are based in New York but borrow ideas from Japan, Africa, India, and the Philippines in both clothing and accessories. *313 Cameron St., Old Town Alexandria, VA, 703/549–0040. Metro: King St.*

designer

6 *a-6*
CHANEL BOUTIQUE
The legendary French house of fashion has an elegant collection of Chanel clothing and accessories in the Willard Inter-Continental Hotel. *1401 Pennsylvania Ave. NW, Downtown, 202/638–5055. Metro: Metro Center.*

2 *b-1*
MICMAC
Micmac is a gem of a boutique. Clothes by Issey Miyake and fab Arche shoes are

arranged in eye-catching displays sure to make you want to buy one of everything. *Chevy Chase Pavillion, 5445 Wisconsin Ave. NW, Upper Northwest, 202/686–9841. Metro: Friendship Heights.*

2 *b-1*

5301 Wisconsin Ave. NW, Upper Northwest, 202/362–6834. Metro: Friendship Heights.

5 *h-4*

RIZIK BROTHERS

A Washington institution, Rizik Brothers combines an excellent inventory of designer clothing, expert service, and not-out-of-sight prices. *1100 Connecticut Ave. NW, Downtown, 202/223–4050. Metro: Farragut North.*

5 *e-5*

SAKS JANDEL

Come to Saks Jandel (not to be confused with Saks Fifth Avenue) for lovely designer clothes *if* money is no object. If it is, come only during sales, as they're quite fabulous. *Watergate Mall, 600 New Hampshire Ave. NW, Foggy Bottom, 202/337–4200. Metro: Foggy Bottom–GWU.*

2 *b-1*

5510 Wisconsin Ave., Chevy Chase, MD, 301/652–2250. Metro: Friendship Heights.

5 *e-5*

ST. LAURENT RIVE GAUCHE

This elegant boutique has marvelous ready-to-wear from one of the world's great designers. *Watergate Mall, 600 New Hampshire Ave. NW, Foggy Bottom, 202/965–3555. Metro: Foggy Bottom–GWU.*

2 *b-1*

5510 Wisconsin Ave., Chevy Chase, MD, 301/656–8868. Metro: Friendship Heights.

discount & off-price

5 *h-4*

FILENE'S BASEMENT

Boston's most famous bargain bin is still a treasure chest: designer clothing by the likes of Christian Dior, Hugo Boss, Burberry, Donna Karan, and many others is deeply discounted. Top the new suit off with cut-rate shoes, handbags, perfumes, and other accessories. The downtown branch is particularly well appointed, with lots of wood and brass. *1133 Connecticut Ave. NW, Downtown, 202/872–8430. Metro: Farragut North.*

6 *a-6*

The Shops at National Place, 529 14th St. NW, Downtown, 202/638–4110. Metro: Metro Center.

2 *b-1*

Mazza Gallerie, 5300 Wisconsin Ave. NW, Upper Northwest, 202/966–0208. Metro: Friendship Heights.

1 *b-8*

FRUGAL FANNIE'S

Renowned for its great prices and a low-key atmosphere, Frugal Fannie's attracts bargain hunters each weekend to its large warehouse-size store. Shop for career clothing, coats, and sportswear bearing price tags that won't eat your paycheck. *5262 Port Royal Rd., Springfield, VA, 703/321–4800. Closed Mon.–Thurs. Metro: Franconia–Springfield.*

1 *b-5*

LOEHMANN'S

Bargain hunters love this place; just don't expect any frills. Designer labels are ripped out to protect the innocent, and their prices slashed to within the reach of mortals. Seek and ye shall (probably) find. *7241 Arlington Blvd., Falls Church, VA, 703/573–1510. Metro: East Falls Church.*

1 *d-6*

MARSHALLS

The vast Marshalls is known for the depth of its discounts on clothes, accessories, household products, and gifts for the entire family, with an impressive selection of women's fashions. *Pentagon Center, 1201 S. Hayes St., Arlington, VA, 703/413–1668. Metro: Pentagon City.*

1 *e-2*

City Place Mall, 8661 Colesville Rd., Silver Spring, MD, 301/495–9566. Metro: Silver Spring.

2 *b-1*

T. J. MAXX

T. J. Maxx is known wherever it sets up shop for quality career clothes, shoes, and sportswear at exciting prices. *5252 Wisconsin Ave. NW, Upper Northwest, 202/237–7616. Metro: Friendship Heights.*

1 *d-8*

773 Richmond Hwy., Alexandria, VA, 703/781–3051.

1 *c-1*

1776 E. Jefferson St., Rockville, MD, 301/881–3857. Metro: Twinbrook.

plus sizes

1 *c-1*

AVENUE

Comfortable, fashionable casual styles in plus sizes run the gamut from hip to straightforward in this store, which also offers evening wear. *Wheaton Plaza, 11160 Viers Mill Rd., Wheaton, MD, 301/949–7707.*

1 *c-7*

Landmark Shopping Center, 6244 Little River Turnpike, Alexandria, VA, 703/941–4557.

1 *c-1*

LANE BRYANT

This store was an institution long before Kathy Najimi became its spokesmodel, and now it's a hipper version of its former self, offering stylish choices in plus sizes. *Federal Plaza, 12274 E. Rockville Pike, Rockville, MD, 301/770–0541. Metro: White Flint.*

1 *a-4*

Tysons Corner Center, 1961 Chain Bridge Rd., McLean, VA, 703/760–9394.

6 *c-6*

STYLISH STOUT SHOP

This downtown shop stocks dresses, suits, and sportswear in sizes 16 to 52 by designers from New York and Italy. *925 F St. NW, Downtown, 202/638–1184. Metro: Gallery Pl.–Chinatown.*

vintage & resale

2 *b-2*

ENCORE OF WASHINGTON

This consignment shop features a wide range of designer fashions in very good condition, by the likes of Escada, Valentino, and Feraud. *3715 Macomb St. NW, Upper Northwest, 202/966–8122. Closed Sun. Metro: Tenleytown–AU.*

6 *b-1*

MOOD INDIGO

Formerly specializing in 1940s clothes and articles, Mood Indigo has expanded its range of eras to sell women's suits, dresses, hats, and accessories from the 1950s to the 1970s. *1214 U St. NW, U*

Street, 202/265–6366. Metro: U St.–Cardozo.

1 *b-5*

NEW TO YOU CONSIGNMENT BOUTIQUE

All of the clothing and accessories in this secondhand shop are less than two years old. You're likely to find Donna Karan, Ralph Lauren, Liz Claiborne, and Gap clothing at excellent prices. *125 N. Washington St., Falls Church, VA, 703/533–1251. Closed Sun. and Mon. Metro: East Falls Church.*

5 *g-3*

SECONDI

With specimens of such labels as Donna Karan, Prada, Ann Taylor, Coach, and, yes, Gap, this is the city's finest consignment shop, with a wide selection of women's clothing, accessories, and shoes, as well as a small but distinctive men's selection. *1702 Connecticut Ave. NW, Dupont Circle, 202/667–1122. Metro: Dupont Circle.*

CLOTHING FOR WOMEN/ SPECIALTIES

furs

1 *c-2*

GARTENHAUS

Gartenhaus has a wonderful collection of furs of every kind, style, size, and price, and holds great sales. *6950 Wisconsin Ave., Bethesda, MD, 301/656–2800. Metro: Bethesda.*

2 *b-1*

NEIMAN MARCUS

For unsurpassed elegance, duck into this small but fine fur salon. Selection and service are both excellent. *Mazza Gallerie, 5300 Wisconsin Ave. NW, Upper Northwest, 202/966–9700. Metro: Friendship Heights.*

1 *a-4*

Tysons Corner Center, 1961 Chain Bridge Rd., McLean, VA, 703/761–1600.

1 *c-2*

ROSENDORF EVANS

Stop here for both a vast collection of furs and excellent storage and care arrangements. *Montgomery Mall, 7125*

Democracy Blvd., Bethesda, MD, 301/469–6888. Metro: Medical Center.

1 *a-4*

Tysons Corner Center, 1961 Chain Bridge Rd., McLean, VA, 703/893–3680.

2 *b-1*

SAKS FIFTH AVENUE

Known throughout Washington for its beautiful fur salon and deluxe personal service, Saks provides all when you're in the market for a precious fur—including great sales. *5555 Wisconsin Ave., Chevy Chase, MD, 301/657–9000. Metro: Friendship Heights.*

1 *a-4*

Tysons Corner Center, 1961 Chain Bridge Rd., McLean, VA, 703/761–0700.

handbags

9 *e-7*

COACH BAGS

Coach's beautiful leather products have many a loyal fan. They are known to age gracefully—or do they just age? Prices are fairly high, but you'll have the piece for a long time. The traditional browns are now being joined by eye-catching hues like lime green. *1214 Wisconsin Ave. NW, Georgetown, 202/342–1772. Metro: Foggy Bottom–GWU.*

1 *c-2*

11301 Rockville Pike, North Bethesda, MD, 301/231–7467. Metro: White Flint.

5 *g-4*

LANE'S LUGGAGE

Lane's is hard to beat for its great prices and fine selection of small leather goods, especially handbags. *1146 Connecticut Ave. NW, Downtown, 202/452–1146. Metro: Farragut North.*

1 *a-4*

WILSON'S LEATHER

Along with fine leather and suede clothing and luggage, Wilson's Leather has a great collection of handbags at reasonable prices. *Tysons Corner Center, 1961 Chain Bridge Rd., McLean, VA, 703/893–1620.*

1 *c-2*

Montgomery Mall, 7125 Democracy Blvd., Bethesda, MD, 301/469–8840. Metro: Medical Center.

hats

9 *e-7*

HATS IN THE BELFRY

From straw boaters to deerstalkers, top hats to fedoras, you'll find the gamut of head coverings here, at reasonable prices. *1237 Wisconsin Ave. NW, Georgetown, 202/342–2006. Metro: Foggy Bottom–GWU.*

8 *g-4*

112 King St., Old Town Alexandria, VA, 703/549–2546. Metro: King St.

9 *e-7*

THE HATTERY

You can top off any outfit or just keep your head warm with an item from this upscale hat shop, whose wares range from the conservative to the funky. *Georgetown Park Mall, 3222 M St. NW, Georgetown, 202/364–4287. Metro: Foggy Bottom–GWU.*

5 *g-3*

PROPER TOPPER

At Proper Topper, stylish headwear ranges from perky wool berets to wide-brimmed, *My Fair Lady* summer hats; accessories extend to gloves, scarves, jewelry, and small cloth handbags. *1350 Connecticut Ave. NW, Dupont Circle, 202/842–3055. Metro: Dupont Circle.*

lingerie & nightwear

2 *b-1*

NEIMAN MARCUS

When you feel the need to blow your allowance on something absurdly luxurious, Neiman Marcus will, of course, oblige. The lingerie feels wonderful, and it makes you look that way, too. *Mazza Gallerie, 5300 Wisconsin Ave. NW, Upper Northwest, 202/966–9700. Metro: Friendship Heights.*

1 *a-4*

Tysons Corner Center, 1961 Chain Bridge Rd., McLean, VA, 703/761–1600.

2 *b-1*

SAKS FIFTH AVENUE

Saks has one of the most extensive selections of beautiful lingerie in the area—always pricey, and usually worth it. *5555 Wisconsin Ave., Chevy Chase, MD, 301/657–9000. Metro: Friendship Heights.*

1 a-4

Tysons Corner Center, 1961 Chain Bridge Rd., McLean, VA, 703/761–0700.

5 g-4

VICTORIA'S SECRET
The retail collection of feminine and sexy intimate apparel includes many items not found in the catalog. Styles range widely enough to satisfy both the pajama girl and the libertine. 1050 Connecticut Ave. NW, Downtown, 202/293–7530. Metro: Farragut North.

9 e-7

Georgetown Park Mall, 3222 M St. NW, Georgetown, 202/965–5457. Metro: Foggy Bottom–GWU.

10 d-2

Union Station, 50 Massachusetts Ave. NE, Capitol Hill, 202/682–0686. Metro: Union Station.

2 b-1

Chevy Chase Pavilion, 5335 Wisconsin Ave. NW, Upper Northwest, 202/686–9165. Metro: Friendship Heights.

maternity

1 c-1

BUY BUY BABY
Whether your needs run to roomy pants or ear swabs, this department store–size emporium will get you from conception to delivery and beyond with brand-name baby clothes, equipment, and clean-up supplies. Hip moms and dads can find diaper bags (and some maternity clothing) that are not covered with little ducks and bunnies. But if it's ducks and bunnies you want, Buy Buy Baby has those, too. Congressional Plaza, Rockville Pike, Rockville, MD, 301/984–1122. Metro: Twinbrook.

1 b-5

IMATERNITY
The selection at this chain is not exactly for future moms looking to make a fashion statement while growing a family. Rather, it offers great prices and a sizable inventory. It's a good place to stock up on basics. 7506 Leesburg Pike, Falls Church, VA, 703/790–1221.

1 c-1

Federal Plaza, 12274 E. Rockville Pike, Rockville, MD, 301/881–1090. Metro: White Flint.

2 b-1

MIMI MATERNITY
This shop refers to itself as "maternity redefined," so you can imagine its attitude toward the clothes. Mimi offers smart, sophisticated wear for the mother-to-be, at reasonable prices. You'll leave here feeling stylish at every stage of your pregnancy. Mazza Gallerie, 5300 Wisconsin Ave. NW, Upper Northwest, 202/362–1400. Metro: Friendship Heights.

1 c-1

White Flint Mall, 11301 Rockville Pike, North Bethesda, MD, 301/770–4313. Metro: White Flint.

1 c-2

Montgomery Mall, 7125 Democracy Blvd., Bethesda, MD, 301/469–0308. Metro: Medical Center.

shoes & boots

1 c-2

DSW
The acronym stands for Discount Shoe Warehouse, but a better name might be the "Filene's Basement of shoe stores." DSW is the secret to keeping your shoe wardrobe up-to-date without emptying your bank account. Not only will you get a kick out of the low prices, but the snappy selection, which includes Cole Haan and Joan & David, will put a swing in your step. Georgetown Rd. at Democracy Blvd., Bethesda, MD, 301/897–0360. Metro: Medical Center.

1 b-8

6644 Loisdale Rd., Springfield, VA, 703/924–5475. Metro: Franconia–Springfield.

10 d-2

NINE WEST
Funky and gorgeous heels, flats, sandals, mules, boots, handbags, and other accessories are the staples of this dependable chain. Union Station, 50 Massachusetts Ave. NE, Capitol Hill, 202/682–0505. Metro: Union Station.

9 e-7

1217 Wisconsin Ave. NW, Georgetown, 202/337–7256. Metro: Foggy Bottom–GWU.

2 d-5

1008 Connecticut Ave. NW, 202/452–9163. Metro: McPherson Sq.

1 *d-6*

NORDSTROM

Recognized throughout the Washington area as the best place to shop for shoes, Nordstrom has everything in all sizes—from sandals to boots to classic pumps to platform heels. The various styles come from designers and labels both domestic and international. *The Fashion Centre at Pentagon City, 1000 S. Hayes St., Arlington, VA, 703/415–2400. Metro: Pentagon City.*

5 *h-5*

PARADE OF SHOES

Specializing in designer knockoffs and Italian imports, this store has a decent selection of women's shoes at great prices. During seasonal clearances, shoes are often marked down as low as $20 a pair. *1020 Connecticut Ave. NW, Downtown, 202/872–8581. Metro: Farragut North.*

9 *e-6*

PRINCE & PRINCESS

The selection of women's shoes includes strappy party shoes, chunky platforms, and stylish pumps from designers such as Via Spiga and Nine West. *1400 Wisconsin Ave. NW, Georgetown, 202/337–4211. Metro: Foggy Bottom–GWU.*

3 *g-8*

SHAKE YOUR BOOTY

Before this store opened, trend-conscious Washingtonians had to go all the way to Manhattan's West Village for these chunky black boots, hip platforms, and strappy evening sandals. *2324 18th St. NW, Adams-Morgan, 202/518–8205. Metro: Woodley Park–Zoo.*

5 *g-3*

SHOE SCENE

Shoe scene's fashionable, moderately priced shoes are imported from Europe and are often difficult to resist. *1330 Connecticut Ave. NW, Dupont Circle, 202/659–2194. Metro: Dupont Circle.*

swimsuits

5 *g-4*

THE BIKINI SHOP

Despite the name, this store also stocks lots of one-piece suits—including sizes for all figures—and men's thongs. The thousands of bikinis, in sizes 4–24 and cups up to D, include novelty items like a white-fur-trimmed red bikini with a Santa hat. *1819 M St. NW, Downtown, 202/331–8372. Metro: Farragut North.*

6 *a-5*

735 15th St. NW, Downtown, 202/393–3533. Closed Sun. Metro: McPherson Sq.

1 *b-8*

FRUGAL FANNIE'S

This discount shop is open only on weekends, but at the moment it's thought to have the best swimsuit selection—and prices—in the area. *5262 Port Royal Rd., Springfield, VA, 703/321–4800. Closed Mon.–Thurs. Metro: Franconia–Springfield.*

1 *d-6*

NORDSTROM

As renowned for its vast swimsuit collection as it is for its shoes, Nordstrom is bound to stock something like what you have in mind. *The Fashion Centre at Pentagon City, 1000 S. Hayes St., Arlington, VA, 703/415–2400. Metro: Pentagon City.*

COINS

5 *g-4*

THE CAPITOL COIN & STAMP COMPANY, INC.

Fittingly, this downtown store specializes in presidential campaign memorabilia, including coins, stamps, buttons, and posters. You'll also find foreign and ancient coins. *1701 L St. NW, Downtown, 202/296–0400. Metro: Farragut North.*

5 *h-4*

LUCIEN BIRKLER & CO.

Birkler caters to the collector with ancient coins, foreign coins, U.S. coins, and paper money. *1100 17th St. NW, Suite 900, Downtown, 202/833–3770. Metro: Farragut North.*

8 *g-4*

OLD TOWN COINS & JEWELRY EXCHANGE

These coins and bills date from 500 BC to the present day, and hail from all over the world. *115 S. Union St., Old Town Alexandria, VA, 703/548–9024. Metro: King St.*

COMPUTERS & SOFTWARE

1 c-7

COMP USA

This national chain offers an immense selection of computers, printers, peripherals, software, and, for the most part, qualified sales help. *5901 Stephenson Ave., Alexandria, VA , 703/212–6610.*

1 c-1

1776 E. Jefferson St., off Rockville Pike, Rockville, MD, 301/816–8963.

8357 Leesburg Pike, Fairfax, VA, 703/821–7700.

MICRO CENTER

Micro Center sells all the computer equipment your heart desires, and offers training classes to make sure you know how to use it. *3089 Nutley St., Fairfax, VA, 703/204–8400. Metro: Vienna/Fairfax–GMU.*

1 c-5

MICROLAND

This vast store carries brand-name computer equipment at reasonable prices. *2901 Wilson Blvd., Arlington, VA, 703/528–5900. Metro: Clarendon.*

COSTUME SALES & RENTALS

1 c-2

ARTISTIC COSTUMES

It's always Halloween at Artistic, which has a friendly sales staff and a wide array of getups for all occasions—whether you're waiting for the Great Pumpkin, looking for a disguise for Mardi Gras, or in need of a costume for your community-theater production. Adult costumes are for rent; costumes for kids are for sale. *4915 Cordell Ave., Bethesda, MD, 301/652–2323. Metro: Bethesda.*

6 h-8

BACKSTAGE, THE PERFORMING ARTS STORE

Considered the best costume-rental shop in the area, this magical store provides just about any costume you might want—from Southern belles to medieval knights to French courtesans to court jesters. The store will complete the outfit with the appropriate hats, swords, and feathers. You name it, they have it.

As an added bonus, you can buy any costume you fall in love with at a discount price. *545 8th St. SE, Capitol Hill, 202/544–5744. Metro: Eastern Market.*

CRAFT & HOBBY SUPPLIES

1 c-2

BRUCE VARIETY

A Washington-area fixture, Bruce carries poster board, notebooks, paints, beads, modeling clay, seeds, and more—everything you need to keep you out of trouble, to get you through a rainy day, or to put you on top of a school project. *Bradley Shopping Center, Arlington St., Bethesda, MD, 301/656–7543. Metro: Bethesda.*

DISCOUNT

BURLINGTON COAT FACTORY

It's not just for coats anymore. Women can find any kind of dress or sportswear, most of it high-quality, in this vast collection. *Potomac Mills Mall, 2700 Potomac Mills Circle, Woodbridge, VA, 703/497–7334.*

1 d-6

MARSHALLS

Dive in for bargain-basement clothing and household items for your whole family. *Pentagon Center, 1201 S. Hayes St., Arlington, VA, 703/413–1668. Metro: Pentagon City. Call for other locations.*

1 e-2

NINE WEST OUTLET

For outlet shopping in a Metro-accessible shopping mall, drop into this popular shoe outlet. The 9 & Co. branch has trendier fare. *City Place Mall, 8661 Colesville Rd., Silver Spring, MD, 301/587–8938. Metro: Silver Spring.*

9 g-7

9 & Co., 3067 M St. NW, Georgetown, 202/338–0686. Metro: Foggy Bottom–GWU.

1 c-2

NORDSTROM RACK

If you like the store, you'll like the Rack. *City Place Mall, 8661 Colesville Rd., Silver Spring, MD, 301/608–8118. Metro: Silver Spring.*

ELECTRONICS & AUDIO

9 e-7

CIRCUIT CITY

Electronics and audio equipment are in ample supply at this national chain. *3222 M St. NW, Georgetown, 202/944–1870. Metro: Foggy Bottom–GWU.*

1 c-2

10490 Auto Park Ave., Bethesda, MD, 301/365–3378. Metro: Bethesda. Call for other locations.

5 g-4

RADIOSHACK

RadioShack sells primarily its own brand of electronics and audio equipment, such as stereos, pagers, and telephones. The products are not top-of-the-line, but are generally solid. *1150 Connecticut Ave. NW, Downtown, 202/833–3355. Metro: Farragut North.*

2 c-3

4531 Wisconsin Ave. NW, Upper Northwest, 202/363–2541. Metro: Tenleytown–AU.

6 a-6

1345 F St. NW, Downtown, 202/737–6055. Metro: Metro Center.

3 g-7

1767 Columbia Rd. NW, Adams-Morgan, 202/986–5008. Metro: Woodley Park–Zoo. Call for other locations.

EROTICA

9 e-7

DREAM DRESSER

The Dream Dresser's always-intriguing window display, with mannequins dressed in upscale fetish wear, is worth passing, if only to take a peek. Inside, there's a wide selection of latex, leather, and vinyl clothing; thigh-high boots with 7-inch heels; whips; and less-dangerous accessories. *1042 Wisconsin Ave. NW, Georgetown, 202/625–0373. Metro: Foggy Bottom–GWU.*

9 e-7

PLEASURE PLACE

From liquid latex and scented body oils to things that tie on and wrap on, this store sells items that make fun gag gifts or aid in serious sexual enhancement. The broad-based clientele includes gay couples, straight couples, singles, married couples, and the occasional gawking tourist. *1063 Wisconsin Ave. NW, Georgetown, 202/333–8570. Metro: Foggy Bottom–GWU.*

5 f-2

1710 Connecticut Ave., Dupont Circle, 202/483–3297. Metro: Dupont Circle.

ETHNIC ITEMS

5 g-2

AFFRICA

African artifacts, masks, carvings, *kinta* cloth (color fabrics used in traditional dress), and furniture line the walls of this appealing shop, a popular destination for collectors and decorators. *2010 R St. NW, Dupont Circle, 202/745–7272. Metro: Dupont Circle.*

4 g-8

AFRICAN HERITAGE GIFT SHOP

African Heritage focuses on African folk art and handicrafts, including wood carvings, jewelry, and some clothing. *2113 Rhode Island Ave. NE, Upper Northeast, 202/269–3113. Metro: Rhode Island Ave.*

8 e-4

BANANA TREE

This charming shop is owned and run by a former foreign-service officer, and his experience shows in the remarkable inventory. You'll find Southeast Asian folk art, rattan pieces, furniture, weavings, bronzes, and garden figures. *1123 King St., Old Town Alexandria, VA, 703/836–4317. Metro: King St.*

1 f-2

INDIA SARI PALACE, INC.

Silks, crafts, brass, artworks, jewelry, and, of course, saris are thrown together in this Indian emporium. *1337 E. University Blvd., Langley Park, MD, 301/434–1350. Metro: College Park–U of MD.*

3 g-8

KHISMET WEARABLE ART SHOWROOM

Traditional garments from West Africa and original fashions for men, women, and children—designed by Millée Spears, who lived in Ghana—fill colorful Khismet. Spears uses ethnic-print fabrics to create garments that are suitable for both work and an evening out; she'll also custom-design clothes. *1800 Belmont Rd. NW, Adams-Morgan, 202/234-7778. Closed Mon.–Fri., except by appointment. Metro: Woodley Park–Zoo.*

5 *g-3*

KOBOS

You'll discover a rainbow of clothing and accessories imported from West Africa. *2444 18th St. NW, Adams-Morgan, 202/332-9580. Closed Sun. Metro: Dupont Circle.*

9 *e-7*

PHOENIX

Jewelry and art pieces (fine and folk) from Mexico are among the items you can find in this store, which also sells contemporary clothing in natural fibers by designers such as Eileen Fisher and Flax. *1514 Wisconsin Ave. NW, Georgetown, 202/244-7197. Metro: Foggy Bottom–GWU.*

EYEWEAR

2 *b-2*

APEX OPTICALS

Can never find just the right frames? Apex feels your pain. This shop will make eyeglass frames and lenses to your own exclusive design, or just show you a diverse selection of frames by designers from around the world. *4200 Wisconsin Ave. NW, Upper Northwest, 202/244-1308. Metro: Tenleytown–AU.*

9 *d-7*

BURTON OPTICIAN

Virginia Burton, the proprietor of this unique vision shop, so despaired of finding attractive eyeglass frames that she went into business selling them. The store is tiny, but it's a virtual treasure trove of unusual and flamboyant eyeglass frames. People with 20/20 vision lament their good fortune when they see this stuff. *3252 Prospect St. NW, Georgetown, 202/965-0346. Metro: Foggy Bottom–GWU.*

5 *g-4*

FOR EYES

This downtown outpost of the national chain stocks contact lenses of every sort, plus a healthy selection of frames and chains. *1725 K St. NW, Downtown, 202/463-8860. Metro: Farragut North.*

5 *g-4*

HOUR EYES

Well stocked, this store has eyewear for everyone in the family. *1775 K St. NW, Downtown, 202/463-6364. Metro: Farragut North.*

1 *d-7*

PEARLE VISION

This national chain has all manner of eyewear for men, women, and children. *Landmark Shopping Center, 5801 Duke St., Alexandria, VA, 703/914-1130. Metro: Van Dorn St.*

1 *e-2*

11213 New Hampshire Ave., Silver Spring, MD, 301/593-5850.

1 *b-5*

6284 Arlington Blvd., Falls Church, VA, 703/237-2131.

11005 Lee Hwy., Fairfax, VA, 703/273-6200.

1971 Chain Bridge Rd., McLean, VA, 703/442-0225.

1 *d-6*

PRICE CLUB

Just across the Potomac River from D.C., this enormous and beloved warehouse store sells numerous contact lenses at discount prices. You must be a member of the Price Club to take advantage, but it's only a matter of buying an immediate annual membership for $30. *Pentagon Center, 1201 S. Hayes St., Arlington, VA, 703/413-2324. Metro: Pentagon City.*

5 *h-5*

VOORTHUS OPTICIANS, INC.

Voorthus provides designer frames for both men and women, along with contacts, exams, and the works. *1035 Connecticut Ave. NW, Downtown, 202/833-9455. Metro: Farragut North.*

5 *g-5*

1825 I St. NW, Downtown, 202/244-7114. Metro: Farragut North.

2 *b-1*

5300 Wisconsin Ave. NW, Upper Northwest, 202/244-7114. Metro: Friendship Heights.

8 *f-4*

530 King St., Old Town Alexandria, VA, 703/683-3822. Metro: King St. Call for other locations.

FABRICS

5 *g-4*

EXQUISITE FABRICS, INC.

Located on bustling K Street, this shop is nonetheless a peaceful place to pour over pattern books, buy notions, and choose among the enviable selection of upscale fabrics. *1775 K St. NW, Downtown, 202/775–1818. Metro: Farragut North.*

1 *c-1*

G STREET FABRICS

This store has a remarkable selection of fabric, buttons, material, notions, and cloth from around the world; the array of styles and colors is dizzying. They also sell sewing machines, hold sewing classes, and even publish a newsletter with updates on the stock and suggested videos on sewing and fashion. *Mid-Pike Plaza, 11854 Rockville Pike, Rockville, MD, 301/231–8998. Metro: White Flint.*

1 *b-5*

Seven Corners Shopping Center, 6250 Arlington Blvd., Arlington, VA, 703/241–1700.

2 *c-2*

MILL END SHOPS

The vast Mill End has an extensive selection of fabric and notions. *4340 Connecticut Ave. NW, Upper Northwest, 202/537–8966. Closed Sun. Metro: Van Ness–UDC.*

6 *b-1*

TRADE SECRETS

The textured wool, velvet, and silk designs in African-inspired patterns are almost too pretty to wear. *1214 U St. NW, U Street, 202/256–6366. Closed Mon. Metro: U St.–Cardozo.*

FLOWERS & PLANTS

florists

8 *f-4*

FLOWERS UNIQUE

Choose from a sound selection of flowers and plants in this Old Town Alexandria shop. *705 King St., Old Town Alexandria, VA, 703/548–4638. Metro: King St.*

9 *d-8*

GREENWORKS

Georgetown is well served by this charming florist. *1052 Potomac St. NW, Georgetown, 202/625–2327. Closed Sun. Metro: Foggy Bottom–GWU.*

2 *c-3*

THE MAIN STEM

This upscale shop pays careful attention to customers and creates distinctive floral designs for weddings and parties. *3416 Idaho Ave. NW, Upper Northwest, 202/244–2121. Closed Sun. Metro: Cleveland Park.*

2 *f-5*

OCIANA GROUP

The flowers and plants at this Capitol Hill shop do wonders for a government office. *1623 Eckington Pl. NE, Capitol Hill, 202/269–5634. Metro: Union Station.*

2 *b-1*

YORK FLOWERS, INC.

York Flowers has supplied Upper Northwest with beautiful flowers and plants for 30 years. *5023 Wisconsin Ave. NW, Upper Northwest, 202/726–2700. Closed Sun. Metro: Friendship Heights.*

nurseries

3 *e-6*

ALLAN WOODS FLOWERS & GIFTS

This lovely nursery has a good selection of both flowers and gardening supplies. *2645 Connecticut Ave. NW, Woodley Park, 202/332–3334. Metro: Woodley Park–Zoo.*

1 *b-7*

CAMPBELL & FERRARA NURSERIES, INC.

Twenty minutes by car from downtown Washington, this nursery is worth the drive for plants, roses, shrubs, flowers, garden furniture, tools, and equipment, not to mention good gardening advice. *6651 Little River Turnike, Alexandria, VA, 703/354–6724.*

2 *b-2*

JOHNSON'S FLOWER & GARDEN CENTER

A Washington institution, Johnson's Flower and Garden Center has supplied the area with beautiful flowers and plants for decades. It's earned its reputation for superb products, reliable delivery, and friendly service. *4200 Wisconsin Ave. NW, Upper Northwest, 202/244–6100. Metro: Tenleytown–AU.*

FOLK ART & HANDICRAFTS

10 *d-2*

APPALACHIAN SPRING

This charming shop specializes in American handmade crafts of all kinds, including quilts, jewelry, weavings, pottery, and blown glass. *Union Station, 50 Massachusetts Ave. NE, Capitol Hill, 202/682–0505. Metro: Union Station.*

9 *e-6*

1415 Wisconsin Ave. NW, Georgetown, 202/337–5780. Metro: Foggy Bottom–GWU.

1 *c-1*

1641 Rockville Pike, Rockville, MD, 301/230–1380. Metro: White Flint.

8 *g-4*

ELDER CRAFTERS' SHOP

This guildlike shop sells handcrafted quilts, dolls, dollhouses, jewelry, scarves, and sweaters made by men and women older than 55 years of age. *405 Cameron St., Old Town Alexandria, VA, 703/683–4338. Metro: King St.*

5 *g-6*

INDIAN CRAFT SHOP

The authentic, handmade Native American crafts sold here include baskets, jewelry, sand paintings, pottery, and weavings from almost two dozen tribes, such as the Navajo, Pueblo, Zuni, Cherokee, Lakota, and Seminole. You'll need a photo ID to get into this shop located inside a federal building. *Dept. of the Interior Bldg., 1849 C St. NW, Downtown, 202/208–4056. Closed weekends, except 3rd Sat. of the month. Metro: Farragut West.*

6 *g-7*

SILK ROAD

Silk Road sells beautiful home furnishings and accessories from mountain communities in South America and Asia. *6224 3rd St., Capitol Hill, 202/723–4793. Metro: Judiciary Sq.*

5 *g-3*

SKYNEAR AND COMPANY

The owners travel the world to find the unusual. Their journeys have been suc-cessful, and here you'll find an extravagant assortment of rich textiles, furniture, and home accessories—all for the art of living. *2122 18th St. NW, Dupont Circle, 202/797–7160. Metro: Dupont Circle.*

8 *g-4*

TORPEDO FACTORY ART CENTER

This converted torpedo factory on the Old Town waterfront is famous as a hotbed of the arts. Here local artists work in small studios, mount exhibitions, and sell their wares, which include paintings, sculptures, jewelry, handicrafts, and wearable-art clothing. *105 N. Union St., Old Town Alexandria, VA, 703/838–4565. Metro: King St.*

FOOD & DRINK

9 *e-7*

DEAN & DELUCA

Straight from SoHo, this gastronomic haven in Georgetown has some of the finest fresh and packaged food in the area. The produce is colorful enough to paint, the sauces countless, the various deli cases a joy to peruse. You'll find yourself willing to pay—not just for the food, but for the pleasure of shopping here. *3276 M St. NW, Georgetown, 202/342–2500. Metro: Foggy Bottom–GWU.*

2 *c-2*

MARVELOUS MARKET

This, well, marvelous market provides organically grown fresh produce as well as fresh-baked breads, fine cheeses, specialty olive oils, fresh pastas, and sauces. The smaller, Dupont Circle branch has less produce. *5035 Connecticut Ave. NW, Upper Northwest, 202/686–4040. Metro: Van Ness–UDC.*

5 *g-2*

1511 Connecticut Ave. NW, Dupont Circle, 202/332–3690. Metro: Dupont Circle.

2 *b-3*

SUTTON PLACE GOURMET

Sutton Place stocks top-of-the-line, sometimes rare products from around the world. It's not the place to bargain-hunt. The suburban outposts offer large selections, while Sutton-on-the-Run outlets in D.C. specialize in gourmet lunches and imported cookies and condiments. *3201 New Mexico Ave. NW, Upper Northwest, 202/363–5800. Metro: Tenleytown–AU.*

2 *b-1*

*4872 Massachusetts Ave., Upper North-
west, 202/966–1740. Metro: Friendship
Heights.*

8 *f-5*

*Franklin and S. Washington Sts., Alexan-
dria, VA, 703/549–6611. Metro: King St.
Call for other locations.*

breads & pastries

1 *d-1*

A & W VAN TOL BAKERY

A & W is an excellent bakery in subur-
ban Maryland. *2516 University Blvd. W,
Wheaton, MD, 301/933–1517. Closed Sun.
Metro: Wheaton.*

2 *b-2*

BRICK OVEN BAKERY

The Brick Oven offers excellent fresh
baked goods at all hours—and at wholesale prices. *4903 Wisconsin Ave. NW,
Upper Northwest, 202/364–0111. Metro:
Tenleytown–AU.*

5 *g-2*

FIREHOOK BAKERY

A sure sign of this bakery's quality: the
French community loves it. Come here
for the bread, made with naturally leav-
ened (yeast-free) sourdough, including
loaves flavored with rosemary, black
olive, thyme, and green olive and sage.
*1909 Q St. NW, Dupont Circle, 202/588–
9296. Metro: Dupont Circle.*

5 *g-3*

*3411 Connecticut Ave. NW, Dupont Circle,
202/362–2253. Metro: Dupont Circle.*

5 *h-4*

*912 17th St. NW, Downtown, 202/429–
2253. Metro: Farragut North.*

8 *e-3*

*214 N. Fayette St., Old Town Alexandria,
VA, 703/519–8020. Closed Sun. Metro:
King St.*

8 *g-4*

*105 S. Union St., Alexandria, VA, 703/519–
8021. Metro: King St.*

1 *c-5*

THE HEIDELBERG PASTRY
SHOPPE

If Black Forest rye bread and sweet
almond pastries make your mouth
water, check out this bakery specializing
in German breads, cakes, pastries, and

cold cuts. Added to the offerings are
"photo cakes," i.e., layer cakes with
photo images airbrushed onto the frost-
ing. *2150 N. Culpeper St., Arlington, VA,
703/527–8394.*

SAMADI SWEETS CAFE

Come here for baklava, halvah, and Mid-
dle Eastern pastries and sweets. *5916
Leesburg Pike, Baileys Crossroads, Falls
Church, VA, 703/578–0606.*

2 *e-2*

SWEDISH PASTRY SHOP

It's an excellent all-around bakery, but
this place specializes in Swedish treats,
like *limpa,* a sandwich bread made with
molasses. *5409 Georgia Ave. NW, Upper
Northwest, 202/723–3191. Metro: Fort Tot-
ten.*

3 *d-4*

UPTOWN BAKERS

Regarded by many as D.C.'s best bread
shop, Uptown has not only miraculous
loaves and pastries but delicious sandwiches to go at lunchtime. *3313 Connecticut Ave. NW, Cleveland Park, 202/362–
6262. Metro: Cleveland Park.*

cheese

10 *g-7*

BOWERS' FANCY CHEESES

The setting is simple, but the cheeses
are international and often quite exotic.
It's fun just to sample. *Eastern Market,
7th St. and N. Carolina Ave. SE, 202/544–
7877. Closed Mon. Metro: Eastern Market.*

2 *c-2*

CALVERT WOODLEY
LIQUORS

Not only does Calvert Woodley carry an
excellent selection of wines and liquors,
but it also offers a wide range of
cheeses and other foods to go with your
drink. It makes for one-stop shopping
for cocktail parties. *4339 Connecticut
Ave. NW, Upper Northwest, 202/966–
4400. Closed Sun. Metro: Van Ness–UDC.*

2 *b-1*

RODMAN'S DISCOUNT
FOODS AND APPLIANCES

Rodman's has a great selection of
cheeses from around the world at discount prices. When you're done picking
those out, head downstairs to the appliance department and grab a refrigerator

or two. *5100 Wisconsin Ave. NW, Upper Northwest, 202/363–3466. Metro: Friendship Heights.*

chocolate & other candy

5 *g-4*

CHOCOLATE MOOSE

These fanciful chocolates and candies appeal to the 5-year-old in everyone. Fun gift packs and loose assortments of bulk candies give you creative leeway. *1800 M St. NW, Downtown, 202/463–0992. Metro: Farragut North.*

9 *e-7*

GODIVA

This internationally beloved chocolatier still makes its top-line product of rich, sinful chocolates, truffles, and other delights, all packaged in the familiar gold box. *Georgetown Park Mall, 3222 M St. NW, Georgetown, 202/342–2232. Metro: Foggy Bottom–GWU.*

10 *e-2*

Union Station, 50 Massachusetts Ave. NE, Capitol Hill, 202/289–3662. Metro: Union Station.

5 *g-3*

1140 Connecticut Ave NW, Dupont Circle, 202/638–7421. Metro: Dupont Circle.

2 *b-1*

KRON CHOCOLATIER

This European chocolate maker has a great sense of whimsical design. Outrageously delicious molded chocolate is coaxed into seasonal forms and shapes inspired by everyday objects. *Mazza Gallerie, 5300 Wisconsin Ave. NW, Upper Northwest, 202/966–4946. Metro: Friendship Heights.*

coffee & tea

1 *c-1*

ASADUR'S

Asadur's specializes in Greek coffee, but sells various other enticing Mediterranean roasts. *5536 Randolph Rd., Rockville, MD, 301/770–5558. Metro: White Flint.*

2 *c-2*

BLUE MOUNTAIN COFFEE

Singled out by *Bon Appetit* as the best coffee shop in the nation, Blue Mountain has the relaxed atmosphere of a campus hangout and a wide selection of coffee beans and loose teas for home brewing. *4224 Fessenden St. NW, Upper Northwest, 202/686–5599. Metro: Friendship Heights.*

5 *g-2*

COFFEE, TEA & THE WORKS

This tiny shop is jam-packed with early morning kitchen items. There's a good selection of bulk coffee beans; Republic of Tea blends, both prepackaged and bulk; brewing accessories; gifts; and specialty cooking utensils. *1627 Connecticut Ave. NW, Dupont Circle, 202/483–8050. Metro: Dupont Circle.*

5 *f-2*

TEAISM

This trendy tea shop and restaurant specializes in bulk tea, with an emphasis on Chinese and Japanese varieties. It also sells beautifully packaged gift sets; tea-ceremony sets; books on tea; and tea-scented soaps, candles, and bath items. *2009 R St. NW, Dupont Circle, 202/667–3827. Metro: Dupont Circle.*

6 *c-6*

400 8th St., Downtown, 202/638–6010. Metro: Archives–Navy Memorial.

5 *g-4*

800 Connecticut Ave., Downtown, 202/835–2233. Metro: Farragut West.

ethnic foods

1 *e-2*

ANGKOR ORIENTAL SUPERMARKET

Angkor has magnificent fresh produce, including vines used in soups. The friendly staff can help explain exactly what to do with it all. *937 University Blvd., Silver Spring, MD, 301/445–4174. Metro: Silver Spring.*

1 *d-1*

ASIAN FOODS

This store has a large selection of Thai take-away foods, many of which you can try before you buy. Among the fresh, frozen, and canned products are Asian sausages, hot chili *sambals*, banana leaves, sweet *kecap manis* sauce, and Indonesian nuts, spices, herbs, and *krupuk* crackers. *2301 University Blvd. W, Wheaton, MD, 301/933–6071. Metro: Wheaton.*

BOMBAY FOODS

This small but complete grocery store carries the delicious imported curries, chutneys, nuts, and spices you need to make Indian favorites, not to mention a large selection of Indian films on video. Particularly appealing are the *samosas* (fried pastries filled with meat, vegetables, or both) and other standbys in the freezer section, as well as the freshly made desserts in the display case. *11213-D Lee Hwy., Fairfax, VA, 703/352–3663.*

6 *c-5*

DA HUA MARKET

You'll find everything you're bound to need to prepare a Chinese or Japanese meal, including wonton wrappers, produce, and noodles of all sorts. *623 H St. NW, Downtown, 202/371–8888. Metro: Metro Center.*

1 *c-1*

DARUMA

Japanese cooks swear by this gourmet shop, which carries particularly hard-to-find ingredients. *1045 Rockville Pike, Rockville, MD, 301/738–1042. Metro: White Flint.*

1 *e-2*

INDIAN SUPER MARKET

All manner of aromatic Indian foods— from curry and ghee to coconut milk and tamarind chutney—is sold here. *8107 Fenton St., Silver Spring, MD, 301/589–8417. Metro: Silver Spring.*

1 *d-1*

KOREAN KORNER

Buy all the ingredients for a great Korean meal, or just opt for a ready-to-cook combination. *12207 Viers Mill Rd., Wheaton, MD, 301/933–2000. Metro: Wheaton.*

LA CUZCATLECA

This shop specializes in Mexican food and produce but also sells a number of other nations' delicacies, such as Philippine banana leaves. La Cuzcatleca also carries the very special Mexican chocolate used to make mole and other sauces. *14452 Jefferson Davis Hwy., Woodbridge, VA, 703/490–4907.*

1 *c-1*

LOTTE ORIENTAL SUPERMARKET

A trove of Korean and other Asian foodstuffs, this store sells thinly sliced meat

for *bulgogi*, jars of kimchi, and a fine selection of fresh whole fish, crustaceans, and mollusks. *11790 Parklawn Dr., Rockville, MD, 301/881–3355. Metro: White Flint.*

1 *a-6*

LUCKY WORLD

At times this huge Asian market seems like a department store, with sushi, freshly cooked fish, fresh and dried produce, a self-serve hot-pickle bar, and a cafeteria serving soups, noodles, and dumplings. There's also an attractive selection of Japanese and Korean china bowls and plates, kitchenware, toiletries, footwear, and videos. *33109 Graham Rd., Falls Church, VA, 703/641–8585. Metro: West Falls Church–VT/UVA.*

MABUHAY ORIENTAL STORE

Collect all the exotic fresh, frozen, or canned products you'll need for a Philippine meal, or cheat and buy a ready-made feast. *6615 Backlick Rd., Springfield, VA, 703/451–8986.*

NIPA HOUSE EMPORIUM

The Nipa House specializes in Philippine products, and it may be the only place in town where you can buy quarts of ice cream made from maize, coconut, purple yam, baby bananas, or jackfruit. *5509 Leesburg Pike, Baileys Crossroads, Falls Church, VA, 703/379–0595.*

1 *c-1*

ORIENTAL MARKET

Have you ever had a peanut-butter popsicle? Mango? Guava? Stop by the Oriental Market and try red-bean paste or taro root, too. You'll also find Asian-cooking staples like wonton wrappers, spices, and condiments. *891F Rockville Pike, Rockville, MD, 301/340–8018. Metro: White Flint.*

1 *c-1*

YANGTZE ORIENTAL

Among Yangtze's array of Asian foods is a particularly strong Indonesian section. *2200 Viers Mill Rd., Rockville, MD, 301/424–1808. Metro: White Flint.*

fish & seafood

All of the following fish markets are packed with fresh, high-quality fish and seafood. Cannon's and Pruitt are particularly well established, and European and Lotte Oriental are known for produce as well as seafood. Pesce is an outgrowth of a successful Dupont Circle restaurant.

1 *b-5*
AMERICA SEAFOOD
4550 Lee Hwy., Arlington, VA, 703/522–8080. Metro: Ballston–MU.

9 *f-8*
CANNON'S SEAFOOD
1065 31st St. NW, Georgetown, 202/337–8366. Metro: Foggy Bottom–GWU.

7 *b-2*
CAPTAIN WHITE SEAFOOD CITY
1100 Maine Ave. SW, Waterfront, 202/484–2722. Metro: Waterfront–SEU.

7 *b-2*
CUSTIS & BROWN
1100 Maine Ave. SW, Waterfront, 202/484–0168. Metro: Waterfront–SEU.

1 *c-1*
EUROPEAN MARKET
17605 Redland Rd., Rockville, MD, 301/417–0788. Metro: White Flint.

7 *b-2*
JESSE TAYLOR SEAFOOD
1100 Maine Ave. SW, Waterfront, 202/554–4173. Metro: Waterfront–SEU.

1 *c-1*
LOTTE ORIENTAL SUPERMARKET
11790 Parklawn Dr., Rockville, MD, 301/881–3355. Metro: White Flint.

5 *f-3*
PESCE
2016 P St. NW, Dupont Circle, 202/466–3474. Metro: Dupont Circle.

7 *b-2*
PRUITT SEAFOOD
1100 Maine Ave. SW, Waterfront, 202/554–2669. Metro: Waterfront–SEU.

gourmet foods

1 *c-1*
EUROPEAN MARKET
This gourmet market has scads of fine products from around the world and is known for its high-quality fresh seafood and produce. 17605 Redland Rd., Rockville, MD, 301/417–0788. Metro: White Flint.

1 *e-2*
GOURMET POLONEZ
In addition to spicy mustards, pickles, and cold cuts, this Polish shop carries various European candies and pastries. 8113 Georgia Ave., Silver Spring, MD, 301/495–2650. Metro: Silver Spring.

1 *c-5*
THE ITALIAN STORE
Stop here for excellent Italian foods, including cheese and produce. The fresh mozzarella is especially tempting, but don't let it keep you from the equally inviting fresh pasta. 3123 Lee Hwy., Arlington, VA, 703/528–6266. Metro: Clarendon.

1 *d-2*
MARCELLA LA BERSAGLIERA
Delicious Italian specialties, including seasonal favorites such as Christmas *pannetone* (traditional cone-shape cake) are sold here. Cheeses, olives, and prepared sauces are particularly wonderful. 8540 Connecticut Ave., Chevy Chase, MD, 301/951–1818. Metro: Medical Center.

1 *b-7*
MEDITERRANEAN BAKERY
This Alexandria shop has quality Middle Eastern food, from fresh pita to homemade hummus and stuffed grape leaves. 352 S. Pickett St., Alexandria, VA, 703/751–0030. Metro: Van Dorn St.

2 *b-2*
SHEMALI'S
Shemali's is worth a trip for top-flight Middle Eastern goodies, fresh and packaged—say, stuffed grape leaves in tins, as well as fresh hummus and feta cheese. Cooking implements encourage you to try making the stuff yourself, but there's a small lunch counter in the back in case it all proves too immediately tempting. The entrance to this well-hidden store is through the parking lot. 3306 Wisconsin Ave. NW, Upper Northwest, 202/686–7070. Metro: Tenleytown–AU.

1 *c-1*
TRADER JOE'S
Absolutely in a class by itself, Trader Joe's is the grocer's answer to the Victo-

ria and Albert Museum—a little of this, a little of that, a little of something you didn't know you couldn't live without. Among the wares collected from an astonishing variety of purveyors, you may find Ghiradelli chocolates, salmon steaks, raw almonds, dried fruit, pet supplies, biscotti, and fresh bread and juice, plus a limited amount of produce. What you won't find are artificial ingredients and high prices. *Federal Plaza, 12268 Rockville Pike, Rockville, MD, 301/ 468–6656. Metro: White Flint.*

1 *b-5*

5847 Leesburg Pike, Falls Church, VA, 703/ 379–5883.

1 *a-4*

7514 Leesburg Pike., Fairfax, VA, 703/288– 0566.

1 *a-5*

WAREHOUSE INTERNATIONAL MARKET
Exotic products and produce line the aisles here. *3815A S. George Mason Dr., Falls Church, VA, 703/845–1526. Metro: West Falls Church–VT/UVA.*

herbs & spices

INDIA FOODS
Saffron at a reasonable price is always a find, and you can find it here. *1355 Holton La., Temple Hills, MD, 301/434–2433.*

1 *c-5*

INDIAN SPICES AND APPLIANCES
This fascinating shop has endless spices and herbs, but also goes beyond such staples to offer delicious takeout dishes in boiling pouches. In case you can't figure out what to do with it all, they also sell cookbooks. *3901 Wilson Blvd., Arlington, VA, 703/522–0149. Metro: Ballston–MU.*

INDO-PAK SPICES
A wonderful collection of Indian herbs and spices awaits you. *424 Elden St., Herndon, VA, 703/709–5842.*

1 *f-2*

THE SMILE HERB SHOP
This shop not only sells unusual herbs and spices, but offers advice and classes on herbal and other therapies. Be prepared if you take the Metro; it's a good walk from the College Park station. *4908*

Berwyn Rd., College Park, MD, 301/474– 8791. Metro: College Park–U of MD.

meat & poultry

1 *e-4*

A. M. BRIGGS
This wholesale warehouse also sells retail; specialties are fresh buffalo (large cuts only), fresh rabbit, squab, quail, and pheasant. They'll deliver to your door. *2130 Queens Chapel Rd. NE, Upper Northeast, 202/832–2600. Metro: Rhode Island Ave.*

1 *c-5*

EL CHAPARREL MEAT MARKET
El Chaparrel specializes in Latin American meats, including a wide selection of tender beef cut specially for fajitas. *2719 Wilson Blvd., Arlington, VA, 703/276– 8336. Metro: Clarendon.*

6 *b-6*

LES HALLES BUTCHER SHOP
Adjacent to the French restaurant Les Halles de Paris, this butcher can provide you with just about any meat—from brains to *onglet* (hanger steak). It's best to call in advance with unusual requests. *1201 Pennsylvania Ave. NW, Downtown, 202/347–6848. Metro: Metro Center.*

SUMMERFIELD FARM
Enthusiasts come to this picturesque bit of countryside for fresh, succulent New Zealand lamb. If you can't make it out here to choose your own quarry, simply call the toll-free number and arrange to have it delivered. *10044 James Madison Hwy., Culpeper, VA, 800/898–3276. Closed Fri.*

pasta & noodles

THE ITALIAN GOURMET DELI
Pasta lovers will drool over the fresh macaroni and delicious frozen pasta dishes at this store. *505 Maple Ave. W, Vienna, VA, 703/938–4141. Metro: Vienna/Fairfax–GMU.*

2 *f-4*

LITTERI'S
Washington's oldest Italian deli is right in the center of the wholesale food market.

517 Morse St. NE, Capitol Hill, 202/544–0184. Closed Sun. Metro: Union Station.

3 *d-4*

VACE

Fine olive oils, roasted peppers, sun-dried tomatoes, olives, and other packaged goods from Italy fill the shelves of this store. Vace also sells thin, crisp pizza, whole or by the slice; or you can pick up some of their fresh-made dough and sauce and roll your own pizza at home. *3315 Connecticut Ave. NW, Cleveland Park, 202/363–1999. Metro: Cleveland Park.*

1 *c-2*

7010 Wisconsin Ave., Bethesda, MD, 301/654–6367. Metro: Bethesda.

1 *c-1*

VIGNOLA PASTA GOURMET

You'll find fresh pasta, cheese, imported tomatoes and olives, and other tasty Italian delicacies here. *113A N. Washington St., Rockville, MD, 301/340–2350. Closed Sun. Metro: White Flint.*

produce

1 *e-2*

BECRAFT'S FARM PRODUCE

This ace produce farm delivers big on Halloween pumpkins; there's even a special pumpkin show on the big day. *14722 New Hampshire Ave., Silver Spring, MD, 301/236–4545. Metro: Silver Spring.*

BUTLER'S ORCHARD

This farm and orchard purveys wonderful produce and throws a pumpkin festival every weekend in October. You can pick your own strawberries, blueberries, and raspberries in the summer. Call to find out what's in season. *22200 Davis Mill Rd., Germantown, MD, 301/972–3299. Closed Nov.–Apr.*

FARMERS' MARKETS

Small farmers' markets are held all over Washington, most on weekends. The produce is fresher than what you see in local grocery chains and is usually much cheaper as well. Farmers will often allow you to sample new items, can usually answer questions on where and how the produce is grown, and may even offer cooking tips. Most markets now also have organic fruit and vegetables. If nothing else, they're a nice way to meet

the neighbors. Arrive early for the best selection.

2 *g-5*

Hit this unusual market for cheap bulk buys and such Southern staples as greens, shucked beans and peas, and pork and ham. It's open Thursday and Saturday year-round. *Oklahoma Ave. and Benning Rd. NE, Parking Lot 6, RFK Stadium, Northeast. Metro: Stadium–Armory.*

1 *c-2*

The Women's Cooperative Market sells produce and general foods Wednesday and Saturday year-round. *7155 Wisconsin Ave., Bethesda, MD. Metro: Bethesda.*

1 *e-3*

If it's organic produce you're after, make your way to the Takoma Park farmers' market, held every Sunday from April to December. *Laurel St. between Eastern and Carroll Aves., Takoma Park, MD. Metro: Takoma.*

8 *g-4*

This charming market is conducted in front of the Old Town Alexandria City Hall by direct edict of George Washington: offering both produce and crafts, it's been held every Saturday morning from 5 to 9 since his day. If you can drag yourself out of bed that early, it's a sight to behold. *301 King St. (in front of City Hall), Alexandria, VA. Metro: King St.*

HOMESTEAD FARM

Berry lovers can pick their own produce all summer long. Come fall, this produce farm offers weekend hayrides. *15600 Sugarland Rd., Poolesville, MD, 301/977–3761.*

JOHNSON'S BERRY FARM

Johnson's is an excellent produce market specializing in berries. *17999 Swanson Rd., Upper Marlboro, MD, 301/627–8316.*

9 *e-5*

NEAM'S OF GEORGETOWN

This Georgetown institution has been supplying elegant matrons with their groceries for decades. It's not large, but this shop packs just about everything delicious and deluxe. *3217 P St. NW, Georgetown, 202/338–4694. Metro: Foggy Bottom–GWU.*

wines & spirits

2 *c-2*

CALVERT WOODLEY LIQUORS

Calvert Woodley has one of the best selections of wine in D.C., and goes beyond that to offer one of the area's best selections of cheese. You can make real finds here. Try Brillat Savarin, from Normandy, in winter; it's one of the most delicious cheeses in the world. The store is open until 8:30 on weekdays for those last-minute hostess gifts. *4339 Connecticut Ave. NW, Upper Northwest, 202/966–4400. Closed Sun. Metro: Van Ness–UDC.*

9 *e-7*

PEARSON'S

Pearson's has one of the largest volumes of discount wines and spirits in the area, and delivers within the District. *2436 Wisconsin Ave. NW, Glover Park, 202/333–6666. Closed Sun.*

10 *h-5*

SCHNEIDER'S OF CAPITOL HILL

Specializing in fine wines, this Capitol Hill shop has a myriad of international wines and spirits. *300 Massachusetts Ave. NE, Capitol Hill, 202/543–9300. Closed Sun. Metro: Union Station.*

1 *b-7*

TOTAL BEVERAGE

An enormous warehouse of wine, spirits, water, and soda, Total Beverage has a truly immense selection, particularly of wines. The proprietors host frequent wine tastings, which can, among other things, make shopping feel like less of a chore. *5240 Little River Turnpike, Alexandria, VA, 703/941–1133. Metro: Van Dorn St.*

FRAMING

All of these shops offer custom framing for a variety of tastes and budgets, and several have ready-made frames on hand as well. Picture Frame Express is particularly amenable to rush orders.

5 *h-5*

B. DAVID'S CUSTOM FRAMING

1001 Connecticut Ave. NW, Downtown, 202/785–1652. Metro: Farragut North.

10 *g-8*

CAPITOL HILL ART & FRAME

623 Pennsylvania Ave. SE, Capitol Hill, 202/546–2700. Closed Sun. and Mon. Metro: Eastern Market.

5 *h-4*

COHEN'S

1703 L St. NW, Downtown, 202/833–8717. Metro: Farragut North.

1 *d-7*

HODGES GALLERY

Belle Vue Shopping Center, Belle Vue Rd., Alexandria, VA, 703/765–0948. Closed Sun. and Mon. Metro: Huntington.

5 *f-3*

PICTURE FRAME EXPRESS

2024 P St. NW, Dupont Circle, 202/833–1112. Metro: Dupont Circle.

9 *f-8*

VEERHOFF GALLERIES

With more than a century's worth of experience in ancient prints and maps, this gallery is one of the best places to take your family treasures or newly acquired antique prints to be framed. *1054 31st St. NW, Georgetown, 202/338–6456. Closed Sun. and Mon. Metro: Foggy Bottom–GWU.*

2 *b-2*

WONDER GRAPHICS PICTURE FRAMING

4622 Wisconsin Ave. NW, Upper Northwest, 202/328–8100. Closed Sun. and Mon. Metro: Tenleytown–AU.

GIFTS & SOUVENIRS

9 *d-4*

A MANO

All of these French and Italian home furnishings are handmade. Concentrations include dinnerware, decorative items, and garden accessories. *1677 Wisconsin Ave. NW, Georgetown, 202/298–7200. Metro: Foggy Bottom–GWU.*

9 *e-7*

BOMBAY COMPANY

You'll find elegant but reasonably priced doorstops, fireplace tools, and furniture inspired by the 19th-century China trade. *Georgetown Park Mall, 3222 M St. NW, Georgetown. 202/333–0852. Metro: Foggy Bottom–GWU.*

1 *c-2*

Montgomery Mall, 7125 Democracy Blvd., Bethesda, MD, 301/469–6800. Metro: Medical Center.

2 *b-2*

DALTON BRODY LTD

Dalton Brody is like a department store of gifts, offering men's and women's personal accessories, fine and costume jewelry, stationery, and children's items, to name just a few. *3412 Idaho Ave. NW, Upper Northwest, 202/244–7197. Metro: Tenleytown–AU.*

6 *c-5*

DISCOVERY CHANNEL STORE

Shopping is just one of the activities at this half store, half museum. You can also play high-tech interactive games, walk through the fuselage of a B-25 bomber, or stand awestruck before a 42-ft cast of the world's largest T-rex. Items for sale include everything from telescopes and science kits to authentic amber jewelry. After browsing, consider slipping into the on-site theater to see the movie *Destination DC* before heading out on the store's 1½-hour "Discover Historic Downtown D.C." tour (available weekends from March to November for $8 per person). *1430 G St. NW, Downtown, 202/639–0908. Metro: Gallery Pl.–Chinatown.*

6 *a-6*

FAHRNEY'S

It all started out as a pen bar—a place to fill your fountain pen before embarking on the day's business. Today, Fahrney's sells pens in silver, gold, and lacquer by the world's leading manufacturers. *1317 F St. NW, Downtown, 202/628–9525. Metro: Metro Center.*

5 *f-2*

GINZA, INC.

This lovely store sells everything Japanese, including sake sets, fans, jewelry, and T-shirts with Japanese inscriptions. *1721 Connecticut Ave. NW, Downtown, 202/331–7991. Metro: Dupont Circle.*

9 *g-7*

KEITH LIPERT

Keith Lipert specializes in fine international gifts, decorative accessories, and unique objets d'art from the classically inspired to the flamboyantly avant-garde. *2922 M St. NW, Georgetown, 202/965–9736. Metro: Foggy Bottom–GWU.*

6 *c-5*

MUSIC BOX CENTER

An exquisite specialty store, the Music Box Center provides listening opportunities with more than 1,500 music boxes that play a total of 500 melodies. *1920 I St. NW, Downtown, 202/783–9399. Metro: Farragut West.*

8 *g-4*

PINEAPPLE

A lovely classic gift shop, Pineapple has traditional as well as unusual gifts for locals and tourists alike. *106 N. Lee St., Old Town Alexandria, VA, 703/836–3639. Metro: King St.*

8 *g-4*

TORPEDO FACTORY ART CENTER

More than 150 artists showcase their creations in this converted factory that was once the nation's major producer of naval torpedoes and parts. The photographers, painters, and sculptors are happy to talk to you about their work while creating masterpieces before your eyes. *105 N. Union St., Old Town Alexandria, VA, 703/838–4565. Metro: King St.*

8 *g-5*

UTICA

This unusual and charming gift shop is a mainstay in Old Town Alexandria. *203 S. Union St., Old Town Alexandria, VA, 703/838–0022. Metro: King St.*

2 *c-3*

WAKE UP LITTLE SUZIE

Clocks shaped like dogs and cats, silver jewelry, funky switch-plate covers, and idiosyncratic ceramics are all here in this boutique of whimsical yet useful gifts. Don't even try to resist buying something for yourself. *3409 Connecticut Ave. NW, Upper Northwest, 202/244–0700. Metro: Cleveland Park.*

HOME FURNISHINGS

1 c-2

ANCIENT RHYTHMS

Often referred to as "seductive," this furniture gallery is itself a lesson in interior design and styling; each item is perfectly placed to create an alluring atmosphere. The staff travels regularly to Southeast Asia for more enticing pieces. *7920 Woodmont Ave., Bethesda, MD, 301/652–2669. Metro: Bethesda.*

1 d-7

A BIT OF BRITAIN

Cozy up to all things British, old and new: fill your rooms with blue-and-white china, antique accessories, floral chintz, country furniture, Lloyd Loom wicker, and Victorian lace. *16 W. Chapman St., Alexandria, VA, 703/836–9129.*

2 b-2

CALICO CORNERS

The friendly, experienced staff at Calico Corners makes choosing fabrics for home decoration a breeze; simply tell them your decorating ideas, and they will get you started. The fabrics are grouped by color, with a wide selection to meet all price ranges. The store also makes its own furniture, which you can order covered in the fabric of your choice. *4400 Jenifer St. NW, Upper Northwest, 202/274–0060. Metro: Friendship Heights.*

9 e-7

CONRAN'S HABITAT

Via London and New York, Conran's is a top international name in contemporary home furnishings. This renovated 18th-century warehouse building is stocked with attractive and colorful housewares, furniture, accessories, and fabrics. *Georgetown Park Mall, 3222 M St. NW, Georgetown, 202/298–8300. Metro: Foggy Bottom–GWU.*

2 b-2

CRATE & BARREL

Come June, Crate & Barrel becomes a mecca for wedding guests—the chain has one of the area's most popular wedding registries. No wonder, since the company turns out affordable and attractive lines of china, glassware, pottery, linens, and kitchenware. The Massachusetts Avenue branch and the International Drive location both carry the company's full line of high-quality furniture. Try the Alexandria outlet store for bargains on last season's remainders. *4820 Massachusetts Ave. NW, Upper Northwest, 202/364–6100. Metro: Tenleytown–AU.*

1 d-6

Pentagon City, 1000 S. Hayes St., Arlington, VA, 703/418–1010. Metro: Pentagon City.

1 c-2

Montgomery Mall, 7125 Democracy Blvd., Bethesda, MD, 301/365–2600. Metro: Medical Center.

8 d-4

1700 Prince St., Alexandria, VA, 703/739–8800. Metro: King St.

1 a-4

Tysons Corner, 1800 International Dr., McLean, VA, 703/891–0090.

3 c-3

ROOMS AND GARDENS

This small, contemporary interior-design company is an offshoot of the SoHo (New York City) antiques store of the same name. Wares include museum-quality 19th-century French furniture, garden objects, and folk art. Interior-and garden-design consultations are available by appointment only. *3677 Upton St. NW, Upper Northwest, 202/362–3777. Metro: Van Ness–UDC.*

architectural artifacts

3 h-8

BRASS KNOB ARCHITECTURAL ANTIQUES AND BACK DOORS WAREHOUSE

Going for the Victorian look? Stop in first at Brass Knob, which has an eclectic mix of lighting fixtures, stained glass, and yes, door knobs. Around the corner on Champlain Street is Back Doors Warehouse, a sister store with larger items such as claw-foot tubs and iron gates. *Brass Knob, 2311 18th St. NW, Adams-Morgan, 202/332–3370; Back Doors, 2329 Champlain St. NW, Adams-Morgan, 202/265–0587. Metro: Woodley Park–Zoo.*

OLD HOUSE PARTS

This fascinating shop only sells to Montgomery County residents who are renovating their pre-1940s homes. You can find everything from doorknobs to bathtubs here. Visit by appointment only. *1000 DeSellum Ave., Gaithersburg, MD, 301/907–3219.*

bedroom & bath

1 *d-6*

LINENS 'N THINGS

Everything for the bedroom, bathroom, and other rooms of the house can be found here. The store packs a robust selection of designer and brand-name bed accessories at discount prices. *The Fashion Centre at Pentagon City, 1000 S. Hayes St., Arlington, VA, 703/413–0993. Metro: Pentagon City.*

2 *b-2*

5333 Wisconsin Ave. NW, Upper Northwest, 202/244–9025. Metro: Friendship Heights.

Potomac Mills Mall, 2700 Potomac Mills Circle, Woodbridge, VA, 703/490–4666.

carpets & rugs

1 *b-7*

AFGHAN MARKET

Specializing in beautiful Afghan rugs, this intriguing shop also sells other Afghan products. *5709 Edsall Rd., Alexandria, VA, 703/212–9529. Metro: Van Dorn St.*

2 *c-4*

GEORGETOWN CARPETS

Interior designers flock to Georgetown Carpets for its wide selection of affordable carpeting and Oriental rugs. *2208 Wisconsin Ave. NW, Glover Park, 202/ 342–2262. Metro: Tenleytown–AU.*

ceramic tiles

8 *g-6*

ADEMAS TILES

Ademas is well-known among local aficionados for its extensive selection of beautiful tiles. The store specializes in exquisite stone and tiles from Portugal, France, and Italy. *816 N. Fairfax St., Old Town Alexandria, VA, 703/549–7806. Metro: King St.*

china, glassware, porcelain, pottery, silver

9 *d-4*

A MANO

A Mano remains a standout in a neighborhood packed with elegant home and gift stores. The pottery, linens, and silver imported from Tuscany and Provence don't come cheap, however. *1677 Wis-*

consin Ave. NW, Georgetown, 202/298–7200. Metro: Foggy Bottom–GWU.

1 *d-7*

A BIT OF BRITAIN

Come here for blue-and-white china, pottery, and other accessories to transform your home into an English country manor. *16 W. Chapman St., Alexandria, VA, 703/836–9129.*

9 *e-6*

LITTLE CALEDONIA

This marvelous store is crammed with unusual, imported, and generally lovely furnishings and accessories. Candles, cards, fabrics, and lamps round out the stock of decorative kitchenware. *1419 Wisconsin Ave. NW, Georgetown, 202/ 333–4700. Metro: Foggy Bottom–GWU.*

8 *e-4*

QUIMPER

This gift shop specializes in the beautiful yellow *faience* produced only in a certain section of Brittany. If you're at all into French porcelain, this store is a must-see. *1121 King St., Old Town Alexandria, VA, 703/519–8339. Metro: King St.*

furniture & accessories

9 *d-7*

BAKER

This century-old North Carolina furniture company went national in 2000, choosing Georgetown for its flagship store. An airy building houses numerous styles of high-end pieces that you'll surely want to pass on to your children. Baker also sells Coach leather furniture. *3330 M St. NW, Georgetown, 202/342–7080. Metro: Foggy Bottom–GWU.*

9 *d-7*

BEE MARKET

Fans of this store refer to it as a little bit of France on M Street. Started by two French expats, Bee Market carries the best furniture and accessories hip French designers have to offer; unfortunately the prices reflect this. But as you stroll around to the sounds of French chansons, you may find that some of the hand-painted porcelain pottery or handmade votive candles fit in your price range. *3300 M St. NW, Georgetown, 202/336–6602. Metro: Foggy Bottom–GWU.*

IKEA

You could furnish an entire home and then some with the items at this Swedish megastore. It sells everything, including the kitchen sink. Shoppers come here for the inexpensive furniture, which consists of beds, desks, dining-room sets, pillows, and much more. Unfortunately, the quality often reflects the low price. You'll also need to assemble most of the furniture yourself. Still, this is a great stop if you're looking to furnish your first apartment without smashing the piggy bank. If you need a break from shopping, try the Swedish meatballs at the Ikea Cafeteria. *Potomac Mills Mall, 2700 Potomac Mills Circle, Woodbridge, VA, 703/494–4532.*

MASTERCRAFT INTERIORS

Quality and price are both agreeable on this large selection of classic and contemporary home furnishings. *10390 Lee Hwy., Fairfax, VA, 703/684–1778.*

8 *e-4*

RANDOM HARVEST

Random Harvest offers a tantalizing mix of antique furniture and new, reproduction accessories; the prices for both are reasonable. All of the antique pieces come covered in white fabric, and you can choose new fabric right at the store. *810 King St., Old Town Alexandria, VA, 703/548–8820. Metro: King St.*

9 *e-6*

1313 Wisconsin Ave. NW, Georgetown, 202/333–5569. Metro: Foggy Bottom–GWU.

1 *c-6*

SAAH UNFINISHED FURNITURE

You'll have to put in some work on this furniture, but you'll still find solid wood pieces of a much higher quality than those at other do-it-yourself stores. The staff will help you choose the paints and stains needed to give your furniture the perfect finishing. *2330 Columbia Pike, Arlington, VA, 703/920–1500. Metro: Pentagon City.*

811 Hungerford Dr., Rockville, MD, 301/424–6911. Metro: Rockville.

2 *b-2*

THEODORE'S

This fun shop has the ultimate in contemporary furniture and accessories, including some seriously one-of-a-kind items. Theodore's own talented designers can help you envision how it will all work in your home. *2233 Wisconsin Ave. NW, Georgetown, 202/333–2300.*

1 *a-4*

THIS END UP

Handsome, rugged, handcrafted yellow-pine furniture is a hallmark of this chain store, and goes for pleasing prices. Choose also from fabrics, lamps, wall hangings, and other accessories. *Tysons Corner Center, 1961 Chain Bridge Rd., McLean, VA, 703/734–5778.*

lamps & lighting

8 *e-4*

THE LAMPLIGHTER

If a blue turtle lamp is your heart's desire, come first to The Lamplighter, a deceptively small shop with both normal and abnormal decorative lighting. You'll find unique styles and shapes of lamps, European snap-in light bulbs, and international styles and sizes of illuminated articles. If you love your outdated lamp, you can bring it here to be spruced up. *1207 King St., Old Town Alexandria, VA, 703/549–4040. Metro: King St.*

LAMPS UNLIMITED MCLEAN

Lamps Unlimited has a vast selection of all kinds of lighting, but its most celebrated attribute is devoted, personalized service. Loyal customers know they'll be greeted and treated by a knowledgeable, friendly staff. *1362 Old Chain Bridge Rd., McLean, VA, 703/827–0090.*

9 *d-5*

REED ELECTRIC

The glass windows surrounding this store reveal its extensive selection of chandeliers—always lighted, like a beacon. The selection also includes Tiffany lamps and table and standing lamps of all types and sizes. *1611 Wisconsin Ave. NW, Georgetown, 202/338–7500. Metro: Foggy Bottom–GWU.*

paint & wallpaper

5 *h-2*

DISTRICT SERVISTAR HARDWARE

A central location makes this a convenient store for city dwellers to buy paint and other home products. Servistar offers a computerized color-matching system. *1623 17th St. NW, Dupont Circle, 202/265–7527. Metro: Dupont Circle.*

WALLS FOR U

If you can't find the wallpaper you want at Walls For U, it probably doesn't exist. The store's wallpaper library contains more than 1,500 sample books, which can be checked out for two days. Stock paper is discounted by as much as 50%, whereas wallpaper selections ordered from the books are reduced by up to 30%. Staff members are even available for at-home consultations. *14025 Lee Jackson Hwy., Chantilly, VA, 703/830–7344.*

HOUSEWARES & HARDWARE

1 *d-7*

HOME DEPOT INC.

A huge warehouse of a store with a no-frills interior, Home Depot supplies heavy-duty items like lumber and building supplies as well as a complete array of tools and household items. *400 S. Pickett St., Alexandria, VA, 703/823–1900. Metro: Van Dorn St.*

1 *f-1*

2300 Broadbirch Dr., Silver Spring, MD, 301/680–3500.

9 *e-7*

RESTORATION HARDWARE

A visit to Restoration Hardware is like a trip down memory lane. Every corner of the store holds items that will take you back in time, from the reproduction Arts and Crafts lamps to the 1950s-style cookie jars. Many of the items make for great conversation pieces or gifts. Restoration also carries paints, fixtures, hardware, and how-to books, but at prices a bit higher than what you'll find at your regular hardware store. *1222 Wisconsin Ave. NW, Georgetown, 202/625–2771. Metro: Foggy Bottom–GWU.*

8 *e-4*

614 King St., Old Town Alexandria, VA, 703/299–6220. Metro: King St.

1 *a-4*

Tysons Corner Center, 1961 Chain Bridge Rd., McLean, VA, 703/821–9655.

2 *b-1*

WILLIAMS-SONOMA

The San Francisco kitchen-supply company is famous for its cookware, but the stores also have cookbooks, a smatter-ing of gourmet foods, and a stylish, well-priced selection of china, bistro ware, wine glasses, flatware, and serving pieces. As one fan put it, Williams-Sonoma stores are not about cooking; they're about lifestyle. Both camps are happy here. *Mazza Galleria, 5300 Wisconsin Ave. NW, Upper Northwest, 202/244–4800. Metro: Friendship Heights.*

1 *a-4*

Tysons Corner Center, 1961 Chain Bridge Rd., McLean, VA, 703/917– 7832, and the Galleria at Tysons II, 2001 International Dr., McLean, VA, 703/917–0005.

1 *c-1*

White Flint Mall, 11301 Rockville Pike, North Bethesda, MD. Metro: White Flint.

JEWELRY

antique & collectible items

5 *h-5*

SHAH & SHAH APPRAISERS

This store looks small, but it has an extensive collection of beautiful jewelry—both new and estate—as well as loose gems and some gift items. Proprietors Michael and Faith Shah make buying jewelry even more of a pleasure than it would normally be. *1001 Connecticut Ave. NW, Downtown, 202/223–6001. Metro: Farragut North.*

8 *g-3*

SILVERMAN GALLERIES

Silverman Galleries has one of the largest collections of antique jewelry in the Washington area. It also specializes in American and European antique furniture and silver. The shop is only open Wednesday and Saturday from 11 to 5, or by appointment. *110 N. St. Asaph St., Alexandria, VA, 703/836–5363. Metro: King St.*

5 *g-4*

TINY JEWEL BOX INC.

Washingtonians love this charming shop, as its baubles are often unique and always of the finest quality. The selection includes estate and antique jewelry as well as beautiful contemporary pieces. *1147 Connecticut Ave. NW, Downtown, 202/393–2747. Metro: Farragut North.*

contemporary pieces

5 *h-5*

ALAN MARCUS & COMPANY

This longtime discount jewelry store features high-end watches and jewelry, including pearls, diamonds, gold, and gemstones. *1200 18th St. NW, Downtown, 202/331–0671. Metro: Farragut North.*

2 *b-1*

CHARLES SCHWARTZ & SON

Long known for fine service and high-quality products. Charles Schwartz specializes in precious stones in both traditional and modern settings. Fine watches are also available. *Mazza Gallerie, 5300 Wisconsin Ave. NW, Upper Northwest, 202/363–5432. Metro: Friendship Heights.*

1 *b-5*

DIRECT JEWELRY OUTLET

The prices you'll find here on fine watches, gold, silver, gemstones, and pearls would make other jewelers blush. *101 E. Broad St., Falls Church, VA, 703/534–2666. Metro: East Falls Church.*

6 *a-5*

GALT & BRO INC.

Galt & Bro sits in the shadow of the White House and has the impeccable reputation to match its surrounding. Established in 1801, this was one of the first jewelry stores in the nation. The store is known for its fine jewelry and estate pieces, and specializes in 18-karat gold and platinum. *607 15th St. NW, Downtown, 202/347–1034. Metro: McPherson Sq.*

8 *f-4*

KING JEWELRY

This full-service store sells fine jewelry, Rolex watches, and custom-made items. Repair service is also available. *609 King St., Old Town Alexandria, VA, 703/549–0011. Metro: King St.*

1 *c-3*

TIFFANY & CO

Tiffany may be as well known for its little blue boxes as it is for its high-end jewelry and gift items. The shop is popular for engagement rings. Although many of the pieces run into the thousands of dollars, some of the beautiful sterling-silver designs are affordably priced. *5500 Wisconsin Ave., Chevy Chase, MD, 301/657–8777. Metro: Friendship Heights.*

costume jewelry

9 *e-7*

IMPOSTORS

Featuring fabulous fakes, Impostors is especially strong on dazzling faux gemstones. You can also find pearls and faux gold. *3270 M St. NW, Georgetown, 202/625–2363. Metro: Foggy Bottom–GWU.*

10 *d-2*

Union Station, 50 Massachusetts Ave. NE, Capitol Hill, 202/842–4462. Metro: Union Station.

LEATHER GOODS & LUGGAGE

GEORGETOWN LEATHER DESIGN OUTLET

Now owned by Wilson's Leather, this outlet has retained its old name along with its extensive selection of leather clothing, bags, and luggage at excellent prices. *Potomac Mills Mall, 2700 Potomac Mills Circle, Woodbridge, VA, 703/497–0521.*

5 *g-4*

LANE'S LUGGAGE

Lane's carries luggage in all sizes for both the business and pleasure traveler. You'll also find small leather products at good prices. *1146 Connecticut Ave. NW, Downtown, 202/452–1146. Metro: Farragut North.*

1 *a-4*

WILSON'S LEATHER

Now owned by Wilson's Leather, this former Georgetown Leather Design store has retained its signature look in fine leather jackets, wallets, gloves, briefcases, and handbags. Designer items by Kenneth Cole and Andrew Marc are also featured. *Tysons Corner Center, 1961 Chain Bridge Rd., McLean, VA, 703/893–1620.*

1 *c-1*

White Flint Mall, 11301 Rockville Pike, North Bethesda, MD, 301/881–4677. Metro: White Flint.

LINENS

2 *b-2*

ABRIELLE

The prices match the quality of the gorgeous linens here—the most beautiful in the city, some say. If you can't find the right item, you can have it made to order from the finest fabrics available. *3301 New Mexico Ave. NW, Upper Northwest, 202/364–6118. Metro: Tenleytown–AU.*

9 *d-7*

APRIL CORNELL

Need some color in your life? April Cornell can bring it to almost any room of your house. The shop prides itself on the colorful tablecloths, napkins, and bed linens, many of which would be at home in a farmhouse in Provence. The same beautiful fabrics are also used to make women's and children's clothing. *3278 M St. NW, Georgetown, 202/625–7887. Metro: Foggy Bottom–GWU.*

1 *d-6*

The Fashion Centre at Pentagon City, 1000 S. Hayes St., Arlington, VA, 703/415–2290. Metro: Pentagon City.

1 *a-4*

Tysons Corner Center, 1961 Chain Bridge Rd., McLean, VA, 703/448–6972.

quilts & duvets

THE QUILT PATCH

It's paradise for quilters—beautiful quilts and all the supplies you need to make them. *10381 Main St., Fairfax, VA, 703/273–6937.*

MAPS

5 *h-5*

ADC MAP STORE

Before your next travel adventure, whether it be to Delaware or Dar es Salaam, make sure you know how to get there. ADC has maps for the four corners of the world as well as the four quadrants of D.C. *1636 I St. NW, Downtown, 202/628–2608. Metro: Farragut North.*

9 *f-7*

OLD PRINT GALLERY

Here is the Washington area's largest collection of maps and old prints, many of which depict the fair city in centuries

past. *1220 31st St. NW, Georgetown, 202/965–1818. Metro: Foggy Bottom–GWU.*

2 *b-2*

TRAVEL BOOKS & LANGUAGE CENTER

Although you can find both city and world maps at Travel Books, the store has so much more to offer, including a comprehensive collection of guidebooks, language tapes, and literature related to countries around the globe. The helpful staff members are intrepid travelers themselves. The store hosts readings by well-known travel writers, and language classes are held in the back room. *4437 Wisconsin Ave. NW, Tenleytown, 202/237–1322. Metro: Tenleytown–AU.*

MEMORABILIA

5 *h-5*

POLITICAL AMERICANA

Both Democrats and Republicans will find something of interest at Political Americana, located in the shadow of the White House. The store is teeming with mugs, T-shirts, posters, and books celebrating the politicians of the past and present. *685 15th St. NW, Downtown, 202/547–1871. Metro: McPherson Sq. or Metro Center.*

MISCELLANY

6 *b-1*

AL'S MAGIC SHOP

This wonderful magic shop has jokes and tricks for pranksters of any age. Resident master of mischief Al Cohen sells everything from a phony faucet (attachable anywhere by suction cup) to a trapped rat that wriggles when you approach. Check out the equipment you need to saw your mate in half. *1012 Vermont Ave. NW, Downtown, 202/789–2800. Metro: McPherson Sq.*

1 *c-2*

BRUCE VARIETY

This is a store for things you can't find anywhere else, from children's plain cotton underwear to needles and thread to science-project supplies—not to mention those rubber and metal clips that attach stockings to garter belts. *Bradley Shopping Center, 6922 Arlington Rd., Bethesda, MD, 301/656–7543. Metro: Bethesda.*

2 *b-2*

G. C. MURPHY

G. C. Murphy is the only extant branch of a chain that used to be known locally as the dime store. It's still a charming, slightly goofy shop where you can buy various items for 99¢, have keys made, get a new pet, have your watch fixed, pick up holiday decorations, or choose a quite nice rug. *3314 Wisconsin Ave. NW, Upper Northwest, 202/537–1155. Metro: Tenleytown–AU.*

MUSIC

cds, tapes, & vinyl

5 *g-4*

BORDERS BOOKS AND MUSIC

Borders has one of the most extensive music selections among the large book-and-music stores in Washington. Fans of folk as well as rock will be pleased with the reasonable prices and the numerous listening stations. Many of the branches also host performances by local musicians in their cafés. *1800 L St. NW, Downtown, 202/466–4999. Metro: Farragut North.*

2 *b-1*

5333 Wisconsin Ave. NW, Upper Northwest, 202/686–8270. Metro: Friendship Heights.

1 *d-6*

The Fashion Centre at Pentagon City, 1000 S. Hayes St., Arlington, VA, 703/418–0166. Metro: Pentagon City.

1 *c-1*

White Flint Mall, 11301 Rockville Pike, Rockville, MD, 301/816–1067. Metro: White Flint.

1 *c-6*

Crossroads Center, 5871 Crossroads Center Way, Baileys Crossroads, Falls Church, VA, 703/998–0404. Call for other locations.

3 *g-8*

DC CD

This upstart music store caters to the club crowd with its late hours and wide selection of indie releases, rock, hip-hop, alternative, and soul. The knowledgeable staff will often open packages, allowing customers to listen before they buy. Local and national bands make occasional appearances. *2423 18th St.*

NW, Adams-Morgan, 202/588–1810. Metro: Woodley Park–Zoo.

5 *g-4*

KEMP MILL MUSIC

Competing with Borders Books and Music and Tower Records, both just blocks away, this local chain sells a great variety of popular CDs and cassettes at reasonable prices. *1900 L St. NW, Downtown, 202/223–5310. Metro: Farragut North.*

5 *f-5*

TOWER RECORDS

It's hard to beat Tower for general power and might wherever it opens up. This mammoth, 16,000-square-ft building houses the District's best assortment of all kinds of music, plus videos, DVDs, and laser discs. Prices are a bit higher than at other stores, but no one beats the selection. *2000 Pennsylvania Ave. NW, Downtown, 202/331–2400. Metro: Foggy Bottom–GWU.*

music boxes

5 *g-5*

MUSIC BOX CENTER

An exquisite specialty store, the Music Box Center enchants with its extraordinary collection of music boxes—more than 1,500 different kinds, with almost as many different melodies. *1920 I St. NW, Downtown, 202/783–9399. Metro: Farragut West.*

musical instruments

8 *g-2*

GORDON KELLER MUSIC

Gordon Keller specializes in pianos, featuring world-famous names like Steinway, Baldwin, and Wurlitzer. You can also shop here for fine violins, cellos, guitars, and other instruments, and the selection of sheet music gives you something to play. *717 N. St. Asaph St., Old Town Alexandria, VA, 703/548–3230. Metro: King St.*

1 *e-3*

HOUSE OF MUSICAL TRADITIONS

If you're looking for a dulcimer or a sitar, or want to learn the difference between bluegrass and blues guitar, this nationally regarded shop carries uncommon instruments as well as books and recordings. *7040 Carroll Ave., Takoma Park, MD, 301/270–9090.*

NEEDLEWORK & KNITTING

IN STITCHES
In Stitches carries an almost overwhelming selection of counted cross-stitch supplies and offers custom framing for needlework. *8800 Pear Tree Ct., Alexandria, VA, 703/360–4600.*

1 c-1

INEZ'S STITCHERY
Inez has a good selection of needlepoint and knitting effects. *3706 Howard Ave., Kensington, MD, 301/942–6040.*

1 a-5

NEEDLEWOMAN EAST
This shop has a friendly, knowledgeable staff and the best supply of needlepoint in northern Virginia. *809C Broad St., Falls Church, VA, 703/241–0316.*

1 c-2

NEEDLEWORK ATTIC
The focuses here are needlepoint and knitting—there's an elegant array of knitting yarns—but the Attic also carries cross-stitch supplies. *4706 Bethesda Ave., Bethesda, MD, 301/652–8688. Metro: Bethesda.*

1 d-6

NIMBLE NEEDLES
For such a small shop, Nimble Needles packs a pretty good selection of cross-stitch charts and supplies. *Crystal City Mall, 1675 Crystal Mall Arc, Arlington, VA, 703/413–6363. Metro: Crystal City.*

2 b-3

THE POINT OF IT ALL
Considered the needlepoint nexus of the D.C. area, this store is positively brimming with gorgeous, hand-painted needlepoint canvases and tapestry yarns and silks. Owner Hyla Hurley will be happy to help you choose the right fibers and stitches for your project. Over the years she has organized professional designers from around the nation to stitch needlepoint ornaments for one of the White House Christmas trees. *3301 New Mexico Ave. NW, Tenleytown, 202/966–9898.*

THE SCARLET THREAD
This suburban shop is well stocked with cross-stitch charts, fabrics, and threads. *10409B Main St., Fairfax, VA, 703/591–4566.*

1 b-4

WOOLY KNITS
Knitters will find a great selection of specialty yarns here, as well as knitted garments on display for inspiration. *6728 Lowell Ave., McLean, VA, 703/448–9665.*

NEWSPAPERS & MAGAZINES

5 g-4

BORDERS BOOKS AND MUSIC
Many readers flock to Borders for its impressive selection of foreign newspapers, magazines, and periodicals. In fact, the area around the magazine racks can get downright crowded at times. Grab a few of your favorite reads and peruse them while sipping coffee in the café. *1800 L St. NW, Downtown, 202/466–4999. Metro: Farragut North.*

2 b-1

5333 Wisconsin Ave. NW, Upper Northwest, 202/686–8270. Metro: Friendship Heights.

1 d-6

The Fashion Centre at Pentagon City, 1000 S. Hayes St., Arlington, VA, 703/418–0166. Metro: Pentagon City.

1 c-1

White Flint Mall, 11301 Rockville Pike, MD, 301/816–1067. Metro: White Flint.

1 c-6

Crossroads Center, 5871 Crossroads Center Way, Baileys Crossroads, Falls Church, VA, 703/998–0404. Call for other locations.

5 h-5

NEWS WORLD
With a good range of the obscure as well as the popular newspapers and magazines, this downtown shop caters to neighboring law firms and media organizations. *1001 Connecticut Ave. NW, Downtown, 202/872–0190. Metro: Farragut North.*

5 f-2

THE NEWSROOM
Every city has a Newsroom: one vast collection of newspapers and magazines

from around the world. This store caters to commuters from the Dupont Circle Metro and to international guests from the Hilton up the street by staying open until 9 every night. *1753 Connecticut Ave. NW, Dupont Circle, 202/332–1489. Metro: Dupont Circle.*

10 *e-7*
TROVER BOOKS
Trover has the area's best selection of both national and international periodicals. *221 Pennsylvania Ave. SE, Capitol Hill, 202/547–2665. Metro: Capitol South.*

PETS & PET SUPPLIES

2 *b-2*
THE ANIMAL HUT
This exotic-pet shop has supplied unique birds, small pets, reptiles, amphibians, and tropical and marine fish to the D.C. area since 1973. *4620 Wisconsin Ave. NW, Upper Northwest, 202/363–1421. Metro: Tenleytown–AU.*

CREATURES 'N' CRITTERS
This Alexandria shop has dogs, cats, birds, reptiles, and tropical and marine fish. *13215 Gordon Blvd., Woodbridge, VA, 703/491–2300.*

1 *b-7*
LANDMARK PET SHOP
Tortoise and tropical-fish buyers can get friendly and helpful advice here along with their quiet new friends. *241 S. Van Dorn St., Alexandria, VA, 703/354–7222. Metro: Van Dorn St.*

2 *d-8*
PETSMART
Everything and anything your aquatic or four-legged friend might need can be found at Petsmart. Rather than selling cats and dogs, the store invites local shelters to bring in homeless animals, usually on weekends, in order to introduce them to potential adoptive families. There are even a veterinarian and groomer on the premises. *3351 Jefferson Davis Hwy., Alexandria, VA, 703/739–4844. Metro: King St.*

1 *b-5*
6100 Arlington Blvd., Falls Church, VA, 703/534–0774.

PHOTO EQUIPMENT

6 *c-6*
PENN CAMERA
Local photographers patronize Penn Camera in part for the expertise of its staff. Penn buys, trades, rents, and repairs equipment; it also offers a popular, high-quality developing service. *915 E St. NW, Downtown, 202/347–5777. Metro: Metro Center.*

5 *g-5*
RITZ CAMERA
Probably the best-known photo store in Washington, Ritz Camera has excellent special offers, especially for card-carrying customers. You can also have film developed here. *1776 I St. NW, Downtown, 202/467–0739. Metro: Farragut West. Call for other locations.*

6 *a-4*
RONCOM
This highly professional store stocks a wide range of cameras and equipment, despite its small size. *1451 L St. NW, Downtown, 202/722–8317. Metro: McPherson Sq.*

SPORTING GOODS & CLOTHING

9 *e-7*
BRITCHES GREAT OUTDOORS
This beloved local store features stylish American sportswear for both men and women—rugby shirts, khaki shorts, that sort of thing. The sales are great opportunities. *1247 Wisconsin Ave. NW, Georgetown, 202/338–3330. Metro: Foggy Bottom–GWU.*

9 *g-7*
EDDIE BAUER
Eddie Bauer is famous for tough, durable, and stylish sports clothes, all priced competitively. It also has a nice selection of luggage and camping equipment. *3040 M St. NW, Georgetown, 202/342–2121. Metro: Foggy Bottom–GWU.*

2 *b-2*
HUDSON TRAIL OUTFITTERS
As the outdoorsy name implies, Hudson Trail provides good-value clothes for a variety of healthy pursuits. *4530 Wiscon-*

sin Ave. NW, Upper Northwest, 202/363–9810. Metro: Tenleytown–AU.

2 *d-8*

THE SPORTS AUTHORITY

No matter what your sport, you'll find the equipment and the fashions to go with it at this superstore. Whether you're looking for something as large as an exercise machine or as small as a golf ball, you've come to the right place. *3601 Jefferson Davis Hwy., Alexandria, VA, 703/684–3204.*

camping & climbing

APPALACHIAN OUTFITTERS

Appalachian outfits you perfectly for camping, hiking, and climbing, among other sports, and offers expert advice in the process. *2938 Chain Bridge Rd., Oakton, VA, 703/281–4324.*

6 *c-6*

SUNNY'S, THE AFFORDABLE OUTDOOR STORE

This chain offers affordable military-surplus clothing, work boots by Timberland, work pants and overalls, and other durable, all-weather items. *912 F St. NW, Downtown, 202/737–2032. Metro: Metro Center.*

golf

2 *b-2*

ANGELO'S GOLF

If you're looking for a new set of clubs or need a repair on your driver, you've come to the right place. The knowledgeable staff can help with custom clubs and fittings. Golf-related books, videos, and gifts are also available. *4930 Wisconsin Ave. NW, Friendship Heights, 202/244–5105. Metro: Friendship Heights.*

riding

DOMINION SADDLERY

This serious tack and equipment shop makes things easy for customers far and wide with its toll-free number, 800/282–2587. *43717 John Mosby Hwy., Chantilly VA, 703/327–4423.*

JOURNEYMAN SADDLERY

In the heart of Virginia horse country, the chic and excellent Journeyman Saddlery draws the area's most beautiful people and sells the finest equestrian

equipment, clothes, and accessories their money can buy. *16 S. Madison St., Middleburg, VA, 540/687–5888.*

THE SADDLERY IN GREAT FALLS, LTD.

Horse lovers of all ages can get equipment, tack, and clothes here. *731-E Walker Rd., Great Falls, VA, 703/759–3500.*

WOODLAWN SADDLERY

Connected to the prestigious Woodlawn Plantation, just down the road from Mount Vernon, Woodlawn Saddlery carries everything the discerning equestrian's heart desires. *8405-J Richmond Hwy., Alexandria, VA, 703/360–2288.*

skiing

2 *b-2*

SKI CENTER

Serious skiers know that it's not just about technique; it's about looking good while you master it. The Ski Center caters to both needs. *4300 Fordham Rd. NW, Upper Northwest, 202/966–5413. Metro: Tenleytown–AU.*

tennis

1 *c-2*

EAST COAST GOLF & TENNIS

This suburban Maryland shop supplies tennis lovers with everything they'll need for court and club. *Hechinger Square, Bethesda, MD, 301/469–7000. Metro: Bethesda.*

2 *b-5*

THE TENNIS FACTORY

The Tennis Factory offers tennis players and players of other racquet sports good equipment at good prices. The store promises to restring racquets in less than 24 hours. *2500 Wilson Blvd., Arlington, VA, 703/522–2700. Metro: Court House.*

STATIONERY & OFFICE SUPPLIES

office supplies

1 *d-4*

OFFICE DEPOT

The robust Office Depot carries office supplies, furniture, business machines, computers, and software. *4455 Connecticut Ave. NW, Upper Northwest, 202/363–5758. Metro: Van Ness–UDC.*

5 *g-4*

1901 L St. NW, Downtown, 202/785–4616. Metro: Farragut West.

9 *d-7*

STAPLES

Billing itself as "The Office Superstore," Staples sells more than 6,000 reasonably priced items, and takes care to distinguish between the corporate and home office. *3307 M St. NW, Georgetown, 202/337–0187. Metro: Foggy Bottom–GWU.*

6 *b-5*

1250 H St. NW, Downtown, 202/638–3907. Metro: Metro Center.

5801 Crossroads Center Way, Falls Church, VA, 703/845–5600.

5 *h-5*

TIME EXPRESS

Time Express is a reliable downtown option for office supplies. *1776 I St. NW, Downtown, 202/223–0450. Metro: Farragut West.*

pens & pencils

6 *a-6*

FAHRNEY'S

This Washington institution has provided both residents and dignity-minded visitors with top-quality pens and elegant writing implements for decades. Brands include Cartier, Mont Blanc, and Waterman. *1317 F St. NW, Downtown, 202/628–9525. Metro: Metro Center.*

stationery

5 *g-4*

COPENHAVER

Stationers to Washingtonians for many a year, this small shop has a lovely selection of fine writing papers. *1301 Connecticut Ave. NW, Dupont Circle, 202/232–1200. Metro: Dupont Circle.*

2 *c-2*

DALTON BRODY, LTD.

This well-known gift shop is particularly strong on stationery. *3412 Idaho Ave. NW, Upper Northwest, 202/244–7197. Metro: Tenleytown–AU.*

9 *d-4*

ROOMS WITH A VIEW

This adorable store proudly features G. Lalo's classic French stationery alongside more modern paper designs. Rooms also has a nice gift selection, particularly for dog lovers and golf enthusiasts. *1661 Wisconsin Ave. NW, Georgetown, 202/625–0610. Metro: Foggy Bottom–GWU.*

THEATRICAL ITEMS

6 *h-8*

BACKSTAGE, THE PERFORMING ARTS STORE

Backstage is Washington's foremost theatrical store. Thespians can find everything from makeup and costumes to scripts, music, and posters. The only thing you can't buy here is acting talent; you'll need to provide that on your own. *545 8th St. SE, Capitol Hill, 202/544–5744. Metro: Eastern Market.*

1 *e-3*

KINETIC ARTISTRY, INC.

Kinetic sells and rents lighting, makeup, stage and studio rigging, wigs, and everything else a thespian is likely to need. *7216 Carroll Ave., Takoma Park, MD, 301/270–6666. Metro: Takoma.*

TOBACCONISTS

9 *f-7*

GEORGETOWN TOBACCO

Georgetown stocks a wide variety of tobacco products as well as accessories. The shop, in business since 1964, is popular with D.C. politicians. *3144 M St. NW, Georgetown, 202/338–5100. Metro: Foggy Bottom–GWU.*

1 *a-4*

Tysons Corner Center, 1961 Chain Bridge Rd., McLean, VA, 703/893–3366.

1 *c-2*

J. B. SIMS FINE TOBACCOS

Discerning pipe, cigar, and cigarette smokers tend to get to know this place. *4914 St. Elmo Ave., Bethesda, MD, 301/656–7123. Metro: Bethesda.*

MARLBORO TOBACCO MARKET

It's a bit of a hike from the District, but this tobacco shop has a large and interesting selection of cigar-, cigarette-, and pipe-smoking effects. *Upper Marlboro, MD, 301/627–3669.*

TOYS & GAMES

collectibles

10 d-2

THE GREAT TRAIN STORE

This unique store in Union Station has a vast collection of trains and train memorabilia for collectors of antique and contemporary trains. Displays include beginners' train sets, train accessories for aficionados of all ages, and a marvelous array of collectors' items, all accompanied by the appropriate train noises, scents, and expert personnel. *Union Station, 50 Massachusetts Ave. NE, Capitol Hill, 202/371–2881. Metro: Union Station.*

new

9 e-7

F. A. O. SCHWARZ

An outpost of the classic New York City toy store, F. A. O. Schwarz contains the makings of any child's wildest dreams. Along with traditional toy-store offerings, the shop has a large section devoted to dolls and stuffed animals. *3222 M St. NW, Georgetown, 202/965–7000. Metro: Foggy Bottom–GWU.*

2 c-3

SULLIVAN'S TOY STORE

Native Washingtonians who shopped here as children now bring their own kids to this classic toy store established in 1954. In an era saturated by digital diversions, bring your tykes here for the reliable standbys of board games, arts-and-crafts kits, and kites. *3412 Wisconsin Ave. NW, Cleveland Park, 202/362–1343. Metro: Tenleytown–AU.*

TOYS R US

The national toy and game emporium supplies tykes throughout the area with this year's playtime rage. *5521 Leesburg Pike, Baileys Crossroads, Falls Church, VA, 703/820–2428.*

8 g-4

WHY NOT?

This shop is a standout, with a nicely edited selection of unique toys, games, clothes, books, hats, and shoes. A tal-ented silhouettist drops in occasionally; a nice silhouette of your favorite young one makes a wonderful gift—for them, their loved ones, or yourself. *200 King St., Old Town Alexandria, VA, 703/548–4420. Metro: King St.*

UMBRELLAS & RAINWEAR

Your best bet for a quick fix in the rain is to buy umbrellas at stands on downtown street corners, especially K Street NW, for $10 or less. More vendors emerge from the woodwork when it rains. You can also find pretty umbrellas, some printed with Impressionist paintings or floral patterns, at Proper Topper, on Connecticut Avenue (*see* Hats *in* Clothing for Women/Specialties, *above*).

5 h-4

BURBERRY

Burberry is, of course, best known for nasty-weather gear: raincoats, umbrellas, and distinctive scarves, all adorned somehow with a Burberry plaid. *1155 Connecticut Ave. NW, Downtown, 202/463–3000. Metro: Farragut North.*

VIDEOS

2 c-4

BLOCKBUSTER VIDEO

Best known for its vast rental selection, this nationwide chain also sells a good number of videos at competitive prices. The best deals are the previously viewed movies, which cost just a few dollars more than a rental. *2332 Wisconsin Ave., Glover Park, 202/625–6200. Metro: Tenleytown–AU.*

3 e-6

3519 Connecticut Ave. NW, Cleveland Park, 202/363–9500. Metro: Cleveland Park.

2 b-1

5440 Western Ave., Chevy Chase, MD, 301/652–7171. Metro: Friendship Heights.

5 h-3

1639 P St. NW, Dupont Circle, 202/232–2682. Metro: Dupont Circle.

10 h-7

400 8th St. SE, Capitol Hill, 202/546–4044. Metro: Eastern Market.

5 *f-5*

TOWER RECORDS

The largest single music and video store in the area, Tower Records has videos to rent as well as buy. *2000 Pennsylvania Ave. NW, Downtown, 202/223–3900.*

5 *f-2*

WASHINGTON VIDEO

This local chain, where you can rent or buy videos, carries a wide selection of foreign and independent films and cult classics as well as popular new releases. They also have a book and computer log that allows you to look up virtually every film released by actor, director, or title. *2012 S St. NW, Dupont Circle, 202/265–1141. Metro: Dupont Circle.*

5 *h-3*

1511 17th St. NW, Dupont Circle, 202/ 667–8868. Metro: Dupont Circle.

7 *c-2*

401 M St. SW, Waterfront, 202/646–0830. Metro: Waterfront–SEU.

WATCHES & CLOCKS

1 *c-2*

ECKERS CLOCK & WATCH SHOP

Eckers focuses on repairs and is known for top-notch service but also sells an assortment of contemporary and antique watches and clocks. *8010 Nor-*

folk Ave., Bethesda, MD, 301/652–0549. Metro: Bethesda.

contemporary

2 *b-1*

CARTIER

Few names symbolize style and elegance more so than Cartier, the world-famous French watchmaker and jeweler. If diamonds are your or your girl's best friend, this is the shop for you. *5454 Wisconsin Ave., Chevy Chase, MD, 301/654–5858. Metro: Friendship Heights.*

1 *a-4*

LILJENQUIST AND BECKSTEAD

McLean's official Rolex jeweler, this store has a large selection of Rolex and other internationally known watches. *The Galleria at Tysons II, 2001 International Dr., McLean, VA, 703/448–6731.*

1 *d-6*

SWATCH

Choose from hundreds of the store brand's eye-catching, waterproof, up-to-the-minute timepieces. *The Fashion Centre at Pentagon City, 1000 S. Hayes St., Arlington, VA, 703/415–3447. Metro: Pentagon City.*

10 *d-2*

Swatch Kiosk, Union Station, 50 Massachusetts Ave. NE, Capitol Hill. Metro: Union Station.

chapter 3

PARKS, GARDENS, & SPORTS

Washington's 69 square mi form a heck of a backyard. There are hundreds of grassy spaces, from the mammoth Rock Creek Park to the tiny Sonny Bono Triangle; from national parks that serve millions each year to little green pockets that cater to a handful of happy dogs. The National Arboretum grows towering pines, miniature bonsai, and everything in-between; Dumbarton Oaks maintains formal French gardens; the C&O Canal is lined with miles of trails for devoted calorie-burners; and the National Mall is perfect for those who just want to lie in the grass and stare at the monuments. When natural beauty isn't enough, consider that Washington maintains 93 recreation centers, 45 public pools, and 156 public tennis courts, all free for D.C. residents. Couch—or stadium—potatoes have a glut of professional sports teams on their doorstep: the Washington Redskins football team, the Washington Wizards basketball team, and the Washington Capitals hockey team, not to mention the relatively new D.C. United soccer team and Washington Mystics women's basketball team. Not every D.C. quarterback works out of an armchair.

parks

You never have to venture far if you're craving a swath of grass or a shade tree: this is one of the greenest metropolitan areas in the country, with park space covering 8,673 acres in the District alone. And just outside the city limits, Maryland's Montgomery County can claim the largest protected urban green space in the United States, a whopping 93,252 acres of virtually car-free land. For general information on any aspect of the urban outdoors or public sports fields, call the D.C. Department of Parks and Recreation at 202/673–7660 or 202/673–7647.

2 g-6
ANACOSTIA PARK
Encompassing more than 1,200 acres along the Anacostia River, this is one of the largest parks in the city, and it's heavily utilized by the surrounding neighborhoods. There's a little something for everyone here: softball fields, basketball courts, tennis courts, picnic facilities, even roller-skating in the Anacostia Park Pavilion. The park also contains the Kenilworth Aquatic Gardens (see Botanical Gardens, below) and the Langston Golf Course (see Golf, below). You can access the river from three concession-operated marinas as well as a public boat ramp. Between S. Capitol St. and Benning Rd. SE, Anacostia, 202/690–5185. Metro: Anacostia.

2 b-3
BATTERY-KEMBLE PARK
Located in a quiet corner of Northwest D.C., Battery-Kemble is a relaxing spread of rolling green where dogs frolic year-round and children sled in the winter. The park served as a military outpost during the Civil War, and you can still see the parapet and gun positions among the honeysuckle and the dogwood and poplar trees. Chain Bridge Rd. between Nebraska Ave. and MacArthur Blvd. NW, Plisades, 202/282–1063.

1 c-4
C&O CANAL NATIONAL HISTORIC PARK
Although it's one of the most popular recreational spaces in the city, this linear stretch is not a park in the conventional sense; it's more like a giant nature trail and exploring path. The grounds extend for 184½ mi, starting in Georgetown (behind the Four Seasons hotel) and continuing to Cumberland, Maryland. The towpath, where mules pulled barges full of coal and other heavy loads in the 19th century, is now a packed-dirt and gravel surface suitable for jogging, running, walking, and biking. Along the way you'll see thick woodlands; a variety of birds and animals, including deer, beavers, and foxes; and hundreds of original locks, lock houses, and aqueducts, reminders of times past. You can picnic, fish, and boat at various points along the canal. Mule-drawn boat rides—guided by National Park Service rangers dressed in period costume are offered from April through November at Georgetown and Great Falls, Virginia. Visitor center: 1057 Thomas Jefferson St. NW, Georgetown, 202/653–5190. Metro: Foggy Bottom–GWU.

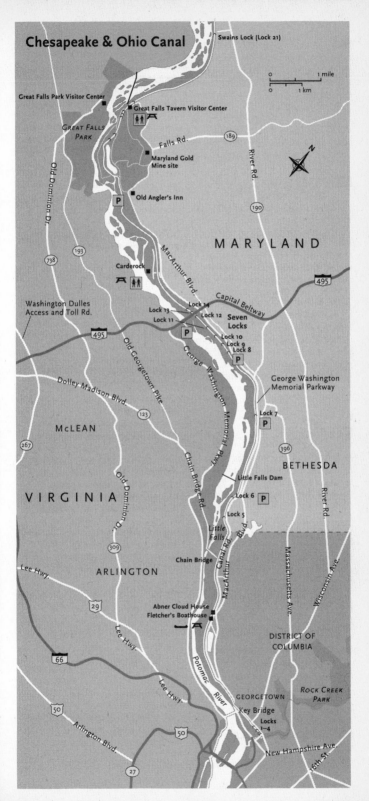

Chesapeake & Ohio Canal

Swains Lock (Lock 21)

Great Falls Park Visitor Center

Great Falls Tavern Visitor Center

GREAT FALLS PARK

Falls Rd.

189

River Rd.

Maryland Gold Mine site

Old Angler's Inn

P

MacArthur Blvd.

190

Old Dominion Dr.

738

193

Carderock

MARYLAND

495

Capital Beltway

Washington Dulles Access and Toll Rd.

Lock 14

Lock 13

Lock 12

Lock 11

Seven Locks

495

Old Georgetown Pike

P

George Washington Memorial Pkwy.

Lock 10

Lock 9

Lock 8

P

Dolley Madison Blvd.

123

George Washington Memorial Parkway

267

McLEAN

Lock 7

P

396

BETHESDA

River Rd.

VIRGINIA

Old Dominion Dr.

Chain Bridge Rd.

Little Falls Dam

Lock 6

P

309

Lock 5

Little Falls

Canal Rd.

MacArthur Blvd.

Massachusetts Ave.

Wisconsin Ave.

Lee Hwy.

ARLINGTON

Chain Bridge

29

Abner Cloud House

Fletcher's Boathouse

DISTRICT OF COLUMBIA

66

Lee Hwy.

Potomac River

GEORGETOWN

Rock Creek Park

50

Key Bridge

Locks 1–4

Arlington Blvd.

50

New Hampshire Ave.

16th St.

27

5 *c-1*

DUMBARTON OAKS PARK

This beautifully landscaped 27-acre park was originally part of the Dumbarton Oaks estate, but today it is administered by the National Park Service. It's especially lovely in spring, when a rainbow of wildflowers bloom. *Enter through Montrose Park, R St. between 31st and 32nd Sts. NW, Georgetown, no phone.*

5 *g-3*

DUPONT CIRCLE

The largest of Washington's traffic-circle parks, this is also one of the busiest and most heavily used green patches in town. Five major roads converge here—Massachusetts, New Hampshire, and Connecticut avenues, and P and 19th streets—throwing people from all walks of life together. Retirees play chess, workers eat their lunches, women minding toddlers chat in groups, teenagers lie in the grass. The circle is also the unofficial meeting place of the city's bike messengers: every weekday at dusk they fill one quadrant of the park, looking like a flock of pigeons descending on bread crumbs. *Metro: Dupont Circle.*

2 *e-6*

7 *b-4*

EAST POTOMAC PARK

An urban jewel, East Potomac Park is a man-made 327-acre peninsula between the Washington Channel and the Potomac River. The perimeter is lined

---

D.C. RECREATION ON-LINE

For great indoor information on the great outdoors, hit some of these colorful and informative Web sites.

D.C. Department of Parks and Recreation
  www.dcrecreation.com

D.C. Online Outdoors/Recreation
  www.washdc.org/rec.html

D.C. Pages.com
  dcpages.com/Recreation

National Capital Parks
  www.nps.gov/nacc

Potomac Appalachian Trail Club
  www.patc.net

Washington D.C. Fun and Recreation
  www.his.com/~matson

---

with cherry trees that bloom about two weeks later than the ones around the Tidal Basin, a nice trick to know if you want to catch the sweet pink blossoms without fighting the crowds. At the southern tip is Hains Point, a popular picnicking and fishing spot as well as the location of the unique *Awakening*, a fantastical sculpture of giant man emerging from the ground. Hains Point is also home to a 6,303-yard golf course, a miniature-golf course, and a 100-stall driving range. Still other attractions are a public pool with changing facilities, tennis courts, picnic facilities, and a 5-mi jogging path. *Ohio Dr. SW, south of Independence Ave., Waterfront, 202/619–7222. Metro: Smithsonian.*

2 *h-6*

FORT DUPONT PARK

Once the site of a Civil War defense fortification, Fort Dupont Park is now used for free jazz concerts in the summer, ice-skating in the winter, and basketball, softball, and picnicking whenever the weather cooperates. *Fort Dupont Dr. and Massachusetts Ave. SE, Dupont Park, 202/426–7723. Metro: Stadium–Armory.*

2 *b-3*

GLOVER-ARCHBOLD PARK

A gift to the city in 1924 from Charles C. Glover and Anne Archbold, these 183 acres of virgin beechwoods, wildflowers, and other greenery provide a shady repose for both birds and people. A nature trail starts at 44th Street and Reservoir Road and crisscrosses the Foundry Branch stream for the 3-mi length of the park. Picnic areas invite alfresco dining. *Between 39th and 44th Sts. from MacArthur Blvd. to Van Ness St. NW, Glover Park, 202/282–1063.*

2 *a-4*

GREAT FALLS PARK

Straddling the Virginia–Maryland border, the Great Falls are 76 ft of rushing Potomac waters cascading down a series of sheer rock cliffs. The view is spectacular, and it draws hundreds of thousands of visitors each year. The falls are popular with rock-climbing enthusiasts, who can choose from 17 different cliff faces. (Anyone can climb; just register on the lower level of the visitors center first.) Swimming and wading are prohibited, but you can fish with a license from D.C., Virginia, or Maryland. Kayakers can often be seen on the river gorge, but they're plenty experienced—the currents here are often deadly. A little less risky are the 15 mi of trails, suitable for bikers, hikers, and horses. The least strenuous, and probably most popular, way to enjoy the park is to plop down with a picnic; there are plenty of tables and grills, and Mother Nature provides unbeatable scenery. Autumn is a particularly brisk time to visit. *9200 Old Dominion Dr., Great Falls, VA, 703/285–2965 or 703/285–2966.*

5 *c-8*
2 *c-6*

LADY BIRD JOHNSON PARK

Situated on an island in the Potomac, this long and narrow park was dedicated to Johnson in 1968 in recognition of her efforts in outdoor beautification. Oaks, maples, and nearly 3,000 flowering dogwoods compete for attention with the springtime bloom of nearly a million daffodils—an incredible sight. *Access from Virginia only, on George Washington Memorial Pkwy. between Memorial Bridge and I–395, no phone.*

2 *e-5*

LAFAYETTE SQUARE PARK

Directly across from the White House and Pennsylvania Avenue, this pretty, petite park makes almost nightly appearances on the evening news as the site of year-round protesters trying to get the president's attention. Once you get past the political travails of the group du jour, however, you'll be rewarded with lovely flower beds and well-tended trees including Norway maples, elms, oaks, and magnolias. Dominating the square is a statue of Andrew Jackson; notwithstanding the name of the park, Lafayette is commemorated with a much smaller monument. *Between Pennsylvania Ave., H St., and Madison and Jackson Pls., Downtown, no phone. Metro: Farragut West.*

2 *c-6*

LYNDON B. JOHNSON MEMORIAL GROVE

When the traffic on the George Washington Memorial Parkway gets to you, duck into this 17-acre grove planted within Lady Bird Johnson Park in honor of LBJ. Breathe deeply among white pine trees, flowering dogwoods, azaleas, and rhododendrons. A 1-mi trail runs through it. *George Washington Memorial Pkwy. between Memorial Bridge and I–395, no phone.*

3 *h-8*

MERIDIAN HILL PARK

Also known as Malcolm X Park (after a speech he gave here in the early '70s), this space provides a lovely respite from the urban and somewhat depressed neighborhood in which it's located. The park was created in the 1920s; its upper portion was designed in the manner of a formal French garden, and the lower level recalls an Italian Renaissance garden. Terraces, a broad stairway, promenades, and cascading waterfalls combine to make these 12 acres enchanting. The thriving 16th Street neighborhood has taken Meridian Hill under its wing, so the park is much safer and more enjoyable now than in years past. *Bounded by 15th, 16th, Euclid, and W Sts. NW, Columbia Heights, 202/ 282–1063. Metro: U St.–Cardozo.*

5 *c-2*

MONTROSE PARK

Once part of the Dumbarton Oaks estate, this park comprises 16 acres of rugged wooded terrain. Dogs love to romp here, but humans also enjoy the tennis courts and picnic facilities, including a screened gazebo. The western boundary, known as Lovers' Lane, is an old cobblestone path that led all the way to Baltimore in the 18th century. *R St. between 30th and 31st Sts., NW, Georgetown, no phone.*

6 *c-7*

NATIONAL MALL

When French architect Pierre Charles L'Enfant designed this fair city, he left plenty of room for a large green expanse, which he pictured as a "Grand Avenue, 400 ft in breadth, and about a mile in length, bordered with gardens, ending in a slope from the houses on each side." In the middle of the 19th century, a horticulturist named Andrew Jackson Downing took a stab at converting the Mall into a large, English-style garden, with disastrous results; fortunately, in 1900, Senator James McMillan hired famed landscape architect Frederick Law Olmsted, Jr., the force behind New York's famed Central Park, to improve the Washington park system. Olmsted rediscovered L'Enfant's original plan, and the National Mall was estab-

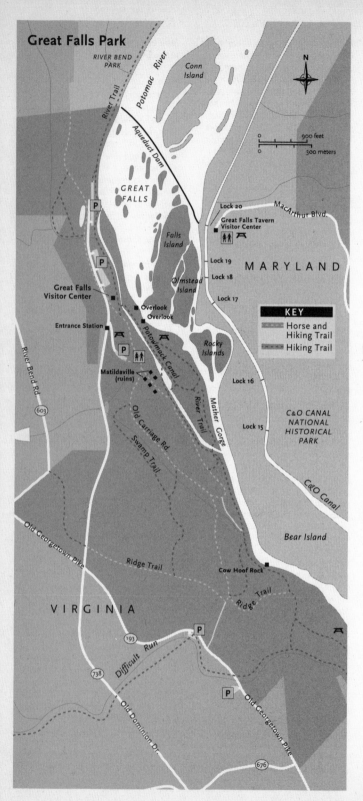

Great Falls Park

RIVER BEND
PARK

Potomac River

Conn
Island

River Trail

Aqueduct Dam

GREAT
FALLS

Lock 20

Great Falls Tavern
Visitor Center

MacArthur Blvd.

Falls
Island

Lock 19

MARYLAND

Great Falls
Visitor Center

Olmstead
Island

Lock 18

Lock 17

Overlook
Overlook

Entrance Station

Patowmack Canal

Rocky
Islands

N

900 feet

300 meters

KEY

Horse and
Hiking Trail

Hiking Trail

River Trail

Mather Gorge

Lock 16

Matildaville
(ruins)

River Bend Rd.

603

Old Carriage Rd

Swamp Trail

Lock 15

C&O CANAL
NATIONAL
HISTORICAL
PARK

C&O Canal

Bear Island

Ridge Trail

Old Georgetown Pike

Ridge Trail

Cow Hoof Rock

VIRGINIA

193

Difficult Run

738

Old Dominion Dr.

Old Georgetown Pike

676

106

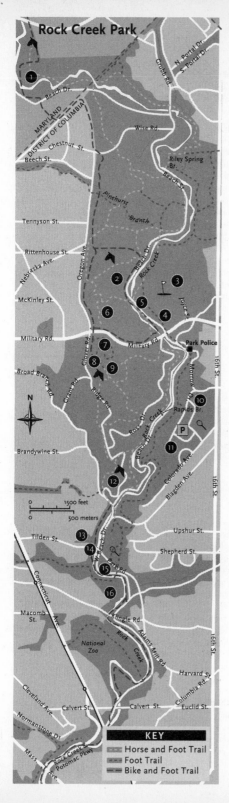

Rock Creek Park

1. Candy Cane City
2. Park Police Stables
3. Public Golf Course
4. Field House
5. Miller Cabin
6. Fort De Russey
7. Planetarium
7. Rock Creek Nature Center
8. Dog Training
8. Park Headquarters
9. Horse Center
10. Brightwood Rec Area
11. Carter Barron Amphitheater
12. Equitation Field
13. Art Barn
14. Pierce Mill
15. Jusserand Memorial
16. Klingle Mansion

KEY

- Horse and Foot Trail
- Foot Trail
- Bike and Foot Trail

lished in all of its grandeur. Today the Mall is a verdant playground, 146 acres bounded by the museums of the Smithsonian Institution and rows of elms, and officially marked by the Washington Monument, to the west, and the U.S. Capitol, to the east.

Just about anything goes on the Mall—within reason of course. (This is still Washington.) You can play catch, bounce a Hacky Sack, fling a Frisbee, or simply jog, bike, or walk the gravel path that runs along the edges of the grassy main area. One challenging and decorative Mall activity is kite-flying near the Washington Monument. (If you forget to bring your own, the shop at the nearby National Air and Space Museum has a nice selection.) Since being transferred to the National Park Service in 1933, the National Mall has hosted celebrations, festivals, demonstrations, and protests. *Bounded by Constitution and Independence Aves. and 1st and 23rd Sts., Downtown, 202/426–6841. Metro: Smithsonian.*

6 *a-6*
PERSHING PARK
Built in 1981 as part of the rehabilitation of Pennsylvania Avenue, this park is a popular downtown retreat. Its central, waterfall-fed pool becomes a public skating rink in winter. *Pennsylvania Ave. between 14th and 15th Sts., Downtown, no phone. Metro: McPherson Sq.*

1 *d-3*
ROCK CREEK PARK
The largest and most impressive park in the Washington area, Rock Creek serves as a giant oasis within the city, occupying 1,800 forested acres that run up to and overlap the Maryland border. Natural, historic, and recreational features all abound, and there are facilities for picnicking, horseback riding, tennis, and golf. A boon for residents: the main traffic artery through the park, Beach Drive, is closed on weekends and holidays between Joyce and Broad Branch roads, providing a safe, if somewhat crowded, path for bikers, in-line skaters, joggers, and hikers. In summer, the Carter Barron Amphitheater (16th Street and Colorado Avenue NW) stages free Shakespeare in the Park and a variety of other performances. Park rangers are headquartered at the Nature Center and Planetarium (Military and Glover roads),

from which they lead nature walks on weekends. *Nature Center: 5000 Glover Rd. NW, Tenleytown, 202/282–1063. Metro: Tenleytown–AU.*

2 *d-5*
2 *d-6*
WEST POTOMAC PARK
This area along the Potomac River leading up to the Lincoln Memorial and surrounding the Tidal Basin is the setting for one of Washington's premier annual events: the blooming of the cherry-blossom trees, donated to the United States by Japan in 1912. Every spring, hundreds of trees blossom right along the water, turning the area into a gentle pink glade. You can rent a paddleboat here and set off for water views of the Lincoln, Jefferson, and FDR memorials. *Bounded by Independence Ave., Ohio Dr., and 15th St., Waterfront, no phone. Metro: Smithsonian.*

botanical gardens

Admission is free unless otherwise noted.

3 *a-6*
BISHOP'S GARDEN
On the grounds of Washington National Cathedral, this medieval-style garden has orchids, boxwood, magnolias, herbs, and a variety of other flowers. It's a restful spot for quiet contemplation. *Wisconsin and Massachusetts Aves. NW, Cathedral Heights, 202/537–6200. Metro: Tenleytown–AU, then bus (call for details).*

2 *d-5*
CONSTITUTION GARDENS
This natural 50-acre setting contains a small lake whose 1-acre island, accessible by footbridge, is inhabited by mallard ducks and turtles. An island memorial commemorates the signers of the U.S. Constitution. The open meadows invite picnics. *West Potomac Park, along Constitution Ave. between 21st and 17th Sts. NW, Waterfront, no phone. Metro: Smithsonian.*

5 *c-1*
DUMBARTON OAKS GARDENS
These 10 acres of breathtakingly beautiful formal gardens in the heart of

Georgetown are part of the Dumbarton Oaks estate and incorporate pools, fountains, and sculpture. Designed by noted landscape architect Beatrix Farrand, the gardens combine elements of the traditional English, Italian, and French styles. A highlight is the Orangery (circa 1810), which contains a variety of potted trees and a fig planted before the Civil War; the fig now covers the walls and beams of the interior, giving it an enchanted feel. There are also a formal rose garden, a towering bamboo stand, and an English country garden. Picnics are not allowed, but lingering for quiet thought and reflection is encouraged. *R and 31st Sts. NW, Georgetown, 202/339–6410. Admission Apr.–Oct. $4; free rest of year. Open Apr.–Oct., daily 2–6; Nov.–Mar., daily 2–5.*

2 *c-2*
HILLWOOD
Designed for cereal heiress Marjorie Merriweather Post, these formal gardens contain more than 3,500 varieties of plants and trees. Among the many delights are a complete Japanese garden with bridges, waterfall, and stone lanterns; a formal French garden; and an extensive rose garden. *4155 Linnean Ave. NW, North Cleveland Park, 202/686–5807. Admission $2 (grounds only). Open Mar.–Jan., Tues.–Sat. 9–5. Metro: Van Ness–UDC.*

3 *c-7*
KAHLIL GIBRAN MEMORIAL GARDEN
Dedicated to the famed Lebanese poet and philosopher, this tiny park features limestone benches with engraved quotations of the poet. The serene environment is nicely conducive to quiet contemplation. *3100 block of Massachusetts Ave. NW, Woodley Park, no phone. Metro: Woodley Park–Zoo.*

2 *h-4*
KENILWORTH AQUATIC GARDENS
The Kenilworth Aquatic Gardens are a magnificent collection of exotic, often giant, flowering aquatic plants on part of the original marshland that became Anacostia Park. Exotic water lilies, lotuses, and hyacinths are just a few of the water-loving species that thrive here, but they're not all: the gardens are home to a variety of wetland animals, including turtles, frogs, and some 40 species of birds. *Anacostia Park, Anacostia Ave. and Douglas St. NE, Anacostia, 202/426–6905. Open: gardens daily 6:30–4; visitor center daily 8–4; garden tour summer weekends at 9, 11, and 1. Metro: Anacostia.*

2 *g-4*
NATIONAL ARBORETUM
Both a research facility and a living museum, the National Arboretum comprises 446 acres of display gardens, special collections, and historical monuments set among native stands of Eastern deciduous trees. Among the highlights are the National Bonsai and Penjing Museum, with miniature trees ranging in age from 20 to 380 years; the Herbarium, with 600,000 dried plants grown in the National Herb Garden; the Gotelli Dwarf Conifer collection, one of the finest groves of conifers in the world; and the Capitol Columns, 22 of the original sandstone Corinthian columns that once stood on the east portico of the U.S. Capitol and now create a picturesque landmark in the arboretum. The arboretum is a favorite warm-weather picnic spot, but keep in mind that picnicking is only allowed in the National Grove of State Trees. Sports are prohibited. *24th and R Sts. NE, off New York Ave., 202/245–2726. Open daily 8–5; bonsai collection daily 10–3:30.*

6 *d-8*
UNITED STATES BOTANIC GARDEN
Within the glass-and-aluminum conservatory are extensive collections of azaleas (more than 90 varieties), lilies, cacti, citrus, orchids, and more than 300 varieties of chrysanthemums. Simulated environments include a jungle, a rain forest, and collections of tropical and subtropical plants. Oddly enough, the Botanic Garden makes a great escape on a rainy day; take a bag lunch and plop down on a bench for a complete change of pace. The new National Garden, scheduled to open in the spring of 2001, will include an environmental learning center and rose, water, and showcase gardens. *1st St. and Maryland Ave. SW, Downtown, 202/225–8333. Open daily 9–5. Metro: Smithsonian.*

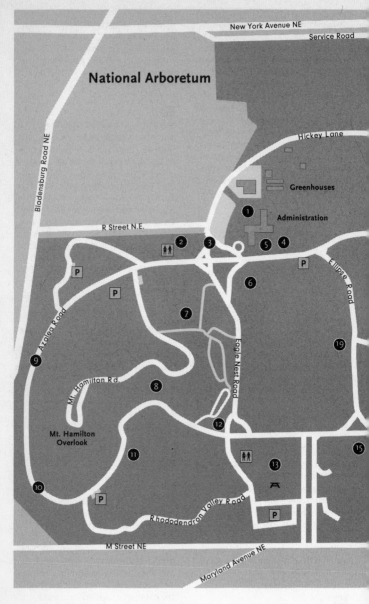

National Arboretum

New York Avenue NE
Service Road

Bladensburg Road NE

Hickey Lane

Greenhouses

Administration

R Street N.E.

Ellipse Road

Azalea Road

Mt. Hamilton Rd.

Eagle Nest Road

Mt. Hamilton
Overlook

Rhododendron Valley Road

M Street NE

Maryland Avenue NE

1 Court of Honor	**9** Crab Apples	**17** Washington Youth Garden
2 Information Center	**10** Viburnum	**18** Fern Valley
3 Friendship Garden	**11** Azalea Valley	**19** National Capitol Columns
4 Bonsai and Penjing Collection	**12** Morrison Azalea Garden	**20** Beech Pond Gazebo
5 Aquatic Gardens	**13** State Trees	**21** Crab Apples
6 Herb Garden	**14** Native Plants	**22** Magnolias
7 Lee Azalea Garden	**15** Shade Trees	**23** Crape Myrtles
8 Azalea Hillside	**16** Shade Trees	

Conifer Road

Visitor's Entrance

Dogwood Circle

Kingman Lake Overlook

Holly Spring Road

Meadow Road

Hickory Hill Overlook

Valley Road

Hickey Run

Beech Spring Pond

Crabtree Road

Hickey Hill Road

Crabtree Road

Kingman Lake Overlook

Anacostia River

N

0   300 feet
0   100 meters

24 Legumes
25 Maples
26 Japanese Maples
27 Dwarf Conifer Collection
28 Gotelli and Watnong Conifer Collection
29 Dawn Redwoods
30 Japanese Woodland

31 Chadwick Overlook
32 Korean Hillside
33 China Valley
34 Garden Club Pagoda

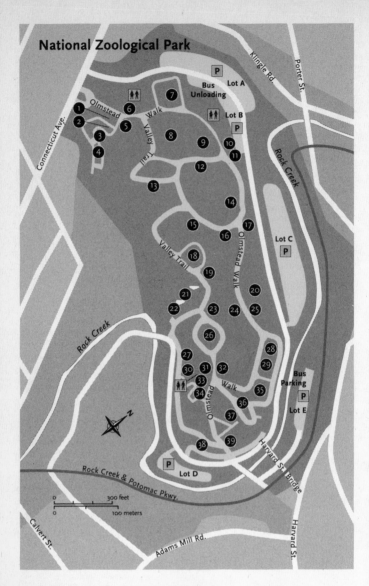

National Zoological Park

1 Tapirs	**14** Hippos & Rhinos	**27** Jaguars
2 Hoofed Animals	**15** Free Ranging Tamarins	**28** Reptile House
3 Wetlands and Eagles	**16** Beavers, Otters, Pumas	**29** Invertebrates
4 Bird House	**17** Concession Stand	**30** Amazonia
5 Bongos	**18** Bison	**31** Prairie Dogs
6 Visitors Center and Gift Shop	**19** Wolves	**32** Monkey Island
7 Cheetahs	**20** Small Mammal House	**33** Police & First Aid
8 Australia Pavilion	**21** Seals & Sea Lions	**34** Mane Restaurant
9 Panda & Panda Cafe	**22** Spectacled Bears	**35** Monkey House
10 Food & Gift Shops	**23** Seal Gift Shop	**36** Lion-Tiger Hill
11 Information & Strollers	**24** Gibbon Ridge	**37** Bats
12 Elephants & Giraffes	**25** Great Ape House	**38** Waterfowl
13 Birds	**26** Bears	**39** Information & Strollers

zoos & aquariums

6 a-7

NATIONAL AQUARIUM

Established in 1873, this is the nation's oldest public aquarium, with more than 1,200 fish and other creatures—such as eels, sharks, and alligators—representing 270 species of fresh- and saltwater life. The exhibits have a somewhat dated look; but the easy-to-view tanks, accessible touching pool (with crabs and sea urchins), low admission fee, and general lack of crowds make this a good outing with children. You'll have to come in through the lackluster entrance in the U.S. Department of Commerce building. *U.S. Department of Commerce Bldg., Room B-037, 14th St. and Constitution Ave. NW, Downtown, 202/482–2825. Admission $3. Open daily 9–5; sharks fed Mon., Wed., and Sat. at 2; piranhas fed Tues., Thurs., and Sun. at 2. Metro: Federal Triangle or Metro Center.*

1 d-4

NATIONAL ZOOLOGICAL PARK

Located at the edge of Rock Creek Park and run by the Smithsonian Institution, the National Zoo is one of the world's greatest. Most animals are housed and exhibited in natural habitats lush with trees, bushes, rocks, and small streams. For years the zoo's most famous residents were the giant pandas Hsing-Hsing and Ling-Ling, donated by China in 1972. Sadly, the female Ling-Ling died in 1993 and was followed by her partner in 1999. At press time, the National Zoo had just acquired on loan for ten years two new pandas, male Tian-Tian and female Mei Xiang, from China. There are literally thousands of animals on display here; you could see everything in one brisk day, but if you live nearby, consider coming to see one favorite exhibit at a time. (Admission is free.) Some suggestions: the Reptile Discovery Center, where amphibians slither and slide; Amazonia, a reproduction of a South American rainforest ecosystem, kept at a steamy 85°F; the Gorilla Outdoor Yard; Komodo dragons, the first to be successfully bred in the West; the Great Flight Cage, a walk-in aviary in which birds fly unrestricted from May to October; the Cheetah Conservation Area; and the Grasslands exhibit, complete with bison and prairie dogs. *3000 block of Connecticut Ave. NW, Wood-ley Park, 202/673– 4800 or 202/673–4717. Open May–mid-Sept., grounds daily 6AM–8PM, animal buildings daily 10–6 (may be open later in summer); mid-Sept.–Apr., grounds daily 6–6, animal buildings daily 10–4:30. Metro: Cleveland Park or Woodley Park–Zoo.*

stadiums

FEDEX FIELD

This 80,000-seat stadium is the home of the Washington Redskins, and moonlights as a stage for concerts and other special events. *Arena Dr., off Capital Beltway (Exit 17), Landover, MD, 301/276–6050.*

6 h-5

MCI CENTER

A state-of-the-art stadium downtown, the MCI Center is home to the NHL's Capitals, the NBA's Wizards, the WNBA's Mystics, and the NCAA Georgetown Hoyas basketball team. The arena also hosts concerts and a wide array of special events. Outside the spotlight, the center houses the National Sports Gallery, an interactive sports memorabilia museum. The massive, four-floor Discovery Channel Store brings the natural world to your shopping bag with everything from gems and minerals to airplane models. *7th and G Sts. NW, Downtown, 202/628–3200. Metro: Gallery Pl.–Chinatown.*

2 g-5

ROBERT F. KENNEDY STADIUM

Still surrounded by a healthy 55,750 seats, the former Redskins field is now used exclusively for professional soccer. D.C. United plays its Major League Soccer matches here, and other international soccer events occasionally breeze through. *See Soccer, below. E. Capitol St. SE, Capitol Hill, 202/547–9077. Metro: Stadium–Armory.*

sports & outdoor activities

With two new sports venues in the Washington, D.C., area—FedEx Field

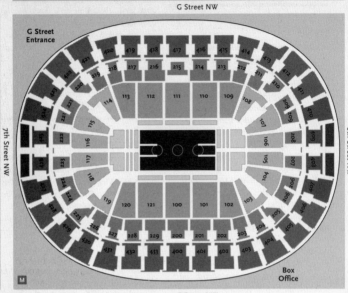

G Street NW

G Street
Entrance

7th Street NW

Box
Office

F Street NW

MCI Center

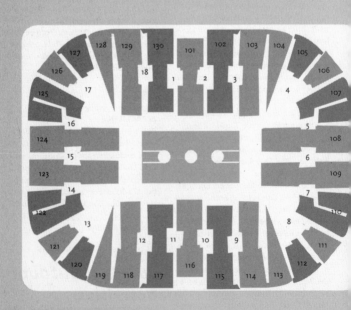

Patriot Stadium

114

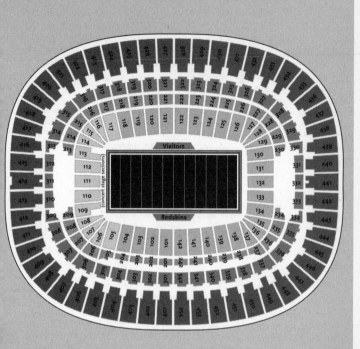

FedEx Field

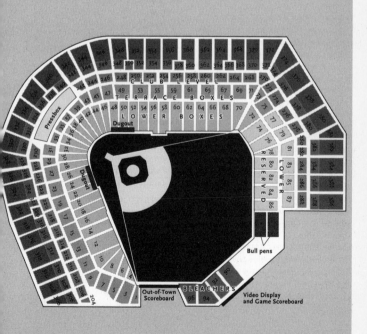

Oriole Park at Camden Yards

and the MCI Center, both born in 1997—sports fans have a lot to cheer about. The Redskins' move from Robert F. Kennedy Stadium to FedEx Field increased the number of fan seats by nearly a third (games, however, still sell out regularly). The 20,000-seat MCI Center brings athletic and special events to the heart of downtown, just outside the Gallery Place metro station; the NBA's Wizards, NHL's Capitals, WNBA's Mystics, and the Hoyas (Georgetown's Division 1 basketball team) play here.

BASEBALL

Alas, D.C. doesn't have a baseball team to call its own. If the ballpark urge strikes, remember that the Baltimore Orioles are just 40 mi north.

teams to watch

BALTIMORE ORIOLES

The closest Washington has to a home team, the Orioles play in the beautiful, 48,000-seat Camden Yards at Oriole Park. Tickets range from $9 for spots in the bleachers to $35 for club level. *333 W. Camden St., Baltimore, MD; tickets in D.C. 202/432–7328.*

BOWIE BAYSOX

The Orioles' Class AA farm team plays in a 10,000-seat stadium in suburban Prince George's County, Maryland, about 45 minutes by car from Washington. Tickets range from $4 to $12, and children ages 6 to 12 wearing Little League uniforms get in free. *Prince George's County Stadium, Rtes. 50 and 301, Bowie, MD, 301/805–6000.*

FREDERICK KEYS

Head northwest on I–270 into Maryland to see the Orioles' Class A Keys in action. Tickets range from $5 to $11, and children ages 5 and under get in free. *Harry Grove Stadium, Market St., Frederick, MD, 301/662–0013.*

HAGERSTOWN SUNS

To watch the Toronto Blue Jays' Class A Hagerstown Suns play, take I–270 north into Maryland. Tickets range from $3 to $7. *Municipal Stadium, 274 E. Memorial Blvd., Hagerstown, MD, 301/791–6266.*

POTOMAC CANNONS

Mark McGwire's eventual replacement may now be on the roster of the St. Louis Cardinals' Class A affiliate, which plays its home games in Manassas, Virginia. Tickets range from $4 to $10. *G. Richard Pfitzner Stadium, 7 County Complex Ct., Manassas, VA, 703/590–2311.*

where to play

There are public baseball diamonds throughout the District. For information on permits and reservations, call the D.C. Department of Parks and Recreation at 202/673–7647.

D.C. METRO MEN'S SENIOR AND ADULT BASEBALL LEAGUE

This serious amateur league for men who don't find softball challenging enough holds games in various fields throughout D.C., Virginia, and Maryland. *Office: 1748 N St. NW, 202/659–2734.*

PONCE DE LEON BASEBALL LEAGUE

This confederation, based on the premise that the real fountain of youth is found on the baseball diamond, operates two distinct divisions with teams throughout the D.C. suburbs: one for men over the age of 30, another for those over 48. It plays down the competitive aspects of the sport—players, for example, are divvied up onto various teams after mass "workouts," not "tryouts," and everybody finds a roster spot. Practices are forbidden during the season, nobody sits out more than one inning in a row, and the league doesn't retain team standings or statistics. There are spring, summer, and fall seasons. *301/989–0945 or 800/808–0244.*

BASKETBALL

teams to watch

5 *f-5*

GEORGE WASHINGTON UNIVERSITY COLONIALS

Washington's "other" Division I team, the Colonials don't have the name recognition of their crosstown rivals, the Hoyas, but they consistently perform well and ignite crowds with their determined attitude. Tickets range from $12 to $18. *Smith Center, George Washington University, Foggy Bottom, 202/994–5779. Metro: Foggy Bottom–GWU.*

6 *c-5*

GEORGETOWN HOYAS
Patrick Ewing and Alonzo Mourning both got their start as Hoyas. The team seems to be on an eternal hot streak, having bid for the NCAA tournament every season for more than 25 years. Now that they play in the 20,000-seat MCI Arena, everyone has a better chance of scoring tickets to see this collegiate powerhouse in action. Tickets range anywhere from $5 to $35. *MCI Center, 601 F St. NW, Downtown, 202/ 628–3200. Metro: Gallery Pl.–Chinatown.*

6 *c-5*

WASHINGTON MYSTICS
This WNBA team draws the biggest crowds in the league—no mean feat, as women's basketball is getting hotter and hotter. Tickets cost between $8 and $38. *MCI Center, 601 F St. NW, Downtown, 202/628–3200. Metro: Gallery Pl.– Chinatown.*

6 *c-5*

WASHINGTON WIZARDS
The Wizards (formerly the Washington Bullets) haven't had a good season in two decades. But things can only get more interesting with the team's new president—basketball's greatest, Michael Jordan. Tickets can cost anywhere from $19 to $125. *MCI Center, 601 F St. NW, Downtown, 202/628–3200. Metro: Gallery Pl.–Chinatown.*

where to play
For the indoor or outdoor basketball court nearest you, call the D.C. Department of Parks and Recreation at 202/673–7647.

HOOPS AFTER DARK
Hoops After Dark is a five-on-five league for players between the ages of 18 and 25. All games are held at Evans Recreation Center, from June to July. Registration costs $150 per team. 202/724–4920.

BICYCLING

With hundreds of miles of bike trails along the C&O Canal towpath, through Rock Creek Park, and throughout the metropolitan area, Washington is very hospitable to cyclists. Downtown is mostly flat terrain, throwing up few obstacles even for cycling commuters. The Metro's Bike-on-Rail program allows riders to take their bicycles on the last car of any train weekdays from 10 to 2 and weekends and holidays after 7PM.

What's the best bike route from your home to your office? How can you see Washington's monuments from your 10-speed? Want to slow down and take a bike tour? The friendly staff at the Washington Area Bicyclist Association (WABA), armed with hundreds of informational pamphlets, can give you safety tips, suggest scenic routes, even put you in touch with the Bicycle Commuter Assistance Program, a network of routing assistants who can help you plot a commute or trip anywhere in the city. In addition, WABA publishes and sells the Greater Washington Area Bicycle Atlas, a definitive listing of 67 scenic tours in the region, complete with maps and expert advice. *733 15th St. NW, Suite 1030, 202/ 628–2500.*

1 *c-4*

C&O CANAL
The towpath along the C&O Canal runs 184½ mi from Georgetown to Cumberland, Maryland, a pretty ambitious ride even for those in great shape. For a more moderate expedition, try the 15-mi trip to Great Falls Park, which passes through grand expanses of woodland, complete with wildlife. The towpath is mostly level terrain, but the packed-dirt and gravel surface is better suited to wide tires than the thin wheels of city bikes.

1 *c-4*

CAPITAL CRESCENT TRAIL
Running from Georgetown to downtown Bethesda on the corridor of the old Georgetown Branch railroad, this trail has an incredibly smooth paved surface. Better still, it has magnificent views of the Potomac River and Key Bridge. The trip is a quick 11 mi, but if you're up for a longer haul, you can take a link in Bethesda to the crushed-stone Georgetown Branch Trail, which extends across Rock Creek Park to Silver Spring and brings the total trip to a little more than 21 mi.

1 *d-6*

MOUNT VERNON TRAIL
Popular with both joggers and cyclists, this trail follows the Potomac River, beginning at Theodore Roosevelt Island, near Key Bridge; passing through Alexandria, Virginia; and then winding

among the 240-acre wetlands of Dyke Marsh. After a very manageable 18½ mi, it ends at George Washington's home, Mount Vernon.

1 *d-3*
ROCK CREEK TRAIL
This 25-mi trail runs from the Lincoln Memorial to Lake Needwood Park in Montgomery County, Maryland. Beloved for its scenery, it often gets congested, especially on sunny weekends; the good news is that Beach Drive from Broad Branch Road to the Maryland border is closed on weekends and holidays. Freed from car traffic, you have only to worry about maiming joggers and in-line skaters.

BILLIARDS

A relaxing alternative to pool tables in crowded bars, billiard clubs rent tables by the hour and provide a more comfortable atmosphere in which to practice your shots or catch a game with friends.

3 *d-4*
ATOMIC BILLIARDS
This popular hall draws a young clientele, who dig the vintage '50s decor and the wide variety of board games with which to pass the time while waiting for one of the six tables. Lessons and leagues are available. *3427 Connecticut Ave. NW, Cleveland Park, 202/363–7665. Metro: Cleveland Park.*

2 *c-3*
BABE'S BILLIARDS
Babe's has an ample 20 tables. *4600 Wisconsin Ave. NW, Tenleytown, 202/966–0082. Metro: Tenleytown–AU.*

3 *g-7*
BEDROCK BILLIARDS
This smaller pool hall has seven tables. *1841 Columbia Rd. NW, Adams-Morgan, 202/667–7665. Metro: Woodley Park–Zoo.*

5 *g-3*
BUFFALO BILLIARDS
The Western-theme Buffalo occupies a whopping 14,000 subterranean square ft. Thirty-one pool tables share space with a snooker table, shuffleboard, dart boards, two bars, and two party rooms. Lessons and leagues are available. *1330 19th St. NW, Dupont Circle, 202/331–7665. Metro: Dupont Circle.*

1 *c-5*
CHAMPION BILLIARDS
Twenty tables are available at Champion Billiards, and if you need any pointers you can ask for Petey. In addition to leagues, there are open eight- and nine-ball tournaments several nights a week. *2620 S. Shirlington Rd., Arlington, VA, 703/521–3800.*

5 *c-4*
GEORGETOWN BILLIARDS
There are 13 tables at Georgetown Billiards. Free lessons are available by appointment on Friday, and there's an open tournament every Monday night. Light food is served at the bar. *3251 Prospect St. NW, Georgetown, 202/965–7665.*

2 *e-3*
JULIO'S BILLIARDS CAFE
There are five tables in Julio's well-attended pizzeria. *1604 U St. NW, U Street, 202/483–8500. Metro: Dupont Circle.*

1 *c-2*
ROCK BOTTOM
A favorite with young locals, Rock Bottom has four tables, two bars, and one restaurant. *7900 Norfolk Ave., Bethesda, MD, 301/652–1311. Metro: Bethesda.*

BIRD-WATCHING

The C&O Canal Park, Glover-Archbold Park, and Rock Creek Park all provide excellent bird-watching opportunities.

1 *c-3*
AUDUBON NATURALIST SOCIETY
A self-guided nature trail winds through this verdant 40-acre estate, the national headquarters of the Audubon Society. Birds are often in abundance here, as the Audubon Society prohibits the use of toxic chemicals in landscaping and leaves most of its grounds in an utterly natural state. *8940 Jones Mill Rd., Chevy Chase, MD, 301/652–9188.*

BOATING

To canoe on the Potomac, you can put in just about anywhere along the river. Kayaking is popular, although dangerous, at Great Falls. The following riverside outfits rent boats to anyone with valid identification; at least one member of your party must be 18 or older.

2 b-4

FLETCHER'S BOATHOUSE

Fletcher's rents both rowboats and canoes for use on the Potomac River. *4940 Canal Rd. NW, Waterfront, 202/ 244–0461.*

1 a-3

SWAIN'S LOCK

Swain's is situated right on the C&O Canal, so it's also convenient to Great Falls. Choose a canoe or a kayak. *River Rd., Potomac, MD, 301/299–9006.*

9 h-8

THOMPSON'S BOATHOUSE

Canoes, rowboats, and rowing sculls, are all available for use on the Potomac. *2900 Virginia Ave. NW, Georgetown, 202/ 333–9543. Metro: Foggy Bottom–GWU.*

BOWLING

Everything old is new again, and bowling is no exception. Sure, the old tenpin game is still kicking around, but many bowling alleys have added some eye-popping gimmicks to create a new generation of bowlers. Such innovations as Rock 'n Bowl nights (with dance music and disco balls) and Cosmic bowling (featuring glow-in-the-dark pins and laser beams) are just a few of the ways this retro pastime is keeping pace with the 21st century.

1 d-7

AMF BOWLING CENTERS

There's something for just about everyone at these friendly bowling alleys, including parties, league nights, and Rock 'n Bowl. *Penn Daw Plaza, 6228-A N. Kings Hwy., Alexandria, VA, 703/765–3633.*

1 b-6

4254 Markham St., Annandale, VA, 703/ 256–2211.

1 d-7

BOWL AMERICA

With more than a dozen locations in the D.C. area and a wide range of promotions and gadgetry, these alleys are the place to be. *100 S. Pickett St., Alexandria, VA, 703/751–1900.*

1 c-2

553 Westbard Ave., Bethesda, MD, 301/ 654–1320.

1 a-5

140 S. Maple Ave., Falls Church, VA, 703/ 534–1370.

1 e-2

8616 Cameron St., Silver Spring, MD, 301/585–6990. Call for other locations.

1 c-5

SHIRLEY PARK BOWL

These 40 top-notch lanes stay open until the wee hours of the morning. *2945 S. Glebe Rd., Arlington, VA, 703/684–5800.*

BOXING

Major professional bouts are held at the MCI Center; for details and information call 202/628–3200.

2 f-5

FINLEY'S BOXING CLUB

More than 40 years old, Finley's is one of the oldest continuously operating boxing gyms in the country. Although it used to cater exclusively to professionals, it now attracts a general, health- conscious crowd looking for an alternative to traditional gyms. Women are welcome, and although few actually step into the ring, the intense cardiovascular workout keeps them coming back for more training. *518 10th St. NE, Capitol Hill, 202/ 543–0976. Metro: Union Station.*

CRICKET

WASHINGTON CRICKET LEAGUE

Particularly popular with West Indian, Pakistani, and Indian immigrants, D.C.'s cricket league has two dozen teams. Games are played on a dozen area fields, including West Potomac Park, Saturday and Sunday at noon or 1PM. If you'd like to try your hand at this beloved Commonwealth pastime, call the league at 888/294–1442, and they'll send you an application form for a nearby team.

CROSS-COUNTRY SKIING

You can actually cross-country ski in the District once there's enough snow to keep joggers and bicyclists off the best trails. Good choices include the Capital Crescent Trail, which runs from George-town to Bethesda; the C&O Canal Tow-path from Georgetown to Great Falls; and the 39 mi of hiking and bridle trails that cover Rock Creek Park.

FENCING

Fencing conjures up images of swash-buckling pirates for many, but it's very much alive as a way of keeping aerobi-cally fit while developing both grace and agility.

1 *e-2*

FOREST GLEN FENCER'S CENTER

Classes and competitions are offered at all levels. Forest Glen is also home to the D.C. Fencers Club, the most promi-nent in the area. *9330 Frasier Ave., Silver Spring, MD, 301/562–1990.*

VIRGINIA ACADEMY OF FENCING

Classes are offered at all levels, and competitions vary widely. *5410 Port Royal Rd., Springfield, VA, 703/321–4922.*

FISHING

The Potomac River is something of an environmental success story: once dan-gerously polluted, it's now beloved by fishing enthusiasts throughout the D.C. area. Largemouth bass, striped bass, shad, and white and yellow perch all live here. Fishing trips are complicated, how-ever, by the fact that the Potomac winds through three jurisdictions—Virginia, Maryland, and the District of Colum-bia—and in Virginia and Maryland you need a license to fish in fresh water. For information on licenses and advice on the physical whereabouts of state bor-ders, call the Maryland Department of Natural Resources at 301/855–1748 or the Virginia Commission of Game and Inland Fisheries at 804/367–1000.

A 5-mi stretch of the Potomac River—roughly from the Wilson Memorial Bridge in Alexandria south to Ft. Wash-ington National Park—is one of the country's best spots for largemouth-bass fishing. It has, in fact, become something of an East Coast mecca for anglers in search of this particular fish. The area around Fletcher's Boat House

(4940 Canal Rd.) is one of the best spots for perch.

FOOTBALL

Washington is a football-crazy town, the object of everyone's desire being a ticket to the see the 'Skins.

team to watch

WASHINGTON REDSKINS

The hometown team now plays at the 80,000-seat FedEx Field (formerly Jack Kent Cooke Stadium), and although the move increased seat capacity by nearly a third over the team's former home, RFK Stadium, it's still almost impossible for the general public to get seats. Both season and individual tickets to Red-skins games have been sold out since the mid-1960s. There is (vague) hope, however, because every now and again a visiting team fails to sell all of its allot-ted tickets; these then become available two hours before kickoff. The ticket office can let you know on the Friday before a Sunday game whether or not they expect any such windfall. *FedEx Field, Arena Dr., off Capital Beltway (Exit 17), Landover, MD, 301/276–6050.*

where to play flag football

Lawyers and insurance companies have all but done away with recreational tackle-football leagues for adults. But if you feel too young to give up the sport altogether, a growing number of area flag-football leagues will allow you to harbor those dreams of Super Bowl glory for a few more years.

ARLINGTON COUNTY FLAG FOOTBALL

The sports division of the county gov-ernment organizes spring and fall flag-football leagues for men's, women's, and co-ed teams. For registration infor-mation call 703/228–4719.

NORTHERN VIRGINIA FLAG FOOTBALL ASSOCIATION

Founded in 1995, the NVFFA calls itself the largest flag-football confederation in the mid-Atlantic region, with more than 100 teams in its ranks. This is a pretty serious operation, with divisions in four-on-four, five-on-five, eight-man eligible, eight-man ineligible, and nine-man ineli-gible. Currently the NVFFA is trying to field a squad of all-stars for a professional flag-football league. No wonder the league's slogan is: "The closest you will get to playing real football." Suit up and judge for yourself. *703/729–7732.*

GOLF

As compact as Washington is, there are still three public golf courses within it, and several dozen public and private courses a short drive from downtown.

washington, d.c.

Although the golf courses in D.C. itself are not the area's most challenging, they're convenient (all three are open every day year-round from dawn until dusk) and economical for those who live nearby. Get in line early for a tee time.

2 *e-6*

EAST POTOMAC PARK GOLF COURSE

Right on the Potomac River and just half a mile from the Jefferson Memorial, this bustling, full-service facility has an 18-hole, par-72 course; a 9-hole, par-34 course; and a 9-hole, par-31 beginner course, all with views of the monuments. There is also a 100-stall, lighted driving range. Greens fees are $15 for 18 holes on weekdays, $9 for 9; on weekends it's $19 and $12.25, respectively. Professional instruction is available. *Hains Point; enter from Ohio Dr. SW, south of Independence Ave., Waterfront, 202/554–7660. Metro: Waterfront–SEU.*

2 *g-5*

LANGSTON GOLF COURSE

An 18-hole, par-72 course situated along the Anacostia River, Langston is home to the annual Capital City Open Golf Tournament. There's also a 25-stall driving range. Greens fees are $13.50 for 18 holes on weekdays, $9 for 9; weekends it's $17 and $10.50, respectively. *26th and Benning Rds. NE, near RFK Stadium, Capitol Hill, 202/397–8638. Metro: Stadium–Armory.*

2 *d-1*

ROCK CREEK PARK GOLF COURSE

This attractive 18-hole, par-65 course is set on rolling and wooded terrain in Rock Creek Park. The challenging last nine holes make this the most attractive public course in D.C. There's also a five-stall driving range with nets. Greens

fees are $15 for 18 holes on weekdays, $9 for 9; weekend fees are $19 and $12.25, respectively. *16th and Rittenhouse Sts. NW, 202/882–7332.*

outside washington, d.c.

BOWIE GOLF & COUNTRY CLUB

This tight, 18-hole, par-70 course has small greens. Greens fees for 18 holes are $25 on weekdays, $30 on weekends. *7420 Laurel- Bowie Rd., Bowie, MD, 301/262–8141.*

1 *d-7*

GREENDALE GOLF COURSE

There are few surprises at this middle-of-the-road 18-hole, par-70 course. Greens fees are $14 for 9 holes and $22 for 18 holes on weekdays, $16 for 9 holes and $26 for 18 holes on weekends. *Telegraph Rd., Alexandria, VA, 703/971–3788.*

GUNPOWDER GOLF COURSE

Traditional in style, the 18-hole, par-70 Gunpowder course has rolling hills and tight greens. Greens fees are $11 on weekdays and $14 on weekends for 9 or 18 holes. *14300 Old Gunpowder Rd., Laurel, MD, 301/725–9861 or 301/725–4532.*

JEFFERSON DISTRICT PARK GOLF COURSE

This short, open, and level nine-hole course has a par of 34. The cost is $15 for nine holes. *7900 Lee Hwy., Falls Church, VA, 703/573–0443.*

MARLBOROUGH COUNTRY CLUB

Fairly tight and with lots of water, this 18-hole course sets par at 71. Fees are $17 Monday through Thursday, $22 on Friday, and $40 on weekends. *4750 John Rogers Blvd., Upper Marlboro, MD, 301/952–1350.*

NEEDWOOD GOLF COURSE

This 18-hole course with large and open greens has an open front 9 and a par of 70. There's also a 9-hole course with a par of 29. Weekday fees are $15 for 9 holes and $24 for 18 holes; weekends fees are $18 for 9 holes and $29 for 18 holes. *Rock Creek Regional Park, 6724 Needwood Rd., Derwood, MD, 301/948–1075.*

PENDERBROOK GOLF COURSE

Penderbrook, with 18 holes and a par of 71, is narrow and tree-lined, with some water. The 5th, 11th, 12th, and 15th holes are exceptional. The fees for 18 holes are $35 Monday through Thursday and $50 Friday through Sunday. *3700 Golf Trail La., Fairfax, VA, 703/385–3700.*

PINECREST GOLF COURSE

This narrow, tree-lined nine-hole course sets par at 35. The cost is $13 on weekdays, $15 on weekends. *6600 Little River Turnpike, Alexandria, VA, 703/941–1061.*

PLEASANT VALLEY GOLF CLUB

Pleasant Valley's pristine 18-hole, par-72 course has hills, hardwood trees, wildflowers, native-grass meadows, and water features. Greens fees are $60 Monday through Thursday, $70 Friday, and $85 on weekends. *4715 Pleasant Valley Rd., Chantilly, VA, 703/631–7904.*

REDGATE GOLF COURSE

This tight and hilly 18-hole course has a par of 71. Greens fees are $25 for 18 holes Monday through Thursday, $15 for 9 holes; Friday through Sunday the fees are $29.50 for 18 holes, $18 for 9 holes. *14500 Avery Rd., Rockville, MD, 301/309–3055.*

RESTON NATIONAL GOLF COURSE

This 18-hole, par-71 parklike course is about a half-hour drive from downtown Washington. Well maintained, it's heavily wooded but not too difficult for the average player. The fees for 18 holes are $52 weekdays and $75 on weekends. *11875 Sunrise Valley Dr., Reston, VA, 703/620–9333.*

ROBIN DALE GOLF CLUB

Flat and open, the 18-hole Robin Dale course has a par of 72. Greens fees are $20 for nine holes and $28 for 18 holes on weekdays; only 18 holes can be played on weekends, and the cost is $38. *15851 McKendree Rd., Brandywine, MD, 301/372–8855.*

1 *e-2*
SLIGO CREEK GOLF COURSE

Terrain on this nine-hole course with a par of 34 is fairly level. Fees are $12 on weekdays, $15 on weekends. *9701 Sligo Creek Pkwy., Silver Spring, MD, 301/585–6006.*

TWIN SHIELDS GOLF COURSE

Par is 70, and the grounds are rolling at this 18-hole course. Greens fees range from $23 to $45, depending on the day and the time. *2425 Roarty Rd., Dunkirk, MD, 410/257–7800.*

1 *f-2*
UNIVERSITY OF MARYLAND GOLF COURSE

Rolling greens and heavy woods fill out these 18 holes, with a par of 71. Greens fees are $32 to $44 on weekdays and $50 on weekends. *University Blvd., College Park, MD, 301/403–4299.*

events

1 *b-2*
KEMPER OPEN GOLF TOURNAMENT

Everyone catches golf fever when this tournament rolls around in May. Some of the biggest names on the tour vie for top prizes. *Congressional Country Club, Bethesda, MD, 301/469–3737.*

HANG GLIDING

1 *f-2*
CAPITOL HANG GLIDER ASSOCIATION

Those who really want to soar should check out this club, which meets the fourth Wednesday of every month to discuss the best places to hang glide around D.C. They sometimes organize group outings. *Lasick's College Inn (lower level), 9128 Baltimore Blvd., College Park, MD, 202/393–2854.*

1 *c-5*
SILVER WINGS INC.

It's a full-service, year-round hang-gliding school, with certified instructors. *6032 N. 20th St., Arlington, VA, 703/533–3244.*

HIKING

There are more than 50 mi of hiking trails in Washington, D.C., most maintained by the Potomac Appalachian Trail Club. Rock Creek Park, the C&O Canal, and Great Falls Park in particular have well-marked paths and moderately steep inclines. Two of the most popular hikes in the metro area are the Billy Goat Trail, which runs along the Potomac River in Montgomery County, Maryland, and the Potomac Heritage Trail, which traverses the narrow riparian edge of the Potomac

Palisades from downtown D.C. The Billy Goat is rough and rocky, so wear appropriate shoes if you decide to tackle it.

1 c-4
C&O CANAL
Strenuous hiking trails include the Billy Goat (trailhead on MacArthur Boulevard, by the Old Angler's Inn) and the Gold Mine (trailhead where Falls Rd. [Rte. 189] enters Great Falls Park).

HOCKEY

team to watch

6 c-5
WASHINGTON CAPITALS
Washington's NHL team always seems destined for greatness, but always falls just shy of the coveted Stanley Cup. The Capitals are installed in the luxurious MCI Center from October through April. Tickets range from $20 to $75. *601 F St. NW, Downtown, 202/628–3200. Metro: Gallery Pl.–Chinatown.*

where to play

FAIRFAX ICE ARENA
Both kids and adults can join beginner and intermediate leagues here. *3779 Pickett Rd., Fairfax, VA, 703/323–1131.*

HOCKEY NORTH AMERICA
This organization will put you in touch with local teams that play in the nationally registered Adult Recreational Hockey League. They also sponsor a beginners' program for adults. *703/471–0932.*

HORSEBACK RIDING

FAIR HILL NATURE CENTER
Located in scenic Elkton, Maryland, the Fair Hill Nature Center offers horseback-riding trails around an all-service equestrian compound; annual races and breeding events, as well as regular riding classes, are held here. There is a $2 park entrance fee per vehicle. *376 Fair Hill Dr., Elkton, MD, 410/398–1246.*

1 d-2
ROCK CREEK PARK HORSE CENTER
Year-round lessons and guided trail rides are available to everyone 12 or older. *Military and Glover Rds. NW, Tenleytown, 202/362–0117.*

WASHINGTON & OLD DOMINION TRAIL
You and your mount will have to share space with bikers and in-line skaters, but this 30-mi bridle trail from Arlington to Purcellville is quite scenic. For maps and rules, contact the Washington and Old Dominion Railroad Regional Park Office and Friends of the W&OD at 703/729–0596.

HORSE RACING

The Washington area has always been a hotbed of Thoroughbred racing. Some of the most powerful figures in U.S. history were dedicated horseplayers during their stays in D.C. President Andrew Jackson, for example, used to race his ponies at a track on the site of what is now Meridien Hill Park on 16th Street, and FBI strongman J. Edgar Hoover was a regular at several local racing strips—the Maryland Jockey Club still holds a stakes race in his honor each year.

where to watch

CHARLES TOWN RACES
A little more than an hour from downtown, just across the West Virginia border from Maryland and near scenic Harpers Ferry, Charles Town Races has year-round racing—with evening post times Thursday through Saturday, afternoon post times on Sunday—as well as slot machines. There is no live racing Monday through Wednesday, but simulcast wagering is available daily. *Rte. 340, Charles Town, WV, 800/795–7001.*

LAUREL PARK
You can watch and wager on Thoroughbreds at Laurel Park from October to March and July to August. Race days are usually Wednesday through Sunday, plus holidays. Simulcast wagering is available every day but Tuesday year-round. *Rte. 198 and Race Track Rd., Laurel, MD, 301/725–0400.*

PIMLICO RACE COURSE
This strip, best known as the home of the Preakness Stakes, is the second oldest track in the country (the oldest is stately Saratoga). It has Thoroughbred racing from early April through late June. Race days are usually Wednesday

through Sunday. Simulcast wagering is available every day but Tuesday year-round. *Hayward and Winner Aves., Baltimore, MD, 410/542–9400.*

ROSECROFT

Fans of harness racing—sort of a *Ben Hur* version of the sport, in which standardbred horses replace Thoroughbreds and drivers replace jockeys—can get their kicks just outside the Beltway at Rosecroft. Race days are usually Thursday through Saturday in a season that runs from February through mid-December. *6336 Rosecroft Dr., Fort Washington, MD, 301/567–4000.*

events

PREAKNESS STAKES

Despite the fact that it takes place in Baltimore, the Preakness Stakes, which is held on the third weekend in May, is the number-one horse event for D.C.'s equestrian crowd. It's the middle jewel in horse racing's Triple Crown, and the muddy fields around the course turn into a giant party on race day. *Pimlico Race Course, Hayward and Winner Aves., Baltimore, MD, 410/837–3030.*

ICE-SKATING

2 *h-6*

FORT DUPONT ICE RINK

This indoor rink is open year-round. *3779 Ely Pl. SE, Anacostia, 202/584–5007.*

6 *c-7*

NATIONAL GALLERY SCULPTURE GARDEN ICE RINK

Located right on the Mall, in front of the National Archives, this outdoor rink is small and lively. *9th St. and Constitution Ave. NW, Downtown, 202/371–5340. Metro: Archives–Navy Memorial.*

6 *a-6*

PERSHING PARK ICE RINK

One block from the White House, this outdoor rink lets you glide in full view of the monuments. The rink is small, but public hours are ample. Lessons are available. *14th St. and Pennsylvania Ave. NW, Downtown, 202/737–6938. Metro: McPherson Sq.*

IN-LINE & ROLLER SKATING

The skater's most pressing need is smooth pavement. Although many trails are shared with joggers and bicyclists, their surfaces are smooth enough that you won't be eating gravel. Some top choices include the Capital Crescent Trail, one of the newest and best-paved trails in the city; the 18½-mi Mount Vernon Trail, with views of the Potomac; Rock Creek Park, where part of Beach Drive is closed to vehicles from 7 AM Saturday to 7 PM on Sunday; and the Rock Creek Hiker-Biker Trail, which stretches ½ mi from the D.C. line to Lake Needwood, in Montgomery County, Maryland.

MARTIAL ARTS

9 *d-2*

WASHINGTON DC SHOTOKAN KARATE CLUB

Instructors at this club, which conducts classes inside the legendary Jelleff Boys and Girls Club in Georgetown, have international competitions under their black belts. Despite their credentials, the counselors volunteer for their sessions for youth karate for students ages 7 to 17. Adults have to pay. *3265 S St. NW, Georgetown, 202/462–0385.*

MINIATURE GOLF

These little 18-hole putt-putt courses may be more challenging than you think.

2 *e-6*

EAST POTOMAC MINI GOLF

The only mini-golf option downtown, this 18-hole course offers little in the way of creative landscaping, but compensates with a beautiful view of the river. *East Potomac Park, 972 Ohio Dr. SW, Waterfront, 202/488–8087. Metro: Waterfront–SEU.*

PUTT-PUTT GOLF, GAMES AND SKATING

Two 18-hole courses have inclines, humps, and bank shots, but no laughing clowns, windmills, or pirate ships. *130 Rollins Ave., Rockville, MD, 301/881–1663.*

WOODY'S GOLF RANGE

It's just like the real thing, on a smaller scale: Woody's 18 holes come complete with rocks, water, and hills. *11801 Leesburg Pike, Herndon, VA, 703/430–8337.*

POLO

A scenic one-hour drive from downtown will take you to the heart of Virginia horse country, where beautiful creatures with two or four legs play a game most easily described as "hockey on horseback."

where to watch

GREAT MEADOW POLO CLUB

Each Friday night from June through early September, the Great Meadow Polo Club offers arena polo, a smaller-scale, more fan-friendly version of the pasture pastime. Games start at 7PM, weather permitting, but you'll want to arrive early to people-watch and to tailgate, both of which are at least as important to the polo culture as the billed competition. Admission is $15 per carload. *5089 Old Tavern Rd., The Plains, VA, 540/253–5156.*

RACQUETBALL & SQUASH

1 *c-2*

BETHESDA SPORT & HEALTH CLUB

Seven courts are used for both racquetball and squash. *4400 Montgomery Ave., Bethesda, MD, 301/656–9570. Metro: Bethesda.*

FAIRFAX RACQUET CLUB

There are five racquetball courts here. *9860 Lee Hwy., Fairfax, VA, 703/273–9276.*

5 *f-4*

FITNESS COMPANY LAFAYETTE CENTER

Seven courts are reserved for squash. *1120 20th St. NW, Dupont Circle, 202/659–9570. Metro: Farragut North.*

2 *e-4*

NATIONAL CAPITAL YMCA

The Y has six racquetball and squash courts. *1711 Rhode Island Ave. NW, Dupont Circle, 202/862–9622. Metro: Farragut North.*

2 *c-3*

TENLEY SPORT & HEALTH CLUB

Four courts can be used for both racquetball and squash. *4000 Wisconsin Ave. NW, Tenleytown, 202/362–8000. Metro: Tenleytown–AU.*

2 *f-5*

WASHINGTON SPORTS CLUB

These four courts are dedicated to squash. *214 D St. SE, Capitol Hill, 202/547–2255. Metro: Union Station.*

RUGBY

Rugby has a large and devoted following inside the Beltway, including players from New Zealand, Australia, and Scotland who appreciate the near-professional level of play.

POTOMAC ATHLETIC CLUB

With 20 adult teams and 18 college squads, the Potomac Athletic Club supports four divisions playing both the traditional, 15-person game and the faster-paced, seven-person version, and will try to place anyone who's interested. Seasons run from August to November and from January to June, with practices continuing almost year-round. Games are played Saturday afternoons on a field at 15th Street and Independence Avenue, across from the Holocaust Memorial Museum.

For hard-core rugbyheads, the Potomac Rugby Club is not only the hottest show in town but also yields one of the best Level I teams in the country. Other local teams of note include Northern Virginia (NOVA), Washington RFC, and the Maryland Exiles. Call 202/659–9414 for more information; if you like, they'll put you on the phone tree that spreads details on games and practices.

RUNNING & WALKING

Affiliated with the Road Runners Club of America, the D.C. Road Runners Club sponsors a year-round schedule of events for runners of all of ages and abilities. *Box 1352, Arlington, VA, 22210, 703/836–0558.*

where to run or walk

1 c-4

C&O CANAL

Maintained by the National Park Service, the 89-mi packed-dirt and gravel C&O towpath is a favorite with both runners and bicyclists. The most popular loop for runners—from a point just north of the Key Bridge, in Georgetown, to Fletcher's Boathouse and back—is about 4 mi long.

1 c-4

CAPITAL CRESCENT TRAIL

The newest and best-maintained trail in the area, the scenic Capital Crescent is built on the corridor of the old Georgetown Branch railroad and climbs from the Potomac River in Georgetown to downtown Bethesda, Maryland, for a total distance of 11¼ mi. It's also an extremely popular bike route.

1 d-6

MOUNT VERNON TRAIL

Just across the Potomac in Virginia, the Mount Vernon Trail is another favorite of D.C. runners. The trail's shorter, 3½-mi northern section begins near the pedestrian causeway leading to Theodore Roosevelt Island and passes Ronald Reagan National Airport, meanders through protected wetlands, and ends in Old Town Alexandria. The longer, 9-mi southern section takes you along the banks of the Potomac from Alexandria all the way to George Washington's birthplace, Mount Vernon.

6 b-7

NATIONAL MALL

The loop around the Capitol and past the Smithsonian museums, Washington Monument, Reflecting Pool, and Lincoln Memorial is the king of all Washington running rails. The 4½-mi gravel path is often packed with joggers, cyclists, and tourists. For a longer run, veer south of the Mall on either side of the Tidal Basin and head for the Jefferson Memorial and East Potomac Park.

1 d-3

ROCK CREEK PARK

Starting at P Street, on the edge of Georgetown, and continuing into Montgomery County, Maryland, Rock Creek Park contains 15 mi of running trails, often shared with cyclists and equestrians. The most popular run is a 4-mi loop along the creek from Georgetown to the National Zoo.

events

GEORGETOWN CLASSIC 10K

Sponsored by the Capital Running Company, this race in early October starts and finishes on Wisconsin Avenue between M Street NW and Potomac Street. Call 301/871–0005 for more information.

MARINE CORPS MARATHON

The premiere race in the Washington area, the marathon attracts thousands of world-class athletes. The route starts and ends at the Marine Corps War Memorial in Arlington, Virginia, and winds through Georgetown and the District. Apply early if you want to run in this event, which takes place in late October. *MCM, Box 188, Quantico, VA 22134, 703/784–2225.*

SAILING

1 d-7

WASHINGTON SAILING MARINA

The top facility in the area for small sailboats, the Washington Sailing Marina is known for extremely sailable flat water with a steady light wind. Conditions are prime from May to September, but the season can be stretched a month or two in either direction. Instruction is available for adults. *George Washington Pkwy., 1½ mi south of Ronald Reagan National Airport, Alexandria, VA, 703/548–9027.*

SCUBA DIVING

The following outfits offer diving instruction and certification.

AMERICAN WATER SPORTS OF VIRGINIA

6182-A Arlington Blvd., Falls Church, VA, 703/534–3636.

ATLANTIC EDGE SCUBA CENTER

213 Muddy Branch Rd, Gaithersburg, MD, 301/990–0223.

THE DIVE SHOP

3013 Nutley St., Fairfax, VA, 703/698–7220.

2 c-2
NATIONAL DIVING CENTER
4932 Wisconsin Ave. NW, Friendship Heights, 202/363–6123. Metro: Friendship Heights.

1 d7
SPLASH DIVE CENTER
3260 Duke St., at Quaker La., Alexandria, VA, 703/823–7680.

SOCCER

where to watch

2 g-5
ROBERT F. KENNEDY STADIUM
When the Washington Redskins moved from RFK Stadium to Jack Kent Cooke (now FedEx Field), soccer became the sport of choice at RFK. This is now the home of the premier squad in Major League Soccer, D.C. United, made up of both top U.S. players and foreign stars. The stadium also hosts special soccer events, such as international tournaments and the women's World Cup. *RFK Stadium, 22nd and E. Capitol Sts., 202/547–9077. Metro: Stadium–Armory.*

where to play
Because of its incredible cultural diversity, the D.C. area is as soccer-friendly a region as you'll find anywhere in the U.S. The downtown adult leagues tend to be made up of teams from embassies or groups of expatriates from the same country. But any soccer mom, soccer dad, or plain-old soccer enthusiast should be able to find a recreational league around town that will suit his or her desires and skills.

If you're just interested in pickup games, contact the D.C. Department of Parks and Recreation at 202/673–7660 or 202/673–7449 to find the location of the field nearest you.

BARCROFT INDOOR SOCCER LEAGUE
Thanks to the advent of indoor soccer, when the summer winds turn cold and drive you off the pitch, you can run inside and keep on kicking. The Barcroft Indoor Soccer League is one of the biggest of its kind in the D.C. area, with teams in men's, women's, and co-ed

divisions. Franchise fees start at $400. *703/228–4716.*

FAIRFAX WOMEN'S SOCCER ASSOCIATION
More than 700 players of various skill levels make up this league. Teams are divided by age: Open is for players 18 and older, Master for 30 and older, and Grand Master for 40 and older. The playing schedule runs from April through November. Games are generally on weekends on Fairfax County soccer fields. Registration is $35 to $55 per player. *703/541–6194.*

MID-MARYLAND MEN'S LEAGUE
The Mid-Maryland Men's League, based in Prince George's County, has three adult divisions. For information on how to join and how much it'll cost you, call *301/261–4505.*

SOFTBALL

There are two very different types of slow-pitch softball played in the D.C. area. First, there is the downtown version played during happy hour after work. These are the so-called beer leagues, in which generally co-ed teams affiliated with a political official, law firm, or advocacy group get together on the Mall for what is generally a casual affair and all in fun. Then there is the game played between squads sponsored by bars, houses of worship, or social clubs in the trophy leagues in surrounding counties and suburbs. This suburban version has the same rules as the downtown leagues, but carries a much more competitive atmosphere, where winning is paramount.

MALL BALL
All fields on the National Mall are under the auspices of the National Park Service. For field availability call *202/619–7225.*

SWIMMING

outdoor public pools
There are more than a dozen outdoor public pools in the District, all open weekdays from 10 to 8 (except as indicated below) and weekends from noon to 7, Memorial Day to Labor Day. All offer swimming lessons, water-safety

classes, lifeguard training, and water aerobics. For general information on swimming programs, call the Division of Aquatic Services at 202/576–6436.

2 g-6

ANACOSTIA

This popular facility is often quite crowded. *Anacostia Dr. SE, Anacostia, 202/645–5043. Closed Mon. Metro: Anacostia.*

2 e-3

BANNEKER

This large pool sponsors an "aqua" day camp for kids in the summer. *2500 Georgia Ave. NW, Mount Pleasant, 202/673–2121. Closed Thurs.*

7 b-2

EAST POTOMAC

East Potomac Park has an Olympic-size pool with diving platforms and a large changing facility. *Ohio Dr. SW, East Potomac Park, 202/727–6523. Closed Wed. Metro: Waterfront–SEU.*

2 h-4

FORT LINCOLN

This large facility offers an "aqua" day camp in the summer and organizes competitive swimming teams. *Ft. Lincoln and Banneker Drs. NE, Fort Lincoln, 202/576–6389. Closed Mon.*

5 e-3

FRANCIS

There's plenty of room to sunbathe at this well-kept pool. *25th and N Sts. NW, Foggy Bottom, 202/727–3285. Closed Tues. Metro: Foggy Bottom–GWU.*

2 g-5

KENILWORTH-PARKSIDE

Summers bring "aqua" day camp to this large pool. *Anacostia Ave. and Ord St. NE, Anacostia, 202/727–0635. Closed Wed. Metro: Anacostia.*

2 d-2

UPSHUR

The newest public pool in the District attracts a lot of school-age swimmers. *14th St. and Arkansas Ave. NW, Mount Pleasant, 202/576– 8661. Closed Fri.*

indoor public pools

Several indoor public pools provide climate-controlled swimming quarters year-round.

2 f-5

CAPITOL EAST NATATORIUM

635 North Carolina Ave. SE, Capitol Hill, 202/724–4495. Metro: Eastern Market.

6 d-3

DUNBAR

1301 New Jersey Ave. NW, Mt. Vernon Square, 202/673–7744. Closed weekends in winter. Metro: Mt. Vernon Sq.–UDC.

3 g-8

MARIE H. REED

2200 Champlain St. NW, Adams-Morgan, 202/673–7771. Closed Sun. Metro: U St.–Cardozo.

2 g-6

THERAPEUTIC RECREATION POOL

This pool is specially equipped for (and restricted to) those with special physical needs. *3030 G St. SE, Greenway, 202/645–3993.*

2 h-3

THURGOOD MARSHALL

Fort Lincoln and Commodore J. Barney Drs. NE, Fort Lincoln, 202/576–6135. Closed weekends in winter.

2 c-2

WOODROW WILSON

Nebraska Ave. and Chesapeake St. NW, North Cleveland Park, 202/286–2216. Metro: Van Ness–UDC.

TENNIS

outdoor public courts

There are 156 public tennis courts spread throughout the city. All are available on a first-come, first-served basis, and no permit is required. Call the sports office at the D.C. Department of Parks and Recreation for more information (202/645–3944 or 202/645–3940). Unless otherwise indicated below, courts are hard and are not lighted.

2 g-6

ANACOSTIA PARK

The large and well-utilized park has a suitably robust tennis facility, with nine lighted courts. *11th St. and Pennsylvania Ave. SE, Anacostia. Metro: Anacostia.*

2 *h-4*

FORT LINCOLN

This neighborhood has a slew of recreational facilities, including eight lighted tennis courts. *Fort Lincoln Dr. NE, Fort Lincoln.*

2 *g-7*

FORT STANTON PARK

There are three lighted courts here. *18th and Erie Sts. SE, Anacostia.*

5 *e-3*

FRANCIS

These four courts, two of which are lighted, are easily accessible. *24th and N Sts. NW, Dupont Circle. Metro: Dupont Circle.*

5 *d-2*

MONTROSE PARK

These four clay courts have a beautiful wooded setting. *30th and R Sts. NW, Georgetown.*

2 *b-3*

PALISADES

There are three courts here. *Dana St. and Sherrier Pl. NW, McLean Gardens.*

6 *a-7*

SOUTH GROUNDS

These two clay courts are right on the Mall. *15th St. and Constitution Ave. NW, Downtown. Metro: Federal Triangle.*

2 *f-2*

TAKOMA

This cluster has six lighted courts. *3rd and Van Buren Sts. NW, Takoma Park, MD. Metro: Takoma.*

2 *f-3*

TURKEY THICKET

Near Catholic University, this facility has eight courts. *10th St. and Michigan Ave. NE, University Heights. Metro: Brookland–CUA.*

indoor courts

1 *c-2*

CABIN JOHN

There's often a long wait for these six indoor courts, as the facilities are first-rate. *7777 Democracy Blvd., Bethesda, MD, 301/469–7300.*

7 *b-4*

EAST POTOMAC PARK

A bubble covers these five courts. *1100 Ohio St. SW, Waterfront, 202/554–5962. Metro: Waterfront–SEU.*

3 *f-3*

ROCK CREEK PARK

Rock Creek also has five courts in a bubble. *3545 Williamsburg La. NW, Cleveland Park, 202/722–5949.*

events

LEGG MASON TENNIS CLASSIC

Washington has been an annual pit stop on the professional tennis tour for decades. In years past, Jimmy Connors and Andre Agassi have been repeat winners in a tournament that has undergone numerous name changes, but now goes by the moniker of sponsor Legg Mason, a financial institution. For any number of reasons, most of them relating to the humidity of August and temporal proximity to the U.S. Open, this competition has never been able to draw more than a few top names in any given year. Organizers have recently hinted that they will try to change to a less sweltering date. In any case, the facility is located in a national park and remains a topflight venue for players and fans alike. Now, if only somebody would invent air-conditioning that would work outside. *William H. G. Fitzgerald Tennis Center, Carter Barron Park, 16th and Kennedy Sts. NW, Brightwood, 202/426–6837.*

VOLLEYBALL

outdoor volleyball

5 *e-7*

UNDERPASS VOLLEYBALL COURTS

Don't be fooled by the sterile name: these 11 public courts—in the shadow of the Lincoln Memorial and Washington Monument, and bordering the Potomac River—form possibly the most idyllic noncoastal volleyball venue you'll ever find. Six of the courts are reserved for those granted permits through the city, and the remaining five are available on a first-come, first-served basis. *26th St. Circle, between Rock Creek Pkwy. and*

Independence Ave. NW, Downtown, 202/ 619–7225. Metro: Foggy Bottom.

indoor volleyball

For players who don't like the feeling of sand between their toes, the Adult Sports Office at the D.C. Department of Parks and Recreation oversees competitive adult volleyball leagues for indoor play. For $225 per team, you can get a net one night a week at a neighborhood recreation center. *202/ 724–4920.*

YOGA

Rapidly gaining in popularity with harried Hill workers, lawyers, and lobbyists, yoga classes are now available at most gyms as well as the centers below. Yoga has several different forms, some concentrating more on breathing and meditation, others somewhat more physically challenging. As with any new physical regime, it's wise to ask lots of questions and try a class or two before you commit to a long-term program. Most centers offer introductory classes for those new to the process.

5 *b-2*

SPIRAL FLIGHT
The emphasis at this "center for yoga and the arts" is on body alignment and meditation. *1726 Wisconsin Ave. NW, Glover Park, 202/965–1645.*

1 *c-2*

UNITY WOODS YOGA CENTER
The best known and most popular area studio, Unity Woods offers classes at all levels and special programs ranging from yoga for pregnant women to yoga for cancer patients. The Bethesda center administers the two other locations. *4853 Cordell Ave., Suite PH- 9, Bethesda, MD, 301/656–8992.*

3 *e-7*

2639 Connecticut Ave. NW, Suite C-102, Adams-Morgan. Metro: Woodley Park– Zoo.

1 *c-5*

4001 N. 9th St., Suite 105, Arlington, VA. Metro: Ballston–MU.

fitness centers, health clubs, & spa services

CLUBS

2 *g-6*

ANACOSTIA WELLNESS/FITNESS RECREATION CENTER
Cardiovascular equipment, aerobics classes, and weightlifting equipment are all available for a nominal fee at this city-sponsored fitness facility. Certified instructors can help you develop a personal workout regimen or a new diet plan. *1800 Anacostia Dr. SE, Anacostia, 202/645–3944. Metro: Anacostia.*

5 *f-4*

BALLY TOTAL FITNESS
This national chain features cardiovascular equipment, free weights, and a wide range of aerobics classes. There is no cap on the number of members, so clubs are often very crowded, with waiting lists for treadmills and stair machines. *2000 L St. NW, Dupont Circle, 202/331–7788. Metro: Dupont Circle.*

HOTEL HEALTH CLUBS

Some of the best clubs in D.C. are in downtown hotels. The amenities are worth the extra cost, and the crowds are deliciously thin.

Capitol Hilton
1001 16th St. NW, 202/393–1000.

Four Seasons
2800 Pennsylvania Ave. NW, 202/ 342–0444.

Hyatt Regency on Capitol Hill
400 New Jersey Ave. NW, 202/737– 1234.

Washington Hilton and Towers
1919 Connecticut Ave. NW, 202/ 483–3000.

Washington Monarch Hotel
2401 M St. NW, 202/429–2400.

Washington Renaissance Hotel
999 9th St. NW, 202/898–9000.

---

1 d-7

6200 Little River Turnpike, Alexandria, VA, 703/658–5000.

2 b-2

BODY COLLEGE

The Body College teaches Joseph Pilates' system of anaerobic exercise, which focuses on posture and body alignment along with strength and flexibility. 4708 Wisconsin Ave. NW, Friendship Heights, 202/237–0080. Metro: Tenleytown–AU or Friendship Heights.

5 e-4

THE FITNESS COMPANY

An upscale chain of health clubs, Fitness Company targets "executives" who appreciate the high-tech workout equipment and one-on-one attention from the well-trained staff. It's an expensive option, but perks abound, such as laundry service, steam rooms, and a VCR on each treadmill. Washington Monarch Hotel, 2401 M St. NW, Georgetown, 202/457–5070. Metro: Foggy Bottom–GWU.

6 a-5

1401 H St. NW, Downtown, 202/408–8283. Metro: McPherson Sq.

5 g-5

1875 I St. NW, Dupont Circle, 202/833–2629. Metro: Farragut North.

2 d-4

RESULTS—THE GYM

Housed in a bright and airy renovated warehouse in the revitalized U Street area, Results is a cutting-edge fitness facility. Its three giant floors contain a bevy of workout options, including a Reebok spinning room with disco balls (picture it!), a yoga room with a gurgling fountain, a conveyor belt–style moving rock wall, and state-of-the-art Nautilus and Cybex equipment, plus free weights. During busy workout times, there is an "abs" class every 30 minutes in the main weight room. Most Results clients are gay men, but the management goes out of its way to make women feel comfortable as well, with a plush locker room and a separate women's Nautilus area. 1612 U St. NW, U Street, 202/518–0001. Metro: U St.–Cardozo.

2 b-2

SPORT & HEALTH CLUB

One of the largest health-club groups in the D.C. area, these are full-service fitness facilities that often add such perks as tennis courts and swimming pools to the standard Nautilus and other cardio-vascular machines. 4001 Brandywine St. NW, Tenleytown, 202/244–6090. Metro: Tenleytown–AU.

5 f-2

Washington Hilton, 1919 Connecticut Ave. NW, Adams-Morgan, 202/483–3000. Metro: Dupont Circle.

6 e-6

WASHINGTON SPORTS CLUB

A full range of workout options and reasonable prices make this local chain quite popular. All clubs have a wide variety of aerobics classes and Nautilus and Cybex equipment, and the Capitol Hill location has squash courts as well. 214 D St. NW, Capitol Hill, 202/547–2255. Metro: Judiciary Sq.

5 f-4

1990 M St. NW, Downtown, 202/785–4900. Metro: Farragut North.

3 a-8

2251 Wisconsin Ave. NW, Cleveland Park, 202/333–2323. Metro: Cleveland Park.

1 c-2

4903 Elm St., Bethesda, MD, 301/657–0600. Metro: Bethesda.

5 h-3

YMCA

If you picture the local YMCA as a dark and musty building filled with old-fashioned medicine balls and free weights, you owe it to yourself to come and see how much things have changed: this YMCA is as modern a workout facility as any fashionable club in the city, and has very reasonable prices. The bright, sun-drenched rooms are filled with modern equipment, and you can take your pick of a 25-meter six-lane pool, an indoor track, a basketball court, and squash and racquetball courts. 1112 16th St. NW, Dupont Circle, 202/862–9622. Metro: Farragut North or Dupont Circle.

DAY SPAS & MASSAGE

There's nothing more luxurious than pampering yourself just because you've decided you deserve it. Create your own holiday: reward yourself for going to the gym, finishing a project, enduring a personal trial, or just being you, and you'll be amazed how quickly thoughts of the outside world will disappear.

5 *h-4*

ANDRE CHREKY

A beauty-conscious crowd flocks to this day spa, located in a bright, attractive town house, for a full range of body services (including massage and reflexology), waxing, and manicures and pedicures, not to mention the hair salon. *1604 K St. NW, Downtown, 202/293–9393. Metro: Farragut North.*

9 *g-7*

EFX SPA

Featuring the latest beautifying trends in its "skin gym," this spa offers massages, traditional and oxygen facials, and waxing to a youngish Georgetown clientele. *3059 M St. NW, Georgetown, 202/965–1300. Metro: Foggy Bottom–GWU.*

5 *d-4*

GEORGE AT THE FOUR SEASONS

Walk into the day spa at this luxury hotel and walk out feeling like a million bucks. Try the healing mud bath, a massage, a facial, an aromatherapy treatment, or any combination thereof. *2828 Pennsylvania Ave. NW, Georgetown, 202/342–1942. Closed Sun. Metro: Foggy Bottom–GWU.*

2 *b-1*

GEORGETTE KLINGER

A Washington tradition for the well-heeled, Georgette Klinger is for some locals the *only* place to go for massages and facials. Men are every bit as welcome as women. Treatments here are pricey, but regular patrons say they are well worth it. *Chevy Chase Pavilion, 5345 Wisconsin Ave. NW, Upper Northwest, 202/686–8880. Metro: Friendship Heights.*

6 *b-5*

THE HEALTHY BACK STORE

To get the knots out quickly, stop here for a seated 15-, 20-, or 30-minute shoulder rub by a certified massage therapist. The shop also sells such products as ergonomic chairs designed to release back stress and relieve aches and pains. *1341 G St. NW, Downtown, 202/393–2225. Closed weekends. Metro: Metro Center.*

1 *c-2*

JOLIE, THE DAY SPA AND HAIR DESIGN

Busy Washington women don't mind leaving the city proper behind for an appointment at this spa, recently named by *Washingtonian* magazine as the best place in D.C. to get a massage. The day spa has 15 private treatment rooms and a full gamut of services—body treatments, massages, facials, hair, nails, and makeup. *7200 Wisconsin Ave., Bethesda, MD 301/986–9293. Metro: Bethesda.*

5 *f-4*

LILLIAN LAURENCE LTD.

This New Age spa offers a full range of holistic, all-natural treatments. The hydrotherapy and aromatherapy sessions are particularly popular. *2000 M St. NW, Downtown, 202/872–0606. Metro: Farragut North.*

5 *g-5*

VICTORIA'S DAY SPA

What it lacks in fancy amenities, Victoria's more than makes up for with its homespun appeal and comparatively low prices. Some of this spa's special services include paraffin manicures, pedicures, and body wraps, as well as seaweed masks. *1926 I St. NW, Downtown, 202/254–0442. Metro: Farragut West.*

chapter 4

PLACES TO EXPLORE

galleries, gargoyles, museums, & more

With internationally acclaimed museums and monuments that are surrounded by cherry trees and vast expanses of green, Washington, D.C., is home to more free attractions than any other city in the nation. That gives residents and tourists alike the freedom to stroll in and out of museums and galleries, spending 10 minutes here and half a day there. Whether you're pondering a Picasso at the Hirshhorn, sampling the food at Adams-Morgan, reading up on Shakespeare at the Folger, or checking out Nixon's resignation letter at the Archives, you'll never run out of ways to discover—and rediscover—D.C.

Admission to museums is free unless otherwise noted.

where to go

ARCHITECTURE

Washington, D.C., and its suburbs contain too many worthy historic buildings to list here. We review some of the most spectacular, including government buildings, museums, libraries, embassies, and mansions. For more information on these structures and their architects, see the *AIA Guide to the Architecture of Washington, D.C.*, published by the American Institute of Architects (1777 Church St. NW, 20036, 202/626–7475) and the Johns Hopkins University Press.

Each site is introduced with the name of its architect and the year the project was completed.

6 c-7
CANADIAN EMBASSY
(Arthur Erickson Architects, 1989) A spectacular edifice of stone and glass, the Canadian Embassy building occupies a prime piece of real estate. The columns of the rotunda represent Canada's 12 provinces and territories. Inside, a gallery periodically displays exhibits on Canadian culture and history. *501 Pennsylvania Ave. NW, The Mall. Metro: Archives–Navy Memorial.*

10 b-6
CAPITOL
(William Thornton, 1793–1802) George Washington himself laid the cornerstone of this building, one of the world's most widely recognized. Dr. Thornton, a physician from the Virgin Islands, penned the original design, but the building has been expanded and changed by nine other architects over the centuries, set back only when it was torched by the British during the War of 1812. Charles Bulfinch (1819–29) connected the existing wings and built a 55-ft dome modeled after his Massachusetts State House. During the Capitol's 1851–65 expansion, Thomas U. Walter created the great dome that now caps the 180-ft-high Capitol Rotunda. The armed lady *Freedom*, Thomas Crawford's 19-ft statue, was placed atop the dome in 1863, at the time of the Emancipation Proclamation. The West Front, the side facing the Mall, was restored in 1988. *East end of Mall, Capitol Hill. Metro: Capitol South.*

5 g-6
DEPARTMENT OF THE INTERIOR
(Waddy B. Wood, 1935) The neoclassical Department of the Interior was the first large federal building with such modern amenities as escalators and central air-conditioning. The building's exterior is somewhat plain, but much of the inside is decorated with art based on the department's work: hallways feature heroic oil paintings of dam construction, gold panning, and cattle drives. *C and E Sts., between 18th and 19th Sts., Downtown. Metro: Farragut West.*

2 d-6
JEFFERSON MEMORIAL
(John Russell Pope, 1943) The Potomac River once flowed here; workmen moved tons of river bottom to create dry land for this tribute to our third president, Thomas Jefferson. The neoclassical, white-marble monument on the shores of the Tidal Basin was inspired by Rome's Pantheon, which Jefferson loved. The monument greets everyone entering the District by the 14th Street Bridge. *See Statues, Murals & Monuments, below. Tidal Basin, south bank, Downtown. Metro: Smithsonian.*

The Capitol

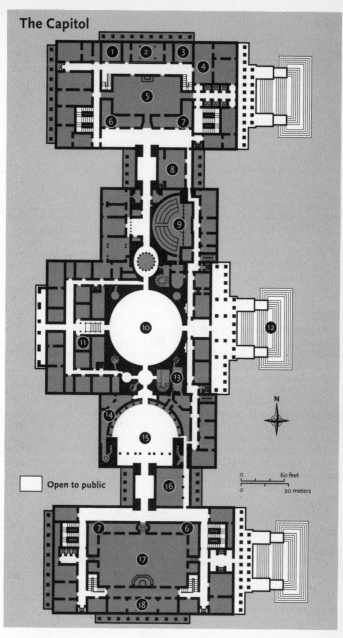

1 President's Room
2 Marble Room (Senators' Retiring Room)
3 Ceremonial Office of the Vice President
4 Senators' Reception Room
5 Senate Chamber
6 Democratic Cloakrooms
7 Republican Cloakrooms
8 Senators' Conference Room
9 Old Senate Chamber
10 Rotunda
11 Prayer Room
12 East Front
13 Congresswomen's Suite
14 House Document Room
15 Statuary Hall
16 House Reception Room
17 House Chamber
18 Representatives' Retiring Rooms

5 | d-6

JOHN F. KENNEDY CENTER FOR THE PERFORMING ARTS

(Edward Durrell Stone, 1971) The rather dull, rectangular design of this white Carrara marble building belies the exciting performances held inside. Those attending an opera, symphony concert, ballet, play, or musical can spend intermission on its wide, riverfront terrace that overhangs the Rock Creek and Potomac Parkway and grants a fabulous view of Georgetown, to the north, and Theodore Roosevelt Island, directly across the Potomac. Beneath 18 one-ton crystal chandeliers in the main foyer stands Robert Berks's massive bronze bust of John F. Kennedy. Guided tours are given weekdays 10–5, weekends 10–1. *New Hampshire Ave. at Rock Creek Pkwy. NW, Foggy Bottom, 202/416–8340. Metro: Foggy Bottom–GWU.*

10 | d-7

LIBRARY OF CONGRESS

(Smithmeyer & Pelz, 1886–92) Based on the design of the Paris Opera House, the Library of Congress's Jefferson Building has stern granite walls supporting a spectacular octagonal copper dome, which rises 160 ft above the marble-and-wood reading room. The Court of Neptune, Roland Horton Perry's fountain at the base of the front steps, rivals some of Rome's finest. *See Libraries, below. 1st St. and Independence Ave. SE, Capitol Hill. Metro: Capitol South.*

5 | e-8

LINCOLN MEMORIAL

(Henry Bacon, 1911–22) Like the Jefferson Memorial, this edifice—inspired by Athens's Parthenon—stands on former swampland. Its 36 columns represent the number of states in the Union during Abraham Lincoln's presidency, and its 48 festoons represent the number of states at the time of the building's completion. It's a perfect counterbalance to the Capitol, at the opposite end of the Mall. *See Statues, Murals & Monuments, below. West end of Mall, Downtown. Metro: Foggy Bottom–GWU.*

6 | d-5

NATIONAL BUILDING MUSEUM/PENSION BUILDING

(Montgomery C. Meigs, 1887) This 400-by 200-ft "barn" was inspired by

Michelangelo's Palazzo Farnese, in Rome, which Montgomery Meigs visited in 1867. Built to administer Civil War pensions, the building contains one of the most astonishing rooms in the District, measuring more than 300 ft long, 116 ft wide, and 159 ft high and ringed by four stories of arcaded passages. The room has hosted more than a dozen inaugural balls and numerous national celebrations. *4th and F Sts. NW, Downtown. Metro: Judiciary Sq.*

6 | c-7

NATIONAL MUSEUM OF NATURAL HISTORY

(Hornblower & Marshall, 1911) On the north side of the Mall is this marble neoclassical gem belonging to the Smithsonian group. The domed roof covers a rotunda dominated by a statue of an enormous bull elephant. *See Science Museums, below. Constitution Ave. between 9th and 12th Sts. NW, Downtown. Metro: Federal Triangle.*

6 | a-5

NATIONAL MUSEUM OF WOMEN IN THE ARTS

(Wood, Donn & Deming, 1908) This elegant limestone-and-granite Renaissance Revival trapezoid was designed by Waddy Wood. Once a men-only Masonic Temple, it was restored in 1987 to house a library and gallery of art by women. *See Art Museums, below. New York Ave. and 13th St. NW, Downtown. Metro: Metro Center.*

5 | h-6

OLD EXECUTIVE OFFICE BUILDING

(Alfred B. Mullett, 1875–88) This 10-acre building adjacent to the White House, originally the State, War and Navy Building, has 900 projecting and superimposed Doric columns and a French mansard roof with chimneys. Detractors criticized the busy French Empire design, which was patterned after the Louvre. Numerous plans to alter the facade foundered because of lack of money. The grand edifice may look like a wedding cake, but its high ceilings and spacious offices are popular with occupants, who include members of the executive branch. The OEOB was the site of both the first presidential press conference, given by President Truman in 1950, and the first televised press conference, given by President Eisenhower in 1955. *Pennsylvania Ave. and 17th*

St. NW, Downtown. Metro: Farragut West.

6 b-6
OLD POST OFFICE/ THE PAVILION

(Willoughby J. Edbrooke, 1899) The spire of this wonderful Romanesque Revival building can be seen far and wide. It was the first major steel-framed structure in town, and when it opened, its 99-by-184-ft interior court was the city's largest uninterrupted enclosed space. Although it was almost demolished several times after the Post Office decamped in 1930, it was restored in 1982 by Arthur Cotton Moore & Associates. Its new, impressive atrium, 160 ft high, takes in seven floors of offices and three floors of shops and restaurants, and is home to the National Endowment for the Arts. 12th St. and Pennsylvania Ave. NW, Downtown. Metro: Federal Triangle.

5 g-7
ORGANIZATION OF AMERICAN STATES

(Albert Kelsay and Paul P. Cret, 1910) This marble structure was built as the headquarters of the OAS, which was founded in 1948 to foster collaboration among the nations of North, South, and Central America. Inside, the upstairs Hall of the Americas contains busts of generals and statesmen from the 34 OAS member nations, as well as each country's flag. The building's patio is adorned with a pre-Columbian-style fountain and lush tropical plants. This tiny rain forest is a cool resting place in the hot Washington summer. 17th St. and Constitution Ave. NW, Downtown. Metro: Farragut West.

6 b-8
SMITHSONIAN INSTITUTION BUILDING ("THE CASTLE")

(James Renwick, 1855) Today one could write a book about each of the Smithsonian museums, but this was the original, and it's now the administrative headquarters of the entire Smithsonian Institution. The red-sandstone building is arguably one of the greatest examples of Gothic Revival design in the nation. Inside is the Smithsonian Information Center (open daily 9–5:30), useful in plotting a course through the various museums. Jefferson Dr. between 9th and 12th Sts. SW, The Mall. Metro: Smithsonian.

6 a-6
TREASURY BUILDING

(Robert Mills, 1836) Obstructing what Pierre-Charles L'Enfant, the French engineer who planned the layout of D.C., termed the "reciprocity of view" between the White House and the Capitol (Andrew Jackson selected the site), the Treasury Building is the oldest of the government's departmental buildings and the largest Greek Revival edifice in Washington. Construction started in 1836 but wasn't completed until 1869. Mills himself was dismissed from the job in 1851 because of political squabbling, but the architectural mastery of the building is his. The 30-piece Ionic colonnade that stretches down 15th Street set the tone for the buildings that followed. The southern facade has a statue of Alexander Hamilton, the department's first secretary. 1500 Pennsylvania Ave. NW, Downtown. Metro: McPherson Sq. or Metro Center.

6 f-5
UNION STATION

(Daniel H. Burnham, 1908) With its 96-ft-high coffered ceiling gilded with eight pounds of gold leaf, the city's train station is one of the capital's great spaces and is used for inaugural balls and other festive events. In 1902 the McMillian Commission—charged with suggesting ways to improve the appearance of the city—recommended that the many train lines that sliced through the capital share one main depot. Beaux Arts–style Union Station was opened in 1908 as the first building completed under the commission's plan. Chicago architect and commission member Daniel Burnham patterned the station after the Roman Baths of Diocletian. The Union Station you see today is the result of a huge 1988 restoration that followed years of neglect. The jewel of the structure is its main waiting room, with 46 statues of Roman legionnaires—one for each state in the Union when the station was completed—ringing the room. Massachusetts Ave. NE, north of the Capitol, Capitol Hill. Metro: Union Station.

5 h-6
WHITE HOUSE

(James Hoban, Benjamin H. Latrobe, and others, 1792) An Irish architect practicing in Charleston, South Carolina, Hoban drew inspiration for the Executive Mansion from Dublin's Leinster

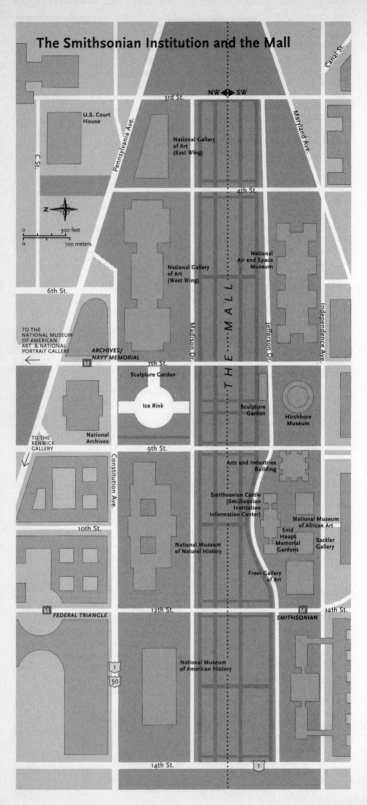

The Smithsonian Institution and the Mall

Canal St.

3rd St.

NW — SW

Maryland Ave.

U.S. Court House

National Gallery of Art (East Wing)

Pennsylvania Ave.

C St.

4th St.

N

300 feet

100 meters

National Gallery of Art (West Wing)

National Air and Space Museum

6th St.

Madison Dr.

Jefferson Dr.

THE MALL

Independence Ave.

TO THE NATIONAL MUSEUM OF AMERICAN ART & NATIONAL PORTRAIT GALLERY

ARCHIVES/ NAVY MEMORIAL

7th St.

Sculpture Garden

Ice Rink

Sculpture Garden

Hirshhorn Museum

TO THE RENWICK GALLERY

National Archives

Constitution Ave.

9th St.

Arts and Industries Building

Smithsonian Castle (Smithsonian Institution Information Center)

Enid Haupt Memorial Gardens

National Museum of African Art

Sackler Gallery

10th St.

National Museum of Natural History

Freer Gallery of Art

FEDERAL TRIANGLE

12th St.

SMITHSONIAN

12th St.

1

50

National Museum of American History

14th St.

1

House and from other English and Irish country houses. Built of Virginia sandstone, the house was first occupied in 1800 by John Adams, torched by the British in 1814, and only saved from total destruction by a fortuitous thunderstorm, which extinguished the flames. Construction was finally completed in 1829, although several presidents have modified the building since then. *See* Historic Structures & Streets, *below. 1600 Pennsylvania Ave. NW, Downtown, 202/456–7041 or 202/619–7222. Metro: Federal Triangle.*

6 a-6
WILLARD INTER-CONTINENTAL HOTEL
(Henry Hardenbergh, 1901) Designed by the same architect who created New York City's Plaza Hotel, the Willard was restored in the early 1980s and reopened in 1986. Just two blocks from the White House, this opulent building has a mansard roof sheltering the penthouses. *14th St. and Pennsylvania Ave. NW, Downtown. Metro: Metro Center.*

ART GALLERIES

Washington's art scene is experiencing a surge of vibrancy and expansion, as evidenced in the growing popularity and sophistication of its galleries. The full gamut of art forms is exhibited—from old master paintings to neon sculpture, from 19th-century photography to postmodern video abstraction. Galleries are generally open Tuesday through Saturday 10–5 or 11–6; some are also open Sunday or Monday, usually with reduced hours. For a comprehensive review of exhibitions, see *galleries* magazine, available in some galleries or by subscription (call 301/270–0180). *Washington City Paper*, the *Washington Post*'s Friday "Weekend" section, and *Washingtonian* magazine also list openings and ongoing exhibitions.

dupont circle
The Galleries of Dupont Circle, a consortium of almost two dozen Dupont art businesses, holds a joint gallery open house with light refreshments on the first Friday of each month from 6 to 8. On the second Saturday of each month, they sponsor a gallery-talk program with short discussions of art-related topics at various galleries. *202/232–3610.*

5 f-2
AFRICA
Stop in here to see fine traditional arts of Africa, including masks, figures, textiles, pottery, and furniture. The gallery's name comes from the continent's spelling on old maps. *2010 R St. NW, 202/745–7272. Closed Sun. and Mon. Metro: Dupont Circle.*

5 f-2
ALEX GALLERY
Victor Gaetan's contemporary painting and sculpture gallery showcases abstractions by Europeans and Americans with firmly established reputations. Although not a member of the Dupont galleries consortium, the gallery does participate in First Friday open houses. *2106 R St. NW, 202/667–2599. Closed Sun. and Mon. Metro: Dupont Circle.*

5 f-2
AMERICA, OH YES!
This gallery features Outsider and Visionary art—the work of self-taught artists. The descriptions accompanying the pieces are often as engaging as the works themselves. *2020 R St. NW, 202/483–9644. Closed Sun. Metro: Dupont Circle.*

5 f-2
ANTON GALLERY
Contemporary art—including paintings, sculpture, ceramics, and photography—with an Asian emphasis characterize this progressive gallery. *2108 R St. NW, 202/328–0828. Closed Mon. Metro: Dupont Circle.*

5 f-2
BURDICK GALLERY
John Burdick's gallery is one of very few in the United States that specializes in contemporary Inuit (Eskimo) sculpture and graphics and prints from the Canadian Arctic. *2114 R St. NW, 202/986–5682. Closed Sun. and Mon. Metro: Dupont Circle.*

5 f-3
BURTON MARINKOVICH FINE ART
The prints and paintings here are from modern and contemporary masters, including Georges Braque, Pablo Picasso, and Fernand Léger. *1506 21st St. NW, 202/296–6563. Closed Sun. (except by appointment) and Mon. Metro: Dupont Circle.*

5 *f-1*

CHAO PHRAYA GALLERY

Works here center on the arts and antiques of Asia; a recent exhibition displayed contemporary Vietnamese lacquer paintings on wood. *2009 Columbia Rd. NW, 202/745–1111. Closed Sun. and Mon. Metro: Dupont Circle.*

5 *f-2*

GALLERY K

Dupont Circle's most popular gallery shows emerging artists from the D.C. area, but the large inventory also includes works by Andy Warhol, Robert Motherwell, and Jackson Pollock. *2010 R St. NW, 202/234–0339. Closed Sun. and Mon. Metro: Dupont Circle.*

5 *g-2*

GALLERY 10 LTD.

In its four rooms right above Kramerbooks, this co-op–managed gallery displays contemporary art by its own members and other local artists. *1519 Connecticut Ave. NW, 202/232–3326. Closed Sun. and Mon. Metro: Dupont Circle.*

5 *f-2*

GEOFFREY DINER

Diner specializes in 20th-century English and American decorative arts and crafts by such notables as Gustav Stickley and Tiffany, among others. The gallery is only open Saturday from 1–6 or by appointment. *1730 21st St. NW, 202/483–5005. Metro: Dupont Circle.*

5 *f-2*

KATHLEEN EWING GALLERY

Internationally renowned photography dealer Kathleen Ewing shows top-notch work—from late-19th-century to contemporary—in a low-key, friendly environment. *1609 Connecticut Ave. NW, 202/328–0955. Closed Sun.–Tues. Metro: Dupont Circle.*

5 *f-2*

L.I.P.A.

The name stands for Links to International Promotion of the Arts, and the gallery shows work by Eastern and Central European artists, such as Metka Krasevec. Hours vary, so call ahead. *1635 Connecticut Ave. NW, 202/238–0007. Metro: Dupont Circle.*

5 *f-2*

MARSHA MATEYKA

Mateyka displays contemporary paintings, sculptures, and works on paper by established living American and European artists. Stephen Talesnik and Nathan Oliveira have shown here. *2012 R St. NW, 202/328–0088. Closed Sun.–Tues. Metro: Dupont Circle.*

5 *f-2*

ROBERT BROWN GALLERY

Brown shows 20th-century American and European prints, etchings, and lithographs. *2030 R St. NW, 202/483–4383. Closed Sun. and Mon. Metro: Dupont Circle.*

5 *g-2*

ST. LUKE'S GALLERY

The area's only old master gallery, St. Luke's specializes in 16th- to 18th-century oils, watercolors, and prints. Chamber music and lectures often accompany exhibitions. *1715 Q St. NW, 202/328–2424. Closed Sun.–Tues. Metro: Dupont Circle.*

5 *f-2*

STUDIO GALLERY

Contemporary paintings, ceramics, and mixed media are all mounted here at this 30-member cooperative gallery. *2108 R St. NW, 202/232- -8734. Closed Sun.–Tues. Metro: Dupont Circle.*

5 *f-2*

THE TARTT GALLERY

Tartt shows 19th- and 20th-century photography and Outsider art. *2017 Q St. NW, 202/332–5652. Closed Sun.–Tues. Metro: Dupont Circle.*

5 *f-2*

TROYER GALLERY

Sally Troyer promotes young, edgy talent, displaying work by local painters, photographers, and sculptors. *1710 Connecticut Ave. NW, 202/328–7189. Closed Sun. and Mon. Metro: Dupont Circle.*

5 *g-3*

VERY SPECIAL ARTS

This nonprofit gallery shows art in all media by professional artists with disabilities. *1300 Connecticut Ave. NW, 202/628–2800. Closed Sun. Metro: Farragut North.*

5 f-2

WASHINGTON PRINTMAKERS GALLERY

As the name implies, you can peruse original contemporary prints here. *1732 Connecticut Ave., Dupont Circle, 202/332–7757. Closed Mon. Metro: Dupont Circle.*

georgetown

Georgetown's galleries range from old guard to cutting edge. Galleries 1054, at 1054 31st Street NW, has several galleries in one building. They host an open house on the third Friday of each month from 6 to 8, with live music in warm weather.

5 b-2

ADDISON/RIPLEY

Addison/Ripley showcases the work of Washington-based artists, including painter Manon Cleary and sculptor John Drayfuss. The gallery also presents group shows by contemporary masters such as painter Manon Cleary and sculptor John Drayfuss. *1670 Wisconsin Ave. NW, 202/333–3335. Closed Sun. and Mon.*

9 f-7

ALLA ROGERS

The area's only gallery specializing in contemporary Eastern European art, Alla Rogers shows the work of artists well-known in their own countries. *1054 31st St. NW, 202/333–8595. Closed Sun. and Mon.*

9 g-7

AMERICAN HAND PLUS

This intriguing collection includes modern pottery, dishes, lamps, and glasses. *2906 M St. NW, 202/965–3273.*

9 d-7

CREIGHTON-DAVIS

Creighton-Davis specializes in fine art prints and also handles some paintings, etchings and small-scale sculpture. Works by Pablo Picasso, Henri Matisse, Marc Chagall, Roy Lichtenstein, Andy Warhol, Robert Rauschenberg, and James McNeil Whistler are presented. *3322 M St. NW, 202/333–3050.*

9 g-7

FINE ART & ARTISTS GALLERY

Works by Roy Lichtenstein, Andy Warhol, Robert Rauschenberg, R. C.

White, and Claes Oldenburg, among others, are shown here. The gallery also exhibits glass, ceramic, and steel multiples. *2920 M St. NW, 202/965–0780 or 800/334–4033.*

9 f-7

FRASER

Established by Catriona Fraser in 1996 as a showcase for less-intimidating contemporary art—"artwork for people"—the Fraser Gallery features one artist each month in addition to an annual juried group show. *1054 31st St. NW, 202/298–6450. Closed Sun. and Mon.*

9 f-7

GALLERY OKUDA INTERNATIONAL

Teruko Okuda shows contemporary painting and sculpture by American, Japanese, and European artists. *1054 31st St. NW, 202/625–1054.*

9 f-7

GEORGETOWN ART GUILD

This gallery has featured a South African collection and work by Pierre Matisse. Wine tastings and wine dinners are nice touches. *1054 31st St. NW, 202/625–1470. Closed Sun. and Mon.*

9 e-5

GEORGETOWN GALLERY OF ART

Works by Pablo Picasso, Henry Moore, and Allan Houser are often shown here, in addition to various important original graphics. *3235 P St. NW, 202/333–6308. Closed Sun. and Mon.*

9 c-7

GOVINDA GALLERY

Owner Christopher Murray shows work by pop and folk artists, but his gallery is best known for its collection of rock and roll photography and paintings. Work includes photos by Annie Liebovitz, Linda McCartney, Astrid Kirchherr, and original Beatle Stuart Sutcliffe. *1227 34th St. NW, 202/333–1180. Closed Sun. and Mon.*

9 d-7

HEMPHILL FINE ARTS

Hemphill features abstract paintings, sculpture, and works on paper by up-and-coming and established artists. Represented artists include painter Steve Cushner, photographer Joseph

Mills, and sculptor Tara Donovan. *1027 33rd St. NW, 202/342–5610. Closed Sun. and Mon.*

9 *f-7*

MUSEUM OF CONTEMPORARY ART (MOCA)

Owned by husband and wife artists Michael Clark and Felicity Hogan, MOCA is the antithesis of the conservative art gallery. The low ceiling and grungy atmosphere complement the innovative, unusual contemporary art shown here—everything from paintings with poetry readings to multimedia video displays. *1054 31st St. NW, 202/342–6230. Closed Sun. and Mon.*

9 *g-6*

SPECTRUM

A cooperative fine arts gallery, Spectrum has been showing abstract and traditional American art, with an abundance of paintings, for 35 years. Female artists are well represented. *1132 29th St. NW, 202/333–0954. Closed Mon.*

9 *g-7*

SUSAN CONWAY

Susan Conway shows her 20th-century American art collection in a four-story, 19th-century Georgetown row house (known as Glackens House). The gallery is a favorite of political cartoon fans—it's home to the world's largest collection of Pat Oliphant's drawings and sculpture. *1214 30th St. NW, 202/333–6343. Closed Sun. and Mon.*

downtown

The Seventh Street arts corridor has a mix of commercial and cooperative galleries that hold joint openings on the third Thursday of the month from 6 to 8, with gallery walks and specials at local restaurants. You can hit several galleries downtown with a stop at 406 7th Street NW, a building housing several galleries.

6 *c-6*

ARTISTS MUSEUM

This commercial gallery rents space to artists, so it has an ever-changing variety of artists and media. *406 7th St. NW, 202/638–7001. Closed Sun. and Mon. Metro: Gallery Pl.–Chinatown or Archives–Navy Memorial.*

6 *c-6*

DAVID ADAMSON

Adamson's collection focuses on the possibilities of computer-generated art, showcasing digital printmaking and photography. Some artists use Adamson's high-fidelity ink-jet color printer in the adjoining studio to create new art from existing works. *406 7th St. NW, 202/628–0257. Closed Sun. and Mon. Metro: Gallery Pl.–Chinatown or Archives–Navy Memorial.*

6 *c-6*

EKLEKTIKOS

eklektikos (Greek for eclectic) has established itself as one of the hottest contemporary art spaces in the District today, with avant-garde creations by local, national, and international artists. *406 7th St., NW, 202/342–1809. Closed Sun. and Mon. Metro: Gallery Pl.–Chinatown or Archives–Navy Memorial.*

6 *c-6*

NUMARK

Numark might be said to specialize in contemporary ethereal prints and works on paper. The gallery also exhibits sculpture. Exhibitions have included the works of Donald Baechler, Mel Bochner, Chuck Close, Tara Donovan, Carroll Dunham, Tony Feher, Greg Hannan, Mary Heilmann, Ellsworth Kelly, Sol Lewitt, and Jeff Spaulding. *406 7th St. NW, 202/628–3810. Closed Sun. and Mon. Metro: Gallery Pl.–Chinatown or Archives–Navy Memorial.*

6 *c-6*

TOUCHSTONE

One of the oldest cooperative galleries in the area, Touchstone deals in minimalist paintings and photography. *406 7th St. NW, 202/347–2787. Closed Mon. and Tues. Metro: Gallery Pl.–Chinatown or Archives–Navy Memorial.*

6 *c-6*

ZENITH

Among the traditional sculpture, furniture, fiber art, or neon showing at Zenith, Ray Wiger's metal mesh occasionally makes an appearance. The gallery also has the area's only annual neon show. *413 7th St. NW, 202/783–2963. Closed Sun. Metro: Gallery Pl.–Chinatown.*

elsewhere

Although Dupont Circle, Georgetown, and 7th Street have the largest concentration of galleries, many others dotted throughout the city are worth a visit.

3 g-8

DISTRICT OF COLUMBIA ARTS CENTER (DCAC)

A combination art gallery and performance space, nonprofit DCAC offers nine cutting-edge visual arts shows a year of regional artists, and hosts offbeat plays, poetry readings, and performance art. *2438 18th St. NW, Adams-Morgan, 202/462–7833. Closed Mon. and Tues. Metro: Dupont Circle.*

6 b-3

SIGNAL 66

Contemporary local artists are featured in this ultrahip gallery housed in a renovated warehouse, which was originally a Civil War livery stable. The gallery's obscure address—hidden down an alley—adds to its appeal. The openings can be worth the trip for the eclectic art scene and club atmosphere. *Blagden Alley, 926 N St. NW, Downtown, 202/842–3436. Closed Sun.–Wed. Metro: Mount Vernon Sq./7th St.–Convention Center.*

8 g-4

TORPEDO FACTORY ART CENTER

Once the site of a torpedo munitions factory, this 72,000-square-ft building was converted in 1973 to artist studios and workshops. About 160 artists—painters, printmakers, sculptors, potters, photographers, and jewelers—work here, and the cooperative Art League holds monthly juried shows. *105 N. Union St., Alexandria, 703/838–4199. Metro: King St.*

ART MUSEUMS

5 h-3

B'NAI B'RITH KLUTZNICK NATIONAL JEWISH MUSEUM

Devoted to the history of Jewish people, this museum has a permanent collection spanning 2,000 years. Displays highlight Jewish festivals and the rituals that mark the various stages of life. There's a wide variety of Jewish decorative art, on such items as spice boxes and Torah covers; and changing exhibitions feature works by contemporary Jewish artists. *1640 Rhode Island Ave. NW, Downtown, 202/857–6583. Suggested donation $2. Open Sun.–Fri. 10–5. Metro: Farragut North.*

5 g-6

CORCORAN GALLERY OF ART

The Corcoran is Washington's largest—and first—nonfederal art museum. It features American and European art, including the famous Gilbert Stuart portrait of George Washington. The permanent collection numbers more than 14,000 works, including paintings by the first great American portraitists John Copley, Gilbert Stuart, and Rembrandt Peale. The Hudson River School is represented by such works as *Mount Corcoran,* by Albert Bierstadt, and *Niagara,* by Frederic Church; there are also portraits by John Singer Sargent, Thomas Eakins, and Mary Cassatt. European art is in the Walker Collection (with works by Gustave Courbet, Claude Monet, Camille Pissarro, and Auguste Renoir, among others) and the Clark Collection (with Dutch, Flemish, and French Romantic paintings, and the entire, restored 18th-century Salon Doré of Paris's Hotel d'Orsay). Be sure to catch *Old House of Representatives,* by Samuel Morse (yes, the original telegrapher), and the sculpture *Greek Slave,* by Hiram Powers, which scandalized 19th-century society. Other strengths include photography and contemporary American art. Docents lead tours daily at noon plus weekends at 10:30 and 2:30 and Thursday at 7:30. *500 17th St. NW, Downtown, 202/639–1700. Suggested donation $3. Open Wed.–Mon. 10–5, Thurs. 10–9. Metro: Farragut North, Farragut West.*

9 e-2

DUMBARTON OAKS

Housed in an 1801 Federal mansion surrounded by 10 acres of formal gardens, this museum is on the site of the 1944 Dumbarton Oaks conference, which led to the establishment of the United Nations. Now maintained by Harvard University, the art collection consists of small but choice collections of Byzantine and pre-Columbian works. Byzantine items include both religious and secular pieces executed in mosaic, metal, enamel, and ivory. Pre-Columbian works—artifacts and textiles from Latin America by such peoples as the Aztec, Maya, and Olmec—are arranged in an enclosed glass pavilion designed by Philip Johnson. *See* Historic Structures & Streets, *below. 1703 32nd St. NW, Georgetown, 202/339–6400. Suggested donation $1. Open Tues.–Sun. 2–5.*

5 f-2
FONDO DEL SOL

Fondo del Sol is a nonprofit artist-run alternative museum devoted to the cultural heritage of Latin America and the Caribbean. Its exhibitions cover contemporary, pre-Colombian, and folk art, and the museum has a program of lectures, concerts, and poetry readings and an annual summer festival. *2112 R St. NW, Dupont Circle, 202/483–2777. Admission $3. Open Wed.–Sat. 12:30–5:30. Metro: Dupont Circle.*

6 b-8
FREER GALLERY OF ART

The Smithsonian's Freer Gallery, one of the world's finest collections of Asian art, was established by an endowment from Detroit industrialist Charles L. Freer, who retired in 1900 and devoted the rest of his life to collecting art. Opened in 1923, four years after its benefactor's death, the collection includes more than 27,000 works—dating from Neolithic times to the 20th century—from the Far and Near East, including Asian porcelains, Japanese screens, Korean stoneware, Islamic art, and Chinese paintings and bronzes. Freer's friend James Whistler, the American painter who introduced Freer to Asian art, is also represented, as are other American artists who Freer felt were influenced by Asian art. One large display is the Peacock Room, a blue and gold dining room designed by Whistler for a British shipping magnate and decorated with leather, wood, and canvas; Freer paid $30,000 for the room and moved the entire thing from London to the United States in 1904. *12th St. and Jefferson Dr. SW, The Mall, 202/357–2700. Open daily 10–5:30 (call for extended summer hours). Metro: Smithsonian.*

6 c-8
HIRSHHORN MUSEUM

In a striking and controversial building that detractors dubbed "the doughnut," the Hirshhorn Museum opened in 1974 and now houses 4,000 paintings and drawings and 2,000 sculptures donated by Joseph Hirshhorn, a Latvian-born immigrant who made his fortune mining uranium in the United States. Artists exhibited include Americans Edward Hopper, Jackson Pollock, Mark Rothko, and Andy Warhol and modern European and Latin masters such as René Magritte, Joan Miró, Francis Bacon, Fernando Botero, and Victor Vasarely. Designed by Gordon Bunshaft, the cylindrical, reinforced-concrete building is a fitting home for contemporary art. Its severe exterior lines were softened in 1992, when the plaza was relandscaped by James Urban; grass and trees now provide a counterpoint to the concrete, and a granite walkway rings the museum and its outdoor sculptures. The impressive sculpture collection is arranged in open spaces between the museum's concrete piers and across Jefferson Drive in the sunken Sculpture Garden; the latter includes one of the nation's largest public collections of works by Henry Moore (58 sculptures) as well as works by Honoré Daumier, Max Ernst, Alberto Giacometti, Pablo Picasso, and Man Ray. Auguste Rodin's *Burghers of Calais* is a highlight. The gift shop is known for its contemporary jewelry. *7th St. and Independence Ave. SW, Downtown, 202/357–2700. Open daily 10–5:30 (call for extended summer hours). Sculpture garden open daily 7:30–dusk. Metro: Smithsonian or L'Enfant Plaza.*

2 b-3
KREEGER MUSEUM

Designed by Philip Johnson, this former residence of Carmen and David Kreeger displays the couple's permanent collection of paintings and sculpture. Highlights include works by Claude Monet, Pablo Picasso, Joan Miró, Henry Moore, and Frank Stella. You need a reservation to view the collection, which is explained on 90-minute guided tours Tuesday through Saturday at 10:30 and 1:30. Children under 12 are not allowed. *2401 Foxhall Rd. NW, Glover Park, 202/337–3050. Suggested donation $5.*

3 h-7
MEXICAN CULTURAL INSTITUTE

This glorious Italianate house, designed by Nathan Wyeth and George A. Fuller, architects of the West Wing of the White House, housed the Embassy of Mexico until 1989. In 1990, the Mexican Cultural Institute moved in, with the aim of promoting Mexican art, culture, and science. The permanent collection includes paintings, graphic arts, sculptures, and photographs of contemporary Mexican artists; the main hall displays six murals painted by Diego Rivera's disciple Roberto Cueva del Rio. The Talavera Tile Courtyard hosts plays, dance performances, and an annual Day of the Dead celebration. The lavishly decorated Music Room holds a concert series. *2829 16th St. NW, Adams-Morgan, 202/ 728–1628. Open Tues.– Sat. 11–5.*

6 *d-7*

NATIONAL GALLERY OF ART

The National Gallery's two magnificent buildings are known, aptly enough, as the West Building and the East Wing and are linked by a paved plaza and an underground concourse. The West Building houses one of the finest art collections in the world, illustrating Western European and American achievements in painting, sculpture, and the graphic arts from the late Middle Ages to the 20th century; holdings include works by Leonardo da Vinci, Peter Paul Rubens, Rembrandt van Rijn, Edgar Degas, Claude Monet, Auguste Renoir, and Mary Cassatt. The East Wing holds both modern art from the permanent collection and major traveling exhibitions from all periods. Highlights are Pablo Picasso's *The Lovers* and *Family of Saltimbanques,* four of Henri Matisse's cutouts, Joan Miró's *The Farm,* and Jackson Pollock's *Lavender Mist.* The National Gallery Sculpture Garden, opened in 1999, has changing exhibitions as well as pieces from the museum's permanent collection on display amid shade trees, flowering trees, and perennials. Entrances to the West Building are on Constitution Avenue at 6th Street NW; Madison Drive at 6th Street NW; and 4th Street between Constitution Avenue and Madison Drive NW. The entrance to the East Building is on 4th Street between Constitution Avenue and Madison Drive NW. *Constitution Ave. between 3rd and 4th Sts. NW, Downtown, 202/737– 4215. Open Mon.– Sat. 10–5, Sun. 11–6. Metro: Archives– Navy Memorial.*

6 *b-8*

NATIONAL MUSEUM OF AFRICAN ART

Founded in 1964 as a private educational institution dedicated to the exhibition, study, and preservation of the traditional arts of Africa, the museum has a permanent collection that

includes more than 7,000 objects from hundreds of African cultures. On display are masks, carvings, textiles, and jewelry, all made from such natural materials as wood, fiber, bronze, ivory, and clay. One exhibition explores the personal objects that were part of daily life in 19th- and early 20th-century Africa, showing how aesthetics were integrated with utility to create works of peculiar beauty. Because many African artworks are made of organic materials, the museum also runs a conservation laboratory, where curators work to arrest the decay of the valuable collection. *950 Independence Ave. SW, The Mall, 202/ 357–2700. Open daily 10–5:30. Metro: Smithsonian.*

6 *c-5*

NATIONAL MUSEUM OF AMERICAN ART

The Smithsonian's National Museum of American Art was the first federal art collection in the United States, beginning as a private collection here in Washington and predating the founding of the Smithsonian itself in 1846. Today the museum's collection, research facilities, exhibits, and public programs acknowledge all of the United States' regions, cultures, and traditions, and the more than 37,500 works of art, in all media, represent 200 years of American artistic achievement. The galleries hold colonial portraiture, 19th-century landscapes, American impressionism, 20th-century realism, New Deal projects, American crafts, contemporary photography, and graphic arts. Located in the Old Patent Office Building, the museum is the largest resource in the world for the study of American art. The entire Old Patent Office Building, including the museum, is slated to be closed for renovations until 2003. *8th and G Sts. NW, Downtown, 202/357–2700. Metro: Gallery Pl.–Chinatown.*

6 *a-5*

NATIONAL MUSEUM OF WOMEN IN THE ARTS

One of the larger Smithsonian museums, the National Museum of Women in the Arts showcases works by prominent female artists from the Renaissance right through the present. In addition to traveling exhibitions, the museum houses a permanent collection that includes paintings, drawings, sculptures, prints, and photographs by such artists as Georgia O'Keeffe, Mary Cas-

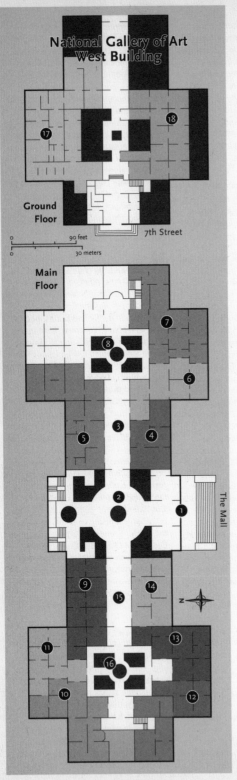

1 Mall Entrance
2 Rotunda
3 East Sculpture Hall
4 French Painting
   (17th & 18th
   Century)
5 French Painting
   (19th Century)
6 British Painting
7 American Painting
8 East Garden Court
9 Renaissance
   Painting (Florence
   & Central Italy)
10 Renaissance
   Painting (Venice &
   Northern Italy)
11 Italian Furniture &
   Sculpture
12 Italian Painting
   (17th & 18th
   Century)
13 Spanish Painting
14 Flemish & German
   Painting
15 Dutch Painting
16 West Sculpture
   Hall
17 European
   Sculpture (West
   Garden Court)
18 Sculpture &
   Decorative Arts

satt, Elisabeth Vigée-Lebrun, Frida Kahlo, and Judy Chicago. *1250 New York Ave. NW, Downtown, 202/783–5000. Suggested donation $3. Open Mon.–Sat. 10–5, Sun. noon–5. Metro: Metro Center.*

6 *c-6*

NATIONAL PORTRAIT GALLERY

The concept of a national portrait gallery is as old as our republic. Charles Willson Peale set about creating a gallery to portray the great men of his era during the Revolutionary War. The first official gesture toward assembling a national portrait collection was made in 1857, when Congress commissioned George Peter Alexander Healy to paint a series of presidential portraits for the White House; but it was not until a century later that the National Portrait Gallery was finally established. The 1962 act of Congress that created the gallery stated that it would function as "a free public museum for the exhibition and study of portraiture and statuary depicting men and women who have made significant contributions to the history, development, and culture of the people of the United States, and the artists who created such portraiture and statuary." The permanent collection consists of 7,000 portraits: Thurgood Marshall, George Marshall, Marian Anderson, Mary McLeod Bethune, W. E. B. DuBois, George Washington Carver, and Gloria Swanson, among others. These are supplemented by an array of special collections and by the valuable Study Collection. With the exception of presidents, whose portraits are admitted to the collection as soon as an appropriate image can be found, portraits may be admitted to the permanent collection only after the subject has been dead at least 10 years. This museum, along with the entire Old Patent Office Building, is slated to be closed for renovations until 2003. *8th and F Sts. NW, Downtown, 202/357–2700. Metro: Gallery Pl.–Chinatown.*

7 *g-3*

NAVY ART GALLERY

The Navy Art Collection has more than 13,000 paintings, prints, drawings, and sculptures, depicting naval ships, personnel, and action from all eras of U.S. naval history. Due to the operation of the Combat Art Program, World War II, the Korean War, the Vietnam War, and Desert Shield/Storm are particularly well represented. *Bldg. 67, Washington Navy Yard, 901 M St. SE, Navy Yard, 202/433–3815. Open Wed.–Fri. 9–4, Sat. 10–6, Sun. noon–6. Metro: Navy Yard or Eastern Market.*

5 *f-3*

PHILLIPS COLLECTION

As the first permanent museum of modern art in the country, the Phillips Collection is unique in both origin and content. In 1918, Duncan Phillips, grandson of a founder of the Jones & Laughlin Steel Company, began to collect art for a museum that would stand as a memorial to his father and brother, who had died within 13 months of each other. Three years later, the Phillips Memorial Gallery opened in two rooms of this Georgian Revival home near Dupont Circle. With no respect for either a painting's market value or its popularity, Phillips searched instead for works that impressed him as outstanding products of an artist's unique vision. Today's holdings include works by Georges Braque, Paul Cézanne, Paul Klee, Henri Matisse, and John Twachtman, and the nation's largest public collection of the work of Pierre Bonnard. Exhibitions change regularly. Permanent highlights include Auguste Renoir's *Luncheon of the Boating Party*, Francisco Goya's and El Greco's *Repentant Peter*, Edgar Degas's *Dancers at the Bar*, Vincent van Gogh's *Entrance to the Public Garden at Arles*, and Cézanne's self-portrait (the painting that Phillips said he would save first if his gallery caught fire). In the 1920s, Phillips and his wife started to support American Modernists, such as John Marin, Georgia O'Keeffe, and Arthur Dove. The museum stays open late on Thursdays, enticing all with chamber music or jazz and with a café that serves light dinners. From September to May the museum hosts a Sunday afternoon concert series at 5 in the music room, free with admission. *1600 21st St. NW, Dupont Circle, 202/387–2151. Admission $6.50 ($7.50 Thurs. night). Open Tues.–Sat. 10–5, Thurs. 10–8:30, Sun noon–7 (noon–5 June–Aug.). Metro: Dupont Circle.*

5 *g-5*

RENWICK GALLERY

A branch of the Smithsonian's National Museum of American Art, this gallery displays the creative achievements of designers and craftspeople in the

147

United States. Two rooms, the Octagon Room and the Grand Salon, are furnished in the styles of the 1860s and 1870s; the rest of the building is devoted to exhibits probing the richness and diversity of this country's heritage in design, crafts, and decorative arts. The permanent collection includes a wealth of distinctly American work made after World War II in a wide range of styles. Optional tours provide a general introduction to the gallery, focusing on the history of the building and the decoration of the two period rooms; tours leave by appointment Tuesday through Thursday at 10, 11, and 1. *Pennsylvania Ave. at 17th St. NW, Downtown, 202/357–2531. Open daily 10–5:30. Metro: Farragut West or Farragut North.*

6 *b-8*

SACKLER GALLERY

When Charles Freer endowed the gallery bearing his name (*see above*), he insisted on a few conditions: objects in the collection could not be loaned out, nor could objects from outside the collections be displayed. Because of the latter restriction it was necessary to build a second, complementary museum to house the Asian art collection of Arthur M. Sackler, a wealthy medical researcher and publisher who began collecting Asian art as a student in the 1940s. Sackler allowed Smithsonian curators to select 1,000 items from his ample collection, then pledged $4 million toward the construction of a museum. The collection includes works from China, Thailand, Indonesia, and the Indian subcontinent, including Persian manuscripts, Chinese ritual bronzes, jade ornaments from the 3rd millennium BC, and Indian paintings in gold, silver, lapis lazuli, and malachite. *1050 Independence Ave. SW, The Mall, 202/357–2700. Open daily 10–5:30. Metro: Smithsonian.*

BRIDGES

Washington has no Golden Gate, but it does have a number of functional and several beautiful bridges. Bridges across the Potomac and Anacostia are necessary, but they're generally not very beautiful, and traffic can make them unpleasant to cross. Some of the newer ones appear to have been built from sections that were ordered from a catalog and shipped to the site on barges; these are recognized in the *AIA Guide to Washington, D.C.* and are worth a look if you're an architecture buff.

5 *e-8*

ARLINGTON MEMORIAL BRIDGE

A classic yet functional beauty with two huge statues on the Lincoln Memorial end, this bridge links the memorial with the main entrance to Arlington National Cemetery and Arlington House (the Custis-Lee mansion). A bridge here was first proposed by President Andrew Jackson; this one is said to have been the result of an impossible traffic jam on Memorial Day, 1921. Colonel U. S. Grant, the general's grandson, supervised its construction from 1926 to 1932. The statues, *Valor* and *Sacrifice,* were cast in bronze in Milan and given to the United States by the people of Italy in 1950.

3 *f-7*

DUKE ELLINGTON BRIDGE

Formerly known as the Calvert Street Bridge, this bridge was renamed for D.C. musician Edward Kennedy Ellington in 1974. Built in 1935, it links the Columbia Road area of Kalorama with Connecticut Avenue and the Woodland Park–Zoo Metro station.

5 *e-2*

DUMBARTON BRIDGE

Known as the Buffalo Bridge (to the chagrin of purists who remind us that America had bison, not buffalo), this bridge was built in 1914 to join Georgetown with the then-developing Kalorama area. It is embellished with four bronze bison; its sides are decorated with busts of Native Americans (best seen from street level). *23rd and Q Sts. NW.*

CHILDREN'S MUSEUMS

In addition to the museums listed below, several Smithsonian museums have featured attractions for children, outlined in a pamphlet available at the Smithsonian Information Center (202/357–2700).

10 *e-1*

CAPITAL CHILDREN'S MUSEUM

It's almost a shame to call it a museum; a house of fun for kids would do it more justice. With such activities as "driving" a Metrobus, creating animated cartoons, climbing through tunnels and caves, and making Mexican hot chocolate, the hands-on, interactive museum encourages children to touch, smell, taste, and even wear the exhibits. The museum also focuses on how people in other cultures live: kids can "visit" houses from around the world. *800 3rd St. NE, Downtown, 202/675–4120. Admission $6 (children under 2 free). Open daily 10–5. Metro: Union Station.*

6 *c-8*

DISCOVERY THEATER

Discovery Theater, a division of the Smithsonian Associates, presents plays for children in its own theater, located in the Smithsonian Arts and Industries Building. Performances are open to the public, but advanced reservations can be arranged for groups. Performances have included original productions, contemporary and traditional live puppetry, dance, storytelling, and musicals—all designed to entertain, educate, and enlighten a young audience. Shows are held weekdays at 10 and 11:30. *900 Jefferson Ave. SW, The Mall, 202/357–1500. Admission $5. Metro: Smithsonian.*

5 *h-4*

NATIONAL GEOGRAPHIC SOCIETY'S EXPLORERS HALL

Explorers Hall is *National Geographic Magazine* come to life. Video touchscreens explain geographic concepts and then quiz you on what you've learned, and the Earth Station One Interactive Theatre sends the audience around the world—an 11-ft-diameter hand-painted globe that floats on a cushion of air. *17th and M Sts. NW, Downtown, 202/857–7588. Metro: Farragut North.*

2 *b-2*

WASHINGTON DOLLS' HOUSE AND TOY MUSEUM

Most of the antique toys and dollhouses at this quaint museum are behind glass, which disappoints younger kids, but older kids and doll enthusiasts will enjoy it. The museum also shows miniature dolls and toys. Dollhouse kits and accessories are sold in the gift shop. *5236 44th St. NW, Georgetown, 202/244–0024. Admission $4. Tues.–Sat. 10–5, Sun. noon–5. Metro: Friendship Heights.*

CHURCHES, MOSQUES, & SYNAGOGUES

Not all religious centers are open to visitors; we indicate hours for those that are.

4 *g-5*

BASILICA OF THE NATIONAL SHRINE OF THE IMMACULATE CONCEPTION

The largest Catholic church in the United States and the eighth-largest in the world, the basilica blends the Romanesque and Byzantine styles and is adorned with mosaics, sculptures, a bell tower, four pipe organs, and more than 60 chapels. Guided tours are available. *Michigan Ave. and 4th St. NE, Northeast, 202/526–8300. Open Apr.–Oct., daily 7–7; Nov.–Mar., daily 7–6. Metro: Brookland–CUA.*

7 *d-1*

EBENEZER METHODIST CHURCH

Ebenezer Methodist was the site of D.C.'s first public school for blacks. *420 D St. SE, Capitol Hill, 202/544–1415. Open weekdays 8:30–3. Metro: Capitol South.*

5 *h-3*

FOUNDRY UNITED METHODIST CHURCH

Founded by Henry Foxall, owner of the Foxall-Columbia Foundry, this church has been attended by Hillary Rodham Clinton. *1500 16th St. NW, Dupont Circle, 202/332–4010. Metro: Dupont Circle.*

5 *c-4*

GRACE EPISCOPAL CHURCH

In the mid- to late 19th century, Gothic Revival Grace Episcopal Church served the boatmen and workers from the nearby C&O Canal. At the time, the area was one of the poorest in Georgetown. *1041 Wisconsin Ave. NW, Georgetown, 202/337–2840.*

5 *b-3*

HOLY TRINITY PARISH

Built in 1794 as the Convent of Mercy, Holy Trinity was the first Catholic church in Washington. Holy Rood Cemetery was established nearby in 1832, at 35th Street and Wisconsin Avenue. *3513 N St. NW, Georgetown.*

5 d-1

ISLAMIC MOSQUE AND CULTURAL CENTER

The Muslim faithful are called to prayer five times daily at the mosque from atop its 162-ft-high minaret. Tours of the ornate interior, which has deep-pile Persian rugs and mosaics depicting verses from the Koran, are available by appointment. *2551 Massachusetts Ave. NW, Dupont Circle, 202/332–8343. Metro: Dupont Circle.*

5 h-4

METROPOLITAN AFRICAN METHODIST EPISCOPAL CHURCH

Completed in 1886, the Gothic-style Metropolitan African Methodist Episcopal Church is one of the most influential black churches in the city. Abolitionist orator Frederick Douglass worshipped here, and Bill Clinton chose the church for both of his inaugural prayer services. *1518 M St. NW, Downtown, 202/331–1426. Metro: Farragut North.*

2 b-2

NATIONAL PRESBYTERIAN CHURCH AND CENTER

Moved to its present site after its founding (as St. Andrew's Church) in a carpenter's shed on the White House grounds, this church counts 14 presidents among its former members. *4101 Nebraska Ave., Tenleytown, 202/537–0800. Metro: Tenleytown–AU.*

6 d-5

OLD ADAS ISRAEL SYNAGOGUE

This is the oldest synagogue in Washington. Originally built in 1876 at 5th and G Streets NW, the brick building was moved to its present location in 1969 to make way for an office building. Exhibitions in the Lillian and Albert Small Jewish Museum inside explore Jewish life in Washington over the years. *3rd and G Sts. NW, Downtown, 202/789–0900. Metro: Judiciary Sq.*

6 a-1

ST. AUGUSTINE

St. Augustine's, founded in 1858, is home to the longest continually active African-American Catholic congregation in D.C. *1419 V St. NW, U Street, 202/265–1470. Metro: U St.–Cardozo.*

5 h-5

ST. JOHN'S CHURCH ("OF THE PRESIDENTS") (EPISCOPAL)

According to the *AIA Guide to the Architecture of Washington, D.C.*, every president since Madison has attended St. John's. Across Lafayette Square from the White House, it was designed by Benjamin Latrobe on a Greek-cross plan in a classical style and completed in 1815. Later additions include the Doric portico and the cupola tower. *16th and H Sts. NW, Downtown, 202/347–8766. Open daily 9– 3. Metro: McPherson Sq.*

5 g-3

ST. MATTHEW'S CATHEDRAL (OF WASHINGTON'S ARCHBISHOP)

This Renaissance-style church was the site of President John F. Kennedy's funeral and is the seat of Washington's Catholic archbishop. Tours are available most Sundays at 2:30. *1725 Rhode Island Ave. NW, Dupont Circle, 202/347–3215. Open weekdays and Sun. 7–6:30, Sat. 7:30–6:30. Metro: Farragut North or Dupont Circle*

3 a-6

ST. SOPHIA CATHEDRAL

Greek Orthodox St. Sophia is noted for its exquisite interior mosaic work and for its lively Greek festival, held each spring and fall. *Massachusetts Ave. at 36th St. NW, 202/333–4730.*

2 c-3

WASHINGTON NATIONAL CATHEDRAL (EPISCOPAL)

Pierre-Charles L'Enfant's original city plan proposed a large national church, but the cathedral wasn't chartered by Congress until 1893. Construction of the enormous Gothic edifice—the sixth-largest cathedral in the world—began in 1906 but was not officially completed, nor was the church consecrated, until 1990. (Actually, work continues, but the "final" stone was laid by President Bush in 1989.) The first service was held in 1912. Like its medieval counterparts, the cathedral has a nave, flying buttresses, transepts, and vaults, all built stone by stone. Expert stone carvers created the fanciful gargoyles. The tomb of Woodrow Wilson, the only U.S. president buried in Washington, is on the south side of the nave. Guided tours are available, and the view of the city from the Pilgrim Gallery is exceptional. Choral programs bring the place especially alive for the Christmas season and other holidays. *Massachusetts and Wisconsin Aves. NW, Cathedral Heights, 202/537–6200; for tour information, 202/537–6207. Open Mon.–Sat. 10–3:15, Sun. 12:30–2:45. Metro: Tenleytown–AU, then bus (call cathedral for details).*

GRAVEYARDS & CEMETERIES

1 *d-5*

ARLINGTON NATIONAL CEMETERY

Some 250,000 U.S. war dead, as well as other notable Americans (including Presidents William Howard Taft and John F. Kennedy), are buried in these 612 acres across the Potomac from Washington. Arlington was established as the national cemetery in 1864, and you're bound to hear a trumpet playing taps or a gun salute while you're here. About 15 funerals are still held here daily; the cemetery is expected to be filled by 2020. The ceremonial changing of the guard on the hour (and on the half-hour as well in summertime), regardless of weather conditions, at the Tomb of the Unknowns is a highlight of the visit. Each sentinel marches exactly 21 steps, then faces the tomb for 21 seconds, symbolizing the 21-gun salute, America's highest military honor. If you're looking for a specific grave, the staff at the visitor center on Memorial Drive can help you find it. You should know the full name of the deceased and, if possible, his or her branch of service and year of death. Tour buses depart from the visitor center from April through September; tickets are $4 and include visits to the Kennedy graves, the Tomb of the Unknowns, and Arlington House. If you decide to walk—for a closer look at the graves and a better feel for these rolling Virginia hills—head west from the visitor center on Roosevelt Drive, then turn right on Weeks Drive. *West end of Memorial Bridge, Arlington, VA, 703/607–8052; to locate a grave, 703/697–2131. Metro: Arlington Cemetery.*

2 *g-6*

CONGRESSIONAL

Established in 1807 "for all denomination of people," Congressional was the first national cemetery created by the government. Mathew Brady, J. Edgar Hoover, John P. Sousa, several Revolutionary War heroes, and 76 members of Congress are among those buried here. Tours are available. *1801 E St. SE, Anacostia, 202/543–0539. Open daily dawn–dusk. Metro: Stadium Armory or Potomac Avenue.*

1 *g-3*

FORT LINCOLN

This 1912 graveyard occupies a large area, including theme gardens. There are many custom graves, a few churches, and miles of driveways. *3401 Bladensburg Rd., Brentwood, MD, 301/864–5090. Open daily 7:30 AM–dark.*

4 *f-7*

GLENWOOD

You can drive through this cemetery, not far from Catholic University, and even take a self-guided tour by following signs. The oldest grave is dated April 3, 1853. The most striking is that of Teresina Vasco, a child who died at age two after playing with matches, immortalized sitting in her favorite rocking chair. *2219 Lincoln Rd. NE, Northeast, 202/667–1016. Open daily dawn–dusk. Metro: Brookland–Catholic University.*

9 *b-1*

HOLY ROOD

On Wisconsin Avenue, uphill from Georgetown, Holy Rood has an excellent view of the city. It was established by the Holy Trinity Parish and is the burial site of about 7,300 people, including slaves, many Irish immigrants, and the widow of Commodore Stephen Decatur. Unfortunately, the cemetery is in poor condition after years of neglect. The oldest extant grave is dated July 27, 1834. *2128 Wisconsin Ave. NW, Georgetown. Pedestrian walkway nearly always open.*

2 *g-4*

MOUNT OLIVET

From its hilltop location, this large cemetery overlooks much of Washington. See if you can find the oldest grave, dated April 21, 1832. *1300 Bladensburg Rd. NE, Northeast, 202/399–3000. Open daily 7 AM–dark.*

9 *g-3*

OAK HILL

Chartered by Congress in 1849 and set on four acres of landscaped terraces

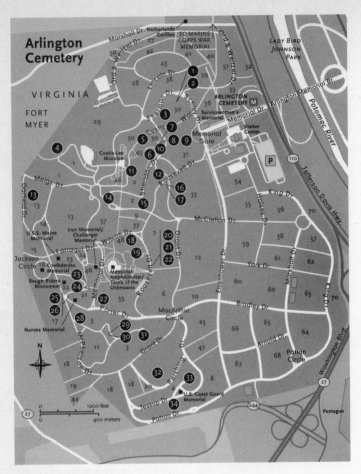

Arlington Cemetery

VIRGINIA

FORT MYER

donated by William Corcoran, this beautiful cemetery overlooks Rock Creek Park. It's worth a visit for the architecture alone: the brick-and-sandstone gatehouse, designed in 1850 by George de la Roche; Oak Hill Chapel, designed in 1850 by James Renwick; and the Van Ness Mausoleum, designed in 1833 by George Hadfield. Cameras and backpacks are not allowed in the cemetery. *3001 R St. NW, Georgetown, 202/337–2835. Open weekdays 10–4.*

4 f-8
PROSPECT HILL
Established in 1858, Prospect Hill is now a deserted graveyard. It shares a fence with Glenwood Cemetery and holds the remains of many Germans from early in U.S. history; many of the tombstones are engraved in German. *2201 N. Capitol St. NE, Northeast, 202/667–0676. Open Thurs.–Mon. 10–4.*

4 e-1
ROCK CREEK
Rock Creek Cemetery is home to one of Washington's most moving memorials, Augustus Saint Gaudens's 1890 statue of a seated, shroud-draped woman. Though its real name is "The Peace of God that Passeth Understanding," it is universally known as "Grief." The piece was commissioned by historian Henry Adams in honor of his wife, after she committed suicide. Don't be misled by the cemetery's name: it's not near Rock Creek. *Rock Creek Church Rd. and Webster St. NW, Upper Northwest, 202/829–0585. Open daily dawn–dark.*

HISTORIC STRUCTURES

9 e-7
CITY TAVERN
This 1796 building is representative of many such taverns on the main post road (the original mail route). It is now a private club. *3206 M St. NW, Georgetown.*

5 b-3
COX'S ROW
These five houses, built between 1815 and 1818 by Georgetown mayor John Cox, are among the purest examples of Federal-era architecture. The flat-front, redbrick house at 3307 N Street NW was the home of then-Senator John F. Kennedy and his family before the White House beckoned. *3327–3339 N St. NW, Georgetown.*

5 h-5
DECATUR HOUSE
This house was built in 1819 by Benjamin Latrobe for Commodore Stephen Decatur, who earned the affection of the nation in battles against the British and Barbary pirates. The redbrick, Federal-style building was the first private residence on President's Park. Now operated by the National Trust for Historic Preservation, the first floor is furnished as it was in Decatur's time. The second floor is furnished in the Victorian style favored by the Beale family, who owned it until 1956. *748 Jackson Pl. NW, Downtown, 202/842–0920. Open Tues.–Sun. noon–4. Metro: Farragut North or Farragut West.*

9 h-5
DUMBARTON HOUSE
Built in 1798, Dumbarton House was originally named Bellevue; one of the largest of Georgetown's old houses, it has been extensively modified and thus does not accurately represent any single period. Eight rooms have been restored to colonial splendor, with period furnishings such as mahogany American Chippendale chairs, hallmark silver, Persian rugs, and a breakfront cabinet filled with rare books. Other notable relics include Martha Washington's traveling cloak and a British redcoat's red coat. Since 1928, it has served as the headquarters of the National Society of the Colonial Dames of America. *2715 Q St. NW, Georgetown, 202/337–2288. Open Tues.– Sat. 10–1; tours 10:15, 11:15, and 12:15. Closed Aug. Suggested donation $3.*

9 e-3
DUMBARTON OAKS
This 1801 mansion has been much tinkered with over the years, but it remains both beautiful and significant: in 1944, representatives of the United States, Great Britain, the Soviet Union, and China met in the music room here to lay the groundwork for the United Nations. Diplomat Robert Woods Bliss and his wife, Mildred, bought the property in 1920 and set about taming the sprawling grounds and removing 19th-century additions that had marred the original Federal lines. In 1940 the couple conveyed the estate to Harvard University, which now maintains world-renowned

collections of Byzantine and pre-Columbian art here. Also on view to the public are the lavishly decorated music room and some of Mildred Bliss's rare illustrated garden books. The 10 acres of formal gardens (enter from 31st and R streets) were designed by noted landscape architect Beatrix Farrand and incorporate the traditional English, Italian, and French styles. *32nd and R Sts. NW, Georgetown, 202/342–3200. Art collection open Tues.–Sun. 2–5, suggested donation $1. Gardens open Apr.–Oct. daily 2–6, Nov.–Mar. daily 2–5. Admission Apr.–Oct. $3, Nov.–Mar. free.*

6 b-6
FORD'S THEATRE
This famous theater was built in 1863 for Baltimore impresario John T. Ford. Alas, after President Abraham Lincoln was assassinated here on April 14, 1865, during a production of *Our American Cousin*, the theater closed and Ford's business dried up. The federal government bought the theater in 1866 for $100,000 and converted it into office space. In 1893 the deteriorated building caved in under the weight of stored government records, killing 22 people. It was remodeled as a Lincoln museum in 1932: the theater was restored to its original appearance and reopened in 1968. The basement museum has such artifacts as Booth's pistol and the clothes Lincoln was wearing when he was shot. Across the street is the former home of tailor William Petersen, where Lincoln died. The theater itself has a full schedule of plays, including holiday favorite *A Christmas Carol. 511 10th St. NW, Downtown, 202/426–6924; box office 202/347–4833. Theater and house open daily 9–5 except during theater matinees (usually Thurs. and Sun.). Metro: Metro Center.*

9 d-7
FORREST-MARBURY HOUSE
This house was built in 1785 by Uriah Forrest and later owned by attorney William Marbury, of the landmark Supreme Court case *Marbury v. Madison*, which held that courts have the power to void acts of Congress when those acts are held to violate the Constitution. In 1791, Forrest hosted an important dinner here, during which George Washington convinced landowners to provide land for the new national capital. It is now a private home. *3350 M St. NW, Georgetown.*

6 h-8
FRIENDSHIP HOUSE SETTLEMENT
Designed by William Lovering in 1795 for William Duncanson, a wealthy planter, this house was later owned by Francis Scott Key, author of "The Star-Spangled Banner." *630 South Carolina Ave. SE, Capitol Hill. Metro: Eastern Market.*

5 f-4
HEURICH HOUSE
Built in 1892 for brewer Christian Heurich, this Romanesque Revival house is now owned by the Historical Society of Washington. The interior is eclectic Victorian, with plaster detailing, carved wooden doors, and painted ceilings. The downstairs breakfast room is decorated like a rathskeller. *1307 New Hampshire Ave. NW, Dupont Circle, 202/785–2068. Admission: $3. Open Wed.–Sat. noon–4. Metro: Dupont Circle.*

5 g-6
OCTAGON HOUSE
Owned by the American Institute of Architects and built in 1801, this is Washington's oldest mansion, and now contains period furnishings and architectural drawings. There are two schools of thought about why this six-sided building is called the Octagon. Some say it is because the main room is a circle, and it was constructed as other round rooms of the time were—by building an octagon and rounding out the sides. Others claim it is for the eight angles formed by the odd shape of the six walls—the true definition of an octagon. James Madison lived here after the White House was burned in the War of 1812, and it was here that he ratified the Treaty of Ghent, which ended the war. Some say this is one of Washington's haunted houses; the ghost of John Tayloe III, the builder of the house, has been heard ringing bells, and the ghosts of his daughter and a murdered slave girl also show up from time to time. Group tours are available by appointment. *1799 New York Ave. NW, Downtown, 202/638–3221. Admission $3. Open Tues.–Sun. 10–4. Metro: Farragut West.*

6 b-6
OLD POST OFFICE BUILDING
When it was completed, in 1899, this Romanesque building on the Federal Triangle was the largest government build-

ing in D.C., the first with a clock tower, and the first with an electric power plant. Despite these innovations, it became old after only 18 years, when a new post office was built near Union Station. Park Service rangers who work here consider a trip to the clock tower's observation deck one of the best-kept secrets in D.C. Although it's not as tall as the Washington Monument, it has almost as great a view, has larger windows (that open!), and it's usually significantly less crowded. On the way down, look at the Congress Bells, cast at the same British foundry that made the bells in London's Westminster Abbey. The bells are rung to honor the opening and closing of Congress and other such solemn occasions, such as a Redskins victory in the Super Bowl. *12th St. and Pennsylvania Ave. NW, Downtown, 202/ 619–7222. Tower open Easter–Labor Day, daily 8 AM–11 PM (last tour at 10:45); Labor Day–Mar., daily 10–6 (last tour at 5:45). Metro: Federal Triangle.*

9 *f-7*

OLD STONE HOUSE

This house, built in 1765, is thought to be the oldest building in D.C. still in its original location. Christopher Layman bought the lot for one pound and three shillings in 1764 and promptly built a home on it; the house is furnished today with objects listed on the inventory of Layman's estate when he died in 1765. Guided tours, craft demonstrations, and programs on colonial life are operated by the U.S. Park Service. *3051 M St. NW, Georgetown. Open Wed.–Sun. 10–4.*

3 *b-4*

ROSEDALE

Built as a farmhouse in 1793 by Uriah Forrest (*see Forrest-Marbury House, above*) on 1,000 acres north of Georgetown, this building is now the home of International Exchange Youth for Understanding. *3501 Newark St. NW, Upper Northwest.*

6 *f-7*

SEWALL-BELMONT HOUSE

Built by Robert Sewall in 1799–1800, this redbrick house has two historical claims to fame: it's the oldest home on Capitol Hill, and it was the only residence burned in Washington during the British invasion of 1814, after a resident fired on advancing British troops from an upper-story window (the only armed

resistance the British met that day). Sewall rebuilt the house in 1820, and it was owned by his descendants until 1922. Since 1929, the house has been the headquarters of the National Woman's Party, and for 43 years it was also the home of the party's founder, Alice Paul, who drafted the Equal Rights Amendment. The house has a museum that chronicles its history and the early days of the women's movement. Susan B. Anthony's desk, where she worked on the 19th Amendment, and a life-size statue of Joan of Arc stand among the marble busts and portraits of such women's suffrage leaders as Lucretia Mott and Elizabeth Cady Stanton. *144 Constitution Ave. NE, Capitol Hill, 202/ 546–3989. Open Jan.–Feb. and Apr.–Oct., Tues.–Fri. 10–3, Sat. noon–4; Mar. and Nov.–Dec., Tues.–Fri. 10–3, Sat. noon–4, Sun. 1–4. Metro: Union Station.*

9 *g-7*

3001–3009 M ST. NW

Built in 1794 by Thomas Lee, a friend of George Washington's, this Georgetown property began as a six-bay town house. It was later divided in two.

9 *e-3*

TUDOR PLACE

Robert Peter—the father-in-law of Martha Washington's granddaughter, also named Martha—was a successful Scottish tobacco merchant and the first mayor of the thriving port city of Georgetown. With the younger Martha's handsome $8,000 legacy from George Washington, she and Thomas Custis Peter purchased the Tudor Place property in 1805; it comprised one city block on the crest of Georgetown Heights. The Peters asked their friend Dr. William Thornton, the first architect of the U.S. Capitol, to design their house, and the resulting neoclassical mansion, with its unique domed portico, was completed in 1816. The house and its contents were cherished by succeeding generations of the family, and during the 180 years of Peter family ownership, the house assumed a fascinating character that could only have come through the repeated cycles of marriage, the purchase of furnishings, and inheritance. Furniture, silver, china, sculpture, portraits, photographs, textiles, and books not only testify to the continuous thread of family life at Tudor Place, but also give rare insight into American social and cul-

The White House

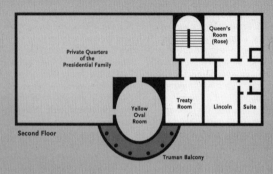

Private Quarters
of the
Presidential Family

Queen's
Room
(Rose)

Treaty
Room

Lincoln

Suite

Yellow
Oval
Room

Second Floor

Truman Balcony

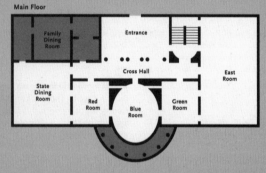

Main Floor

Family
Dining
Room

Entrance

Cross Hall

East
Room

State
Dining
Room

Red
Room

Blue
Room

Green
Room

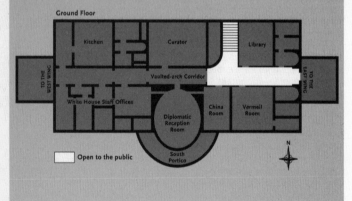

Ground Floor

Kitchen

Curator

Library

TO THE
WEST WING

Vaulted-arch Corridor

TO THE
EAST WING

White House Staff Offices

Diplomatic
Reception
Room

China
Room

Vermeil
Room

Open to the public

South
Portico

N

tural history. One of the highlights of the collection is a group of more than 100 objects that belonged to George and Martha Washington, from fine furniture down to a piece of soap. The Peter family also laid out a garden with formal parterres, sweeping lawns, and graceful trees and shrubs, which was enriched by succeeding family members over the years. Each area of the garden has its own charm, and something of interest is in bloom every season. *1644 31st St. NW, Georgetown, 202/965–0400. Suggested donation: $6. House tours Tues.–Fri. 10, 11:30, 1, and 2:30.*

5 *h-5*

THE WHITE HOUSE

Every occupant of this legendary house has modified it somehow. Thomas Jefferson added terraces to the east and west wings; Andrew Jackson installed running water; James Garfield put in the first elevator; and between 1948 and 1952, Harry Truman had the entire house gutted and restored, adding a second-story porch to the south portico. Most recently, George Bush installed a horseshoe pit, and Bill Clinton, a customized jogging track.

You'll enter through the East Wing lobby, walking past the Jacqueline Kennedy Rose Garden. The large, white-and-gold East Room is the site of presidential news conferences. In 1814 Dolley Madison saved the room's full-length portrait of George Washington from pyromaniac British soldiers by cutting it from its frame, rolling it up, and spiriting it out of the house. The Federal-style Green Room is used for informal receptions and photo ops with foreign heads of state. Notable furnishings here include a New England sofa that once belonged to Daniel Webster, and portraits of Ben Franklin, John Quincy Adams, and Abigail Adams. The elliptical Blue Room, the most formal space in the house, is furnished with a gilded, Empire-style settee and chairs that were ordered by James Monroe. The White House Christmas tree is placed here each year. Another well-known elliptical room, the president's Oval Office, is in the White House's semidetached West Wing, along with other executive offices.

The Red Room is decorated as an American Empire–style parlor of the early 19th century, with furniture by the New York cabinetmaker Charles-Honoré Lannuier. The State Dining Room, which can seat 140 guests, is dominated by G. P. A. Healy's portrait of Abraham Lincoln, painted after the president's death. The stone mantel is inscribed with a quotation from one of John Adams's letters: "I pray heaven to bestow the blessings on this house and all that shall hereafter inhabit it. May none but honest and wise men ever rule under this roof." In Teddy Roosevelt's day, a stuffed moose head hung over the mantel.

Guided tours examine selected first- and second-floor rooms Tuesday through Saturday from 10 to noon; pick up timed tickets at the White House Visitors Center, on E Street between 14th and 15th streets. Note that the White House is occasionally closed for official functions. *1600 Pennsylvania Ave. NW, Downtown, 202/456–7041 or 202/208–1631. Metro: Metro Center, Farragut West, or Federal Triangle.*

HISTORY MUSEUMS

2 *g-7*

ANACOSTIA MUSEUM

The Anacostia Museum is a national resource for African-American history and culture in Washington, D.C., and areas of the rural South. The museum also examines contemporary issues such as housing, land loss, health care, and economic development. Throughout its nearly three decades of work in cultural documentation and preservation, the museum has also encouraged and facilitated widespread community involvement in projects. *1901 Fort Pl. SE, Anacostia, 202/357–1300. Open daily 10–5. Metro: Anacostia.*

5 *h-4*

CHARLES E. SUMNER SCHOOL MUSEUM AND ARCHIVES

Built in 1872 for the education of black children, this school takes its name from the Massachusetts senator who delivered a blistering attack against slavery in 1856 and was savagely caned as a result by a congressman from South Carolina. The building was design by Adolph Cluss, who created the Arts and Industries Building on the Mall. It's typical of D.C.'s Victorian-era public schools. Beautifully restored in 1986, the museum hosts an array of exhibitions and has in its permanent collection the first African-American history map of the United States. *1201 17th St. NW, Downtown, 202/727–3419. Open Tues.– Fri. 10–5. Metro: Farragut North.*

5 *g-6*

DAR MUSEUM

A Beaux Arts–building serving as headquarters of the Daughters of the American Revolution, Memorial Continental Hall was the site each year of the DAR's congress until the larger, Russell Pope–designed Constitution Hall was opened around the corner. The DAR Museum's 33,000-piece collection includes fine examples of colonial and Federal furniture, textiles, quilts, silver, china, porcelain, stoneware, earthenware, and glass. Thirty-three period rooms are decorated in styles representative of various U.S. states, ranging from an 1850 California adobe parlor to a New Hampshire attic filled with toys from the 18th and 19th centuries. Two galleries—one a permanent exhibition and the other a rotating one—display decorative arts. Docents are available for tours weekdays 10–2:30 and Sunday 1–5. Youngsters will especially love the "Colonial Adventure" tours, which are usually held the first and third Sundays of the month. Costumed docents lead children through the museum, explaining the exhibits and describing life in colonial America. You need to make reservations at least 10 days in advance. *1776 D St. NW, Downtown, 202/879–3241. Open weekdays 8:30–4, Sun. 1–5. Metro: Farragut West.*

5 *f-6*

DEPARTMENT OF STATE

Here the U.S. Diplomatic Corps has its headquarters, and U.S. foreign policy is hammered out and administered by battalions of domestic analysts. The opulent Diplomatic Reception rooms are decorated in the manner of the great halls of Europe and the rooms of colonial American plantations. The museum-quality furnishings include a Philadelphia highboy, a Paul Revere bowl, and the desk on which the Treaty of Paris was signed. The largest room has a specially loomed carpet so vast and weighty that it had to be airlifted in by helicopter. The rooms are used 15 to 20 times a week to entertain foreign diplomats and heads of state. You'll have to register for a tour well in advance, up to three months ahead in summer; they're given weekdays at 9:30, 10:30, and 2:45. The building is closed to visitors during official functions. *2201 C St. NW, The Mall, 202/647–3241. Metro: Foggy Bottom–GWU.*

6 *b-6*

FEDERAL BUREAU OF INVESTIGATION

One of the most popular attractions in D.C. is the one-hour tour of the J. Edgar Hoover FBI Building, which affords a glimpse of how the FBI works. The tour covers famous cases, the FBI's ten most-wanted fugitives, a visit to the FBI's scientific laboratory, and a firearms demonstration by a Special Agent. *10th St. and Pennsylvania Ave. NW (enter on E St. between 9th and 10th Sts. for tours), Downtown, 202/324–3447. Open weekdays 8:45–4:15. Metro: Federal Triangle.*

2 *f-7*

FREDERICK DOUGLASS NATIONAL HISTORIC SITE

Born in slavery, Douglass lived through the Civil War and became an outstanding author, orator, and champion of civil rights. He lived here, at Cedar Hill, from 1877 until his death, in 1895. Original furnishings in the home represent Douglass's late years, when he was U.S. Minister to Haiti. The visitor center is separate and shows a film on Douglass's life. *14th and W Sts. SE, Anacostia, 202/426–5961. Admission $3. Open mid-Oct.–mid-Apr., daily 9–4 (last tour at 3); mid-Apr.–mid-Oct., daily 9–5 (last tour at 4); tours on the hr (except noon). Metro: Anacostia, then Bus B2.*

7 *h-3*

MARINE CORPS MUSEUM

This museum tells the story of the Marine Corps from its inception in 1775 to its role in Operation Desert Storm. The collection includes a variety of artifacts, from uniforms and weapons to documents and photographs. *Bldg. 58, Washington Navy Yard, 901 M St. SE, Navy Yard, 202/433–3534. Metro: Navy Yard or Eastern Market.*

5 *h-4*

MARY MCLEOD BETHUNE COUNCIL HOUSE

Exhibits in this Victorian town house museum focus on the achievements of black women. The building was the last D.C. residence of Mary McLeod Bethune, who founded Florida's Bethune-Cookman College, established the National Council of Negro Women, and served as an adviser on African-American affairs to four presidents. The visitors' center shows a video on Bethune's life. *1318 Vermont Ave. NW, Downtown, 202/673–2402. Open Mon.–Sat. 10–4. Metro: McPherson Sq.*

6 c-7
NATIONAL ARCHIVES

If the Smithsonian Institution is the nation's attic, the National Archives is the nation's basement, charged with cataloging and preserving important government documents and related items. In the Rotunda, you can see the U.S. Declaration of Independence, Constitution, and Bill of Rights—in a case made of bulletproof glass, illuminated with green light, and filled with helium gas (for preservation). At night, the documents are lowered into a 50-ton vault to shield them from vandals and nuclear attack. Other holdings include bureaucratic correspondence, military and immigration records, treaties, and such miscellany as Richard Nixon's resignation letter and the rifle Lee Harvey Oswald used to assassinate John F. Kennedy. Hours are extended in summer. Call at least three weeks in advance to arrange a behind-the-scenes tour. *Constitution Ave. and 8th St., Downtown, 202/501–5000. Open early Sept.–Mar., daily 10–5:30; Apr.–early Sept., daily 10–9. Metro: Archives–Navy Memorial.*

6 d-5
NATIONAL BUILDING MUSEUM

This museum is devoted to architecture and the building arts. Its permanent exhibition, "Washington: Symbol and City," outlines the capital's architectural history, from monumental core to residential neighborhoods. Temporary exhibitions have covered the rebuilding of Oklahoma City after the bombing of its federal building, and the dome as a symbol of American democracy. Tours are available weekdays at 12:30 and 1:30. *Pension Bldg., 4th and F Sts. NW, Downtown, 202/272–2448. Open Mon.–Sat. 10–4, Sun. noon–4. Metro: Judiciary Sq.*

6 c-7
NATIONAL MUSEUM OF AMERICAN HISTORY

This museum explores the nation's cultural, political, technological, and scientific past through a wealth of artifacts that have no doubt contributed to the Smithsonian's nickname "the nation's attic." Here you have Muhammad Ali's boxing gloves, the Fonz's leather jacket, and the Bunkers' living-room furniture from "All in the Family." The science and technology displays include farm machines, antique cars, early phonographs, and a 280-ton steam locomotive. "Science in American Life" covers such breakthroughs as the mass production of penicillin, the development of plastics, and the birth of the environmental movement. Other exhibits include ceramics, money, graphic arts, musical instruments, photography, and news reporting. Hands-on history and science rooms invite you to do it yourself—sort mail, 19th-century style; ride a high-wheel bike; explore DNA fingerprinting. *Constitution Ave. between 12th and 14th Sts. NW, The Mall, 202/357–2700. Open daily 10–5:30. Metro: Smithsonian or Federal Triangle.*

5 g-2
NATIONAL MUSEUM OF AMERICAN JEWISH MILITARY HISTORY

Under the auspices of the Jewish War Veterans of the USA, this museum documents the contributions of Jewish Americans to the peace and freedom of the United States and to the fight against anti-Semitism. On display from every war the nation has fought are American Jews' weapons, uniforms, medals, recruitment posters, and other military memorabilia. The few specifically religious items—a camouflage yarmulke, rabbinical supplies fashioned from shell casings and parachute silk—underscore the strains placed on religion during war. *1811 R St. NW, Dupont Circle, 202/265–6280. Open weekdays 9–5, Sun. 1–5. Metro: Dupont Circle.*

10 c-2
NATIONAL POSTAL MUSEUM

Drawing on its vast postal history and philatelic collection, the museum includes six major exhibition galleries touching on a range of topics, from the earliest history of the post office to the art of letter writing and the history of stamp collecting. An impressive atrium features three suspended airmail planes and is one of five exhibit galleries. The museum also has a library and research center, which includes a rare-book reading room, an audiovisual room, and a workroom for viewing items from the collection. Educational programs include a Discovery Center for children. *2 Massachusetts Ave. NE, Capitol Hill, 202/257–2700. Open daily 10–5:30. Metro: Union Station.*

6 c-6
NAVY MEMORIAL AND NAVAL HERITAGE CENTER

The huge, outdoor Navy Memorial plaza includes a granite map of the world and sculptor Stanley Bleifeld's statue, *The Lone Sailor*. Next door to the plaza, in the Market Square East building, the Naval Heritage Center has a gift shop and a Log Room, where you can look up the service records of Navy veterans. A 30-minute, 70-mm film, *At Sea* (brought to you by the makers of *To Fly*), provides a visually stunning look at life on board a modern aircraft carrier. *701 Pennsylvania Ave. NW, Downtown, 202/737–2300. Open Mon.–Sat. 10–6 (10–5 Nov.–Mar.), Sun. noon–5. Metro: Archives–Navy Memorial.*

7 h-3
NAVY MUSEUM

Housed in a long shop building that was once the Naval Gun Factory, this collection features the foremast fighting top from the USS *Constitution*, the bathyscaphe *Trieste*, large ship and aircraft models, medals, uniforms, statues, newspapers, photographs, other naval memorabilia, and fine art. Outside the building are guns, rockets, and a submarine sail. The USS *Barry* (named for the commodore, not the mayor) is open for exploration, and kids will enjoy the working submarine periscopes. *Bldg. 76, Washington Navy Yard, 901 M St. SE, Navy Yard, 202/433–4882. Open weekdays 9–4 (9–5 in summer), weekends 10–5. Metro: Navy Yard or Eastern Market.*

1 c-5
NEWSEUM

The first museum dedicated to the news business opened in Arlington in 1997. Here you can relive the defining moments in recent history; learn how the business of journalism evolved; try your hand at reporting, anchoring, and weathercasting; and see artifacts like Ernie Pyle's typewriter and Columbus's letter to Queen Isabella about his fateful discovery. Experience news as it's breaking by hearing radio reports from around the world, watching a video screen with images culled from 300 sources, and watching a "zipper" with headlines from 70 different newspapers.

1101 Wilson Blvd., Arlington, VA, 703/284–3700 or 888/639–6386. Open Wed.–Sun. 10–5. Metro: Rosslyn.

10 b-6
UNITED STATES CAPITOL

Let's clear up the confusion: the building is the Capitol; the city is the capital. The leading figures in American history have passed through the imposing halls of the former: George Washington laid the cornerstone in a Masonic ceremony in 1793, and President John Adams addressed the first joint session of Congress in the Senate chamber on November 22, 1800. The twin-shelled dome, a marvel of 19th-century engineering, rises 285 ft above the ground and weighs 9 million pounds; it expands and contracts up to 4 inches a day depending on the temperature outdoors. The fresco in the center of the dome indoors was completed by the Italian artist Constantino Brumidi in 1856; the figures in the inner circle represent the 13 original states of the union, with those in the outer ring symbolizing arts, sciences, and industry. The frieze around the rim of the Rotunda, begun by Brumidi but finished by fellow Italian Filippo Costaggini and American Allyn Cox, depicts 400 years of American history. You'll also see eight immense oil paintings here, four of them scenes of the American Revolution by John Trumbull. Optional tours depart the rotunda every few minutes from 9 to 3:45. You can obtain visitor passes to the House and Senate galleries from the office of your member of Congress (call 202/224–3121 for information). The grounds, landscaped by Frederick Law Olmsted (of Central Park fame), are as impressive as the building. Hours are extended in summer. *East end of Mall, Capitol Hill, 202/224–3121. Open daily 9–4:30. Metro: Capitol South or Union Station.*

6 a-8
UNITED STATES HOLOCAUST MEMORIAL MUSEUM

Designed by James Ingo Freed, the Holocaust Memorial Museum tells the stories of the 11 million Jews, Gypsies, Jehovah's Witnesses, homosexuals, political prisoners, and others killed by the Nazis during the years 1933–45. The presentation is as unique as the subject matter: upon arrival, you are handed an "identity card" containing the biographical information of a real person killed in the Holocaust; as you move through the museum, you read sequential updates on your card. Documentary films, audio- and videotaped oral histories, and a collection of objects complete the experience. The museum can be profoundly disturbing, and is not recommended for children under 11. The Hall of Remembrance provides a space for quiet reflection after the displays themselves. *14th St. and Raoul Wallenberg Pl., The Mall, 202/488–0400. Open daily 10–5:30. Metro: Smithsonian.*

10 *d-6*

U.S. SUPREME COURT BUILDING

The highest tribunal in the land was established by Article III of the Constitution. The court was originally composed of a chief justice and five associates, appointed by the president with the advice and consent of the Senate; today the court has nine members who hear 125–170 cases annually—from among almost 6,000 petitions. The court moved to its present location in 1935, when Charles Hughes was chief justice; the building is of white marble, with twin rows of Corinthian columns designed by Cass Gilbert. Lectures are given on the half hour until 3:30 when the court is not in session. Seating for oral arguments is granted on a first-come, first-served basis. *1st St. and Maryland Ave. NE, Capitol Hill, 202/479–3000. Open weekdays 9–4:30. Metro: Capitol South.*

5 *f-2*

WOODROW WILSON HOUSE

Woodrow Wilson is one of only two presidents who stayed in Washington after leaving the White House (Bill Clinton is the second). He and his second wife, Edith Bolling Wilson, retired in 1920 to this Georgian Revival house, designed by Waddy B. Wood (who also designed the Department of the Interior building and the National Museum of Women in the Arts) and built in 1915 for a carpet magnate. Wilson suffered a stroke toward the end of his second term, in 1919, and the years he spent on this quiet street were his last—he died in 1924. On view inside are such items as a Gobelin tapestry, a baseball signed by King George V, and the shell casing from the first shot fired by U.S. forces in World War I. The house also contains memorabilia related to the short-lived League of Nations, including the colorful flag Wilson hoped it would bear. *2340 S St. NW, Dupont Circle, 202/387–4062. Admission $5. Open Tues.–Sun. 10–4. Metro: Dupont Circle.*

LIBRARIES

10 *e-6*

FOLGER SHAKESPEARE LIBRARY

The Folger Library's collection of works by and about Shakespeare and his time is the finest in the world, a haven for researchers. The white-marble Art Deco building, designed by Paul Philippe Cret, is decorated with scenes from the Bard's plays. Inside is a reproduction of an inn-yard theater, which is used for chamber music, baroque opera, and readings as well as plays; and a gallery, designed to resemble an Elizabethan great hall, which houses rotating exhibits from the library's collection. *201 E. Capitol St. SE, Capitol Hill, 202/544–7077. Open Mon.–Sat. 10–4 (guided tour at 11). Metro: Capitol South.*

10 *d-7*

LIBRARY OF CONGRESS

The library was established in 1800, but when the British burned the Capitol in 1814, its books were destroyed—so Thomas Jefferson sold his library of 6,500 volumes to the government at cost. His collection was the genesis of this massive facility, now the largest and best-equipped library in the world, its 108 million items including books, manuscripts, prints, films, photographs, sheet music, and the world's largest collection of maps. The books alone fill 575 mi of shelves. Originally designed as a research aid to Congress, the library was later opened to scholars and the general public, although it is not a lending library; researchers must work on-site. The copper-domed Thomas Jefferson Building is the oldest of the three buildings that make up the library; the Adams Building, on 2nd Street, was added in 1939, and the James Madison Building, on Independence Avenue, opened in 1980. Exhibit halls in the Jefferson Building contain some of the most treasured items of U.S. history and priceless examples of early printing, including one of only three perfect Gutenberg Bibles; displays change frequently. *1st and 2nd Sts. SE, between E. Capitol and C Sts., Capitol Hill, 202/707–8000. Open Mon.–Sat. 10–5 (tours 11:30, 1, 2:30, and 4 from Great Hall). Metro: Capitol South.*

6 *b-5*

MARTIN LUTHER KING MEMORIAL LIBRARY

Designed by Ludwig Miës van der Rohe, this is the largest public library in the city with five floors of books, periodicals, and other reference materials. A mural on the first floor depicts the life of the Nobel Prize–winning civil rights activist. Used books are almost always on sale at bargain prices in the library's gift shop. *901 G St. NW, Downtown, 202/727–1111. Open Mon.–Thurs. 10– 9, Fri.–Sat. 10–5:30. Metro: Gallery Pl.–Chinatown or Metro Center.*

SCIENCE MUSEUMS

6 *c-8*

ARTS AND INDUSTRIES BUILDING

The Smithsonian's Arts and Industries Building (originally known as the U.S. National Museum) was designed in a high Victorian style by the Washington architectural firm Cluss & Schulze. Opened in 1881, just in time for the inaugural ball of President James A. Garfield, the building was built to exhibit materials acquired from the nation's Centennial Exposition, in Philadelphia. The museum's name was derived from the theme of that exposition: the statue above the entrance depicts the figure of Columbia protecting the two seated figures of Science and Industry.

Over the years the Arts and Industries Building has hosted a number of special exhibitions, from First Ladies' gowns (now in the Museum of American History) to the Wright brothers' *Spirit of St. Louis* (now in the National Air and Space Museum). In 1976, it was partially restored for the nation's bicentennial; also re-created then were the geometric stencils of rich Victorian yellow, red, green, and blue on the rotunda and hall spandrels. Surrounded by seasonal plants, the working fountain in the Rotunda makes for a quiet respite in a picturesque setting. The Discovery Theater stages programs for children. *900 Jefferson Dr. SW, The Mall, 202/357–1300. Open daily 10–5:30. Metro: Smithsonian.*

6 *d-8*

NATIONAL AIR AND SPACE MUSEUM

The Smithsonian's National Air and Space Museum (NASM) maintains the largest collection of historic air and spacecraft in the world, and is a vital center for research on the history, science, and technology of aviation and space flight. Hundreds of artifacts are on display, including the Wright brothers' original 1903 Flyer, the *Spirit of St. Louis*, the Apollo 11 command module, and a lunar rock sample that you can touch. The museum's Samuel P. Langley Theater shows IMAX films on a five-story-high screen—including *Cosmic Voyage, To Fly!* and *Mission to Mir*—that usually feature surprisingly realistic swooping aerial scenes. The Albert Einstein Planetarium, which charges a small fee, projects images of celestial bodies on a domed ceiling. *Jefferson Dr. and 6th St. SW, The Mall, 202/357–2700. Open daily 10–5:30 (call for extended summer hours). Metro: Smithsonian.*

1 *d-3*

NATIONAL MUSEUM OF HEALTH AND MEDICINE

Originally established during the Civil War as the Army Medical Museum, the center collected specimens for research in military medicine and surgery. In 1989, it became the National Museum of Health and Medicine, chronicling the history of medicine. The museum has a wide variety of objects in its historical and anatomical collections—many of them not for the squeamish. *Walter Reed Army Medical Center, 6825 16th St. NW, Adams-Morgan, 202/782–2200. Open daily 10–5:30.*

6 *b-7*

NATIONAL MUSEUM OF NATURAL HISTORY

Washington has one of the greatest natural history museums in the world, filled with bones, fossils, stuffed animals, and other relics, for a total of 120 million specimens. Displays also explore the ways in which humans have adapted to their various environments. The first-floor rotunda is dominated by a stuffed, 8-ton African bull elephant, one of the largest ever found. (The tusks are fiberglass: the ivory ones were too heavy for the stuffed animal to support.) Off to the right is the popular Dinosaur Hall. The west wing has exhibits on birds, mammals, and sea life, many from the collection bagged by Teddy Roosevelt on his trips to Africa. Not everything is dead, though: the sea-life display features a living coral reef, complete with fish, plants, and simulated waves. The

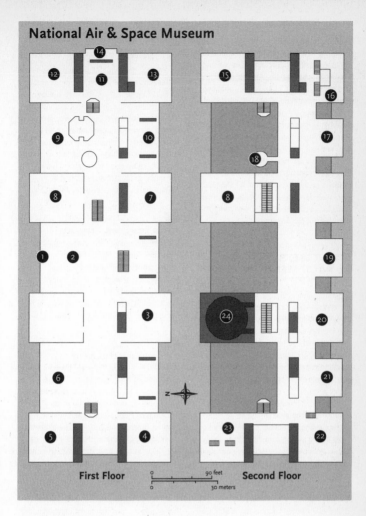

National Air & Space Museum

First Floor

Second Floor

0   90 feet
0   30 meters

1   Main Entrance
2   Milestones of Flight
3   Early Flight
4   Golden Age of Flight
5   Vertical Flight
6   Air Transportation
7   Flight Tests
8   Langley Theater
9   Space Hall
10   Looking at Earth
11   Lunar Rovers
12   Space Flight & Rockets
13   Astronomical Devices
14   Dining Room
15   Flight in the Computer Age
16   Art and Flying
17   Apollo Equipment & Artifacts
18   Skylab Workshop
19   Pioneers of Flight
20   Planetary Exploration
21   World War I Aviation
22   World War II Aviation
23   Naval Aviation
24   Einstein Planetarium

halls north of the rotunda contain tools, clothing, and other artifacts from a variety of cultures, including those of the Americas, the Pacific, Asia, and Africa. The second floor houses the fantastic mineral and gem collection, with the largest sapphire on public display in the country, largest uncut diamond, and the Hope Diamond, a blue gem from India. Also on this floor is the O. Orkin Insect Zoo. Hours are extended in summer. Recent renovations have spruced up exhibits and have added a 3D IMAX theater. *10th St. and Constitution Ave. NW, The Mall, 202/357–1300. Open daily 10–5:30. Metro: Smithsonian.*

STATUES, MURALS, & MONUMENTS

6 *b-1*

AFRICAN AMERICAN CIVIL WAR MEMORIAL

The nation's first and only national memorial to the United States Colored Troops (USCT) brings recognition to the black soldiers who served in the Civil War. Unveiled in 1998, the centerpiece of the granite-paved plaza is the sculpture *Spirit of Freedom*, designed by Ed Hamilton. One side of the 10-ft-high bronze piece depicts three infantry soldiers and a sailor, and the other shows a family group with the soldier son leaving for war. A bas-relief on the concave inner surface of the sculpture shows the faces of women, children, and elders. Around the plaza is the Wall of Honor, listing the names of 209,145 USCT Civil War soldiers and the 7,000 white officers who served with them. A directory lists individual names by regiment. *1000 U St. NW, Shaw. Metro: U St.–Cardozo.*

6 *e-8*

BARTHOLDI FOUNTAIN

Frederic-Auguste Bartholdi, sculptor of the more famous Statue of Liberty, created this delightful fountain—with its aquatic monsters, sea nymphs, tritons, and lighted globes (which were once gas)—for the Philadelphia Centennial Exhibition of 1876. The U.S. government purchased the fountain after the exhibition and installed it on the grounds of the old Botanic Garden on the Mall. It was moved to its present location in 1932 and was restored in 1986. *1st St. and Independence Ave. SW, Capitol Hill. Metro: Federal Center.*

2 *c-4*

CHURCHILL STATUE

In front of the British Embassy on Massachusetts Avenue is a plain statue of Sir Winston Churchill, with his right hand making the "V" gesture of victory. The statue was erected to commemorate John F. Kennedy's confirmation of honorary American citizenship on Churchill in 1963, and its base contains a time capsule to be opened in 2063. *British Embassy, 3100 Massachusetts Ave. NW, Glover Park. Metro: Woodley Park–Zoo.*

5 *f-7* .

EINSTEIN MEMORIAL

On the grounds of the National Academy of Sciences, Robert Berks's 21-ft-high sculpture of Albert Einstein ponders the universe. It's a favorite of kids, who like to sit on the physicist's lap. *22nd St. and Constitution Ave. NW, Downtown. Metro: Foggy Bottom–GWU.*

2 *d-6*

FRANKLIN DELANO ROOSEVELT MEMORIAL

Unveiled in May 1997, the 7½-acre memorial to FDR has waterfalls, reflecting pools, four outdoor galleries (one for each of FDR's terms as president) and 10 bronze sculptures. The granite passageways connecting the galleries are decorated with engravings of some of Roosevelt's most famous quotes, including "The only thing we have to fear is fear itself." Of course the memorial has its critics; FDR is not portrayed here with his omnipresent cigarette, nor is he pictured in the wheelchair that he used for the last 24 years of his life. Moreover, the President requested a simple memorial, and this one is anything but. *Tidal Basin, west bank, The Mall, 202/619–7222. Open 24 hrs; staffed daily 8 AM–midnight. Metro: Smithsonian.*

6 *e-7*

GRANT MEMORIAL

The 252-ft-long memorial to the 16th American president and commander in chief of the Union forces during the Civil War is the largest sculpture group in the city, but is often overlooked because of its position behind the Capitol. The pedestal statue of Ulysses S. Grant on horseback, flanked by Union artillery and cavalry, conveys a sense of the composure the general maintained in the face of chaos. The soldiers and horses are notable for their realism; sculptor Henry

Shrady spent 20 years researching and completing the memorial. *Near 1st St. and Maryland Ave. SW, Capitol Hill. Metro: Federal Center or Union Station.*

2 *d-6*

JEFFERSON MEMORIAL

Dedicated in 1943, this memorial evokes the classical style so admired by Thomas Jefferson, and employed in his designs of the University of Virginia and his estate at Monticello. Inside are a 19-ft bronze statue of Jefferson and carved excerpts from four of his writings. Japanese cherry trees surround the memorial and the Tidal Basin. National Park rangers are happy to discuss the structure and its history. *Ohio Dr., Tidal Basin, south bank, 202/426–6821. Rangers available daily 8 AM–midnight, 202/426–6841. Metro: Smithsonian.*

5 *f-8*

KOREAN WAR VETERANS MEMORIAL

This is one of Washington's newest public memorials, dedicated in 1995. It honors those killed in action, listed as missing, or held as prisoners of war in Korea. A raised granite curb lists the 22 nations that participated in this first United Nations conflict. The 19 statues in the triangular Field of Service depict multiethnic, poncho-clad foot soldiers on patrol in rugged Korean terrain heading toward an American flag. To the south of the soldiers stands a 164-ft-long granite wall etched with the faces of 2,400 unnamed service men and women with a silver inlay reading "Freedom is Not Free." The adjacent Pool of Remembrance honors all who were killed, captured, wounded, or missing is action. *West Potomac Park, Independence Ave. at Ohio Dr., The Mall, 202/619–7222. Open daily 8 AM–midnight. Metro: Smithsonian.*

5 *e-7*

LINCOLN MEMORIAL

This monument of white Colorado marble was designed by Henry Bacon and completed in 1922; the 36 Doric columns represent the 36 states of the Union at the time of Lincoln's death. (Their names appear on the frieze above the columns. Above the frieze are the names of the 48 states of the Union when the memorial was dedicated.) Daniel Chester French's somber statue of the seated president, which comprises 28 interlocking pieces of Georgia marble, looks out over the Reflecting Pool. When the monument was first built, some objected to the commemoration of the humble Lincoln with what is essentially a Greek temple. Lincoln's Gettysburg and Second Inaugural addresses are carved on the walls inside. The lower lobby has a permanent exhibition on Lincoln's legacy of justice, equality, and civil rights. *West end of Mall, at 23rd St. NW, The Mall, 202/619–7222. Staffed daily 8 AM–midnight. Metro: Foggy Bottom–GWU.*

6 *e-7*

PEACE MONUMENT

Erected in 1878 to commemorate naval deaths during the Civil War, sculptor Franklin Simmons's neoclassical white marble Peace Monument depicts two classically robed female figures facing the Capitol. Grief weeps in mourning over the sailors lost at sea onto the shoulder of History, who holds a tablet inscribed with the simple words, "They died so that their country might live." The base of the 44-ft monument shows classical figures representing science, literature, and art, signifying the progress of civilization made possible by peace. *Traffic circle at 1st St. and Pennsylvania Ave. NE, Capitol Hill. Metro: Union Station.*

5 *g-7*

VIETNAM VETERANS MEMORIAL

Renowned for its aesthetic power, the Vietnam Veterans Memorial was conceived by Jan Scruggs, a former infantry corporal who had served in Vietnam; designed by then 21-year-old Maya Lin, whose plan was selected in a competition; and completed in 1982. These polished black-granite walls are inscribed with the names of the more than 58,000 men and women who gave their lives or remain missing in the Vietnam War. Names are inscribed "in the order they were taken from us." Alphabetical directories around the memorial help visitors find names by panel and line number. Tents are often set up near the wall by veterans' groups, some to provide information on soldiers still missing in action, others to help fellow vets deal with the sometimes overwhelming emotions that grip them when visiting the wall for the first time. *21st St. and Constitution Ave., Downtown, The Mall, 202/619–7222. Staffed daily 8 AM–midnight. Metro: Foggy Bottom–GWU.*

5 g-7

VIETNAM WOMEN'S MEMORIAL

After years of debate over its design and necessity, the Vietnam Women's Memorial was finally dedicated on Veterans' Day 1993. Sculptor Glenna Goodacre's stirring bronze group depicts two uniformed women caring for a wounded male soldier while a third woman kneels nearby. The eight trees around the plaza commemorate each of the women who died in Vietnam. *21st St. and Constitution Ave., The Mall, 202/619–7222. Staffed daily 8 AM–midnight. Metro: Foggy Bottom–GWU.*

5 h-8

WASHINGTON MONUMENT

Pierre-Charles L'Enfant, architect of the city of Washington, chose the site for this obelisk in the late 1700s, while George Washington was alive. The tallest masonry structure in the world, built of American granite and faced with Maryland marble, it went up in stages 100 yards south of the spot he chose (due to marshy conditions), delayed by many factors. In 1854 members of the anti-Papist "Know-Nothing" party stole and destroyed a memorial block donated by Pope Pius IX; combined with a lack of funds and the onset of the Civil War, this action delayed the completion of the monument considerably. In 1876 Congress finally appropriated $200,000 to finish it, and the Army Corps of Engineers took over construction, capping it off in 1884 with a 7½-pound piece of aluminum, then one of the most expensive metals in the world. *See Viewpoints, below. Constitution Ave. and 15th St. NW, The Mall, 202/619–7222. Metro: Smithsonian.*

VIEWPOINTS

6 a-6

HOTEL WASHINGTON

Check out this seasonal rooftop restaurant and bar atop the nation's oldest continuously operating hotel for a fabulous view of the Treasury Building, the Washington Monument, and the White House. *515 15th St. NW, Downtown, 202/638–5900. Metro: Metro Center.*

5 b-8

MARINE CORPS WAR MEMORIAL

Just north of Arlington Cemetery, in Rosslyn, the slight elevation here provides a view of the Mall, Georgetown, the Potomac River, Key Bridge, and Upper Northwest. Free parking is available.

6 b-6

OLD POST OFFICE PAVILION

Although not as tall as the Washington Monument, the observation deck in the clock tower of the Old Post Office offers nearly as impressive a view. Even better, it's usually not as crowded, the windows are bigger, and—unlike the monument's windows—they open, allowing cool breezes to waft through. The tour is about 15 minutes long. *12th St. and Pennsylvania Ave. NW, Downtown, 202/289–4224. Metro: Federal Triangle.*

5 h-8

WASHINGTON MONUMENT

This is the best vantage point for all of Washington, really: the Mall, the city, Georgetown, Arlington Cemetery, and the Potomac and Anacostia rivers. When the monument first opened to visitors in 1888, four years after its completion, only men were allowed to take the 20-minute steam-elevator ride to the top; women had to walk the 898 steps, as the elevator was thought too dangerous for them. These days no one is allowed to make this hike; vandalism and a disturbing number of heart attacks en route convinced the park service otherwise. The elevator zips you up in a minute flat. *See Statues, Murals & Monuments, above. Constitution Ave. and 15th St. NW, The Mall, 202/619–7222. Open Apr.–early Sept., daily 8AM–midnight, Sept.–Mar. daily 9–5. Limited number of free timed tickets (good for a specified half-hour period) available at kiosk on 15th St. daily beginning at 7:30AM Apr.–early Sept. and 8:30AM Sept.–Mar.; limit six per person. No tickets required after 8PM (3PM off season). Advance tickets available from Ticketmaster (202/432–7328) for $1.50 service charge. Metro: Smithsonian.*

guided tours

BICYCLE TOURS

BIKE THE SITES

See Washington up close at a leisurely pace on this three-hour tour, in which entertaining guides lead you down scenic paths and trails while instructing you on history, architecture, and scandal. Other tours include Mount Vernon, Gettysburg, and Antietam. Bikes and helmets are provided. Children under 9 are not allowed. *202/966–8662.*

BOAT TOURS

5 *c-5*

CAPITOL RIVER CRUISES

Capitol departs from Washington Harbour (also known as Georgetown Harbour) for a 50-minute tour. *Georgetown, 301/460–7447.*

7 *c-3*

CRUISE BOAT ODYSSEY

Trips depart from Gangplank Marina on Water Street (daily in summer) and feed you brunch, lunch, or dinner. *Waterfront, 888/822–5991. Metro: Waterfront–SEU.*

POTOMAC RIVERBOAT COMPANY

Three different boats explore Washington, Mount Vernon, and Alexandria. *703/548–9000.*

5 *c-5*

SHORE SHOT CRUISES

Do you love to speed? This cruise of Washington Harbour is right up your alley: the boat goes fast, and you're done in a jiffy. *202/554–6500 or 301/593–0780.*

7 *c-3*

SPIRIT CRUISES

This company offers trips to Mount Vernon and dinner cruises in season. *Pier 4, 6th and Water Sts. SW, Waterfront, 202/554–8000. Metro: Waterfront–SEU.*

BUS TOURS

ALL ABOUT TOWN

This outfit offers full-day, half-day, and evening sightseeing tours of Washington, Georgetown, and points in nearby Virginia in glass-topped sightseeing coaches, with free pickup at most hotels. Reserve a day in advance. *202/393–3696.*

10 *d-2*

GRAY LINE

The well-known Gray Line departs from Union Station for tours of Georgetown,

Lafayette Park, Dupont Circle, and Embassy Row. Hotel pickups can be arranged. *202/289–1995.*

OLD TOWN TROLLEY TOURS

This company is a good bet for two-hour narrated tours with 18 stops for museums, shopping, and dining, both day and night. *202/832–9800.*

TOURMOBILE

This company offers day and night tours and a two-day package that combines the major sights of Washington with Arlington and Mount Vernon or a Frederick Douglass tour. *202/554–5100 or 888/868–7707.*

HELICOPTER TOURS

2 *d-7*

CAPITAL HELICOPTERS

Capital offers a narrated 18- to 20-minute flight over all of D.C.'s important buildings and monuments, leaving from the general aviation terminal at Ronald Reagan National Airport. Take the Metro to the airport, use the free valet parking at Signature Flight Support, or use Capital's free hotel or business pickup service. *703/417–2150.*

2 *f-6*

LIBERTY HELICOPTER TOURS OF NEW YORK

Don't let the name confuse you: a whirl here will show you the best of aerial D.C. Tours run from 4½ to 22 minutes. There is free parking and free van pickup from the Washington Navy Yard Metro (Half Street) or L'Enfant Plaza Metro stations. *1724 S. Capitol St. SE, Navy Yard, 202/484–8484.*

SPECIALIZED TOURS

6 *a-8*

BUREAU OF ENGRAVING AND PRINTING

Paper money has been printed here since 1914. Despite the fact that there are no free samples, the 35-minute guided tour—which takes you past presses that turn out some $696 million a day—is one of the city's most popular. Stamps, military certificates, and presidential invitations are printed here, too.

Be prepared for a long wait to enter. *14th and C Sts. SW, The Mall, 202/874–3019. Same-day timed-entry passes issued starting 8 AM at Raoul Wallenberg Pl. SW entrance. Open weekdays 9–2, plus 5–7:30 June–Aug. Metro: Smithsonian.*

DC DUCKS

And now for something completely different: DC Ducks offers land and water tours of the city aboard restored amphibious trucks from World War II. *202/966–3825.*

5 *h-5*

DECATUR HOUSE

Built for naval hero Commodore Stephen Decatur in 1819, Decatur House was the first neighbor to the President. Follow this 19th-century historic house on its 170-year journey from private home to rental property, Civil War supply depot to public museum. The tour, which is required for entry, departs every half hour; walking tours of Lafayette Square are also available by appointment. *See* Historic Structures & Streets, *above. 748 Jackson Pl. NW, Downtown, 202/842 -0920. Admission $4. Open Tues.–Fri. 10–3, weekends noon–4. Metro: Farragut West or Farragut North.*

5 *h-5*

OLD EXECUTIVE OFFICE BUILDING

Reservations are required for these guided Saturday morning tours. *Pennsylvania Ave. and 17th St., Downtown, 202/395–5895. Metro: Farragut West.*

2 *c-6*

THE PENTAGON

The massive size of this 34-acre office complex begs comparative statistics: it's twice the size of the Merchandise Mart in Chicago, three times the floor space of the Empire State Building, and as wide as three Washington Monuments laid end to end. The Pentagon is a virtual city, with 23,000 employees, 131 stairways, 284 restrooms, and 7,754 windows. Built in just two years during World War II to consolidate the 17 buildings of the War Department, the building is surprisingly efficient. Despite 17½ mi of corridors, it only takes seven minutes to walk between any two points in the building. The 75-minute tour takes you past only those areas meant to be seen by visitors. In other words, you

won't see situation rooms, communications centers, or gigantic maps showing troop positions. But you will see hallways lined with portraits of military leaders, scale models of U.S. Air Force planes and Navy ships, and the Hall of Heroes, where the names of all the winners of the Congressional Medal of Honor are inscribed. The tour is led by uniformed service personnel, who walk backwards the entire way, lest anyone slip away down a corridor. A photo ID is required for admission; children under 16 must be accompanied by an adult. Tickets are distributed for the day's tours at 8:45 AM, but go early; it's a very popular tour. *Off I–395, Arlington, VA, 703/695–1776. Tours weekdays every hour 9–3. Metro: Pentagon.*

WALKING TOURS

Specialized tours of various neighborhoods can be arranged with Jeanne Fogle (703/525–2948), Abill Hasson and Phil Ogilvie (202/829–8246), Steve Hoglund (202/387–8907), Ed Smith (202/885–1192), historian Anthony Pitch (Adams-Morgan, Georgetown; 301/294–9514), Ruth Ann Overbeck (Capitol Hill; 202/546–3395), Mary Drabkin (Kalorama; 202/557–9083), and James O'Connor (geology; 301/946–7277).

1 *c-4*

CIVIL WAR TOUR OF GEORGETOWN

This one-hour tour is offered irregularly by the National Park Service in the C&O Canal National Historical Park. *Georgetown, 202/653–5190.*

SMITHSONIAN ASSOCIATES

The Smithsonian Associates operate infrequent tours of various neighborhoods, including nearby suburbs. *202/357–3030.*

events

Sponsored by various organizations throughout D.C., these festivities go some way toward representing the city's local, regional, and national pride. Where no phone number is listed, or for more information on these and other events, call the Washington, D.C., Convention and Visitors Association at 202/

789–7000. Admission is free unless otherwise noted.

JANUARY

2 *e-5*

CHINESE LUNAR NEW YEAR CELEBRATION

Chinatown lights up in late January or early February, complete with a cacophony of firecrackers and a dragon-led parade. 202/638–1041.

5 *e-8*

MARTIN LUTHER KING JR. BIRTHDAY OBSERVANCE

Visit the Lincoln Memorial in mid-January for a public commemoration of King, including a recitation of his "I have a dream" speech.

5 *e-8*

ROBERT E. LEE BIRTHDAY CELEBRATION

The Confederate general's birthday is celebrated with 19th-century music at Arlington House (the Custis-Lee mansion) in Arlington National Cemetery. 703/557–0613.

FEBRUARY

AFRICAN-AMERICAN HISTORY MONTH

Celebrate all month long with cultural programs, museum exhibitions, performances, and other special events. 202/727–1186.

2 *f-7*

FREDERICK DOUGLASS'S BIRTHDAY

Douglass is commemorated on the Friday closest to his birthday (February 7) with a wreath-laying ceremony at the Frederick Douglass National Historic Site in Anacostia.

1 *d-7*

GEORGE WASHINGTON'S BIRTHDAY

On Presidents' Weekend a parade heads down Washington Street in Old Town Alexandria. Tours examine historic homes, and scenes from the Revolutionary War are reenacted. 703/780–2000.

5 *e-8*

LINCOLN'S BIRTHDAY

Don't miss the wreath-laying ceremony and reading of the Gettysburg Address at the Lincoln Memorial on Lincoln's actual birthday, February 12. 202/619–7222.

MARCH

2 *d-6*

NATIONAL CHERRY BLOSSOM FESTIVAL

For two weeks beginning in late March or early April, Washington rallies around its famous cherry trees, which surround the Tidal Basin in East and West Potomac Parks. The festival includes the traditional lighting of the 300-year-old Japanese lantern, with dignitaries including the Japanese Ambassador, the festival princesses, and top federal and city officials. Events include the Festival Parade and the Cherry Blossom Classic 10K race. 202/728–1137.

ST. PATRICK'S DAY PARADE

Show your green side in D.C.'s version of the St. Paddy's Day Parade, which runs down Constitution Avenue from 7th to 17th streets on the weekend nearest March 17. 202/637–2474.

5 *h-8*

SMITHSONIAN KITE FESTIVAL

In late March, the sky above the Washington Monument blooms with kites of every hue. Kite fliers, kite makers, and enthusiasts of all ages show up. 202/357–2600.

APRIL

2 *d-6*

THOMAS JEFFERSON'S BIRTHDAY

Jefferson's birthday is celebrated with military drills and a wreath-laying service at his memorial. 202/619–7222.

5 *h-6*

WHITE HOUSE EASTER EGG ROLL AND HUNT

The day after Easter, children ages three to six fill the South Lawn and older kids are entertained in the Ellipse at this beloved event. 202/456–2200.

5 *h-6*

WHITE HOUSE SPRING GARDEN AND HOUSE TOUR

The gates to the famous grounds are thrown open in mid-April; you can see the Rose Garden and the South Lawn, as well as public rooms in the White House. *202/456–2200.*

MAY

10 *b-6*

MEMORIAL DAY CONCERT

The National Symphony Orchestra's 7:30PM concert on the Capitol's West Lawn officially welcomes summer to D.C. *202/619–7222.*

2 *c-3*

WASHINGTON NATIONAL CATHEDRAL FLOWER MART

Gardeners revel in plants and outdoor entertainment on the first weekend in May on the cathedral grounds. *202/537–6200.*

JUNE

2 *d-5*

FESTIVAL OF AMERICAN FOLKLIFE

The theme varies from year to year, but this festival always involves food and performances inspired by regional cultures from different parts of the United States and around the world. Sponsored by the Smithsonian, it's held on the Mall around the end of June and beginning of July. *202/357–2700. Metro: Smithsonian.*

JAZZ ARTS FESTIVAL

From late June to early July, catch this showcase of some of the world's most accomplished and innovative musicians in free concerts throughout the D.C. area. *202/783–0360.*

MILITARY BAND SUMMER CONCERT SERIES

From June through Labor Day, the United States' military bands perform free outdoor concerts at various sites including the east steps of the Capitol, the Sylvan Theater (on the grounds of the Washington Monument), the Navy Memorial, the Marine Barracks (8th and I Sts. SE), and the Marine Corps War Memorial, in Rosslyn. Chairs are not provided, so bring a folding chair or, if applicable, sit on the Capitol steps. Call before you go, as some bands send an ensemble instead of their full entourage, so you might find a bluegrass band when you expected an orchestra. Moreover, warm summer weather tends to spawn thunderstorms, in which case some concerts are canceled. *Navy 202/433–2525, Air Force 202/767–5658, Marine Corps 202/433–4011, Army 703/696–3399.*

10 *b-6*

NATIONAL SYMPHONY ORCHESTRA OUTDOOR CONCERTS

Summer weekends mean free orchestral music on the West Lawn of the Capitol. *202/619–7222.*

JULY

2 *e-4, e-5*

NATIONAL 4TH OF JULY CELEBRATION

Celebrate independence in high style with a National Symphony Orchestra concert at the Capitol end of the mall, followed by fireworks over the Reflecting Pool. *202/619–7222.*

SEPTEMBER

2 *d-3, d-4*

ADAMS-MORGAN DAY

Celebrate the African-American and Latin American elements of this unique neighborhood in early September with live music, crafts, and, of course, food. *202/332–3292.*

5 *h-7*

BLACK FAMILY REUNION

The city celebrates the African-American family with entertainment, exhibits, and food on the grounds of the Washington Monument in early September. *202/737–0120.*

1 *b-3*

GLEN ECHO LABOR DAY ART EXHIBITION

Glen Echo Park's annual and highly successful showcase of local art attracts artists and art lovers from all over the Washington area. More than 100 artists' works are shown in the park's historic Spanish Ballroom, and most items are for sale. *7300 MacArthur Blvd. NW, Glen Echo, MD, 301/320–5331.*

2 *d-4*
KALORAMA HOUSE TOUR
Tour private homes, including ambassadors' residences and the Woodrow Wilson House (*see* History Museums, *above*), in mid- September. *202/387–4062. Admission: $20. Metro: Dupont Circle.*

2 *e-5*
LABOR DAY WEEKEND CONCERT
The National Symphony Orchestra plays a free concert at the Capitol end of the Mall. *202/619–7222.*

OCTOBER

5 *b-8*
MARINE CORPS MARATHON
Held on the fourth Sunday in October, this race begins at the United States Marine Corps War Memorial in Rosslyn. *703/784–2225.*

TASTE OF DC
Various Washington restaurants present their best, with live music enhancing the international atmosphere. Tasting tickets are sold on site. Sponsored by the DC Committee to Promote Washington, the festival is held on or around Columbus Day weekend. *202/724–5430.*

5 *h-6*
WHITE HOUSE FALL GARDEN TOUR
Fall forward into the President's backyard. Dates vary; call for details. *202/456–2200.*

NOVEMBER

2 *c-6*
VETERANS DAY CEREMONIES
On November 11, a small American flag is placed on each grave in Arlington National Cemetery. The President lays a special wreath at the Tomb of the Unknowns. *202/619–7222.*

DECEMBER

5 *d-6*
JOHN F. KENNEDY CENTER HOLIDAY FESTIVALS
From early December through New Year's Day, free musical performances are given almost daily in the foyer of the Kennedy Center for the Performing Arts. *202/467–4600.*

5 *h-6*
NATIONAL CHRISTMAS TREE LIGHTING/ PAGEANT OF PEACE
In mid-December (usually the second Thursday), the President lights the National Christmas Tree at dusk on the Ellipse, just south of the White House, accompanied by holiday music and caroling. For the next few weeks the Ellipse grounds are the site of nightly choral performances, a crèche, a burning Yule log, and, surrounding the national tree itself, a display of lighted smaller trees representing each state and territory. *202/619–7222.*

5 *h-6*
WHITE HOUSE CHRISTMAS CANDLELIGHT TOURS
See the nation's most famous house in a whole new light—a warm glow, in fact—in late December. *202/456–2200.*

day trips out of town

ANNAPOLIS, MARYLAND
Founded in 1684, Annapolis received its city charter in 1708 and became a major port, particularly for the export of tobacco. Although it has long since been overtaken by Baltimore as the Chesapeake's aquatic hub, Annapolis is still a popular pleasure-boating destination. The city's enduring nautical reputation derives largely from the presence of the U.S. Naval Academy, whose uniformed midshipmen throng city streets in summer whites or winter navy blues. In April and October, commercial boat shows attract national attention. Eighteenth-century architecture abounds here, including 50 pre–Revolutionary War buildings: that's more surviving Colonial buildings than any other place in the country. *40 mi east of Washington on U.S. Rte. 50 (exit Rowe Blvd.). Visitor center: 26 West St., 410/280–0445. Greyhound (800/231–2222), Dillons (800/673–8435), and MTA (800/543–9809) provide bus service.*

FREDERICKSBURG, VIRGINIA

Fredericksburg is a popular destination for history buffs because it was the linchpin of the Confederate defense of Richmond and, as such, the inevitable target of Union assaults. By war's end, fighting in Fredericksburg and on the nearby Chancellorsville, Wilderness, and Spotsylvania Court House battlefields (all of which you can visit) resulted in more than 100,000 dead or wounded. Fredericksburg's cemeteries hold the remains of 17,000 soldiers from both sides. The town's 40-block historic district contains more than 350 original 18th- and 19th-century buildings, including the house George Washington bought for his mother, Mary; the Rising Sun Tavern; and Kenmore, the magnificent 1752 plantation home of Washington's sister. Antiques collectors will also enjoy themselves here; dealers line Caroline Street, on land once favored by Indian tribes as fishing and hunting ground. If that's not enough, the short drive across the Rappahannock to Chatham Manor and Belmont, two lovely Georgian homes, nets splendid views of all of Fredericksburg. *50 mi south of Washington in I–95 (Exit 130A), near falls of Rappahannock River. Visitor center: 706 Caroline St., 540/373–1776. Amtrak (800/872–7245) and Virginia Rail Express (VRE, 800/743–3873) provide train service; Greyhound (800/231–2222) provides bus service.*

MOUNT VERNON, VIRGINIA

The shores of the Potomac River were divided into plantations by wealthy traders and gentleman farmers long before the city of Washington sprang up. Most vestiges of the Colonial era disappeared as the capital grew in the 19th century, but not George Washington's home. Mount Vernon and the surrounding lands had been in the Washington family for nearly 90 years by the time George inherited it all, in 1761, and transformed the main house from an ordinary farm dwelling into what was, for its time, a grand mansion. Small groups are ushered through the interior by a guide, who describes the furnishings in detail. The building's best feature is the view from its back: the dramatic riverside porch looks onto a lawn that slopes to the Potomac, and in spring the river is framed by the blossoms of wild plum and dogwood. Protocol requires U.S. ships and foreign navies to salute when passing the house. You can stroll the grounds and gardens and visit the kitchen, carriage house, workshops, reconstructed slave quarters, and, down the hill, the tombs of George and Martha Washington. *Southern end of George Washington Pkwy., Mt. Vernon, VA, 703/780–2000. Admission: $8. Open Mar., Sept., and Oct., daily 9–5; Apr.–Aug., daily 8–5; Nov.–Feb., daily 9–4. The Fairfax County Connector (703/339–7200) runs bus service. The Potomac Spirit (202/554–8000) runs boat service, which includes a meal.*

chapter 5

ARTS, ENTERTAINMENT, & NIGHTLIFE

From military pomp to hard-core punk, opera to experimental theater, and abstract modern dance to down-home folk routines, Washington packs both high culture and subculture. The Kennedy Center showcases not only its resident orchestra, the National Symphony, but Broadway plays and musicals, ballet, modern dance, opera, and more. Half a dozen or so plucky theaters spread out around 14th Street and downtown—our own "Broadway"—offer new works and new twists on old ones. Art museums augment their stationary exhibits with highly regarded chamber-music series.

As for nightlife, D.C. does have its share: the area surrounded by Georgetown, Adams-Morgan, U Street, and Dupont Circle is a whirl of barhopping, band-watching, and dancing after dark. Downtown is filled with suits by day, but after hours its pricey restaurants become exclusive nightclubs, and large warehouses open their doors to club kids.

The free weekly Washington City Paper hits the stands on Thursday and handily covers the nightlife scene. The "Weekend" section of Friday's Washington Post is the best guide to events for that weekend and the following week. The Post's daily "Guide to the Lively Arts" also covers cultural events. The Washington Times' "Weekend" section comes out on Thursday. You might also consult the "City Lights" section in the monthly Washingtonian magazine, and the weekly digest mw for gay and lesbian events.

arts

CONCERTS IN CHURCHES

4 g-5

BASILICA OF THE NATIONAL SHRINE OF THE IMMACULATE CONCEPTION
Choral and church groups often perform in this impressive space. *Michigan Ave.*

and 4th St. NE, Brookland, 202/526–8300. Metro: Brookland–CUA.

3 a-5

WASHINGTON NATIONAL CATHEDRAL
Choral music is wonderful in this grand cathedral. There's often a performance after the cathedral's "Tour and Tea," every Tuesday and Wednesday afternoon. *Wisconsin and Massachusetts Aves. NW, Upper Northwest, 202/537–6200. Metro: Tenleytown–AU.*

DANCE

4 h-5

DANCE PLACE
A combination studio and theater that presented its first performance in 1980, Dance Place hosts a wide assortment of modern and ethnic dance most weekends and offers dance classes daily. *3225 8th St. NE, Brookland, 202/269–1600. Metro: Brookland–CUA.*

2 b-2

JOY OF MOTION
A dance studio by day, Joy of Motion is also a showcase for several area troupes, who perform in the studio's Jack Guidone Theatre. Companies include the City Dance Ensemble (modern), Spanish Dance Ensemble (flamenco), J.O.M. Jam Crew (funk), and JazzDanz (you guessed it). *5207 Wisconsin Ave. NW, Friendship Heights, 202/387–0911. Metro: Friendship Heights.*

2 b-4

MOUNT VERNON COLLEGE
The In Series at this small, women's liberal arts college presents performance art, theater, classical music, and dance companies in the fall and spring. Past participants in the dance series have included the troupes of Robert Small and Nancy Meehan. *2100 Foxhall Rd. NW, Glover Park, 202/625–4655.*

6 b-8

SMITHSONIAN ASSOCIATES PROGRAM
This group presents both national and international dance groups, often at various Smithsonian museums (see Performance Venues, below). *1000 Jefferson Dr. SW (on the Mall), Downtown, 202/357–3030. Metro: Smithsonian.*

5 *d-6*

6 *b-6*

WASHINGTON BALLET

Between September and May, the company presents classical and contemporary ballets from such choreographers as George Balanchine, Choo-San Goh, and artistic director Septime Webre at the Kennedy Center and the Warner Theatre (*see* Performance Venues, *below*). December brings that eternal holiday favorite, *The Nutcracker*. 202/362–3606.

FILM

programs and theaters

10 *d-2*

AMC UNION STATION 9

AMC Union Station 9 shows big-budget flicks on nine screens and offers three-hour validated parking. *Union Station, Capitol Hill, 202/842–3757. Metro: Union Station*.

5 *d-6*

AMERICAN FILM INSTITUTE

More than 700 different movies—including classic and contemporary foreign and American films—are shown each year at the American Film Institute's theater in the Kennedy Center. Filmmakers and actors are sometimes on hand to discuss their work. *John F. Kennedy Center for the Performing Arts, New Hampshire Ave. and Rock Creek Pkwy. NW, Foggy Bottom, 202/785–4600. Metro: Foggy Bottom–GWU*.

2 *b-7*

ARLINGTON CINEMA 'N' DRAFTHOUSE

A suburban-Virginia alternative to movie theaters in the capital, this theater-cum-pub serves various libations and hot dogs, pizza, and other snacks so you can munch while you watch. You must be 21 or over, or with a parent. *2903 Columbia Pike, Arlington, VA, 703/486–2345*.

1 *c-3*

BETHESDA THEATRE CAFÉ

Think dinner theater for the average joe: you watch movies from tables while the waitstaff delivers pizza, nachos, beer, and cocktails. You must be at least 21 or come with a parent, except during the family matinees, when all ages are welcome and admission is only $1.50. *7719 Wisconsin Ave., Bethesda, MD, 301/656–3337. Metro: Bethesda*.

3 *d-5*

CINEPLEX ODEON UPTOWN

You don't see places like this old beauty anymore. It's got one huge, multiplex-dwarfing screen, art deco flourishes, a wonderfully huge balcony that seems to deposit you right in the movie, and—in one happy concession to modernity—crystalline Dolby sound. *3426 Connecticut Ave. NW, Cleveland Park, 202/966–5400. Metro: Cleveland Park*.

6 *c-8*

HIRSHHORN MUSEUM

For lovers of avant-garde and experimental film, the Hirshhorn screens movies weekly—often first-run documentaries, features, and short films—absolutely free. *7th St. and Independence Ave. SW (on the Mall), Downtown, 202/357–2700. Metro: Smithsonian or L'Enfant Plaza*.

6 *c-7*

NATIONAL ARCHIVES

Historical films and documentaries are shown here every day. Call or consult the archives' calendar of events for listings. *8th and Constitution Aves. NW, Downtown, 202/501–5000. Metro: Archives–Navy Memorial*.

6 *d-7*

NATIONAL GALLERY OF ART–EAST BUILDING

Classic and international films, usually related to current exhibits, are shown free in the museum's large auditorium. Stop by and pick up the film calendar for listings. *4th and Constitution Sts. NW (on the Mall), Downtown, 202/737–4215. Metro: Archives–Navy Memorial*.

5 *h-4*

NATIONAL GEOGRAPHIC SOCIETY

The renowned society screens educational films with a scientific, geographic, or anthropological bent. *17th and M Sts. NW, Downtown, 202/857–7588. Metro: Farragut North*.

festival

FILMFEST D.C.

An annual citywide celebration of international cinema, the D.C. International Film Festival (a.k.a. Filmfest) takes place in late April and early May. Films are shown at various venues throughout the city. *Box 21396, Washington, DC 20009, 202/724–5613.*

OPERA

2 *b-4*

MOUNT VERNON COLLEGE

Rarely produced chamber operas are staged in the college's intimate Hand Chapel in winter and spring. *2100 Foxhall Rd. NW, Glover Park, 202/625–4655.*

1 *c-6*

OPERA THEATER OF NORTHERN VIRGINIA

This company presents three operas a season, all in English, at a community theater and other venues in Arlington, Virginia. In December they switch to a one-act opera aimed especially at youngsters. *703/528–1433.*

4 *h-4*

SUMMER OPERA THEATER COMPANY

An independent professional troupe, the Summer Opera Theater Company stages one major opera in June and one in July, with English subtitles if appropriate. *Hartke Theater, Catholic University, Brookland, 202/526–1669. Metro: Brookland–CUA.*

5 *d-6*

WASHINGTON OPERA

D.C.'s opera company presents eight operas in their original languages (with English surtitles) between November and March in the Kennedy Center's Opera House and Eisenhower Theater. Performances are often sold out to subscribers, but you can buy returned tickets an hour before curtain time. Standing-room tickets go on sale at the box office each Saturday at 10 AM for performances the following week. *John F. Kennedy Center for the Performing Arts, New Hampshire Ave. and Rock Creek Pkwy. NW, Foggy Bottom, 202/295–2400 or 800/876–7372. Metro: Foggy Bottom–GWU.*

ORCHESTRAS & ENSEMBLES

5 *h-8*

10 *b-6*

ARMED FORCES CONCERT SERIES

From June to August, service bands from all four military branches perform Monday, Tuesday, Thursday, and Friday evenings on the East Terrace of the Capitol and several nights a week at the Sylvan Theater on the Washington Monument grounds. The traditional band concerts include marches, patriotic numbers, and some classical music. The Air Force celebrity series features popular artists such as Earl Klugh and Keiko Matsui. The bands often perform free concerts at other locations throughout the year. *202/767–5658 Air Force; 703/696–3718 Army; 202/433–2525 Navy; 202/433–4011 Marines.*

5 *d-6*

NATIONAL SYMPHONY ORCHESTRA

The season at the Kennedy Center is from September to June. In summer the NSO performs at Wolf Trap and gives free concerts at the Carter Barron Amphitheatre and, on Memorial Day and Labor Day weekends and July 4, on the West Lawn of the Capitol. The cheapest way to hear the NSO perform in the Kennedy Center Concert Hall is to get $13 second-tier side seats. Call 202/416–8100 for information.

PERFORMANCE VENUES

3 *g-1*

CARTER BARRON AMPHITHEATRE

Tall, lush trees surround this 4,250-seat outdoor theater in Rock Creek Park. The summer fare includes pop, jazz, and R&B concerts as well as National Symphony performances and free plays from Shakespeare in the Park. *16th St. and Colorado Ave. NW, Upper Northwest, 202/426–6837; off season, 202/426–6893.*

10 *d-7*

COOLIDGE AUDITORIUM

Famous for its commissions by the likes of Martha Graham and Aaron Copland, not to mention its excellent acoustics, this Library of Congress hall presents both classical and new music—contemporary composers and avant-garde jazz—in a space that's intimate, elegant, and generally well designed. *1st St. and Independence Ave. SE, Capitol Hill, 202/707–5502. Metro: Capitol South.*

5 *g-6*

CORCORAN GALLERY OF ART

Hungary's Takács String Quartet and the Cleveland Quartet are some of the illustrious chamber groups in the Corcoran's Musical Evening Series, with concerts one Friday each month from October to May, and occasionally in summer. Each performance is followed by a reception with the artists. *500 17th St. and New York Ave. NW, Downtown, 202/639–1700. Metro: Farragut West.*

4 *c-7*

CRAMPTON AUDITORIUM

Crampton, on the campus of Howard University, presents regular jazz, gospel, and R&B concerts and various special events. *2455 6th St. NW, Shaw, 202/806–7198. Metro: Shaw–Howard Univ.*

5 *g-6*

D.A.R. CONSTITUTION HALL

This 3,700-seat hall once denied the stage to African-American opera singer Marian Anderson, but it now hosts the likes of female rocker Ani DiFranco and sexual provocateur The Artist. *18th and C Sts. NW, Downtown, 202/628–4780. Metro: Farragut West.*

5 *h-3*

D.C. JEWISH COMMUNITY CENTER

The JCC presents everything from dance and theater to lectures and workshops. Performances are not always Jewish in content, but the educational value is consistently high. *1529 16th St. NW, Dupont Circle, 202/518–9400. Metro: Dupont Circle.*

10 *e-6*

FOLGER SHAKESPEARE LIBRARY

The Folger Shakespeare Library's internationally acclaimed resident chamber music ensemble, the Folger Consort, regularly presents a selection of instrumental and vocal pieces from the medieval, Renaissance, and baroque periods in a season that runs from October to May. *201 E. Capitol St. SE,*

Capitol Hill, 202/544–7077. Metro: Capitol South.

2 *h-6*

FORT DUPONT

Fort DuPont is one of D.C.'s best-kept summer secrets: groove under the stars to jazz and big bands, presented by the National Park Service. Bring a blanket and cooler and claim your space. *Minnesota Ave. and F St. SE, Anacostia, 202/426–7723 or 202/619–7222.*

1 *a-7*

GEORGE MASON UNIVERSITY

The GMU campus in suburban Virginia is home to the ambitious Center for the

---

CULTURE FOR KIDS

Try to feed your kids some highbrow entertainment before someone tells them they're not supposed to like it.

Dance Place (Dance)
Sunday matinees often feature storytellers and children's dance theater.

John F. Kennedy Center for the Performing Arts (Performance Venues)
Storytellers and folk musicians from around the world are bound to please.

Lincoln Theatre (Performance Venues)
Major jazz artists often play matinees for young audiences before the main event.

National Geographic Society (Film)
Films delight youngsters with outer space or ferocious wildlife.

National Theatre (Theater)
The Saturday series brings in jugglers, storytellers, mimes, and musicians.

Opera Theater of Northern Virginia (Opera)
A special one-act opera for children premieres every December.

Smithsonian Institution: Museum of Natural History (Performance Venues)
Introduce them to music from around the world, both old and new.

Washington Ballet (Dance)
Kids can't resist The Nutcracker—nor can adults.

Arts, a glittering complex made up of a 1,900-seat concert hall, the 500-seat proscenium Harris Theatre, and the intimate, 150-seat Black Box Theatre. Performances range from edgy, unconventional plays to ballet and modern dance to classical music. Also on campus is the 9,500-seat Patriot Center, which hosts pop acts and sporting events. *Rte. 123 and Braddock Rd., Fairfax, VA, 703/993–8888, 703/993–3000, or 202/432–7328.*

5 *d-6*

JOHN F. KENNEDY CENTER FOR THE PERFORMING ARTS

Any search for highbrow entertainment should start at the John F. Kennedy Center for the Performing Arts, the United States' national cultural center. With five stages under one roof, the "KenCen" has a little bit of everything: the Concert Hall, home of the National Symphony Orchestra; the 2,200-seat Opera House, the setting for ballet, modern dance, opera, and large-scale musicals; the Eisenhower Theater, usually devoted to drama; the Terrace Theater, designed by Philip Johnson, which showcases chamber groups and experimental works; and the Theater Lab, which offers cabaret-type performances. (The hit audience-participation mystery *Shear Madness* has been playing here since 1987.) You can also catch a free performance every evening—world music, perhaps, or family fare—at 6 PM at the Millennium Stage in the Kennedy Center's Grand Foyer. *New Hampshire Ave. and Rock Creek Pkwy. NW, Foggy Bottom, 202/467–4600 or 800/444–1324. Metro: Foggy Bottom–GWU.*

6 *b-1*

LINCOLN THEATRE

From the 1920s to the 1940s, the 1,250-seat Lincoln hosted the same performers as New York's Cotton Club and Apollo Theatre: Cab Calloway, Lena Horne, Duke Ellington, and all the rest. It's still heavy on jazz, along with other special events. *1215 U St. NW, Shaw, 202/328–6000. Metro: U St.–Cardozo.*

5 *f-5*

LISNER AUDITORIUM

A 1,500-seat theater on the campus of George Washington University, Lisner Auditorium programs pop, classical, and choral music as well as modern dance and musical theater. *21st and H Sts. NW, Foggy Bottom, 202/994–6800. Metro: Foggy Bottom–GWU.*

6 *c-5*

MCI CENTER

Smack in the middle of downtown, this 19,000-seat arena is the home of the Washington Wizards and Mystics (basketball) and the Capitols (hockey). It also hosts rock concerts, big-top circuses, and ice-skating shows. *601 F St. NW, at 7th St., Chinatown, 202/628–3200. Metro: Gallery Place–Chinatown.*

5 *f-7*

NATIONAL ACADEMY OF SCIENCES

The academy's 670-seat auditorium is acoustically near-perfect and hosts free performances October through May. Both the National Musical Arts Chamber Ensemble and the United States Marines Chamber Orchestra play often. *2101 Constitution Ave. NW, Foggy Bottom, 202/334–2436. Metro: Foggy Bottom–GWU.*

6 *c-7*

NATIONAL GALLERY OF ART

Free concerts by the National Gallery Orchestra, conducted by George Manos, plus performances by outside recitalists and ensembles are held in the venerable West Building's West Garden Court on Sunday evenings from October to June. Most of the performances are classical, but April's American Music Festival often brings jazz into the mix. *6th St. and Constitution Ave. NW (on the Mall), Downtown, 202/842–6941 or 202/842–6698. Metro: Archives–Navy Memorial.*

5 *f-3*

PHILLIPS COLLECTION

Duncan Phillips's mansion is more than just an art museum: from September through May, the long, paneled music room hosts Sunday-afternoon recitals, which are covered in the price of admission to the gallery. Chamber groups from around the world perform here, and May is devoted to performing artists from the Washington area. Concert time is 5 PM; arrive early for decent seats. *1600 21st St. NW, Dupont Circle, 202/387–2151. Metro: Dupont Circle.*

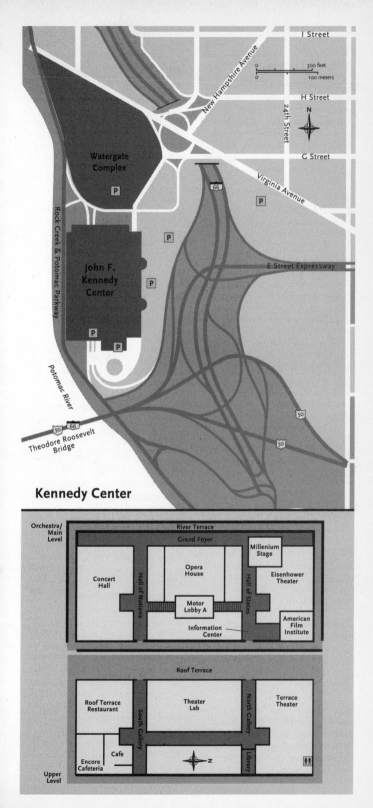

Kennedy Center

Orchestra/Main Level

River Terrace

Grand Foyer

Concert Hall

Hall of Nations

Opera House

Millenium Stage

Eisenhower Theater

Hall of States

Motor Lobby A

Information Center

American Film Institute

Upper Level

Roof Terrace

Roof Terrace Restaurant

South Gallery

Theater Lab

North Gallery

Terrace Theater

Library

Cafe

Encore Cafeteria

Z

1 *f-5*

ROBERT F. KENNEDY STADIUM

Now that the Redskins have moved to FedEx field, RFK tends to host festival-type events like the Tibetan Freedom Concert, monster-truck rallies, and large-scale powwows such as 1997's Promise Keepers conference. *22nd and E. Capitol Sts. SE, Downtown, 202/546–3337. Metro: Stadium–Armory.*

6 *b-8*

SMITHSONIAN INSTITUTION

The Smithsonian presents a rich assortment of music, both free and ticketed. American jazz, musical theater, and popular standards are performed in the National Museum of American History. In the Hall of Musical Instruments, on the museum's third floor, musicians periodically perform on historic instruments from the museum's collection. In warm weather, performances are held in the courtyard between the National Portrait Gallery and the National Museum of American Art. The Smithsonian Associates Program (202/357–3030) offers everything from a cappella groups to Cajun zydeco bands; many perform in Baird Auditorium, at the National Museum of Natural History. *1000 Jefferson Dr. SW (on the Mall), Downtown, 202/357–2700. Metro: Smithsonian.*

6 *b-6*

WARNER THEATRE

There's not a bad seat in the house at this elegant, 1920s-era theater in the heart of downtown. Performances run the gamut: jazz, comedy, modern dance, musicals, and the occasional European-style circus (i.e., one featuring people rather than animals). *13th and E Sts. NW, Downtown, 202/783–4000. Metro: Metro Center.*

WOLF TRAP FARM PARK

Just off the Dulles Toll Road, about half an hour from downtown, Wolf Trap is the only national park dedicated to the performing arts. The Filene Center, an outdoor theater, presents pop, jazz, opera, ballet, and other dance performances June through September. The rest of the year the intimate, indoor Barns at Wolf Trap (703/938–2404) hosts folk, jazz, rock, chamber, opera, and other music. For shuttle information, call the Metro (202/637–7000). *1551 Trap Rd., Vienna, VA, 703/255–1860. Metro: Vienna (then shuttle).*

THEATER

5 *g-3*

CHURCH STREET THEATER

Housed within a converted gymnasium built in 1905, this space has been a mainstay for up-and-coming independent producers and playwrights since the '70s. *1742 Church St. NW, Dupont Circle, 202/265–3748. Metro: Dupont Circle.*

3 *g-8*

DISTRICT OF COLUMBIA ARTS CENTER

Known to area artists as DCAC, this cross-genre space presents avant-garde performance art and experimental plays in its small, black-box theater. The adjacent art gallery has changing exhibits. *2438 18th St. NW, Adams-Morgan, 202/462–7833. Metro: Woodley Park–Zoo.*

6 *b-6*

FORD'S THEATRE

Looking much as it did when President Lincoln was shot at a performance of *Our American Cousin*, Ford's is host to both plays and musicals, many with family appeal. The holiday season brings Dickens's *A Christmas Carol. 511 10th St. NW, Downtown, 202/347–4833. Metro: Metro Center.*

3 *h-5*

GALA HISPANIC THEATRE

Gala mounts Spanish classics as well as contemporary Spanish and Latin American plays, in either Spanish or English (often with simultaneous translation via headphones). *1625 Park Rd. NW, Mount Pleasant, 202/234–7174.*

6 *a-6*

NATIONAL THEATRE

The National, which has been around for more than 150 years, presents touring Broadway shows and free children's shows on Saturdays. In winter and spring, the theater has a colorful program of free Monday-night shows that run the gamut from Asian dance to performance art to a cappella cabarets. *1321 Pennsylvania Ave. NW, Downtown, 202/628–6161. Metro: Metro Center.*

OLNEY THEATRE

Musicals, comedies, and summer stock are presented here in a converted barn, an hour from downtown in the Maryland countryside. *2001 Olney-Sandy Spring Rd., Olney, MD, 301/924–3400.*

6 *a-2*

SOURCE THEATRE

The recently renovated 125-seat Source Theatre mounts established plays with a sharp satirical edge and modern interpretations of classics. In July and August, Source hosts the Washington Theater Festival: a series of new plays, many by local playwrights. *1835 14th St. NW, Dupont Circle, 202/462–1073. Metro: Dupont Circle.*

companies

7 *c-2*

ARENA STAGE

Established in 1950, Arena Stage is D.C.'s most respected resident company, and was the first theater outside New York to win a Tony award. Its three venues—the Fichandler Stage, the proscenium Kreeger, and the cabaret-style Old Vat Room—present a wide-ranging season. *6th St. and Maine Ave. SW, Waterfront, 202/488–3300. Metro: Waterfront.*

6 *c-6*

SHAKESPEARE THEATRE

Five plays—three by the Bard and two classics from the same era—are staged each year by the acclaimed Shakespeare Theatre troupe in a state-of-the-art 450-seat space. For two weeks each June, the company stages its own version of New York's Shakespeare in the Park: a free play under the stars at Carter Barron Amphitheatre. *450 7th St. NW, Downtown, 202/547–1122. Metro: Gallery Place–Chinatown.*

1 *d-6*

SIGNATURE THEATRE

This plucky group performs in a 126-seat black-box theater in a converted bumper-plating facility in suburban Virginia. Signature and Stephen Sondheim are known to share a mutual admiration for each other. *3806 S. Four Mile Run Dr., Arlington, VA, 703/820–9770.*

6 *a-3*

STUDIO THEATRE

Presenting an eclectic season of both classic and offbeat plays, the Studio Theatre is one of Washington's best small, independent companies. With two 200-seat theaters, the Mead and the Milton, as well as the 50-seat Secondstage, used for particularly experimental works, it's one of the busiest performance spaces in the city. *1333 P St. NW, Dupont Circle, 202/332–3300. Metro: Dupont Circle.*

6 *a-2*

WASHINGTON STAGE GUILD

Washington Stage Guild performs both the classics and more contemporary fare—George Bernard Shaw is a specialty. The group shares space with the Source Theater. *1835 14th St. NW, Dupont Circle, 202/529–2084. Metro: Dupont Circle.*

6 *a-3*

WOOLLY MAMMOTH

Unusual, imaginatively produced shows have earned Woolly Mammoth many a positive review and favorable comparisons to Chicago's Steppenwolf. The company is using alternative venues during a planned multiyear renovation of its Church Street theater. Call for locations. *1401 Church St. NW, Dupont Circle, 202/393–3939. Metro: Dupont Circle.*

TICKETS

You can obtain tickets to most arts events by calling or visiting each theater's box office, but tickets for all events are usually available for a small surcharge through Tickets.Com or Ticketmaster. Tickets.Com (703/218–6500, www.tickets.com) takes phone orders for events at Arena Stage, Ford's Theatre, the Holocaust Museum, the 9:30 Club, and Signature Theatre; you can also buy tickets in selected Waxie Maxie's record stores. Ticketmaster (202/432–7328 or 800/551–7328) takes phone orders for events at most venues around the city, and has outlets at all Hecht's department stores. No refunds or exchanges are allowed.

From a booth at the Old Post Office Pavilion, TicketPlace (1100 Pennsylvania Ave. NW, 202/842–5387) sells half-price tickets to selected shows on the day of the performance; a "menu board" lists the shows available that day. There is a 10% service charge. The booth is open Tuesday through Saturday from 11 to 6 (tickets for Sunday and Monday performances are sold on Saturday) and is also a full-price Ticketmaster outlet (only cash is accepted for full-price tickets).

nightlife

BARS & LOUNGES

3 g-8

ASYLUM

Asylum is one of the last vestiges of D.C.'s underground rock scene, but since it relocated from U Street to somewhat swankier digs in Adams-Morgan, the bar is less a live-music venue than a place for scenesters to drink beer and play pool. 2471 18th St. NW, Adams-Morgan, 202/319–9353. Metro: Woodley Park–Zoo.

5 g-3

THE BIG HUNT

The faux animal heads on the wall suggest a safari, but most of the hunting going on here consists of college guys trying to score a few phone numbers. The bar food is decent, and the prices are fair. There are 17 beers on tap. 1345 Connecticut Ave. NW, Dupont Circle, 202/785–2333. Metro: Dupont Circle.

3 g-8

BLUE ROOM

This bar offers a lounge vibe with a film noir edge. Area DJs spin cool, mood-setting sounds most nights. This is a good place to hang out with a couple of friends on a long sofa or relax with a special someone in a shadowy nook. On Sundays, the Blue Room hosts free screenings of cult films such as La Femme Nikita and 2001: A Space Odyssey. 2321 18th St. NW, Adams-Morgan, 202/332–0800. Metro: Woodley Park–Zoo.

5 h-5

THE BOTTOM LINE

Because several news bureaus have offices nearby, journalists are the mainstay of this simple bar, located in a fairly dry part of town. 1716 I St. NW, Foggy Bottom, 202/298–8448. Metro: Foggy Bottom–GWU.

10 d-8

BULLFEATHERS

Bullfeathers caters mainly to congressional aides and other Capitol Hill professionals, who turn out for happy-hour specials. 410 1st St. SE, Capitol Hill, 202/543–5005. Metro: Capitol South.

9 e-7

CHAMPIONS

Its walls covered with jerseys, pucks, bats, balls, and a big-screen TV showing the game of the moment, this popular Georgetown establishment is an oasis for sports fans. Ballpark-style food enhances the mood. 1206 Wisconsin Ave. NW, Georgetown, 202/965–4005. Metro: Foggy Bottom–GWU.

2 d-4

CHI CHA LOUNGE

Groups of stylish twentysomethings relax here on sofas and armchairs. Homemade sangria and cocktails complement the bar's menu of Andean appetizers, and for a small price Sunday through Wednesday, you can indulge in Turkish water pipes filled with imported honey-cured tobacco. 1624 U St. NW, U Street, 202/234–8400. Metro: U St.–Cardozo.

3 g-8

CHIEF IKE'S MAMBO ROOM

There's no mambo, and nobody knows who Chief Ike is, but Adams-Morgan residents know that this is a great place to relax with friends, listen to good local musicians, and maybe even dance a bit. The schedule is eclectic, mixing rock, blues, funk, and more. 1725 Columbia Rd. NW, Adams-Morgan, 202/332–2211. Metro: Woodley Park–Zoo.

5 f-3

THE CHILDE HAROLD

By day it's a nice lunch spot, where suits and ties munch on Caesar salads under the awning. By night, the same crowd sheds its workaday duds and gets into a retro groove. 1610 20th St. NW, Dupont Circle, 202/483–6701. Metro: Dupont Circle.

3 g-8

DAN'S CAFE

This bar takes do-it-yourself to new levels. Ask for Bacardi and Coke and you'll get a can of soda, an airline-size nip, a glass, and your own personal ice bucket. Nothing trendy here. 2315 18th St. NW, Adams-Morgan, 202/265–9241. Metro: Woodley Park–Zoo.

5 g-3

DRAGONFLY

With its frosted glass window and pure white interior, Dragonfly gives new meaning to the term "cool." The sleek, minimalist design, sushi-only menu, and projections of kung fu flicks on the wall create a futuristic landscape for hipsters who believe less is more. *1215 Connecticut Ave. NW, Dupont Circle, 202/331–1775. Metro: Dupont Circle.*

10 *b-3*
DUBLINER
Snug, paneled rooms, thick Guinness, and nightly live entertainment make Washington's premier Irish pub popular with Capitol Hill staffers. *520 N. Capitol St. NW, Capitol Hill, 202/737–3773. Metro: Union Station.*

6 *a-2*
ELEVENTH HOUR
Slightly stiffer than other area lounges, Eleventh Hour is a good place to strike a pose in your finest retro attire. *1520 14th St. NW, U Street, 202/234–0886. Metro: U St.–Cardozo.*

5 *f-2*
FAIRFAX BAR
Located in the Westin Fairfax, this is a classic Washington hotel bar, where the moneyed make quiet deals and power brokers unwind. *2100 Massachusetts Ave. NW, Dupont Circle, 202/293–2100. Metro: Dupont Circle.*

3 *g-8*
FELIX
The huge chrome-and-neon sign outside this restaurant and bar conjures up 1980s decadence, and the slick decor inside does nothing to dispel the notion. Felix is known for its grand martinis as well as its trendy menu. Live jazz and funk entertain on the weekends. *2406 18th St. NW, Adams-Morgan, 202/483–3549. Metro: Woodley Park–Zoo.*

8 *g-4*
FISHMARKET
There's something different in just about every room in the Fishmarket, a multilevel space in Old Town Alexandria—from piano-bar crooner to ragtime piano shouter to guitar strummer. The operative word here is "boisterous." *105 King St., Alexandria, VA, 703/836–5676.*

10 *e-8*
HAWK AND DOVE
A friendly neighborhood bar in a 'hood dominated by the Capitol and the Library of Congress, Hawk and Dove

attracts a repeat crowd of politicos, lobbyists, and well-behaved marines from a nearby barracks. *329 Pennsylvania Ave. SE, Capitol Hill, 202/543–3300. Metro: Eastern Market.*

5 *g-3*
LUCKY BAR
Visually, anyway, the latest incarnation of this below-Dupont staple has a Las Vegas theme. Mondays are Latin dance nights, with free salsa lessons followed by general cutting loose. Other nights, DJs play Top 40. *1221 Connecticut Ave. NW, Dupont Circle, 202/466–2336. Metro: Dupont Circle.*

3 *g-8*
MADAM'S ORGAN
The mural of a buxom redheaded woman painted high on Madam's exterior has caused some controversy, but most regard it as a local landmark. This comfortable, three-story establishment has good live music, a decent bar, and a pool table. Once a month, the everglamorous DJ Stella Neptune hosts a disco-funk party. Redheads get $2 Rolling Rock all the time. *2461 18th St. NW, Adams-Morgan, 202/667–5370. Metro: Woodley Park–Zoo.*

3 *g-8*
MILLIE AND AL'S
This bar is very divey, but has seriously good pizza and is one of the few places in the neighborhood where you can successfully avoid trendy crowds. *2440 18th St. NW, Adams-Morgan, 202/387–8131. Metro: Woodley Park–Zoo.*

10 *g-8*
MR. HENRY'S
Roberta Flack got her start at this Capitol Hill institution. A comfortable neighborhood bar, it has an outdoor patio and features live jazz weekends. *601 Pennsylvania Ave. SE, Capitol Hill, 202/546–8412. Metro: Eastern Market.*

3 *g-8*
PHARMACY BAR
Like something out of *Clockwork Orange*, the tiny Pharmacy Bar seems to celebrate chemical concoctions while sticking to legal libations. An intriguing array of multicolored pills and tablets fills the glass-covered table tops, but otherwise it's a pretty friendly neighborhood bar for indie-rock types. *2337 18th St. NW,*

Adams-Morgan, 202/483–1200. Metro: Woodley Park–Zoo.

2 *d-4*

POLLY'S

Polly's is the quintessential U Street hangout, an intersection of all the different cliques and subcultures that frequent the area's clubs. It's open late, the food is excellent and affordable, the bartenders are friendly, and the jukebox is always playing the right song. *1342 U St. NW, U Street, 202/265–8385. Metro: U St.– Cardozo.*

3 *h-6*

THE RAVEN

If longevity had monetary value, this dive bar would be platinum. It gets its winning, no-frills, 1950s charm from a combination of comfortable booths, crotchety bartenders, and really cheap drinks. *3125 Mt. Pleasant St. NW, Mount Pleasant, no phone.*

6 *c-5*

THE ROCK

This huge downtown sports bar has excellent stats: 42 beer taps, 65 TVs, 5 pool tables, and 1 roof deck. Located near the MCI Arena, it's a sports fan's dream. *717 6th St. NW, Downtown, 202/842–7625. Metro: Gallery Place–Chinatown.*

10 *b-3*

SENATORS

Named after the only baseball team Washington's ever had, the long-defunct Senators, this sports bar in the Holiday Inn on the Hill serves as a shrine to what was. Twenty-one TVs keep local sports lovers from taking the loss too hard. *415 New Jersey Ave. NW, Capitol Hill, 202/347–7678. Metro: Union Station.*

5 *g-4*

SIGN OF THE WHALE

The best hamburger in town is served at the bar of this well-known haven for postpreppie neo-yuppies. *1825 M St. NW, Downtown, 202/785–1110. Metro: Farragut North.*

2 *d-4*

STETSON'S

A local hangout for the postcollege crowd, Stetson's is also a good preconcert or preclub meeting spot. The open patio in back is surprisingly pretty compared to the stale, beer-scented front room. *1610 U St. NW, U Street, 202/667–6295. Metro: U St.–Cardozo.*

9 *d-7*

THE TOMBS

It's doubtful that anyone comes back to this dark, basement bar after finishing college; attendance seems to be a degree requirement for most local students. *1226 36th St. NW, at Prospect St., Georgetown, 202/337–6668.*

5 *g-4*

TOWN & COUNTRY LOUNGE

Part of the ritzy Renaissance Mayflower hotel, the Town & Country draws local lawyers and execs in dark suits, along with a good number of business travelers. *1127 Connecticut Ave. NW, Downtown, 202/347–3000. Metro: Farragut North.*

3 *g-8*

TRYST

This coffeehouse-bar manages to be at once ultrahip and unpretentious. Homemade waffles are served fresh all day, as are fancy Italian sandwiches and exotic coffee creations. *2459 18th St. NW, Adams-Morgan, 202/232–5500. Metro: Woodley Park–Zoo.*

10 *e-8*

TUNE INN

The young and politically hungry come here to ease their frustrations after a day of interning and aide-ing with those already in power. *331 Pennsylvania Ave. SE, Capitol Hill, 202/543–2725. Metro: Eastern Market.*

2 *e-4*

VELVET LOUNGE

Rock-star dreams and big martinis come together at this cozy local bar on the end of the U Street corridor. Upstairs, local bands break onto the music scene on the small stage; downstairs, regulars relax with oversize drinks. *915 U St. NW, U Street, 202/518–8944. Metro: U St.–Cardozo.*

5 *g-3*

XANDO

This hip chain is both coffee bar and real bar, serving up rum-laced lattes and make-your-own s'mores (complete with flame and skewers) along with the usual caffeinated options. *1350 Connecticut*

Pack an easy way to reach the world.

Wherever you travel, the MCI WorldCom Card℠ is the easiest way to stay in touch. You can use it to call to and from more than 125 countries worldwide. And you can earn bonus miles every time you use your card. So go ahead, travel the world. MCI WorldCom℠ makes it even more rewarding. For additional access codes, visit **www.wcom.com/worldphone**.

EASY TO CALL WORLDWIDE

1. Just dial the WorldPhone® access number of the country you're calling from.

2. Dial or give the operator your MCI WorldCom Card number.

3. Dial or give the number you're calling.

Aruba (A) ✣	800-888-8
Australia ◆	1-800-881-100
Bahamas ✣	1-800-888-8000
Barbados (A) ✣	1-800-888-8000
Bermuda ✣	1-800-888-8000
British Virgin Islands (A) ✣	1-800-888-8000
Canada	1-800-888-8000
Costa Rica (A) ◆	0800-012-2222
New Zealand	000-912
Puerto Rico	1-800-888-8000
United States	1-800-888-8000
U.S. Virgin Islands	1-800-888-8000

(A) Calls back to U.S. only.   ✣ Limited availability.   ◆ Public phones may require deposit of coin or phone card for dial tone.

EARN FREQUENT FLIER MILES

Limit of one bonus program per customer. All airline program rules and conditions apply. © 2000 WorldCom, Inc. All Rights Reserved. The names, logos, and taglines identifying WorldCom's products and services are proprietary marks of WorldCom, Inc. or its subsidiaries. All third party marks are the proprietary marks of their respective owners.

© 2000 Visa U.S.A. Inc.

When it Comes to Getting Cash at an ATM,

Same Thing.

Whether you're in Yosemite or Yemen, using your Visa® card or ATM card with the PLUS symbol is the easiest and most convenient way to get cash. Even if your bank is in Minneapolis and you're in Miami, Visa/PLUS ATMs make getting cash so easy, you'll feel right at home. After all, Visa/PLUS ATMs are open 24 hours a day, 7 days a week, rain or shine. And if you need help finding one of Visa's 627,000 ATMs in 127 countries worldwide, visit **visa.com/pd/atm**. We'll make finding an ATM as easy as finding the Eiffel Tower, the Pyramids or even the Grand Canyon.

It's Everywhere You Want To Be.

Ave. NW, Dupont Circle, 202/296–9341.
Metro: Dupont Circle.

5 *f-2*

1647 20th St. NW, Dupont Circle, 202/
332–6364. Metro: Dupont Circle.

10 *e-8*

301 Pennsylvania Ave. SE, Capitol Hill,
202/546–5224. Metro: Eastern Market.

BREWPUBS & MICROBREWERIES

5 *f-3*

BRICKSKELLER

Brickskeller is the place to go when you
want something more exotic than a Bud
Lite—they sell more than 800 brands of
beer, from African lagers to micro-
brewed American ales. 1523 22nd St. NW,
Dupont Circle, 202/293–1885. Metro:
Dupont Circle.

6 *b-5*

CAPITAL CITY BREWING COMPANY

Gleaming copper accents decorate both
Capital City locations, and the Postal
Square branch still has trappings of its
former days as a functioning post office.
Young professionals come to sample
the changing beer list, with everything
from bitters to bock. 1100 New York Ave.
NW, Downtown, 202/628–2222. Metro:
Metro Center.

6 *f-6*

2 Massachusetts Ave. NE, Downtown,
202/842–2337. Metro: Union Station.

6 *c-6*

DISTRICT CHOPHOUSE AND BREWERY

Not your typical dark-panel steak house,
this bustling restaurant serves an array
of fresh entrées. Walk upstairs to watch
brew masters mix barley and hops while
monitoring gleaming metal vats filled
with tasty brews. 509 7th St. NW, Downtown, 202/347–3434. Metro: Gallery
Place–Chinatown.

1 *c-5*

NINGALOO

Formerly known as Bardo Rodeo, Ninga-
loo traded in its beloved Tex-Mex menu
for hit-and-miss Asian fusion offerings.
But you can play pool for free, and you
can still get Bardo's namesake brew
along with a strong selection of micro-

brews on tap. 2001 Clarendon Blvd.,
Arlington, VA, 703/599–3400. Metro:
Courthouse.

1 *c-5*

ROCK BOTTOM

Despite the name, this brewery-restau-
rant is tops with a young professional
crowd looking to blow off steam. A
changing selection of special brews, an
all-American menu, and live bands every
Saturday keep the crowds coming. 4238
Wilson Blvd., Arlington, VA, 703/516–
7688. Metro: Ballston.

CIGAR BARS

3 *d-4*

AROMA

One of the less pretentious cigar bars in
D.C., Aroma has decor that swings
between retro and futuristic. Scotch-
and cigar-tasting nights draw huge thir-
tysomething crowds. More mellow
weeknights may feature live jazz or a DJ
spinning ambient grooves. 3417 Connecticut Ave. NW, Cleveland Park, 202/
244–7995. Metro: Cleveland Park.

5 *g-3*

BUFFALO BILLIARDS

This upscale pool hall has 30 pool tables
along with snooker and darts. Clouds of
cigar smoke appear in the air above
small enclaves of sofas where groups of
friends talk and drink microbrews. 1330
19th St. NW, Dupont Circle, 202/331–
7665. Metro: Dupont Circle.

6 *b-5*

BUTLERS

Butlers, located in the Grand Hyatt, is
the quintessential cigar bar, done up in
marble, dark wood, and brass accents. A
state-of-the-art ventilation system keeps
the smoke from building up. Patrons
can choose from a changing menu of
cigars and order one of 30 martinis. For
the real aficionado, the bar rents personal humidors. 10th and H Sts. NW,
Downtown, 202/637–4765. Metro: Metro
Center.

5 *g-4*

OZIO

A favorite with the young, European ex-
pat crowd and other people who don't
seem to work 9 to 5, Ozio appropriately
takes its name from the Italian for

"leisure." Bossa nova tunes provide the backdrop to martini drinking and tapas eating. Cigar lovers will appreciate the smoking menu with 25 to 30 cigars. *1813 M St. NW, Dupont Circle, 202/822–6000. Metro: Dupont Circle.*

3 g-8
RUMBA CAFE
South American emigrants pack the bar at this tiny Adams-Morgan spot, where cigar smokers are welcome and red meat is considered a virtue. Latin bands crammed onto the impossibly tiny stage entertain patrons enduring the wait for the restaurant's excellent Argentinian food. *2443 18th St. NW, Adams-Morgan, 202/588–5501. Metro: Woodley Park–Zoo.*

COMEDY

1 d-5
CAPITOL STEPS
The musical political satire of the Capitol Steps—a group of current and former Hill staffers—is presented on Friday and Saturday at Petitbones restaurant and occasionally at other spots around town. *Capitol Steps, 703/683–8330; Petitbones, 1911 Ft. Myer Dr., Rosslyn, VA, 703/527–7501.*

GROSS NATIONAL PRODUCT
After years of spoofing Republican administrations with such shows as *Man Without a Contra* and *BushCapades*, then aiming its barbs at the Democrats in *Clintoons* and *All the President's Women*, the satirical comedy troupe Gross National Product has most recently performed *Bushwacked* and *Gore More Years*. For locations and reservations, call GNP at 202/783–7212.

2 a-1
HEADLINERS
Intimate rooms in this suburban hotel host national talent on weekends, local and regional acts on weekdays. *Holiday Inn, 8120 Wisconsin Ave., Bethesda, MD, 301/942–4242.*

5 g-4
IMPROV
A heavyweight on the Washington comedy scene, the Improv is descended from the club that sparked the stand-up boomlet of the '80s in New York and then across the country. Big-name headliners are common. *1140 Connecticut Ave. NW, Downtown, 202/296–7008. Metro: Farragut North.*

JOKES ON US
Jokes On Us hosts stand-up six nights a week. Such jokesters as Martin Lawrence, Tommy Davidson, and Jimmie Walker play here when they're in town. Athletic wear is verboten. *312 Main St., Laurel, MD, 301/490–1993.*

WASHINGTON IMPROV THEATER (WIT)
This group of 10 upstart improvisators falls more into the realm of *MADtv* or *Kids in the Hall* than the usual political-oriented humor prevalent in D.C. Using audience suggestions, the members of WIT create funny, sometimes bizarre, laugh-out-loud stories and vignettes. For locations and reservations, call WIT at 202/244–8630.

DANCE CLUBS

2 d-4
THE CAGE
This haven for fans of the departed Cellar club plays Top 40 on one level and '70s and '80s music on another. Cheap drinks along with discount admission for interns and people with military ID feed the meat-market atmosphere. *1811 14th St. NW, U Street, 202/262–9190. Metro: U St.–Cardozo.*

3 g-8
CLUB HEAVEN AND HELL
This split-personality club offers danceable retro music and celestial decor upstairs, a red-room basement bar with rock and cheap beer downstairs. *2327 18th St. NW, Adams-Morgan, 202/667–4355 or 703/522–4227 (event line). Metro: Woodley Park–Zoo.*

3 g-8
CRUSH
A fun spot where groups of friends come to dance (rather than hunt), Crush draws a twentysomething crowd with a mixture of house, Top 40, and R&B. *2323 18th St. NW, Adams-Morgan, 202/319–1111. Metro: Woodley Park–Zoo.*

6 b-6
DC LIVE
The clientele tends to vary according to who's the DJ and what style of music is

played on a given night. Cliques ranging from young black professionals to white suburbanites will wait in block-long lines for happy hour events and to dance to Top 40, hip-hop, R&B, and reggae. *932 F St. NW, Downtown, 202/347–7200. Metro: Metro Center.*

7 *f-2*
THE EDGE
A bit off the beaten path, the Edge is home to a unique underground club scene. Ravers and B-boys happily coexist while jungle, house, and hip-hop pound through the wee hours. *56 L St. SE, Navy Yard, 202/488–1200. Metro: Navy Yard.*

5 *g-3*
18TH STREET LOUNGE
This lounge is too hip—ultrahip—to announce itself by marquee or sign. Ever stylish, the young crowd swings to a mix of bossa nova, electronica, and mellow dance grooves. On weekends, a live Brazilian or jazz combo plays upstairs. The patio bar offers relief from the heat. *1212 18th St. NW, Dupont Circle, 202/466–3922. Metro: Dupont Circle.*

1 *b-3*
GLEN ECHO PARK
The Spanish Ballroom at Glen Echo is one of the few places where you can learn *contra* (a form of folk) dancing and practice with a live band and dance caller. The swing dance nights, featuring bands such as Peaches O'Dell & Her He-Man Orchestra, are also immensely popular with serious dance lovers. *7300 MacArthur Blvd., Glen Echo, MD, 301/ 492–6229, 301/340–9732 (swing), 202/ 216–2116 (folk dance hot line).*

3 *g-8*
HABANA VILLAGE
No matter the temperature outside, it's always balmy inside Habana Village. The tiny dance floor is packed nightly with couples dancing to the latest salsa and merengue. Cool off with a Cuban drink in one of several lounges. *1834 Columbia Rd. NW, Adams- Morgan, 202/462–6310. Metro: Woodley Park–Zoo.*

1 *e-1*
HOLLYWOOD BALLROOM
This is the place for people who believe dancing should be done cheek to cheek. Live bands play for dance parties, which

are often preceded by a free dance lesson. Classes in tango, waltz, cha-cha, mambo, salsa, and the hustle cater to all levels. *2126 Industrial Pkwy., Silver Spring, MD, 202/462–6310.*

3 *g-8*
LATIN JAZZ ALLEY
Not as long-established as Habana Village, Latin Jazz Alley positions itself as slightly more exclusive because it offers higher cover prices, live bands, and quality dance lessons and lectures. Incredibly, the dance floor is even smaller than Habana's, all the more reason to stay close to your partner. *1721 Columbia Rd. NW, Adams-Morgan, 202/ 328–6190. Metro: Woodley Park–Zoo.*

5 *g-3*
LUCKY BAR
Monday is Latin dance night, with free salsa lessons followed by general cutting loose. Other nights DJs play Top 40. The club hosts occasional theme nights devoted to current fads such as swing and disco. *1221 Connecticut Ave. NW, Downtown, 202/466–2336. Metro: Dupont Circle.*

6 *b-6*
PLATINUM
Known for years as the Bank, this upscale dance venue always keeps up with the trends. Now the multilevel club with three dance floors and a VIP lounge

---

DINING & DANCING

Just remember, for best results wait one full hour after eating before stepping onto the dance floor.

Habana Village (Dance Clubs)
Fortify yourself with good Cuban food before spinning the night away.

Platinum (Dance Clubs)
They say sushi is an aphrodisiac.

Republic Gardens (Dance Clubs)
The food may be elegant, but the dance floor is all about getting your groove on.

Sesto Senso (Dance Clubs)
It's all about looking good. Don't even think about breaking a sweat.

Yacht Club (Dance Clubs)
A classic place for men and women who believe dancing requires two hands.

bills itself as a sushi bar, and the DJs play techno, house, and Latin music. That may change in six months, but there's guaranteed to be some kind of party happening. 915 F St. NW, Downtown, 202/737–3250 or 202/737–3177 (hot line). Metro: Metro Center.

6 b-6

POLLY ESTHER'S

Polly Esther's is the Hard Rock Cafe of dance clubs, with outlets in New York and Miami. Focusing on popular '70s and '80s tunes, it caters to a crowd barely old enough to remember the end of disco: you can sing out loud here to your favorite Bee Gees song while striking a John Travolta pose, and no one will look twice. Tennis shoes and baseball caps are verboten. 605 12th St. NW, Downtown, 202/737–1970. Metro: Metro Center.

5 g-3

RED

A basement club with what you might call basement music, Red stays open late and features the area's best house-music DJs. Votive candles flicker in the chapel-like alcoves along the walls. 1802 Jefferson Pl. NW, Dupont Circle, 202/466–3475. Metro: Dupont Circle.

2 d-4

REPUBLIC GARDENS

Beautifully designed, with exposed-brick walls and bronze accents, this upscale, trilevel bar has a restaurant, pool tables, and a sports bar. Current R&B and rap hits lure a young black professional crowd to the dance floor. 1355 U St. NW, U Street, 202/232–2710. Metro: U St.–Cardozo.

5 g-4

SESTO SENSO

At night this pricey Italian restaurant reopens its doors to a youthful, upscale international clientele that moves to fast-pace Europop. 1214 18th St. NW, Dupont Circle, 202/785–9525. Metro: Dupont Circle.

6 b-6

THE SPOT

This downtown nightclub near the FBI Building faithfully adheres to the warehouse-club model by offering several different types of music in its seven rooms, including retro disco hits, trance, Top 40, and live soul bands. 919 E St. NW,

Downtown, 202/638–2582. Metro: Metro Center.

2 d-4

STATE OF THE UNION

State draws a young, eclectic crowd dressed in the requisite wide-leg jeans. Far from a meat market, the place attracts serious music fans who come to dance or hold down a spot at the bar while the city's best DJs spin a mix of house, drum-and-bass, hip-hop, and classic R&B. 1357 U St. NW, U Street, 202/588–8926. Metro: U St.– Cardozo.

6 c-1

2K9

This newcomer to the scene bridges the gap between pricey, exclusive nightclubs and low-cover neighborhood spots. Part of the converted warehouse's place-to-be look, including huge overhead cages with live dancers, was created by one of the original designers of Studio 54. Pass the velvet ropes outside to enter. 2009 8th St., U Street, 202/575–2009. Metro: Shaw–Howard Univ.

1 c-2

YACHT CLUB

Enormously popular with well-dressed older (30 to 55) singles, this suburban Maryland lounge is the brainchild of irrepressible entrepreneur and matchmaker Tommy Curtis (he's behind 90 marriages so far). Jacket with tie or turtleneck is required. 8111 Woodmont Ave., Bethesda, MD, 301/654–2396.

6 a-5

ZEI

Pronounced "zee," this New York–style dance club in a former electric power substation draws an international crowd, ranging from dark-suited "hiplomats" to young, affluent exchange students who move to the relentless thump of Europop. Tennis shoes are not allowed. 1415 Zei Alley NW, off 14th St. between H and I Sts. NW, Downtown, 202/842–2445. Metro: McPherson Square.

FOLK & ACOUSTIC

1 d-6

BIRCHMERE

Birchmere is one of the best places this side of the Blue Ridge Mountains to hear acoustic folk and bluegrass acts.

Audiences come to listen, and the management politely forbids distracting chatter. *3701 Mt. Vernon Ave., Alexandria, VA, 703/549–7500.*

1 *e-1*

CERRIDWIN'S COFFEE HOUSE

This monthly gathering of goddess worshippers and ex-hippies creates a genuine community. Artisans sell their wares before the concerts. Celtic music is a favorite, but regardless of the genre, the level of musicianship is always quite high. *10309 New Hampshire Ave., Silver Spring, MD 301/946–3731.*

6 *c-5*

FADO IRISH BAR

Inside this wood-paneled restaurant bedecked with portraits of famous Irish writers, solo folk singers and small duos clear off the tables and perform in a cozy nook. *808 7th St. NW, Downtown, 202/789–0066. Metro: Gallery Place–Chinatown.*

2 *c-3*

IRELAND'S FOUR PROVINCES

This bar caters to a mostly college crowd, so folk shows are no sedate spectacle. *3412 Connecticut Ave. NW, Upper Northwest, 202/244–0860. Metro: Cleveland Park.*

5 *g-3*

KRAMERBOOKS

In the heart of Dupont Circle, this bookstore and bar stays open late on weekends, when solo acoustic singer-songwriters occupy a tiny loft space, sometimes creating the illusion of music falling from the sky. *1517 Connecticut Ave. NW, Dupont Circle, 202/387–1400. Metro: Dupont Circle.*

5 *d-6*

MILLENNIUM STAGE AT THE JOHN F. KENNEDY CENTER FOR THE PERFORMING ARTS

Some of the best folk and acoustic artists in the country land at the Millennium Stage in the Kennedy Center's Grand Foyer. Best of all, it's always free. *New Hampshire Ave. and Rock Creek Pkwy. NW, Foggy Bottom, 202/467–4600 or 800/444–1324. Metro: Foggy Bottom–GWU.*

2 *c-3*

NANNY O'BRIENS IRISH PUB

Less prefab than some of the city's other Irish pubs, Nanny's is also the real thing when it comes to music. There's live music most nights, including a Celtic jam session on Monday. *3319 Connecticut Ave. NW, Cleveland Park, 202/686–9189. Metro: Cleveland Park.*

5 *f-3*

SOHO TEA AND COFFEE

This coffee bar is one of the few venues where just-starting performers can find an audience. Midweek open mikes offer guitar-carrying singer-songwriters a chance to perform, interact, and connect. Soho lives up to its name in other ways by exhibiting the work of local painters. At night, hungry clubgoers come for a caffeine fix and a post-midnight snack. *2150 P St. NW, Dupont Circle, 202/463–7646. Metro: Dupont Circle.*

GAY & LESBIAN BARS & CLUBS

5 *f-3*

BADLANDS

One of the best things about Badlands is that unlike most other clubs, it's open on weeknights. Men will find a definite meat-market vibe here, but with less attitude than you'll find at the larger haunts. *1432 22nd St. NW, Dupont Circle, 202/296–0505. Metro: Dupont Circle.*

5 *h-2*

CLUB CHAOS

Club Chaos mixes it up with ongoing dance parties, regular drag shows, Broadway sing-along nights, and a tasty bistro menu that satisfies both men and women. *17th and Q Sts. NW, Dupont Circle, 202/232–4141. Metro: Dupont Circle.*

2 *f-3*

DELTA ELITE

African-American men sweat it out to hard-core house classics at this Paradise Garage–style club, where the people are the primary decor. *3734 10th St. NE, Brookland, 202/529–0626. Metro: Brookland–CUA.*

5 f-3
THE FIREPLACE
The fire is always burning in the glass window of this long-established men's bar. Inside, music videos or the occasional *Ab Fab* episode entertain a mostly over-thirty crowd. *2161 P St. NW, Dupont Circle, 202/293–1293. Metro: Dupont Circle.*

5 g-5
HUNG JURY
Count on the women at the Hung Jury to make the most of their dance floor, where you're just as likely to hear the innuendo-laden lyrics of rapper Lil' Kim as you are a Top 40 dance track. *1819 H St. NW, Downtown, 202/785–8181. Metro: Farragut West.*

10 g-8
REMINGTON'S
Remington's is your basic cowboy bar, where a mostly male clientele in denim and shiny boots steps to country-and-western tunes. *639 Pennsylvania Ave. SE, Capitol Hill, 202/543–3113. Metro: Eastern Market.*

LIVING-ROOM BARS

Sink into plush sofas and easy chairs, and dream that your house is as stylish as these lounges.

Blue Room (Bars & Lounges)
Take a seat on a leather sofa and make believe you're a dot-com millionaire.

Chi Cha Lounge (Bars & Lounges)
Arrive early to get a comfortable sofa and have a hookah all to yourself.

18th Street Lounge (Dance Clubs)
This jazz-drenched lounge started the whole trend in D.C.

Eleventh Hour (Bars & Lounges)
Doll yourself up in preparation.

Tryst (Bars & Lounges)
The coffeehouse of the moment if you also want a drink drink.

Velvet Lounge (Bars & Lounges)
It's not as slick as the others, but it's comfortable and neighborly.

7 f-2
WET
Go-go boys in showers mix with liquid beats for good clean fun at this club just blocks away from the Navy barracks. *52 L St. SE, Navy Yard, 202/488–1200. Metro: Navy Yard.*

7 f-2
ZIEGFELD'S-SECRETS
The perfect place for gay men to take their straight best female friends, this two-part club features gorgeous go-go boys on one side and top DJs and a dance floor on the other. *1345 Half St. SE, Navy Yard, 202/554–5141. Metro: Navy Yard.*

JAZZ & BLUES

9 e-7
BLUES ALLEY
The kitchen turns out Creole cooking while such national performers as Nancy Wilson, Joshua Redman, and Stanley Turrentine perform on stage. You can come for just the show, but those who dine get better seats. *1073 Wisconsin Ave. NW (rear), Georgetown, 202/337–4141.*

3 g-8
CAFÉ ARISTIDE
The Toulouse-Lautrec decor, French food, and Continental atmosphere are almost enough to evoke the Left Bank of the Seine rather than the right bank of the Potomac. Cool cats play straight-ahead jazz nightly. *2431 18th St. NW, Adams-Morgan, 202/238–9018. Metro: Woodley Park–Zoo.*

3 g-8
COLUMBIA STATION
Amber lights illuminate the brass instrument–theme artwork adorning the walls of this restaurant and bar. The nightly live music usually features a good local jazz or blues band; either way, you're more likely to hear an electric bass than an upright, wailing tune funky enough to dance to. *2325 18th St. NW, Adams-Morgan 202/462–6040. Metro: Woodley Park–Zoo.*

3 g-8
FELIX
Felix is known for its grand martinis as well as its trendy menu. On warm-

weather weekends they open up the windows, allowing the sounds of live jazz and funk to spill out onto the street. Even during cool weather, hot bands keep Felix steamy. *2406 18th St. NW, Adams-Morgan, 202/483–3549. Metro: Woodley Park–Zoo.*

2 *d-4*
HR-57
The name comes from the congressional resolution declaring jazz a national treasure. The music comes straight from the heart of the city's best homegrown jazz musicians. *1610 14th St. NW, U Street, 202/667–3700. Metro: U St.–Cardozo.*

6 *a-3*
NEW VEGAS LOUNGE
No pretensions or airs are allowed at the New Vegas Lounge; blues are belted from deep within the gut for an appreciative, dressed-down crowd of regulars. *1415 P St. NW, Dupont Circle, 202/483–3971. Metro: Dupont Circle.*

5 *e-4*
ONE STEP DOWN
A small, intimate club with a low ceiling and the best jazz jukebox in town, One Step Down books talented local artists and the occasional national act, and is the venue of choice for many New York jazz masters. It's frayed and smoky, as a jazz club should be. *2517 Pennsylvania Ave. NW, Foggy Bottom, 202/995–7141. Metro: Foggy Bottom–GWU.*

1 *e-3*
TAKOMA STATION TAVERN
Located in the shadow of its elevated Metro namesake, the Takoma Station Tavern hosts local favorites along with the occasional national artist stopping by to jam. Jazz happy hours pack the joint starting at 6:30 Wednesday through Friday. There's reggae on Saturday and comedy on Monday. Athletic wear is not allowed. *6914 4th St. NW, Takoma, 202/829–1999. Metro: Takoma.*

2 *e-2*
TWINS LOUNGE
This out-of-the-way spot owned by twin sisters hides the best straight-ahead jazz in D.C. and an atmosphere of serious music appreciation. The twins' tasty Ethiopian food eases the sting of the club's sometimes pricey table minimum. *5516 Colorado Ave. NW, Upper Northwest, 202/882–2523.*

1 *c-2*
TWIST AND SHOUT
A great place for blues, Cajun, and zydeco, Twist and Shout hosts such cult favorites as Koko Taylor, Wayne Toups and Zydecajun, and Junior Wells in addition to local heroes. *4800 Auburn Ave., Bethesda, MD, 301/652–3383. Metro: Bethesda.*

8 *g-4*
219 BASIN STREET LOUNGE
Across the Potomac in Old Town Alexandria (above the restaurant 219), jazz combos perform Tuesday through Saturday in an attractive, Victorian-style bar. Musicians from local service bands often drop by to sit in. *219 King St., Alexandria, VA, 703/549–1141.*

2 *d-4*
UTOPIA
An intimate bistro-style restaurant with an eclectic Mediterranean menu, Utopia offers a range of live music from festive Brazilian jazz to standards sung by smoky-voiced torch singers. *1418 U St. NW, U Street, 202/483–7669. Metro: U St.–Cardozo.*

PIANO BARS & CABARET

8 *g-4*
CATE'S BISTRO
Couples enjoy dinner by candlelight at this romantic spot where the elegant vocals of singer-pianist Suzy Francis complete the intimate atmosphere each weekend. *715 King St., Alexandria, VA, 703/549–0533. Metro: King Street.*

5 *h-2*
CLUB CHAOS
Judy, Barbra, and Liza: eat your heart out. Nobody does Broadway show tunes like Club Chaos. Open mikes allow amateurs to take their turn on the stage at this gay and lesbian club. *17th and Q Sts. NW, Dupont Circle, 202/232–4141. Metro: Dupont Circle.*

5 *c-4*
MR. SMITH'S
Legend has it that Tori Amos tickled the ivories here as a teen. It's doubtful that this restaurant will yield another platinum-selling superstar, but regulars

enjoy singing along to standards regardless of who's at the piano. *3104 M St. NW, Georgetown, 202/333–3104.*

5 *h-4*

TOWN & COUNTRY LOUNGE

Pianists in the lounge lighten the clubby atmosphere of this cigar-friendly, power-broker classic hotel bar in the Mayflower Hotel. *1127 Connecticut Ave. NW, Downtown, 202/347–3000. Metro: Farragut North.*

6 *a-5*

TUSCANA WEST

Happy hour at this posh bar comes with live piano music and earlybird dinner specials. On Thursdays be sure to catch their "Italian cabaret evening," better known as Opera Night. *1350 I St. NW, Downtown, 202/289–7300. Metro: Metro Center.*

POP/ROCK/ HIP-HOP

6 *a-2*

BLACK CAT

Catch the latest local bands as well as a few up-and-coming indie stars from labels like Teenbeat and Dischord Records. The postpunk crowd kills time

---

RETRO REVIVAL

Some people just can't let go of the past—especially those who never actually lived it.

Club Heaven and Hell (Dance Clubs)
  Duran Duran tops the charts on '80s night.

Felix (Bars & Lounges)
  It's as if 1989 never happened at this high-rolling bar.

Glen Echo Park (Dance Clubs)
  Dust off your two-tone shoes and join the swank crowd on the dance floor.

Jaxx (Pop/Rock/Hip-Hop)
  And you thought heavy metal was dead: big hair and black leather still rule here.

Polly Esther's (Dance Clubs)
  A disco flashback for those barely old enough to remember the real thing.

---

in the Red Room, a side bar with pool tables, an eclectic jukebox, and no cover charge. Chefs provide tasty veggie bar food. *1831 14th St. NW, U Street, 202/667–7960. Metro: U St.– Cardozo.*

3 *g-8*

BUKOM CAFE

This small West African restaurant in Adams-Morgan hosts live music every night, with no cover charge. It's got the city's best reggae as well as high-life, zouk, and more. *2442 18th St. NW, Adams- Morgan, 202/265–4600. Metro: Woodley Park–Zoo.*

5 *g-4*

THE GARAGE

The Garage's fluctuating name—it's been known as Ozone, The Roxy, and briefly as Steel—hasn't deterred those seeking a good live show from up-and-coming hip-hop, alternative, and R&B acts. *1214 18th St. NW, Dupont Circle, 202/293–0303. Metro: Dupont Circle.*

2 *c-3*

GROG AND TANKARD

A college-age crowd downs cheap pitchers to the tunes of exuberant local rock bands in this small, comfortably disheveled nightspot. *2408 Wisconsin Ave. NW, Glover Park, 202/333–3114.*

JAXX

Jaxx is one of the last bastions for long-hair bands and the people who love them. Acts like Todd Rundgren, Quiet Riot, and Nelson crank up their guitars to a head-banging crowd of devoted fans. *6355 Rolling Rd., Springfield, VA, 703/569–5940.*

2 *e-4*

KAFFA HOUSE

This eclectic spot, with its regular spoken-word nights and DJ parties, caters to a bohemian hip-hop crowd, with a few mods thrown in for good measure. Live reggae bands perform regularly, and the city's best reggae sound systems make for crowded dance parties every weekend. *1212 U St., U Street, 202/462–1212. Metro: U St.– Cardozo.*

MERRIWEATHER POST PAVILION

In Columbia, Maryland, less than an hour's drive north of Washington, this outdoor pavilion with some covered seating hosts big-name pop acts in warmer months. *Broken Land Pkwy., Exit 18B off Rte. 29 N, 301/982–1800; off season, 301/596–0660.*

6 *a-2*
METRO CAFE
This live music club's roster of local bands, up-and-coming stars, and comeback acts draws music-loving twentysomethings. *1522 14th St. NW, U Street, 202/588–9118. Metro: U St.–Cardozo.*

7 *e-3*
NATION
One of the largest spaces for alternative and rock music in Washington, Nation holds 1,000 people and hosts such performers as Cherry Poppin Daddies, Jamiroquai, and Fugees Allstars. On Friday night the warehouse becomes Sting, a massive rave featuring the latest permutations of techno and drum-and-bass. *1015 Half St. SE, Navy Yard, 202/554–1500. Metro: Navy Yard.*

2 *e-4*
9:30 CLUB
9:30 books an eclectic mix of local, national, and international artists, most of whom fall into the "alternative" category—from Fiona Apple to Portishead to Erykah Badu. There's a large dance floor in front of the stage and a balcony on three sides above, so you can get a view from almost anywhere. *815 V St. NW, U Street, 202/393–0930. Metro: U St.–Cardozo.*

NISSAN PAVILION AT STONE RIDGE
This 25,000-seat venue in rural Virginia, about an hour from downtown Washington, hosts major pop acts as well as music festivals of all kinds. *7800 Cellar Door Dr., Bristow, VA, 703/754–6400 or 202/432–7328.*

2 *d-4*
STATE OF THE UNION
The city's best underground hip-hop acts call State their home along with reggae bands, funked-up jazz, and the occasional acoustic performer. *1357 U St. NW, U Street, 202/588–8926. Metro: U St.–Cardozo.*

1 *h-5*
US AIRWAYS ARENA
Formerly known as the Capital Centre, the US Airways Arena seats 20,000 and is now the region's main venue for big-name pop, rock, and rap acts. *1 Harry S. Truman Dr., Landover, MD, 301/350–3400 or 202/432–7328.*

7 *c-2*
ZANZIBAR ON THE WATERFRONT
After a long hiatus following many years as a world-music hot spot in Adams-Morgan, Zanzibar reopened in swank digs on the waterfront. Here you can listen to live music ranging from reggae to smooth jazz to soulful vocals, or chill out on the deck overlooking the Potomac. *700 Water St., Waterfront, 202/554–9100. Metro: Waterfront.*

WINE BARS

1 *c-3*
GRAPESEED
At Grapeseed you can indulge in a little wine tasting by ordering shot-size samplers from a list of more than 20 by-the-glass wines. The small, tightly packed tables may remind some people of a European bistro, but claustrophobics should skip this popular restaurant. *4865 Cordell Ave. NW, Bethesda, MD, 301/986–9592. Metro: Bethesda.*

1 *c-3*
MENDOCINO GRILLE
As the name suggests, this restaurant brings a West Coast sensibility to the politics-saturated D.C. scene. Much of the wine list, including 23 by-the-glass selections, consists of California varietals. On a warm day, sit by the window and imagine the Golden Gate bridge in the distance. *2917 M St. NW, Georgetown, 202/333–2912.*

1 *c-5*
RHODESIDE GRILL
This casual restaurant offers something for everyone: outdoor tables, live music, original artwork, sandwiches, pool tables, and more than 20 wines by the glass. *1836 Wilson Blvd., Arlington, VA, 703/243–0145. Metro: Clarendon.*

3 *g-8*

ROCKY'S CAFE

This Caribbean restaurant serves 15 wines by the glass. Outdoor seating provides a good place to people-watch while washing down spicy appetizers with chilled wine. *1817 Columbia Rd. NW, Adams-Morgan, 202/387–2580. Metro: Woodley Park–Zoo.*

chapter 6

HOTELS

Washington, D.C., has some of the most elegant hotels in the nation. It has to—the guest registers are filled with the signatures of presidents, diplomats, sultans, royalty, and prime ministers. The city's poshest properties offer meticulous service, deluxe accommodations, and high price tags.

If high-end prices aren't in your, or your guests', vacation budget, don't automatically assume that a luxury stay is out of the question. Weekend, off-season, and special rates (such as American Automobile Association and American Association for Retired Persons discounts) can make deluxe rooms more affordable. If that doesn't work out, try a simple walk through the lobbies of some historic lodgings, still a treat for the senses. People-watching in the lobby lounge of a swish hotel is the next best thing to staying there—and a very affordable option for residents and tourists alike. (A word to the wise: dress the part.)

The D.C. area has more than 340 places to stay, encompassing more than 63,000 guest rooms in every price category. Hotels are often full of conventioneers, politicians in transit, or families and school groups in search of museums and monuments, so book as early as possible. Rates increase around the time of the Cherry Blossom Festival in April. D.C. is a bit calmer during the congressional recess, in August, so encourage guests to visit then, if they can stand the tropical weather. Rates drop in late December and January, except around a presidential inauguration. Most hotels have weekend rates that can be substantially lower than weekday rates; discounted group and corporate rates may also be available.

price categories

Most hotels in the Very Expensive and Expensive categories have concierges, as do some in the Moderate group. Because Washington is in effect a world capital, many hotel staffs are multilingual. Every hotel listed here is air-conditioned, and many have facilities for business travelers. Nearly all of the finer hotels have superb restaurants with prices to match. Parking fees range from free (usually in the suburbs) to $24 a night; the high-end hotels sometimes offer valet parking, with its implied additional gratuities. Street parking is free on Sunday and often free after 6:30PM, but there are always more seekers than spaces available. Parking is prohibited on many streets during weekday rush hours; illegally parked cars will be towed.

CATEGORY	COST
Very Expensive Lodgings	over $240
Expensive Lodgings	$170–$240
Moderately Priced Lodgings	$100–$170
Budget Lodgings	under $100

All prices are for a standard double room, excluding room tax (14.5% in D.C, 12% in MD, and 6.5 to 9.75% in VA) and occupancy tax of $1.50 per night in D.C.

VERY EXPENSIVE LODGINGS

5 *f-3*

CLARION HAMPSHIRE HOTEL

Nestled among office buildings, embassies, and other fine hotels, the Hampshire is near Dupont Circle as well as shops and restaurants. Many rooms have excellent views of the city, Rock Creek Park, and Georgetown; most have a kitchenette, and all have a microwave oven and refrigerator. The lobby is compact, but the Peacock Bistro is open and sunny. Guests get free passes to the nearby YMCA. *1310 New Hampshire Ave. NW, Dupont Circle, 20036, 202/296–7600 or 800/368–5691, fax 202/293–2476. 82 rooms. Restaurant, bar, outdoor café, in-room data ports, refrigerators, business services, meeting rooms, parking (fee). AE, D, DC, MC, V. Metro: Dupont Circle.*

5 *f-3*

EMBASSY SUITES

Classical columns, plaster lions, and wrought-iron lanterns decorate this modern hotel's skylighted atrium, where there are waterfalls, tall palms, and plants cascading over balconies. Embassy Suites is within walking distance of Georgetown, the Kennedy Center, and Dupont Circle. Good for business travelers and families alike, each spacious two-room suite has a wet bar, refrigerator, coffeemaker, and microwave oven. A cooked-to-order breakfast is complimentary, and at the nightly manager's reception, beverages are free. The Italian restaurant, Panevino, serves lunch and dinner. *1250 22nd St. NW, Downtown, 20037, 202/857–3388 or 800/ 362–2779, fax 202/293–3173. 318 suites. Restaurant, bar, refrigerators, room service, indoor pool, health club, laundry service, parking (fee). AE, D, DC, MC, V. Metro: Foggy Bottom–GWU, Dupont Circle.*

9 g-7
FOUR SEASONS

Whatever the season, impeccable service and a wealth of wonderful amenities have made pampering guests an art form at this perennial favorite among celebrities, hotel connoisseurs, and families. The hotel overlooks the C&O Canal and Rock Creek at the White House edge of Georgetown. Rich mahogany paneling, antiques, spectacular flower arrangements, and extensive greenery abound. Rooms are spacious and bright, with fine marble baths (some with sunken tubs) and original artwork. An expansive state-of-the-art fitness center offers personal trainers, yoga and exercise classes, a whirlpool, a sauna, and a lap pool. There's live music six days a week in the Garden Terrace, the site of a popular Sunday brunch and daily afternoon tea. Seasons restaurant offers formal dining. *2800 Pennsylvania Ave. NW, 20007, 202/342–0444 or 800/332–3442, fax 202/342–1673. 205 rooms, 55 suites. 2 restaurants, lobby lounge, room service, pool, health club, parking (fee). AE, DC, MC, V. Metro: Foggy Bottom–GWU.*

6 b-5
GRAND HYATT WASHINGTON

The fanciful interior of this high-rise hotel contains a waterfall-fed blue lagoon with a small island on which a pianist plays Cole Porter tunes. The hotel's location can't be beat: it's across from the Washington Convention Center, two blocks from the MCI Center, and just steps from downtown shops and theaters. You can enter Metro Center—the hub of D.C.'s subway system—directly from the lobby. Rooms that face the atrium have windows that open indoors; if you don't want to be bothered by restaurant noise, ask for a room above the first few floors. Weekend brunch here is very popular. *1000 H St. NW, Downtown, 20001, 202/582–1234 or 800/233–1234, fax 202/637–4781. 900 rooms, 60 suites. 4 restaurants, 2 bars, minibars, room service, indoor lap pool, health club, business services, meeting rooms, parking (fee). AE, DC, MC, V. Metro: Metro Center.*

5 h-5
HAY–ADAMS HOTEL

This Italian Renaissance–style landmark, built in 1928, is directly across Lafayette Park from the White House. For the city's best view of the great mansion and, behind it, the Washington Monument, reserve a room on the south side well in advance. The eclectic grandeur of the interior will charm you with European and Asian antiques; Doric, Ionic, and Corinthian touches; carved walnut wainscoting; and intricate ornamental ceilings. It stands on the site of houses owned by statesman and author John Hay and diplomat and historian Henry Adams. Attentive staff assures that you receive warm, congenial service immediately upon your arrival. The Lafayette restaurant, which serves elegant contemporary American cuisine, is a favorite spot for English-style high tea. *1 Lafayette Sq. NW, Downtown, 20006, 202/638–6600 or 800/424–5054, fax 202/638–2716. 125 rooms, 18 suites. Restaurant, bar, room service, laundry service, parking (fee). AE, DC, MC, V. Metro: McPherson Square or Farragut North.*

6 b-4
HENLEY PARK HOTEL

A Tudor-style building adorned with 119 gargoyles, this National Historic Trust hotel has the cozy charm of an English country house. The highly acclaimed Coeur de Lion restaurant has a leafy atrium, stained-glass windows, and an American menu. The hotel lobby is warm and inviting with a fireplace and grandfather clock. Guest rooms vary in size, but all have a floral-pattern decor. Some of the thoughtful complimentary perks of staying here include shoe shines, morning delivery of the *Washington Post*, and weekday morning car service to any downtown destination. The hotel is a one-block walk to the Washington Convention Center, three blocks from Smithsonian museums, and a five-block walk to the MCI Sports Arena. *926 Massachusetts Ave. NW, Downtown, 20001, 202/638–5200 or 800/222–8474, fax 202/638–6740. 96 rooms, 17 suites. Restaurant, bar, minibars, room service, parking (fee). AE, DC, MC, V. Metro: Metro Center or Gallery Place–Chinatown.*

5 *f-2*

HOTEL SOFITEL WASHINGTON

All rooms in Washington's only French boutique hotel include a small work area, and because of the building's excellent hilltop location, many guest rooms have excellent views of Washington. The Trocadero Café serves three meals daily. *1914 Connecticut Ave. NW, Adams-Morgan, 20009, 202/797–2000 or 800/424–2464, fax 202/462–0944. 107 rooms, 37 suites. Restaurant, bar, mini-bars, room service, exercise room, laundry service, parking (fee). AE, DC, MC, V. Metro: Dupont Circle.*

6 *a-6*

HOTEL WASHINGTON

Washingtonians bring visitors to the outdoor rooftop bar here—open May through October—for cocktails and a spectacular panorama that includes the White House grounds and the Washington Monument. (The hotel has been known for its view ever since it opened, in 1918.) Now a National Landmark, the Washington sprang from the drawing boards of John Carrère and Thomas Hastings, who designed the New York Public Library. Elvis Presley stayed in Suite 506 whenever he passed through. Guest rooms have mahogany furniture and Italian marble bathrooms. Rooms in the interior portion of the hotel are small. *515 15th St. NW, Downtown, 20004, 202/638–5900, fax 202/638–1594. 344 rooms, 16 suites. 2 restaurants, bar, deli, lobby lounge, room service, exercise room, laundry service, business services, parking (fee). AE, DC, MC, V. Metro: Metro Center.*

1 *c-2*

HYATT REGENCY BETHESDA

The Hyatt Regency is conveniently located on Wisconsin Avenue, the main artery between Bethesda and Georgetown, atop the Bethesda Metro station. Its atrium lobby, with ferns and glass elevators, is reminiscent of those in other Hyatt Regencies. All rooms are nicely appointed and have coffeemakers; some also have fax machines and minibars. The sights of downtown Washington are about 15 minutes away by Metro. An adjacent plaza has a small ice rink, open in winter, and a huge indoor food court. *1 Bethesda Metro Center (on 7400 block of Wisconsin Ave.), Bethesda, MD 20814, 301/657–1234 or 800/233–1234, fax 301/657–6453. 371 rooms, 10 suites. Bar, café, lobby lounge, in-room data ports, indoor pool, exercise room, laundry service, business services, convention center, meeting rooms, parking (fee). AE, DC, MC, V. Metro: Bethesda.*

10 *b-4*

HYATT REGENCY ON CAPITOL HILL

Guest rooms at the 11-story Hyatt Regency, near Union Station and the Mall, are well lighted and furnished with artwork, new desks, and upgraded electric and telephone connections. Suites on the south side have a view of the Capitol dome, as does the rooftop Capitol View Club restaurant, a private club open to hotel guests at lunch and to the public for dinner. *400 New Jersey Ave. NW, 20001, 202/737–1234, fax 202/737–5773. 834 rooms, 31 suites. Restaurant, lobby lounge, pub, in-room safes, room service, pool, barbershop, beauty salon, health club, meeting rooms, parking. AE, DC, MC, V. Metro: Union Station or Judiciary Square.*

6 *a-6*

J. W. MARRIOTT

This modern flagship hotel of the Marriott group has a prime location, next to the National Theatre and near the White House. The spacious, columned lobby includes a four-story atrium, marble and mahogany accents, and Oriental rugs. The plush guest rooms have dark wood furnishings, floral bedspreads, and burgundy and cream interior accents; those on the Pennsylvania Avenue side have the best views. Guests have indoor access to National Place, which has 80 shops and 18 restaurants and cafés. *1331 Pennsylvania Ave. NW, Downtown, 20004, 202/393–2000 or 800/228–9290, fax 202/626–6991. 772 rooms, 34 suites. 2 restaurants, 2 bars, room service, indoor pool, health club, laundry service, parking (fee). AE, DC, MC, V. Metro: Metro Center.*

5 *h-4*

JEFFERSON HOTEL

Federal-style elegance abounds in this small luxury hotel, next door to the National Geographic Society and opposite the Russian Embassy. Each room has antiques, original art, VCRs, and CD players; you may borrow from the hotel's video and CD libraries. A high staff-to-guest ratio ensures outstanding service: employees greet you by name, and laundry is hand-ironed and delivered in wicker baskets. The restaurant is a favorite of high-ranking politicos and film stars; its American cuisine includes game and seafood. *1200 16th St. NW, Downtown, 20036, 202/347–2200 or 800/368–5966, fax 202/785–1505. 68 rooms, 32 suites. Restaurant, bar, room service, in-room VCRs, laundry service, parking (fee). AE, DC, MC, V. Metro: Farragut North.*

2 *e-5*

LOEWS L'ENFANT PLAZA

This hotel was named for the architect who designed Washington, Pierre L'Enfant. Appropriately, the guest rooms—which occupy the top four floors, above a shopping mall–office complex and a Metro stop—have spectacular views of L'Enfant's handiwork. Rooms look out on either monuments, the river, or the Capitol. Just two blocks from the Smithsonian museums, the hotel is also near several government agencies (the USDA, USPS, USIA, and DOT), making it popular with business travelers as well as tourists. All rooms have coffeemakers, and both bedrooms and bathrooms have TVs and phones. The Club rooms have fax machines. *L'Enfant Plaza SW, Downtown, 20024, 202/484–1000 or 800/223–0888, fax 202/646–4456. 348 rooms, 22 suites. Restaurant, 2 bars, in-room VCRs, minibars, room service, indoor pool, health club, parking (fee). AE, DC, MC, V. Metro: L'Enfant Plaza.*

5 *h-4*

MADISON HOTEL

Old-world luxury and meticulous service prevail at the Madison (named for the fourth U.S. president), which may be why the signatures of dignitaries and heads of state fill the guest register. Deceptively contemporary on the outside, the 14-story building, four blocks from the White House, contains a world-class collection of antiques; a rare Chinese Imperial altar table and a Louis XVI palace commode are on display in the lobby. The European-style guest rooms are average size and have pink, navy, burgundy, and green color schemes. Each suite is individually decorated. The Retreat restaurant serves three meals a day as well as high tea. *15th and M Sts. NW, Downtown, 20005, 202/862–1600 or 800/424–8577, fax 202/785–1255. 318 rooms, 35 suites. 2 restaurants, bar, room service, massage, sauna, steam room, exercise room, business services, parking (fee). AE, DC, MC, V. Metro: McPherson Square.*

3 *d-7*

MARRIOTT WARDMAN PARK

The largest hotel in town is a veritable city on a hill. You may soon know your fellow guests' names, though, because many will be wearing convention name tags as they wander through the vast corridors searching for their meeting room. The Marriott Wardman is surrounded by 16 parklike acres and is just two blocks from the National Zoo. The 1920s brick Wardman Tower used to be an apartment building, home to presidents, cabinet members, and senators. Guest rooms and public areas of the 10-story old section include traditional furnishings; rooms in the newer convention-ready main complex are contemporary, with chrome and glass touches and data ports. *2660 Woodley Rd. NW, Woodley Park, 20008, 202/328–2000, fax 202/234–0015. 1,338 rooms, 125 suites. 2 restaurants, bar, coffee shop, room service, 2 pools, spa, health club, baby-sitting, laundry service, meeting rooms, parking (fee). AE, DC, MC, V. Metro: Woodley Park–Zoo.*

3 *f-7*

OMNI SHOREHAM HOTEL

This immense facility, with seven ballrooms, has hosted the world's rich and famous since 1930, when its art deco– and Renaissance-style lobby opened its doors for business. Guest rooms have marble-floored baths with phones and hair dryers, traditional cherry furniture, and floral spreads with dust ruffles. The hotel is a moderate walk from Rock Creek Park, Adams-Morgan, and the National Zoo. *2500 Calvert St. NW, Woodley Park, 20008, 202/234–0700 or 800/843–6664, fax 202/756–5145. 812 rooms, 24 suites. Restaurant, bar, deli, in-room data ports, minibars, room service, pool, exercise room, dry cleaning, laundry service, parking (fee). AE, D, DC, MC, V. Metro: Woodley Park–Zoo.*

5 *e-4*

PARK HYATT

Original works of art, some by Picasso, Matisse, and Calder, grace the guest rooms and public spaces of this elegant and luxurious modern hotel, about four blocks from the eastern end of Georgetown, just off M Street. Guest rooms, in shades of sage, cream, and taupe, have built-in armoires, goose-down duvets, and specially commissioned artwork. Guests can enjoy the on-site fitness center (with swimming pool) and Rendez-Vous day spa. Melrose restaurant, specializing in seafood dishes, features a Picasso at its entryway and offers courtyard dining with a cascading fountain. *1201 24th St. NW, Foggy Bottom, 20037, 202/789–1234 or 800/233–1234, fax 202/457–8823. 93 rooms, 131 suites. Restaurant, café, lobby lounge, refrigerators, room service, pool, beauty salon, hot tub, massage, sauna, spa, steam room, health club, parking (fee). AE, DC, MC, V. Metro: Foggy Bottom–GWU.*

5 *f-3*

RADISSON BARCELÓ HOTEL

The Barceló was once an apartment building, so its spacious rooms, with fluffy bedspreads and large sitting areas, are especially good for families. It's convenient to Dupont Circle and Georgetown, and the second-floor outdoor swimming pool has a lovely setting—a brick courtyard enclosed by the walls of the hotel and the backs of a row of century-old town houses to the east. The restaurant, Gabriel, serves Spanish fare. *2121 P St. NW, Dupont Circle, 20037, 202/293–3100, fax 202/857–0134. 235 rooms, 65 suites. Restaurant, bar, tapas bar, room service, pool, exercise room, parking (fee). AE, D, DC, MC, V. Metro: Dupont Circle.*

5 *g-4*

RENAISSANCE MAYFLOWER HOTEL

A National Historic Landmark, this 10-story hotel four blocks from the White House opened in 1925 for Calvin Coolidge's inauguration. Franklin Delano Roosevelt wrote "The only thing we have to fear is fear itself" in Suite 776, and J. Edgar Hoover ate here at the same table every day for 20 years. Sunlight spills into its majestic skylighted lobby, causing the gilded trim to gleam, and Oriental rugs splash the floors with color. Guest rooms are filled with antiques and have marble bathrooms. Contemporary Mediterranean cuisine is served amid silver, crystal, and artful flower arrangements at the Café Promenade restaurant. *1127 Connecticut Ave. NW, Downtown, 20036, 202/347–3000 or 800/468–3571, fax 202/466–9082. 660 rooms, 80 suites. Restaurant, bar, room service, sauna, exercise room, parking (fee). AE, DC, MC, V. Metro: Farragut North.*

2 *c-7*

RITZ-CARLTON PENTAGON CITY

The 18-story Ritz-Carlton at Pentagon City is more convenient to downtown Washington than many D.C. hotels. Guest rooms are well lighted and have mahogany traditional furniture and quilted bedspreads in muted colors. Public areas are decorated in a Virginia hunt country motif. Many upper rooms on the Potomac side have views of the monuments across the river. The lobby lounge serves meals, includes a small bar, and has an entrance to the Fashion Centre shopping mall, which has cinemas, a food court, 150 shops, and an underground Metro station. *1250 S. Hayes St., Arlington, VA 22202, 703/415–5000 or 800/241–3333, fax 703/415–5060. 345 rooms, 21 suites. Bar, in-room safes, minibars, room service, indoor lap pool, health club, business services, convention center, meeting rooms, parking (fee). AE, DC, MC, V. Metro: Pentagon City.*

5 *h-4*

ST. REGIS

The luxurious St. Regis, formerly the Carlton Hotel, looks like an updated Italian Renaissance mansion, with gilded ornamental ceilings and Louis XVI furnishings. In a bustling business sector near the White House, it offers unpretentious but attentive service, including day and night butler service on the top two floors. Rooms offer special touches such as cordless phones, Frette sheets, and bottled drinking water. Children stay free in their parents' room, and the St. Regis Kids program offers cookies and milk on arrival, accredited baby-sitting, and a small children's video library. *923 16th St. NW, Downtown, 20006, 202/638–2626 or 800/325–3535, fax 202/638–4231. 179 rooms, 14 suites. Restaurant, lobby lounge, room service, exercise room, meeting rooms, parking (fee). AE, D, DC, MC, V. Metro: McPherson Square.*

5 *e-5*

SWISSÖTEL WASHINGTON WATERGATE

The Watergate is accustomed to serving the world's elite. The lobby sets a genteel tone with its classic columns, Oriental rugs on black-and-white checkerboard marble, subdued lighting, and soothing classical music. The hotel is on the Potomac River, across the street from the Kennedy Center, and a short walk from the State Department and Georgetown. Originally intended as apartments, the guest rooms are large, and all have walk-in closets, fax machines, kitchens or wet bars, and refrigerators. The riverside restaurant, Aquarelle, serves sophisticated Euro-American cuisine. There's complimentary limousine service weekdays 7 AM–10 AM. *2650 Virginia Ave. NW, Downtown, 20037, 202/965–2300 or 800/424–2736, fax 202/337–7915. 104 rooms, 146 suites. Restaurant, bar, in-room safes, refrigerators, room service, indoor pool, health club, parking (fee). AE, DC, MC, V. Metro: Foggy Bottom–GWU.*

10 *b-3*

WASHINGTON COURT HOTEL

Terraced marble stairs lead to a skylighted atrium lobby with an indoor waterfall and glass elevators at this luxury hotel, which is near Union Station and sits firmly in the Capitol's sight line. Guest rooms are equipped with modern, luxurious furnishings and high-speed modem access. *525 New Jersey Ave. NW, Downtown, 20001, 202/628–2100, fax 202/879–7918. 252 rooms, 11 suites. Restaurant, bar, in-room data ports, refrigerators, room service, health club, laundry service, business services, parking (fee). AE, D, DC, MC, V. Metro: Union Station.*

5 *e-4*

WASHINGTON MONARCH HOTEL

Formerly the ANA, this hotel at the Georgetown end of downtown Washington is a stylish combination of contemporary and traditional. The glassed lobby and about a third of the bright, airy rooms have views of the central courtyard and gardens, which are popular for weddings. The hotel's informal restaurant, the Bistro, serves contemporary American cuisine and offers courtyard dining. The Colonnade room hosts a Sunday champagne brunch. A deluxe fitness center is one of the best in the city. *2401 M St. NW, Georgetown, 20037, 202/429–2400 or 877/222–2266, fax 202/457–5010. 406 rooms, 9 suites. Restaurant, bar, café, lobby lounge, in-room data ports, in-room safes, minibars, room service, indoor lap pool, sauna, steam room, health club, parking (fee). AE, DC, MC, V. Metro: Foggy Bottom–GWU.*

5 *f-3*

WESTIN FAIRFAX

This intimate hotel, originally built as an apartment building, was owned by the Gore family and was the childhood home of Al Gore. It has an English hunt-club theme and complimentary butler service. The Fairfax is close to Dupont Circle and not far from Georgetown and the Kennedy Center. Rooms have views of Embassy Row or Georgetown and the National Cathedral. The renowned Jockey Club restaurant, with its half-timber ceilings, dark wood paneling, and red-checkered tablecloths, serves three meals daily in an intimate atmosphere. The Fairfax Bar is a cozy spot for a drink beside the fire, with piano entertainment some evenings. *2100 Massachusetts Ave. NW, Downtown, 20008, 202/293–2100 or 800/325–3589, fax 202/293–0641. 154 rooms, 59 suites. Restaurant, bar, in-room data ports, in-room safes, in-room VCRs, minibars, room service, massage, sauna, exercise room, meeting room, parking (fee). AE, DC, MC, V. Metro: Dupont Circle.*

6 *a-6*

WILLARD INTER-CONTINENTAL

Popular with those who expect nothing less than perfection, the Willard has long been a favorite of American presidents and other news makers. Martin Luther King Jr. drafted his famous "I Have a Dream" speech here. Superb service and a wealth of amenities are a hallmark of the hotel, just two blocks from the White House. The spectacular beaux arts main lobby features great columns, sparkling chandeliers, mosaic floors, and elaborate ceilings. Renovations are currently underway to coincide with the 2001 centennial celebration of the hotel, and include newly updated guest rooms in warm green and gold hues, sleek marble bathrooms, and an expanded fitness center. The Kids in Tow program features an activity package for children. The hotel's formal dining room, the Willard Room, has won nationwide acclaim. *1401 Pennsylvania Ave. NW, Downtown, 20004, 202/628–9100, or 800/327–0200, fax 202/637–7326. 302 rooms, 38 suites. Restaurants, 2 bars, café, minibars, room service, health club, laundry service, meeting rooms, parking (fee). AE, DC, MC, V. Metro: Metro Center.*

EXPENSIVE LODGINGS

5 *h-3*

CANTERBURY HOTEL

On a quiet street near the embassies of Massachusetts Avenue and Dupont Circle, the Canterbury was built in 1901 as an apartment building. Rooms have 18th-century European reproduction furnishings and interiors, with queen-, double queen–, or king-size beds, and separate dressing areas. Some rooms have stoves or microwave ovens on request. The hotel offers free access to the nearby YMCA and serves a Continental breakfast. *1733 N St. NW, 20036, 202/393–3000 or 800/424–2950, fax 202/785–9581. 99 rooms. Restaurant, bar, in-room safes, minibars, refrigerators, laundry service, business services, meeting rooms, parking (fee). AE, D, DC, MC, V. Metro: Dupont Circle.*

6 *f-8*

CAPITOL HILL SUITES

On a quiet residential street beside the Library of Congress, this all-suites hotel's proximity to the House office buildings means that it often fills with visiting lobbyists when Congress is in session. Guest rooms, which are actually renovated apartments with full-size kitchens, are cozy and large; the sun-filled lobby has a fireplace. *200 C St. SE, 20003. 202/543–6000 or 800/424–9165, fax 202/547–2608. 152 suites. Kitchens, lobby lounge, in-room data ports, health club, dry cleaning, laundry service, meeting rooms, parking (fee). AE, DC, MC, V. Metro: Capitol South.*

1 *d-6*

CRYSTAL CITY MARRIOTT

This business hotel is in a tall row of office buildings near Ronald Reagan National Airport and the Pentagon. The Smithsonian-lined Mall is just minutes away by Metro. The lobby, with its lush plants, marble floor, and art deco–style fixtures, is more luxurious than the rooms, which are tidy and have traditionally styled furniture. *1999 Jefferson Davis Hwy., Arlington, VA 22202, 703/413–5500 or 800/228–9290, fax 703/413–0185. 336 rooms, 9 suites. Restaurant, bar, room service, indoor pool, health club, business services, meeting rooms, airport shuttle, parking (fee). AE, D, DC, MC, V. Metro: Crystal City.*

1 *c-1*

DOUBLETREE HOTEL

The soothing sounds of the one-story waterfall in the soaring atrium can be heard throughout the hotel's corridors. The atrium also includes a 200-seat dining room and a gazebo large enough for a bar and large-screen television. In the rooms, a floral spread covers the bed and floral prints adorn the walls. If you don't care for the coffee in your room, buy a mug of your favorite from Starbucks, offered every morning from 6:30 to 11. More than a dozen restaurants are within walking distance of the hotel. The Twinbrook Metro station is nearby. Rates drop considerably on weekends. *1750 Rockville Pike, Rockville, MD 20852, 301/468–1100 or 800/222–8733, fax 301/468–0163. 298 rooms, 17 suites. Restaurant, indoor-outdoor pool, health club. AE, D, DC, MC, V. Metro: Twinbrook.*

8 *d-4*

EMBASSY SUITES OLDE TOWN ALEXANDRIA

This modern, all-suites hotel sits across from the landmark George Washington Masonic Temple. The extensive, light-filled atrium lobby has hanging foliage, waterfalls, and gazebos. Suites are decorated in green and burgundy with mahogany furniture. If you're a train buff, request a suite overlooking the historic Alexandria train station, where Amtrak and freight trains still pass. (The Amtrak station and Metro are about 100 yards across the street.) A free shuttle transports guests to the scenic Alexandria riverfront, with its myriad shops and restaurants. A cooked-to-order breakfast is complimentary, as is the cocktail reception every evening. *1900 Diagonal Rd., Alexandria, VA 22314, 703/684–5900 or 800/362–2779, fax 703/684–1403. 268 suites. Restaurant, in-room data ports, refrigerators, indoor pool, hot tub, sauna, exercise room, laundry service, business services, meeting rooms, parking (fee). AE, D, DC, MC, V. Metro: King St.*

5 *e-5*

GEORGE WASHINGTON UNIVERSITY INN

This boutique-style hotel is a few blocks from the Kennedy Center and the State Department. It's also two blocks from George Washington University, where you have complimentary use of the university's fitness center. You enter the hotel through gray wrought-iron gates into a courtyard; beveled-glass doors open into a small lobby with gray marble floors. Guest rooms have colonial-style furniture, refrigerators, microwaves, coffeemakers, and fully equipped kitchenettes. Zuki Moon, a Japanese noodle house and tea garden, is off the lobby. *824 New Hampshire Ave. NW, Foggy Bottom, 20037, 202/337–6620 or 800/426–4455, fax 202/298–7499. 48 rooms, 31 suites, 16 efficiencies. Restaurant, kitchenettes, refrigerators, coin laundry, laundry service, meeting rooms, parking (fee). AE, D, DC, MC, V. Metro: Foggy Bottom–GWU.*

6 d-8
HOLIDAY INN CAPITOL

You can't sleep any closer to the Smithsonian museums than this large hotel, only one block from the National Air and Space Museum (NASM). The Holiday Inn Capitol is both family-friendly and well equipped for business travelers. Guest rooms are attractively decorated in forest green and tan, with mahogany furniture, paisley bedspreads, and richly textured upholstery. A sightseeing trolley will pick you up here, and you can buy discounted tickets for the Air and Space Museum's IMAX movies at the front desk. Relax in the lounge, and, with the purchase of a drink, enjoy an all-you-can-eat buffet from 4:30 to 6:30 for just a few dollars. *550 C St. SW, 20024, 202/479–4000, fax 202/488–4627. 505 rooms, 24 suites. Restaurant, bar, food court, in-room data ports, no-smoking floors, room service, pool, exercise room, coin laundry, meeting rooms, parking (fee). AE, D, DC, MC, V. Metro: L'Enfant Plaza.*

5 a-5
KEY BRIDGE MARRIOTT

A short walk across the Key Bridge from Georgetown, this Marriott is three blocks from a Metro stop for easy access to Washington's major sights; the hotel provides a shuttle to the station. Rooms on the Potomac side have excellent Washington views, as does the rooftop restaurant. *1401 Lee Hwy., Arlington, VA 22209, 703/524–6400 or 800/ 228–9290, fax 703/243–3280. 564 rooms, 20 suites. 2 restaurants, 2 bars, lobby lounge, room service, indoor-outdoor pool, barbershop, beauty salon, health club, coin laundry, business services, meeting rooms, parking (fee). AE, D, DC, MC, V. Metro: Rosslyn.*

6 b-5
MARRIOTT AT METRO CENTER

This Marriott's interior virtues include a marble lobby, original artwork, and the popular Metro Grille and Regatta Raw Bar—a handsome two-level mahogany, oak, brass, and marble facility serving new American cuisine. The room decor is simple and contemporary, with dark wood furnishings, and the location is central. *775 12th St. NW, Downtown, 20005, 202/737–2200, fax 202/824–6106. 456 rooms, 3 suites. Restaurant, bar, room service, indoor pool, health club, laundry service, business services, meeting rooms, parking (fee). AE, DC, MC, V. Metro: Metro Center.*

1 c-2
MARRIOTT RESIDENCE INN BETHESDA

Only 3 mi from Marriott's corporate headquarters, this all-suites hotel is designed for extended stays. Each room has a living room and fully equipped kitchen, which the staff will stock with groceries. A Continental breakfast is served every morning. Social hours are held Monday, Tuesday, and Wednesday evenings, and dessert nights are held on Thursdays. Your cat or dog is also welcome. The longer you stay, the more your rates go down. *7335 Wisconsin Ave., Bethesda, MD 20814, 301/718–0200 or 800/331–3131, fax 301/718–0679. 187 suites. Pool, exercise room. AE, D, DC, MC, V.*

2 c-7
MARRIOTT RESIDENCE INN PENTAGON CITY

This all-suites high-rise has a magnificent view across the Potomac of the D.C. skyline and the monuments. Adjacent to the Pentagon, it's one block from the upscale Pentagon City Fashion Centre mall, which has cinemas, a food court, 150 shops, and a Metro stop. All suites have kitchens equipped with dishwashers, ice makers, microwaves, coffeemakers, toasters, dishes, and utensils. Complimentary services include grocery shopping, daily newspaper, breakfast, light dinner Monday to Wednesday, dessert buffet on Thursday evenings, and transportation to Ronald Reagan National Airport. *550 Army Navy Dr., Arlington, VA 22202, 703/413–6630, fax 703/418–1751. 299 suites. In-room data ports, kitchenettes, no-smoking rooms, indoor pool, hot tub, exercise room, coin laundry, laundry service, meeting rooms, airport shuttle, parking (fee). AE, D, DC, MC, V. Metro: Pentagon City.*

8 f-4
MORRISON HOUSE

The architecture, parquet floors, crystal chandeliers, sconces, and furnishings in the Morrison House are so faithful to the style of the Federal period that the hotel is often mistaken for a renovated period building rather than one built in 1985. Guest rooms blend the early American charm of four-poster beds and armoires with modern conveniences such as data ports and VCRs. The popular Elysium restaurant serves contemporary American cuisine. In the heart of Old Town Alexandria, the hotel is seven blocks from the train and Metro station. *116 S. Alfred St., Alexandria, VA 22314, 703/838–8000 or 800/367–0800, fax 703/684–6283. 42 rooms, 3 suites. 2 restaurants, piano bar, room service, parking (fee). AE, DC, MC, V. Metro: King St.*

6 c-4
MORRISON–CLARK INN

This inn was formed by the merger of two 1864 Victorian town houses, one of which has a 1917 Chinese Chippendale porch. The antiques-filled public rooms have marble fireplaces, bay windows, 14-ft pier mirrors, and porch access. Guest rooms have either neoclassical, French-country, or Victorian furnishings and offer comfy robes and in-room data ports. In 1923, the town houses were transformed into the Soldiers, Sailors, Marines and Airmen's Club, which served as a military establishment for 57 years; first ladies Mamie Eisenhower and Jacqueline Kennedy volunteered regularly here. The inn's highly regarded restaurant serves American cuisine with Southern and other regional influences. *Massachusetts Ave. and 11th St. NW, Downtown, 20001, 202/898–1200 or 800/332–7898, fax 202/289–8576. 54 rooms. Restaurant, minibars, in-room data ports, room service, exercise room, laundry service, parking (fee). AE, D, DC, MC, V. Metro: Mount Vernon Square–UDC.*

10 b-3
PHOENIX PARK HOTEL

Named for an historic park in Dublin, the Phoenix Park is an Irish-style hotel and home to the Dubliner Pub, where Irish entertainers perform nightly. Across the street from Union Station and only four blocks from the Capitol,

the hotel is popular with lobbyists, business travelers, and tourists alike. Three penthouse suites have balconies that overlook Union Station; three duplex suites have spiral staircases. Regular rooms, which vary in size, have a Celtic theme, with Irish linen and original artwork. *520 N. Capitol St. NW, Capitol Hill, 20001, 202/638–6900 or 800/824–5419, fax 202/393–3236. 150 rooms, 6 suites. Pub, in-room data ports, minibars, exercise room, laundry service, parking (fee). AE, D, DC, MC, V. Metro: Union Station.*

6 c-4
WASHINGTON RENAISSANCE HOTEL

Opposite the Washington Convention Center, the Renaissance was designed as a business hotel and has all the requisite meeting and supporting facilities, including a business center. The hotel is just a block from the MCI Center and a 10-minute walk from the Smithsonian. Accommodations here include free access to the 10,000-square-ft fitness center and its lap pool. For an additional $20 per night you become a member of the Renaissance Club, which includes complimentary breakfast, evening hors d'oeuvres in the Club lounge, coffeemakers and robes in your room, and morning newspaper delivery. Restaurants include Florentine, a casual place with regional American cuisine, and Caracalla, which serves Italian fare. A food court is just outside the lobby. *999 9th St. NW, Downtown, 20001, 202/898–9000 or 800/228–9898, fax 202/789–4213. 779 rooms, 21 suites. 2 restaurants, 2 bars, deli, in-room data ports, minibars, refrigerators, room service, indoor lap pool, health club, parking (fee). AE, DC, MC, V. Metro: Gallery Place–Chinatown.*

MODERATELY PRICED LODGINGS

1 c-2
BETHESDA RAMADA HOTEL AND CONFERENCE CENTER

Just south of the National Institutes of Health and the Naval Medical Center, this hotel is particularly popular with government employees and business travelers. But with its bright and cheery rooms in rich navy with gold accents, and heavily discounted weekend rates, the hotel also appeals to vacationers who don't mind being just outside of D.C. Amenities include an outdoor

Olympic-size swimming pool; a fitness room; and a washer, dryer, and microwave on each floor. The popular Chatters Restaurant and Sports Bar has wide-screen TVs, a pool table, a jukebox, and outdoor dining. *8400 Wisconsin Ave., Bethesda, MD 20814, 301/654–1000 or 800/272–6232, fax 301/986–1715. 160 rooms. Restaurant, in-room data ports, pool, exercise room, coin laundry, meeting rooms, parking (fee). AE, D, DC, MC, V. Metro: Medical Center.*

2 e-6
CHANNEL INN
The only hotel on D.C.'s waterfront, this property overlooks Washington Channel, the marina, and the Potomac River. Guest rooms have small balconies and a European feel. All are decorated with either Laura Ashley or similar-style fabrics. Public areas and meeting rooms have a nautical motif with mahogany panels and marine artifacts. The terrace allows scenic cocktail quaffing and dining in warm weather. The Mall, Smithsonian, Treasury, and several other government offices are nearby. Guests can use a nearby health club free of charge. *650 Water St. SW, Downtown, 20024, 202/554–2400 or 800/368–5668, fax 202/863–1164. 100 rooms, 4 suites. Restaurant, bar, café, pool, meeting rooms, free parking. AE, D, DC, MC, V. Metro: Waterfront.*

1 d-6
DAYS INN CRYSTAL CITY
An eight-story full-service hotel in Crystal City, on Route 1 between the Pentagon and National Airport, the Days Inn is only four Metro stops from the Smithsonian and provides shuttle service to nearby shopping and Ronald Reagan National Airport. The Crystal City Underground, with its many shops, restaurants, and a Metro stop, is a very short walk away. The hotel holds Days Inn's highest quality rating for service and cleanliness. *2000 Jefferson Davis Hwy. (Rte. 1), Arlington, VA 22202, 703/920–8600, fax 703/920–2840. 242 rooms, 3 suites. Restaurant, bar, room service, pool, exercise room, laundry service, airport shuttle, car rental, free parking. AE, D, DC, MC, V. Metro: Crystal City.*

5 e-5
DOUBLETREE GUEST SUITES
Don't be deceived by the small, European-style lobby: the Doubletree's suites are large, with full kitchens, coffeemakers, irons, ironing boards, a hair dryer, and sofa beds for extra guests. The bedroom is separate from the living room–dining room, which has a writing desk and conference-size dining table. Service is friendly and efficient. The outdoor rooftop pool has great views of the D.C. skyline and Georgetown. This building is on a quiet stretch of New Hampshire Avenue, near the Kennedy Center. *801 New Hampshire Ave. NW, Downtown, 20037, 202/785–2000 or 800/222–8733, fax 202/785–9485. 101 suites. In-room data ports, kitchenettes, room service, pool, coin laundry, dry cleaning, parking (fee). AE, D, DC, MC, V. Metro: Foggy Bottom–GWU.*

5 h-2
EMBASSY INN
Set amid beautiful old churches, homes, and office buildings, this small, three-story hotel is somewhat reminiscent of Fawlty Towers—without the crazy innkeeper. The staff is pleasant and efficient. There's no elevator, but the stairs are easy and quaint. Afternoon sherry is served in the cheery downstairs lobby. *1627 16th St. NW, Dupont Circle, 20009, 202/234–7800 or 800/423–9111, fax 202/234–3309. 38 rooms. Lobby lounge. AE, DC, MC, V. Metro: Dupont Circle.*

9 e-6
GEORGETOWN INN
With an atmosphere reminiscent of a gentleman's sporting club, this quiet, Federal-era, redbrick hotel has an 18th-century flavor. Guest rooms are large and have colonial-style decor. The hotel is in the heart of historic Georgetown, near shopping, dining, galleries, and theaters. Free passes to a nearby fitness center are provided. *1310 Wisconsin Ave. NW, 20007, 202/333–8900 or 800/424–2979, fax 202/625–1744. 86 rooms, 10 suites. Restaurant, bar, in-room data ports, room service, parking (fee). AE, DC, MC, V. Metro: Foggy Bottom–GWU.*

9 g-7
GEORGETOWN SUITES
Located in a brick courtyard one block south of M Street, in the heart of Georgetown, the Georgetown Suites is a real find. No cramped and overpriced rooms here: the affordable suites come in various shapes and have large kitchens and separate sitting rooms. A Continental breakfast is included in the

rate. *1111 30th St. NW, 20007, 202/298–7800 or 800/348–7203, fax 202/333–5792. 216 suites. Kitchenettes, exercise room, laundry service, parking (fee). AE, DC, MC, V. Metro: Foggy Bottom–GWU.*

1 c-2

GOLDEN TULIP BETHESDA COURT HOTEL

Bright burgundy awnings frame the entrance to this comfortable, intimate, three-story hotel that features a lovely, well-tended, European-style courtyard. The hotel, two blocks from the Bethesda Metro and set back from busy Wisconsin Avenue, offers a relaxed environment. Rooms have amenities such as in-room coffeemakers, refrigerators, cable TV, safes, and fax machines. An evening tea with cookies and chocolates is complimentary, as are limousine service and shuttles to the National Institutes of Health research center. *7740 Wisconsin Ave., Bethesda, MD 20814, 301/656–2100 or 800/874–0050, 301/986–0375. 75 rooms, 1 suite. In-room data ports, in-room safes, exercise room, coin laundry, free parking. AE, D, DC, MC, V. Metro: Bethesda.*

1 c-3

HOLIDAY INN CHEVY CHASE

A short walk from the Friendship Heights Metro on the D.C. border, this comfortable hotel is in the heart of an upscale shopping district and contains the Avenue Deli and Julian's restaurant. The nearby Chevy Chase Pavilion and Mazza Gallerie malls have extensive family-dining options, and you'll find a wealth of gastronomic choices one Metro stop away in Bethesda, or a 10-minute drive down Wisconsin Avenue into Georgetown. Rooms have bright floral linens and mocha- or coral-color bathroom tile. A large outdoor swimming pool is set near the hotel's beautiful rose garden terrace, a popular spot for weddings. *5520 Wisconsin Ave., Chevy Chase, MD 20815, 301/656–1500, fax 301/656–5045. 206 rooms, 10 suites. Restaurant, bar, deli, room service, pool, exercise room, coin laundry, meeting rooms, free parking. AE, D, DC, MC, V. Metro: Friendship Heights.*

9 d-2

HOLIDAY INN GEORGETOWN

On the edge of Georgetown, this Holiday Inn is a short walk to dining, shopping, Dumbarton Oaks, the National Cathedral, and Georgetown University. The guest rooms have new furnishings and all the usual amenities, including hair dryers and irons and ironing boards. Because the building is uphill from Georgetown, many rooms have scenic views. There's complimentary coffee every morning in the lobby. *2101 Wisconsin Ave. NW, 20007, 202/338–4600 or 800/465–4329, fax 202/338–4458. 296 rooms. Restaurant, bar, no-smoking floors, room service, pool, exercise room, coin laundry, meeting room, parking (fee). AE, DC, MC, V. Metro: Foggy Bottom–GWU.*

10 b-3

HOLIDAY INN ON THE HILL

You can expect clean, comfortable, upgraded rooms in this hotel convenient to Union Station and the Capitol building. Hotel amenities include high-speed modem access, a newly expanded fitness room, and a Discovery Zone site for younger guests with supervised educational games, snacks, and contests. *415 New Jersey Ave. NW, Capitol Hill, 20001, 202/638–1616 or 800/638–1116, fax 202/638–0707. 342 rooms. Restaurant, bar, in-room data ports, room service, pool, sauna, exercise room, business services, meeting rooms, parking (fee). AE, D, DC, MC, V. Metro: Union Station.*

5 a-6

HOLIDAY INN ROSSLYN

Comfortable, budget-friendly, and conveniently located, this hotel is just two blocks from the Rosslyn Metro and a leisurely stroll across Key Bridge to Georgetown; the Newseum, Fort Myer, and Arlington National Cemetery are also very close. Its greatest asset may be the view of Washington's monuments from the panoramic windows of the Vantage Point restaurant. *1900 N. Fort Myer Dr., Arlington, VA 22209, 703/807–2000 or 800/368–3408, fax 703/522–8864. 306 rooms. Restaurant, café, in-room data ports, indoor pool, health club, coin laundry, laundry service, meeting rooms, free parking. AE, D, DC, MC, V. Metro: Rosslyn.*

8 g-4

HOLIDAY INN SELECT OLD TOWN

The distinctive mahogany-paneled lobby of this well-known chain hotel suggests a club room, and guest-room decor follows this motif with hunting-and-horse prints on the walls. Bathrooms have marble floors and tubs, and the phones have computer-modem capabilities. The hotel chain has decreed this member to be one of its 20 best worldwide, in large part because of the extraordinary service: the staff will bring exercise bicycles to rooms on request and provide touring bicycles for use in the area without charge. Guests in some rooms on the fifth and sixth floors can enjoy a picturesque roofscape of 18th- and 19th-century buildings and the river beyond—but only in the winter, after the trees have shed their leaves. *480 King St., Alexandria, VA 22314, 703/549–6080 or 800/368–5047, fax 703/684–6508. 227 rooms. Restaurant, lobby lounge, in-room data ports, indoor pool, barbershop, beauty salon, sauna, bicycles. AE, D, DC, MC, V. Metro: King St.*

5 g-3

HOTEL TABARD INN

Formed by the consolidation of three Victorian town houses, the Hotel Tabard Inn, which is named after the inn in Chaucer's *Canterbury Tales*, is one of the oldest continuously running lodgings in D.C. It's furnished throughout with well-worn Victorian and American Empire antiques. Although the wooden floorboards are creaky and the plumbing is old-fashioned, the hotel exudes a quaint charm. Room size and facilities vary considerably (one guest room alternates as a private dining room, and many share bathrooms), so prices differ widely. Passes are provided to the nearby YMCA, which has extensive fitness facilities. The contemporary restaurant is popular with locals. *1739 N St. NW, Downtown, 20036, 202/785–1277, fax 202/785–6173. 40 rooms, 25 with bath. Restaurant, bar, lobby lounge. AE, D, DC, MC, V. Metro: Dupont Circle.*

5 e-1

JURYS NORMANDY INN

A small, quaint European-style hotel on a quiet street in the embassy area of Connecticut Avenue, this hotel was formerly the Doyle Normandy. Rooms are neat, cozy, and attractively decorated; all have refrigerators and coffeemakers. Each Tuesday evening a wine-and-cheese reception is held for guests. You can select a book from the small library and read by the fireplace in the lobby while enjoying the complimentary coffee

and tea in the morning and afternoon. *2118 Wyoming Ave. NW, Adams-Morgan, 20008, 202/483–1350 or 800/424–3729, fax 202/387–8241. 75 rooms. In-room data ports, in-room safes, library, parking (fee). AE, D, MC, V. Metro: Dupont Circle.*

9 g-7

LATHAM HOTEL

"George's town," the Potomac River, and the C&O Canal are visible at treetop level from most of the rooms in this small, Federal-style hotel on the historic district's fashionable main drag. The Latham is a favorite of diplomats. The facilities are impeccable, the rooms beautifully decorated. The polished brass and glass lobby leads to Citronelle, one of Washington's best restaurants, and there's a branch of La Madeleine coffee shop on-site. *3000 M St. NW, Foggy Bottom, 20007, 202/726–5000 or 800/368–5922, fax 202/337–4250. 122 rooms, 21 suites. Restaurant, bar, coffee bar, room service, pool, parking (fee). AE, DC, MC, V. Metro: Foggy Bottom.*

5 e-4

ONE WASHINGTON CIRCLE HOTEL

The combination of elegant rooms and facilities and an upscale address makes this hotel a great bargain. Rooms resemble very well furnished apartments, with five different floor plans, all including separate bedrooms. Every room has a balcony, refrigerator, and at least a microwave; most have kitchenettes. The hotel is currently undergoing renovations and may have a name change in the near future. The American-style West End Café has live music Tuesday through Saturday nights and during the Sunday brunch buffet. *1 Washington Circle NW, 20037, 202/872–1680 or 800/424–9671, fax 202/223–3961. 151 suites. Restaurant, bar, kitchenettes (some), minibars, refrigerators, room service, pool, exercise room, piano, coin laundry, laundry service, meeting rooms, parking (fee). AE, D, DC, MC, V. Metro: Foggy Bottom.*

5 f-2

WASHINGTON COURTYARD BY MARRIOTT

Many guest rooms here offer excellent skyline views because of the hotel's elevation on upper Connecticut Avenue. In the compact but comfortable lobby, complimentary cookies and coffee await you each afternoon. *1900 Connecticut Ave. NW, Dupont Circle, 20009, 202/332–9300 or 800/842–4211, fax 202/328–7039. 147 rooms. Restaurant, bar, lobby lounge, in-room safes, pool, exercise room, baby-sitting, coin laundry, laundry service, meeting rooms, parking (fee). AE, D, DC, MC, V. Metro: Dupont Circle.*

5 *h-1*
WINDSOR INN

This small, older, three-story hotel in two buildings (neither with elevator) is just up New Hampshire Avenue from Dupont Circle. The lobby is art deco, and most guest rooms—either rectangular or L-shape—have marble-top furniture, floral bedspreads, and mauve-and-green color schemes. Most of the bathrooms have showers; a few have bathtubs. Afternoon sherry is served in the lobby. *1842 16th St. NW, Dupont Circle, 20009, 202/667–0300 or 800/423–9111, fax 202/667–4503. 46 rooms. Lobby lounge. AE, D, DC, MC, V. Metro: Dupont Circle.*

5 *e-1*
WINDSOR PARK HOTEL

The Windsor Park is a short walk from the National Zoo, Dupont Circle, and Adams-Morgan. Guest rooms have reproduction Victorian furniture. Street parking can be difficult, but a reasonably priced garage is two blocks away. *2116 Kalorama Rd. NW, Adams-Morgan, 20008, 202/483– 7700 or 800/247–3064, fax 202/332–4547. 38 rooms, 5 suites. Refrigerators. AE, DC, MC, V. Metro: Woodley Park–Zoo.*

BUDGET LODGINGS

3 *g-7*
ADAMS INN

Think cozy and rustic and you've captured the essence of this European-style bed-and-breakfast in the heart of the city. Spread throughout three residential buildings not far from Adams-Morgan, the zoo, and Dupont Circle, the rooms are small, but comfortable, and Victorian style. Many rooms share baths; those that do have a sink in the room. A shared kitchen and limited garage parking are available. *1744 Lanier Pl. NW, Woodley Park, 20009, 202/745–3600 or 800/578–6807, fax 202/319–7958. 27 rooms, 16 with bath. Breakfast room, parking. AE, DC, MC, V. Metro: Woodley Park–Zoo.*

1 *c-2*
AMERICAN INN OF BETHESDA

At the north end of downtown Bethesda, the American Inn has clean, well-furnished, bright, and budget-friendly rooms. Guests enjoy complimentary Continental breakfast and free e-mail. All rooms have data ports and telephones with voice mail. The hotel houses Guapo's restaurant, serving moderately priced Tex-Mex fare. Many other restaurants and nightclubs are within walking distance, and the Bethesda Metro is a 10-minute walk away. *8130 Wisconsin Ave., Bethesda, MD 20814, 301/656–9300 or 800/323–7081, fax 301/656–2907. 75 rooms, 1 suite. Restaurant, bar, breakfast room, refrigerators, pool, coin laundry, laundry service, business services, meeting rooms, free parking. AE, D, DC, MC, V. Metro: Bethesda.*

1 *d-6*
BEST WESTERN PENTAGON

Just 4 mi from the Smithsonian, this hotel has a free shuttle service to three nearby Metro stops and the attractions around them. Three two-story buildings have outside entrances and conventional motel rooms. The tower section has a new restaurant and meeting rooms on the ground floor, and brand-new furnishings in the guest rooms, many of which have nice views. *2480 S. Glebe Rd., Arlington, VA 22206, 703/979–4400 or 800/426–6886, fax 703/685–0051. 326 rooms. Restaurant, bar, in-room safes, refrigerators, room service, pool, exercise room, laundry service, airport shuttle, free parking. AE, D, DC, MC, V. Metro: Pentagon City, Crystal City, or Ronald Reagan National Airport.*

6 *a-3*
BRAXTON HOTEL

A favorite among the youthful and backpack sets, the Braxton Hotel is a good value and is just a 15-minute walk from the White House. Room sizes vary considerably, and some are quite small. All rooms have cable TV. *1449 Rhode Island Ave. NW, 20005, 202/232–7800 or 800/350–5759, fax 202/265–3725. 60 rooms. Parking (fee). AE, MC, V. Metro: Dupont Circle or McPherson Square.*

2 *c-5*
DAY'S INN ARLINGTON

Easy to find, on U.S. Route 50 across from Fort Myer, this Day's Inn isn't frilly, but is reasonable and accommodating. You could walk to a Metro station, but a shuttle is provided during the busiest daytime hours. *2201 Arlington Blvd. (Rte. 50), 22201, 703/525–0300, fax 703/525–5671. 128 rooms. Restaurant, bar, pool, no-smoking rooms, recreation room, meeting rooms. AE, D, DC, MC, V. Metro: Rosslyn.*

6 *b-4*

HOSTELLING INTERNATIONAL–WASHINGTON D.C.

This well-kept hostel, formerly the Washington International AYH-Hostel, has bunk beds, a kitchen, a small grocery and souvenir shop, and a living room. Rooms are generally dormitory style, without private bathrooms, but families are given their own room if the hostel is not full. Towels and linens are provided at no additional fee. The maximum stay is 14 days. College-age travelers predominate, and July through August is the busiest period. *1009 11th St. NW, Downtown, 20001, 202/737–2333, fax 202/737–1508. 250 beds. Coin laundry. MC, V. Metro: Metro Center.*

6 *b-6*

HOTEL HARRINGTON

Although only three blocks from the J. W. Marriott and Grand Hyatt, the Harrington is miles away in price. One of Washington's oldest continuously operating hotels, the Harrington doesn't offer many frills, but it does have low prices and a prime location—right in the center of everything. It's very popular with springtime high school bus tours and with families who like the two-bedroom, two- bathroom deluxe family rooms. *436 11th St. NW, Downtown, 20004, 202/628–8140 or 800/424–8532, fax 202/347–3924. 236 rooms, 24 family rooms. Restaurant, pub, room service, coin laundry, meeting rooms, parking (fee). AE, D, DC, MC, V. Metro: Metro Center.*

1 *c-5*

QUALITY INN IWO JIMA

Within walking distance of the Marine Corps War Memorial and the Rosslyn Metro, the Quality Inn Iwo Jima is a consistently well-regarded budget hotel with easy access to Georgetown, the Pentagon, and Ronald Reagan National Airport. There are two sections; the older original section has outside entrances and larger rooms with double-sink bathrooms. The high-rise rooms

are business-class with work tables and data ports. *1501 Arlington Blvd. (Rte. 50), Arlington, VA 22209, 703/524–5000 or 800/221–2222, fax 703/522–5484. 141 rooms. Restaurant, bar, room service, indoor pool, laundry service, free parking. AE, D, DC, MC, V. Metro: Rosslyn.*

2 *b-7*

TRAVELODGE CHERRY BLOSSOM

A modestly priced, three-story lodging less than 2 mi from the Pentagon, Pentagon City Fashion Centre mall, and two Metro stations, the Cherry Blossom can even be reached by a city bus that stops out front. Wallpapered rooms are decorated in navy and wine-colored fabrics and have standard motel furniture. Local calls, HBO, a microwave oven on request, and Continental breakfast are included, and rooms with kitchenettes are available. The Rincome, a Thai restaurant, is on the premises, and more than 50 other restaurants are within walking distance. *3030 Columbia Pike, Arlington, VA 22204, 703/521–5570, fax 703/271–0081. 76 rooms. Restaurant, bar, kitchenettes (some), refrigerators, exercise room, free parking. AE, D, DC, MC, V. Metro: Pentagon.*

B&B RESERVATION SERVICES

Bed 'n' Breakfast Accommodations Ltd. of Washington, D.C. Staffed 10 to 5, this company handles about 85 different properties in the area. *Box 12011, 20005, 202/328–3510.*

Bed and Breakfast League, Ltd. Write for a list of member properties with accommodations priced to please. *Box 9490, 20016.*

chapter 7

CITY SOURCES

getting a handle on the city

basics of city life

other locations and hours, call 703/838–3000.

BANKS

The following banks have two or more branches in D.C.; we list only those with the longest hours. For ATMs that accept Cirrus cards, call 800/424–7787; for those that accept Plus, call 800/843–7587. Banks sometimes change names, so you might want to call ahead.

Adams National Bank (1627 K St. NW, 202/466–4090): Mon.–Thurs. 9–3, Fri. 9–5.

Allfirst (5630 Connecticut Ave. NW, 202/537–8280): Mon.–Thurs. 9–4, Fri. 9–5, Sat. 9–1.

Bank of America (3 Dupont Circle NW, 202/624–4370): Mon.–Thurs. 9–3, Fri. 9–5, Sat. 9–noon.

Chevy Chase Bank (1545 Wisconsin Ave. NW, 202/337–4540): Mon.–Wed. 9–3:30, Thurs.–Fri. 9–6, Sat. 9:30–3. For other locations and hours, call 301/598–7100.

First Union (5701 Connecticut Ave. NW, 800/275–3862): Mon.–Thurs. 9–3, Fri. 9–5, Sat. 9–noon.

Riggs (800 17th St. NW, 202/835–6767): weekdays 9–5. For other locations and hours, call 301/887–6000.

SunTrust (formerly Crestar; 1445 New York Ave. NW, 202/879–6308): Mon.–Thurs. 9–3, Fri. 9–5, Sat. 9–noon. For

---

ESSENTIAL NUMBERS

Dial-A-Park (202/619–7275): up-to-date information on monuments, parks, and special events.
ENCORE (301/718–2525): tickets for concerts, theater, and sporting events.
Metro Information (202/637–7000).
Metro Special Events Hotline (202/783–1070): weekly information on local events and how to reach them by Metro.
MovieFone (202/333–FILM): movie show times and information.
TicketMaster (800/551–SEAT): tickets for concerts, theater, and sporting events.
Time (202/844–2525).
Weather (202/936–1212).

DRIVING

Public transportation in D.C. is easily accessible and reaches most destinations, but many people still drive, especially in the suburbs. Washington does not have any unusual driving rules; the speed limit on most city streets is 25 mph, and you may turn right on red unless a sign indicates otherwise. The biggest hurdles to owning a car are the bureaucratic registration process, the parking game, confusing street layouts, and escalating gasoline prices. Streets are logically named: east-to-west downtown streets are lettered alphabetically, and north-to-south streets are numbered. Diagonal avenues are named for states. However, numerous traffic circles and rotaries bisect the otherwise straight streets, and the state-named streets radiate from these circles. Rock Creek Park, bridges, the Potomac and Anacostia rivers, and other natural features further disrupt the logical flow. And alas, inept signage adds to the confusion.

licenses

Proof of residence in the District of Columbia is required for all motor vehicle transactions; this can take the form of a lease, homeowners' deed, utility bill, payroll stub, tax return, or voter-registration card. You can convert an out-of-state license for $20 at the Bureau of Motor Vehicle Services, 301 C Street NW, Room 1157, Window 7. Bring your current license and social-security card, and be prepared to take a written test of driving rules (study guide available) and an eye test. For more information, call 202/727–5000.

REGISTRATION

Vehicles must be titled and registered within 30 days of moving into D.C. Bring the out-of-state title and lien contract, if financed. Provide your insurance company's name and policy or binder number, your car's odometer reading, and your photo ID. You must have your car inspected (see below) prior to registration; a five-day temporary registration is available. Fees: $20 for title, $15 for lien, and $10 for inspection. The type and weight of your vehicle determine the license-plate tax; you'll also be charged an excise tax of 6% or 7% based on weight and value. For more information, call the Department of Motor Vehicle Services at 202/727–5000.

VEHICLE INSPECTION

Before your car can be registered, it must be inspected at 1101 Half Street SW, and reinspected annually thereafter. Extended inspection hours are weekdays 6 AM–10 PM and Saturday 7–3 (no appointment necessary). If your car fails inspection, you must take it to a designated station for repair and reinspection.

traffic

The morning rush hour for traffic entering downtown D.C. begins as early as 7 and peaks around 8:30; the heaviest afternoon traffic leaving the city runs from approximately 4:15 to 6:30. The increase in traffic affects inbound bridges in particular, causing backups on the approaching highways. Because Washington has only a few bridges, it's hard to avoid these delays. Adding to the congestion are numerous potholes and street closures due to seemingly endless repair work. A few years ago, the stretch of Pennsylvania Avenue in front of the White House was closed indefinitely as an antiterrorist measure. Public transportation during these hours is also crowded, and fares are higher.

GAS STATIONS

Brookland Citgo (2800 12th St. NE, 202/269–1558).

Brown and Vaz's Exxon (5501 South Dakota Ave. NE, 202/832–6220).

Capitol Hill Citgo (2300 Pennsylvania Ave. SE, 202/581–7080).

Capitol Hill Exxon (339 Pennsylvania Ave. SE, 202/547–4054).

Columbia Heights Exxon (3540 14th St. NW, 202/234–0026).

Compass Shell (4321 Nannie Helen Burroughs Ave. NE, 202/398–7750).

Connecticut Avenue Amoco (5001 Connecticut Ave. NW, 202/244–6975).

Distad's Amoco (823 Pennsylvania Ave. SE, 202/543–0200).

East Capitol Exxon (4501 Benning Rd. NE, 202/397–5340).

Eastover Exxon (4650 S. Capitol St. SE, 202/562–0493).

Embassy Mobil Service Center (22nd and P Sts. NW, 202/659–8560).

Georgetown Amoco (2715 Pennsylvania Ave. NW, 202/338–0400).

Georgetown Exxon (1601 Wisconsin Ave. NW, 202/333–0538).

Georgia Ave Shell Service Center (4140 Georgia Ave. NW, 202/829–2557).

Navy Yard Exxon (1022 M St. SE, 202/543–4211).

P&A Exxon Service (1201 Pennsylvania Ave. SE, 202/546–6146).

South Capitol Exxon (3900 Martin Luther King Jr. Ave. SW, 202/574–9413).

Stadium Exxon (2651 Benning Rd. NE, 202/396–6125).

Texaco (1022 Pennsylvania Ave. SE, 202/543–6725).

White House Mobil Gas Station (1442 U St. NW, 202/265–2444).

GEOGRAPHY

The interstate highway circling Washington and its closer suburbs is called the Capital Beltway. It used to be I–495, but to make the eastern (Maryland) portion into a stretch of I–95 for north–south travelers, that portion is labeled I–95. It crosses the Potomac River on the south via the Wilson Bridge and on the north via the American Legion Bridge (formerly the Cabin John Bridge).

Washington's layout recalls the radiating boulevards of Paris—perhaps because it was designed by the French-born Pierre L'Enfant. The city is divided into compass quarters with the U.S. Capitol at the center. From there all streets and districts derive their orientation (e.g., Southeast, Northwest). The segments are very uneven, with the southern two taking up only a fraction of the area of the northern ones. (The southern quarters lost all of the land ceded to the District from Virginia in the 1847 retrocession.)

The National Mall, with the Capitol at one end and the Lincoln Memorial and Reflecting Pool at the other, forms an "off-center" center of the city. Most of the area south of the Mall consists of government-owned or -leased offices, with a large residential neighborhood in the Southeast. Since the retrocession to Virginia, the Potomac River forms D.C.'s southwest border with Virginia (the water belongs to the District). Breaking up the southeastern quarter of the city is the Anacostia River, which flows into the Potomac southwest of the Capitol. A considerable part of the Northwest is devoted to the sprawling Rock Creek Park and the National Zoo. Rock Creek itself flows from Maryland into the Potomac next to the Watergate complex.

Washington has a sort of north–south/east–west street setup with a sometimes radial system of diagonal streets named for states overlaying (or interfering, if you prefer, which you may after negotiating a circle or square during rush hour). The Mall runs east–west as do the lettered streets; numbered streets run north–south. North of W Street the names are organized alphabetically beginning with two-syllable names followed by three-syllable names. Navigation can be a challenge, but you'll know you've earned a drink if you've made it back home after battling District traffic.

neighborhoods

There are several distinct and interesting neighborhoods within the District, and, of course, many indistinct ones. Although it houses the House and Senate offices, Capitol Hill is mainly a residential neighborhood with many down-home watering holes and upscale restaurants. Union Station, with its boutiques, restaurants, and movie theaters, is north of the Capitol on Massachusetts Avenue NE. Across from the station is the National Postal Museum, with some fascinating permanent and temporary exhibits. Chinatown, around 7th and H streets NW, is known for its restaurants, Asian markets, and Chinese churches and societies; it now packs the MCI Center as well. The Southwest waterfront has a bustling fish market, some ho-hum seafood restaurants, and a yacht harbor. Anacostia, separated by the Anacostia River from downtown, is mainly residential. Foggy Bottom/West End, the area between downtown and Georgetown, is partly residential. It houses George Washington University, the State Department, the Kennedy Center, the Watergate complex, and a number of restaurants.

Dupont Circle is Washington's most artistic area, with clusters of shops, art galleries, museums, and restaurants. Parking here is almost impossible. The circle itself—with a lovely fountain in the center—is a popular park where residents and office workers eat lunch, soak up the sun, and watch the world go by. Dupont Circle has also been the site of some serious chess matches. North of Dupont Circle is Adams-Morgan, a diverse, vibrant neighborhood with a concentration of Caribbean and Latin American immigrants. Centered along Columbia Road and 18th Street NW, Adams-Morgan has restaurants serving Ethiopian, Italian, Spanish, Brazilian, Mexican, Indian, and more. The nearby U Street corridor is being revitalized, although progress seems stalled at the moment. The neighborhood, with some of the hippest bars in the District, quirky vintage stores, small but lively nightclubs, and numerous cafés, draws a young crowd day and night.

Georgetown, a major Maryland shipping port in Colonial times, predates Washington as a city. Its boundaries are blurred, but most agree the region is roughly bounded by S Street and Reservoir Road to the north, the Potomac River to the south, Rock Creek to the east, and Georgetown University's sprawling campus to the west. Now a fashionable (and expensive) neighborhood, Georgetown is jam-packed with swank shops and trendy restaurants and bars. Sprawled along the Georgetown waterfront is the multiuse Washington Harbour complex, which affords a spectacular view of the Potomac. Upper Northwest is mainly residential, with embassies lined up along stately Massachusetts Avenue NW. It also has Washington National Cathedral and parts of Rock Creek Park. Woodley Park is full of wonderful old apartment buildings and a few restaurants near the National Zoo. Just north of the zoo is Cleveland Park, a mainly residential neighborhood with grand old apartment buildings and restaurants along Connecticut Avenue. Tenleytown, an older area consisting of mostly single-family dwellings, sits west of the intersection of Wisconsin and Nebraska avenues.

HOLIDAYS

Because Washington is a federal city, it observes only federal holidays.

New Year's Day (January 1).

Martin Luther King Day (3rd Monday in January).

Presidents' Day (3rd Monday in February).

Memorial Day (last Monday in May).

Independence Day (July 4).

Labor Day (1st Monday in September).

Columbus Day (2nd Monday in October).

Veterans' Day (November 11).

Thanksgiving (4th Thursday in November).

Christmas (December 25).

LIQUOR LAWS

Alcoholic beverages may be served from 8 AM to 2 AM Monday through Thursday, 8 AM to 2:30 AM Friday and Saturday, and 10 AM to 2 AM Sunday. Liquor stores are closed on Sunday, but wine and beer can be sold in markets every day. In Virginia, many supermarkets and drugstores carry beer and wine.

The minimum drinking age is 21. Proof of age is an official identification issued by a government agency (local, state, federal, or foreign) containing at least your name, date of birth, signature, and photograph.

For more information, contact the D.C. Alcohol Beverage Control Board at 202/442–4445.

NO SMOKING

In D.C. it is illegal to smoke in an elevator (except in a single-family dwelling); in a retail store (except a tobacco shop or a store selling smoking equipment); in a government assembly or hearing room; in an educational facility; while transporting passengers in a government vehicle, or in a for-hire vehicle unless all passengers consent; in a health-care facility; and in a designated no-smoking area of a restaurant or bar.

PARKING

Parking in D.C. is often a challenge, but it can also be a game. It is sometimes impossible to find street parking in the city center without driving in circles, watching for someone to leave a legal space. Here's a trick: if you see a spot, have your passenger jump out of the car and hold the slot while you turn around and park there.

However you manage to secure a legal space, do not stay longer than the nearest sign allows, usually two hours. Parking enforcers have been known to hide in bushes waiting for meters to expire.

rules and enforcement

Weekend and evening parking in D.C. has been largely free ever since the city decided more than 10 years ago that it needed to attract more shoppers and diners from the suburbs. There are still pockets in the city where you must always pay, such as the Convention Center, but away from the city center there are many areas where parking is always free—when you can find a spot. Spaces on the Mall are always free, but do pay attention to the signs telling you when and for how long (usually three hours) you can park. Avoid the spots reserved for taxis, police cars, and people with disabilities. Mall spaces are hardest to find on weekends, when suburbanites descend on the Smithsonian.

Read all street signs carefully. If you don't follow the signs, you risk having your car towed and impounded. Cars have been known to sustain damage while in the care of the D.C. Police and their storage lots. Pay particular attention in the afternoon: every weekday afternoon, a battalion of tow trucks deploys just before 4 to remove cars parked on streets where rush-hour parking is prohibited. If your car is towed, you must contact the Bureau of Traffic Adjudication at 202/727–5000 to pay the towing and storage fees, plus any outstanding tickets. Cars that are towed on weekends cannot be retrieved until Monday.

If your vehicle is ticketed, read the back of the ticket for details on paying the fine. You can contest a parking ticket by mail—within 15 days—by writing to the District of Columbia Government, Department of Public Works, Bureau of Adjudication, Box 2014, Washington, D.C. 20013. For more information, call 202/727–5000. If you think you were wrongly ticketed for an offense other than parking, you can request a hearing

215

with an adjudicator, either in person or in writing. You might need to wait several weeks for a hearing, but it's worth the effort if there's a lot of money involved and you can wait for it.

If your car is booted—that is, immobilized by a tire lock—do not attempt to move it while the boot is in place. Read the warning notice, and call 202/727–5000 to proceed. You must pay all outstanding fines, plus a boot fee, before your car will be released. Good luck.

Abandoned Vehicles (202/535–5800).

Adjudication (202/727–5000).

Booted Vehicles (202/727–5000).

Handicapped Parking Permits (202/727–5525).

Parking Tickets (202/727–5000).

Residential Parking Permits (202/724–4952).

Towed/Impounded Vehicles (202/727–5000).

parking lots

Parking is available at many suburban Metrorail stations. You'll pay a fee during the week (bring quarters), but it's free on weekends and holidays. The following lots are private:

Central Parking Systems (Union Station, 30 Massachusetts Ave. NE, 202/898–1221; 1130 20th St. NW, 202/496–4200).

City Park (2341 Champlain St. NW, 202/986–4973).

Colonial Parking Inc. (Office: 1050 Thomas Jefferson St. NW, Ste. 100; call 202/295–8100 for locations throughout the city.)

Doggett Parking Co. (719 10th St. NW, 202/638–2770).

Georgetown Parking Inc. (518 H St. NW, 202/682–2107).

InterParking, Inc. (1828 L St. NW, 202/466–4300).

Maiden Lane Parking Co. (400 14th St. SW, 202/554–2879).

Monument Parking Co. (1828 L St. NW, 202/833–9357).

Potomac Parking Alliance (700 13th St. NW, 202/393–3012).

Quik Park Inc. (1331 Pennsylvania Ave. NW, 202/393–3650; 2033 K St. NW, 202/775–1980; 1001 G St. NW, 202/393–3650).

PERSONAL SECURITY

Take the same safety precautions in D.C. as you would in any other major city. Most areas are safe during the day, and those around federal buildings, major hotels, theaters, and restaurants are usually safe day and night. Avoid places frequented by streetwalkers and drug dealers, or by anyone else hanging around with no apparent business. You'll know you're in such an area if cars pass slowly and people on the sidewalks take an interest in the occupants. Travel with others at night, especially if you're visiting a specific neighborhood for the first time.

PUBLIC TRANSPORTATION

If you don't have a car, it's still fairly easy to get around the city. The Metro (subway) is cool and clean and has an amusingly Space Age feel to it when the floor lights blink to signal incoming trains. Those areas lacking Metro stations, such as Georgetown and Adams-Morgan, are served by bus. On weekdays there is also extensive, cheap commuter-rail service to Union Station from Virginia, West Virginia, and Maryland. Discount passes offer frequent bus, subway, and commuter-rail users unlimited travel within a specified period, usually two weeks. For general information on the bus and rail systems, including fares, passes, and schedules, call the Washington Metropolitan Area Transit Authority at 202/637–7000.

The Washington taxi system confuses even the hardiest natives, so trust your luck when you hail a cab, and hope that you're charged a fair fare for the number of zones you cross.

bus

If the subway won't take you where you need to go, the bus probably will (it just might take longer). Note that you'll need either exact change or a Metro Flash Pass (see By Subway, below) to ride the bus, as drivers do not make change. The base fare for most Metrobus trips is $1.10, but surcharges and state and zone crossing fees can increase your fare. If you're transferring from Metrorail to Metrobus in D.C. or Virginia, get a 25¢ transfer from the machine at the station where you enter the system, and give it to the driver when you board the bus. Senior citizens and persons with disabilities who show their Metro ID (or Medicare) cards to the driver pay a flat fare of only 50¢, plus any applicable surcharges. A bus-to-bus transfer, valid for one use, is free. Be sure to request a transfer ticket when you first board the bus; hand it to the operator of the second bus. You must pay for transfers after the first one. The transfer charge does not apply to senior citizens and persons with disabilities with official Metro ID or Medicare cards, nor does it apply to D.C. students who pay their fares with school tokens or tickets (in the summer).

subway

The ride on the escalator taking you down to the Metro's subterranean stations may seem endless, but what awaits is one of the cleanest subway systems in the world—and most of the cars are carpeted! As you glide up and down those escalators, though, remember to stand on the right and walk on the left or risk public ire from your harried fellow riders. Flashing lights along the edge of the platform indicate the approach of a train. Be sure to check the destination (displayed on the side of the car) before boarding. Do NOT attempt to board after the chimes have sounded; another train will probably be along shortly. Eating or drinking on the Metro is strictly prohibited and is punishable by a fine; this law is often enforced. There's good news for night owls: as part of a year-long test run, Metro hours were extended in June 2000 until around 2 AM (times vary slightly from station to station) on Friday and Saturday nights. If the extension of hours is successful, trains will continue to run until 2 AM after June 2001; otherwise, the Metro will shut down at 1 AM.

To use the Metro, purchase your Farecard from a machine out front. Then, at the turnstile, swipe your Farecard once on the way in and again on the way out. The card will pop up from a slot as you pass through the turnstile. The time of day and the distance you've traveled determine your fare. Peak fares are in effect weekdays 5:30–9:30 AM and 3–7

PM; off-peak fares are charged at all other times, including holidays. Fares are posted in all Metrobuses and at all Metro station kiosks. Up to two children 5 years or younger ride free when accompanied by a paying adult.

Each passenger must have a magnetically encoded Farecard or pass to ride. You may purchase Farecards at any Metro station for as little as $1.10 or for as much as $45. You receive a 10% discount if you purchase a Farecard worth $20 or more. You can also pay a flat fee for a Flash Pass, which will then allow you unlimited access to the Metro or Metrobus for a set amount of time. You must use the same Farecard to enter and exit the system. If your card doesn't have enough value for the trip, insert it into an Add Fare machine, located just before the exit gate, and insert money as needed. If you're buying your card or adding fare from a machine, keep in mind that although you can insert both bills and coins, the machines give change in coins only, and the most change they'll return is $5. Be careful with your Farecard; it has a magnetic strip that may interfere with strips on ATM cards and credit card, so keep the cards separated in your pocket or wallet.

Qualified senior citizens (65 years or older) and people with disabilities can use specially encoded $3 or $10 Farecards and pay half the peak fare, not to exceed $1.60, regardless of the time of day. You must show your Metro ID card to buy the $3 and $10 Farecards, and must also have it with you when using the system. The special Farecards are available at all Metro sales offices and other retail locations; they are not sold at Metro stations. To get a Metro ID, a person with disabilities must go to 600 5th Street NW. However, if you have a Medicare card, you don't need anything else: you can obtain a free Metro Senior Citizen ID card without having to wait— just bring proof of age, such as your birth certificate, driver's license, or passport, to any Metro sales office or any branch of the public library.

Students under age 19 who live in the city and attend District public, private, or parochial schools may purchase school bus tokens or tickets. Tokens (during the school year) and tickets (during the summer) enable students to ride one way on the WMATA bus and subway systems. With proper identifica-

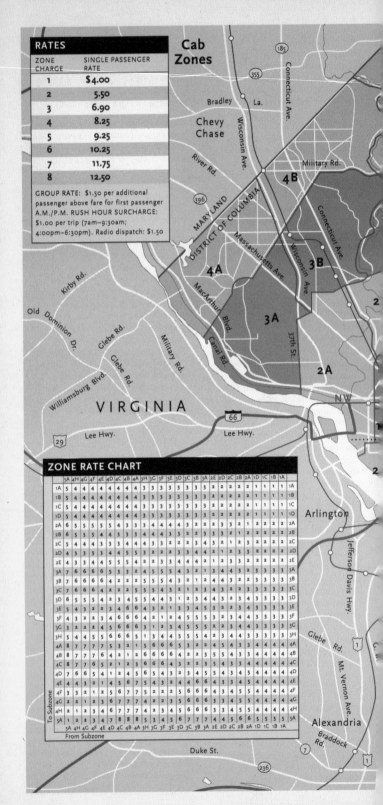

RATES

ZONE CHARGE	SINGLE PASSENGER RATE
1	$4.00
2	5.50
3	6.90
4	8.25
5	9.25
6	10.25
7	11.75
8	12.50

GROUP RATE: $1.50 per additional passenger above fare for first passenger A.M./P.M. RUSH HOUR SURCHARGE: $1.00 per trip (7am–9:30am; 4:00pm–6:30pm). Radio dispatch: $1.50

Cab Zones

ZONE RATE CHART

tion and $5.50, students can buy 10 bus tokens or tickets (in the summer) or one Farecard (valid for 10 rides).

taxi

Hailing a taxi on the streets of Washington is not usually a problem in well-traveled areas. What happens once you enter the cab is a different story, as the city's cabs are governed by a byzantine system of zones, surcharges, and rules. Trying to figure these out can be difficult; almost every year there is a clamor for the government to abandon the zone system and adopt meters. There are eight taxi zones in D.C. The base fare for one zone is $4, with a $1.50 charge for additional passengers and a $1 surcharge during the 7–9:30 AM and 4–6:30 PM rush hours. The maximum fare between any two points in the city is $12.50. Drivers are required to display the zone map and a license (with photo) in a prominent place. Phoning for a cab adds $1.50 to the fare. The helpful D.C. Taxicab Commission can be reached at 202/645-6006. If you need to phone a cab, they'll direct you to the source nearest you. Two companies worth trying are Yellow Cab (202/544–1212), in the District, and Red Top (202/328–3333), for transportation to National and Dulles airports. Beware of rip-off cabbies lurking at area airports; always agree on a fare in advance.

commuter rail

There are many options for traveling in and out of D.C. from Maryland, Virginia, and beyond.

Amtrak (800/872–7245): Amtrak operates from Union Station, serving destinations near and far.

DASH (Alexandria) (703/370–3274): the Alexandria Transit Company's DASH system provides safe and reliable bus service within the City of Alexandria. It connects with Metrobus, Metrorail, Virginia Railway Express, and the Fairfax Connector, serving all Metrorail stations within the City of Alexandria and the Pentagon Metrorail during rush hour.

Fairfax Connector (703/339–7200): the Fairfax Connector covers Fairfax County, with about 25 routes. The system accepts Metrobus Flash Passes, tokens, and commuter tickets.

MARC (Maryland Rail Commuter System) (800/325–7245): Maryland's commuter rail operates weekdays and connects with many Metro stations. Weekly and monthly passes are available.

Montgomery County Transit System (301/217–2184).

VRE (Virginia Railway Express) (703/684–0400 or 800/743– 3873): the VRE/WMATA Transit Link Card offers unlimited travel on VRE and Metrorail; call 703/413–4287 for information.

PUBLICATIONS

the georgetowner

The oldest tabloid paper in Washington, this twice-monthly publication focuses on Georgetown, but also touches on other neighborhoods with coverage of social events, restaurants, shopping, community concerns, and politics.

journal newspapers

Six daily local newspapers circulate in the suburban counties of Virginia and Maryland surrounding the District: the *Alexandria Journal, Arlington Journal, Fairfax Journal, Montgomery Journal, Prince George's Journal,* and *Prince William Journal.*

legal times

This weekly publication serves Washington's enormous number of lawyers, covering business, politics, and other developments of particular interest to the legal profession.

national geographic magazine

Most of the nation's major magazines are published in New York, but this yellow-bordered classic is published here in Washington by the National Geographic Society, and has the fourth-highest circulation of any magazine in the United States.

national journal

The focus of this national weekly is government, federal policy, and politics.

roll call

A Hill fixture since 1955, *Roll Call* is avidly read by members of Congress, staffers, some residents, and obsessed Congress-watchers. In addition to hard legislative news, this biweekly covers social events, real estate, restaurants, and even gossip.

senior beacon of greater washington

This monthly newspaper for residents over age 50 covers news, health, entertainment, and lifestyle topics.

smithsonian magazine

A glossy, well-written monthly serves as a guide to the myriad activities of the Smithsonian and provides fascinating feature articles on related subjects.

washington afro-american

The area's largest publication serving the African-American community, this weekly covers national and international news as well as sports and entertainment.

washington blade

Serving the gay and lesbian community, this lively weekly covers local and national news, political developments, health, and entertainment.

washington city paper

With extensive and reliable nightlife listings and long feature articles, this weekly tabloid speaks to the young on urban topics.

washington hispanic

This Spanish-language weekly addresses the metropolitan area's burgeoning Hispanic population, covering local, national, and international news as well as sports and entertainment.

washington informer

This weekly newspaper serves the area's African-American community. In addition to local, national, and international news, the paper's coverage includes entertainment, sports, and feature articles.

washington jewish week

Distributed throughout the metropolitan area, this newspaper contains local, national, and international news of particular interest to the Jewish community. It also includes entertainment and feature articles.

washington post

The metropolitan area's major daily provides national, international, and local coverage of major and not-so-major events. The Style section keeps readers up-to-date with the arts and entertainment world; the Weekend (Friday) section and Sunday magazine are loaded with restaurant and entertainment tips.

washington times

The Washington Times is the city's second major daily and is by far the more conservative of the two. It is beautifully designed and has strong sports and metro coverage.

washingtonian

This stylish monthly concentrates on area celebrities, shopping, restaurants, travel, and feature articles.

RADIO STATIONS

fm

88.1 WMUC Progressive

88.5 WAMU American University (talk/music)

89.3 WPFW Pacifica (public)

90.1 WCSP C-SPAN

90.9 WETA NPR/classical/talk

91.9 WGTS Christian music

92.7 WMJS Easy listening

93.9 WKYS Urban hits

94.3 WUPP Country

94.7 WARW Classic rock

95.5 WPGC Urban hits

96.3 WHUR Urban adult

97.1 WASH Soft rock

98.7 WMZQ Country

99.1 WHFS Alternative

99.5 WGAY Easy listening

99.9 **WFRE** Country

100.3 **WBIG** Oldies

101.1 **WWDC** Rock

102.3 **WMMJ** Urban adult

103.5 **WGMS** Classical

103.9 **WWVZ** Top 40

104.1 **WWZZ** Top 40

105.1 **WAVA** Christian talk

105.9 **WJZQ** Smooth jazz

106.7 **WJFK** Talk sports

107.3 **WRQX** Adult contemporary

107.7 **WTOP** News

am

570 **WWRC** Business

630 **WMAL** News/talk

730 **WBZS** Business

780 **WABS** Contemporary Christian

820 **WQSI** Country

900 **WILC** Contemporary Spanish-language

930 **WFMD** News/talk

950 **WCTN** Christian

980 **WTEM** Sports

1030 **WWGB** Gospel

1050 **WKDL** Latin/Caribbean music

1120 **WUST** Ethnic

1150 **WMET** Business

1220 **WFAX** Christian

1260 **WWDC** Nostalgia/standards

1310 **WDCT** Korean

1340 **WYCB** Gospel

1390 **WZHF** Success/lifestyles talk

1450 **WOL** Talk

1460 **WKDV** Latin/Caribbean music

1490 **WPWC** Country & Western

1500 **WTOP** News

1540 **WACA** Spanish-language music/news

1560 **WKIK** Classic rock

1580 **WPGC** Gospel

1600 **WINX** Top 40

RECYCLING

Recycling bins are large and burgundy, and recyclable items are picked up on the same designated days as regular trash. Recyclables include corrugated cardboard (flattened and tied in a bundle); newspapers (including inserts), office paper, and magazines (each tied in a separate bundle); plastic and glass bottles with tops removed; and metal cans.

For general information on recycling, trash collection, and illegal dumping, call 202/727–1000.

TAX & TIP

sales tax and beyond

Taxes are an unpleasant fact of life, and Washington area residents pay their share. Rates vary according to region (D.C., Maryland, and Virginia) and are subject to change.

Sales tax on nonfood items is 5.75% in the District and 5% in Maryland. Virginia tax on grocery items is 4%; the tax on nonfood items is 4.5%.

Restaurant–carry-out taxes are 10% in the District and 5% in Maryland. Expect to pay anywhere from 2% to 9% in Virginia, depending on jurisdiction and whether it's carryout or a full-service restaurant.

Hotel tax is 14.5% in the District. Rates vary in the suburbs; Montgomery County room tax is 12% and northern Virginia room tax is 6.5%.

tipping

In restaurants good service should be rewarded with 15% of the tab; excellent service with 20%. In District restaurants, double the tax to figure out a decent tip. Skycaps and doormen are usually tipped about $2. Taxi and tour-bus drivers should be tipped around 15%.

TELEVISION STATIONS

network

Channel 4 WRC (NBC)

Channel 5 WTTG (Fox)

Channel 7 WJLA (ABC)

Channel 9 WUSA (CBS)

Channel 22 WMPT (PBS: Maryland Public Broadcasting from Annapolis)

Channel 26 WETA (PBS: Public Broadcasting from Arlington)

cable

Channel 8 All News

Channel 10 Disney

Channel 15 Discovery

Channel 20 Univision (Spanish)

Channel 21 Encore

Channel 36 HTS (Sports)

Channel 38 C-SPAN

Channel 40 BET

Channel 42 CNN

Channel 47 FOX (Family)

Channel 48 Nickelodeon

Channel 49 TNT

Channel 54 Bravo

Channel 57 Home Shopping Network

Channel 62 The Weather Channel

Channel 65 History

VOTER REGISTRATION

Call 202/727–2525 for information 24 hours.

WEATHER

Washington summers can be hot, steamy, and unrelenting. Spring and autumn are generally the loveliest times to enjoy the city; spring brings the famous cherry blossoms (and occasionally rain), and autumn is peaceful because most of the tourists have left and the heat has lifted. Winters are usually relatively mild, but unexpected snowstorms can bring this not-quite-northern, not-quite-southern city to a standstill.

Air-quality report (202/645–0417).

Current temperature and forecast (202/936–1212).

resources for challenges & crises

BABY-SITTING SERVICES

Capital Kids, Inc. (1250 24th St. NW, 202/293–1460): child care for infants to 5-year-olds in state-of-the-art, secure surroundings.

Capitol Hill Child Development Center (525 A St. NE, 202/543–9189): provides care for children aged 2 to 12 years.

Washington Child Development Council (202/387–0002): helps District residents locate licensed child-care providers.

CATERING

grown-up parties

B&B (202/829–8640): customized menus are available for a wide variety of cuisines for parties from 10 to 15,000, usually in homes, government buildings, or outdoor venues.

Becky Hamill Catering (202/965–1817): creative menus are available for groups ranging from 10 to 1,000; events can be corporate, political, or private gatherings.

Catering Company of Washington (202/364–8883): the American chef custom-designs a menu for each client; parties can range from 12 to 800 guests, usually in homes, historic buildings, museums, or outdoor venues.

La Bernoise Catering (202/333–2433): this Upper Northwest company applies the artistry of a Swiss chef to parties of 2 to 2,000 guests, usually in homes, public buildings, or corporate venues. Menus are custom-designed for each client's needs.

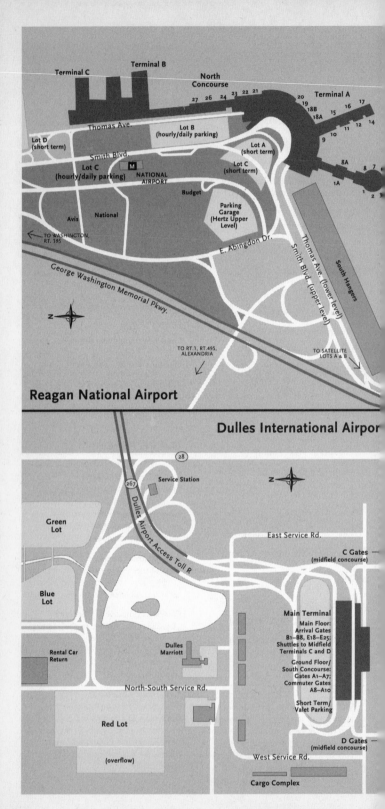

Reagan National Airport

Terminal C

Terminal B

North Concourse

Terminal A

27 26 24 23 22 21 20 19 18B 18A 15 16 17 14 12 13 11 10 9 8A 8 7 1A 1 2 3

Thomas Ave.

Lot B (hourly/daily parking)

Lot D (short term)

Smith Blvd.

Lot C (hourly/daily parking)

M NATIONAL AIRPORT

Lot A (short term)

Lot C (short term)

Budget

Parking Garage (Hertz Upper Level)

Avis

National

← TO WASHINGTON, RT. 395

E. Abingdon Dr.

George Washington Memorial Pkwy.

Thomas Ave. (lower level)

Smith Blvd. (upper level)

South Hangers

N

TO RT.1, RT.495, ALEXANDRIA

TO SATELLITE LOTS A & B

Dulles International Airport

28

267

Service Station

N

Dulles Airport Access Toll R

Green Lot

East Service Rd.

C Gates — (midfield concourse)

Blue Lot

Rental Car Return

Dulles Marriott

Main Terminal

Main Floor: Arrival Gates B1–B8, E18–E25; Shuttles to Midfield Terminals C and D

Ground Floor/ South Concourse: Gates A1–A7; Commuter Gates A8–A10

Short Term/ Valet Parking

North-South Service Rd.

Red Lot

(overflow)

West Service Rd.

D Gates — (midfield concourse)

Cargo Complex

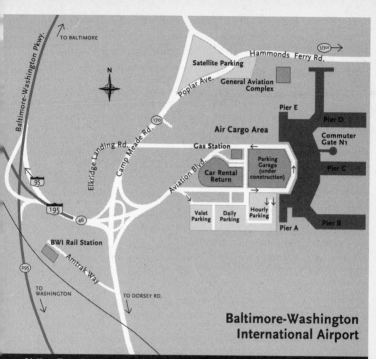

**Baltimore-Washington
International Airport**

Airline Terminals

AIRLINES	REAGAN/NAT'L	DULLES	BWI
Aeroflot ☎ 800/955-5555		B	
Air Canada ☎ 800/776-3000	B	C	
Air France ☎ 800/321-4538		B	
Air Jamaica ☎ 800/523-5585			E
Air Tran ☎ 800/247-8726		D	
All Nippon (ANA) ☎ 800/235-9262		B	
America West ☎ 800/235-9292	B	B	C
American ☎ 800/433-7300	B	D	C
American Eagle ☎ 800/433-7300	B		
British Airways ☎ 800/247-9297		D	E
Continental ☎ 800/525-0280	B	B	C
Continental Express ☎ 800/525-0280	B	B	
Delta ☎ 800/221-1212	B	B	B
DeltaConnection ☎ 800/221-1212	B	B	
Delta Shuttle ☎ 800/221-1212	B		
El Al Israel ☎ 800/352-5747			E
Icelandair ☎ 800/223-5500			E
KLM ☎ 800/374-7747		B	
Lufthansa ☎ 800/645-3880		C	
Mexican ☎ 800/531-7921			E
Midway ☎ 800/446-4392	A		C
Midwest Express ☎ 800/452-2022		A	
Northwest ☎ 800/225-2525	A	B	C
Saudi Arabian ☎ 800/472-8342		A	
Southwest ☎ 800/435-9792			C
Spanair ☎ 888/545-5757		A	
TWA ☎ 800/221-2000	A	D	D
United ☎ 800/241-6522	B	C, D	A, B
United Express ☎ 800/241-6522		A	
US Airways ☎ 800/428-4322	B, C	B	D
US Airways Express ☎ 800/428-4322	C		
US Airways Shuttle ☎ 800/428-4322	C		
Virgin Atlantic ☎ 800/468-8621		B	

Occasions (202/546–7400): this full-service company caters seated dinner parties, weddings, corporate events, and theme parties; they can accommodate anywhere from 10 to 3,000 guests.

Ridgewell's (301/652–1515): the sight of Ridgewell's distinctive purple trucks is a tip-off that someone is having a party; this venerable caterer has served Washingtonians for decades. Parties, usually at homes, offices, historic sites, government buildings, and outdoor venues, can range from 8 to 5,000.

Susan Gage Catering (301/839–6900): the company turning out this fresh, innovative, American cuisine is in constant demand by diplomats, political luminaries, corporate executives, private entertainers, and museums. Party sizes can range from 2 to 2,000.

kids' parties

Amusements Unlimited (301/681–8060): sure to please children young and old this firm rents carousels and other carnival rides for kiddie birthday parties, company picnics, corporate openings, and other events.

CHARITIES

Capital Area Food Bank (645 Taylor St. NE, 202/526–5344): collects food from companies, stores, and farms and donates it to local feeding programs at schools, churches, and social-service agencies. The group regularly solicits cash and food donations.

Community for Creative Non-Violence (CCNV; 425 2nd St. NW, 202/393–1909): provides food and shelter for the homeless and offers drug and alcohol counseling. Blankets, warm clothing, and food donations are all welcome.

Goodwill Industries (2200 South Dakota Ave. NE, 202/636– 4233): trains people with disabilities to repair and sell donated merchandise. For general donation information, contact the number above; to donate a car, call 202/636–4237.

Salvation Army (Administrative offices: 2626 Pennsylvania Ave. NW, 202/756–2600): donate your gently used clothing and furniture to the Salvation Army stores throughout the area; you can also call to schedule a pickup. For furniture pickups in Virginia, call 703/642–9270; in Maryland and in the District, call 301/277–7878.

Share Our Strength (733 15th St. NW, Suite 640, 202/393– 2925 or 800/969–4767): provides direct food assistance and job training to enable low-income earners to become economically self-sufficient.

CHILD CRISIS

The following agencies investigate cases of child abuse and neglect.

Child Abuse and Neglect (Department of Human Services, 202/576–6762).

Child and Family Services Agency (202/671–5683): government agency dealing with child abuse and neglect; also recruits foster and adoptive homes.

District of Columbia Office of Early Childhood Development (717 14th St. NW, 202/727–1839): city agency determines which children are eligible for various community services.

Foster Care (Department of Human Services; 202/724–2023).

CITY GOVERNMENT

complaints

Employment Discrimination (202/724–1385).

Pest Control (202/645–6188).

Restaurant Complaints (202/442–5919).

Sewer Emergency (202/673–6600).

Tenant Management/Public Housing (202/535–1141).

Utility Work Repair (Electric 202/833–7500, Gas 202/750– 1000).

COAST GUARD

For information, call 800/418–7314.

CONSUMER PROTECTION

Better Business Bureau (202/393–8000).

Consumer Complaints (202/727–7770).

Consumers Union (202/462–6262).

Fraud Hotline (202/727–0267).

Public Citizen Consumer Information Center (202/588–1000).

COUNSELING & REFERRALS

aids
Agency for HIV/AIDS (202/727–2500).

HIV/AIDS Hotline (202/332–1437): 24-hour service.

Whitman-Walker Clinic (202/797–3500).

alcoholism treatment
Alcohol Abuse Hotline (888/294–3572).

Alcohol and Drug Abuse Services Administration (202/727– 0668).

Alcoholics Anonymous: for 24-hour meeting information in D.C. and Maryland call 202/966–9115; in Virginia, call 703/876–6166.

crime victims
Adult Protective Services (202/727–2345).

Child Protective Services (202/671–7233).

Crime Solvers (202/393–2222).

Crisis Prevention: 24-hour hot lines are available in Montgomery County (301/738–2255), Prince George's County (301/864–7161), and Northern Virginia (703/527–4011).

drug abuse treatment
Alcohol and Drug Hotline (202/783–1300).

Alcohol and Drug Abuse Services Administration (202/727–0668).

Drug Treatment Referrals (800/662–4357).

Prevention and Treatment Information (800/729–6686).

mental health
Emergency Psychiatric Services Hotline (202/673–9319).

Youth Crisis Hotline (800/448–4663).

rape victims
D.C. Rape Crisis Center (202/333–7273): 24-hour hot line.

National Organization for Victim Assistance (202/232–6682).

DOCTOR & DENTIST REFERRALS

D.C. Dental Society (202/547–7615).

George Washington University Hospital (888/449–3627).

Prologue (202/362–8677): locates doctors, dentists, and urgent-care clinics in the greater Washington area.

EMERGENCIES

ambulance
Dial 911.

hospital emergency rooms
Alexandria Hospital (4320 Seminary Rd., Alexandria, VA, 703/504–3000).

Children's National Medical Center (111 Michigan Ave. NW, 202/884–5000).

D.C. General Hospital (19 Massachusetts Ave. SE, 202/675–7888).

George Washington University Hospital (901 23rd St. NW, 202/994–4911).

Greater Southeast Community Hospital (1310 Southern Ave. NW, 202/574–5641).

Howard University Hospital (2041 Georgia Ave. NW, 202/865–1141).

National Hospital Medical Center (2455 Army Navy Dr., Arlington, VA, 703/553–2417).

Northern Virginia Community Hospital (601 S. Carlin Springs Rd., Arlington, VA, 703/671–1200).

Providence Hospital (1150 Varnum St. NE, 202/269–7000).

Suburban Hospital (8600 Old Georgetown Rd., Bethesda, MD, 301/896–3100).

Washington Adventist Hospital (7600 Carroll Ave., Takoma Park, MD, 301/891–7600).

Washington Hospital Center (110 Irving St. NW, 202/877–5515).

poison control centers

D.C. (202/625–3333).

Lead Poisoning Control Unit (202/442–5828).

suicide prevention

Crisis Hotline (202/561–7000).

Northern Virginia Hotline (703/527–4077).

Prince George's County Hotline (301/731–0004).

FAMILY PLANNING

Planned Parenthood (202/347–8512).

GAY & LESBIAN CONCERNS

Gay Community (Human Rights) (202/724–1385).

Gay and Lesbian Hotline (7–11 PM) (202/833–3234).

HIV/AIDS Hotline (202/332–1437).

HOUSECLEANING AGENCIES

Jiffy Maids (202/638–7703).

Maid Brigade (800/515–6243): for Northwest and Waterfront, call 301/946–5550; for Southeast, Northeast, and Capitol Hill, call 703/823–1726.

Maid to Clean (202/424–3099).

Merry Maids (202/244–6773).

INTERIOR DESIGNER & ARCHITECT REFERRALS

American Institute of Architects (Washington Chapter, 1777 Church St. NW, 202/667–1798).

American Society of Interior Design (Washington Metropolitan Chapter, 300 D St. SW [Design Center], 202/488–4100).

LANDLORD/ TENANT ASSISTANCE

Landlord Tenant Court (202/879–1156).

Tenant Rights/Landlord Relations (202/442–4610).

Tenant's Advocacy Coalition (202/628–3688).

LEGAL SERVICES

American Civil Liberties Union (ACLU; 202/544–1681).

AYUDA (202/387–4848): serves the Hispanic community.

Legal Aid Society of the District of Columbia (202/628–1161).

LOST & FOUND

at airlines & airports

Baltimore-Washington International Airport (410/859–7387).

Dulles International Airport (703/572–2954; after two days call 703/572–8479).

Ronald Reagan National Airport (703/417–8560).

on other public transportation

Amtrak (800/872–7245 or 202/484–7540.)

MARC (800/325–7245).

Metro (202/962–1195): leave message.

Virginia Rail Express (703/658–6200).

lost animals

Animal Shelter/Animal Control (202/576–6664).

lost credit cards

American Express (800/843–2273).

Discover Card Services (800/347–2783).

MasterCard International (800/962–3364).

Visa USA (800/336–8472).

lost traveler's checks

American Express (800/221–7282).

Thomas Cook (800/223–7373).

ON-LINE SERVICES

Many of these services come and go. For the latest list, consult the Computer Services Directory of the *Washington Post*'s Monday business insert or "Internet Services" in the Yellow Pages.

AOL (703/265–1000).

Bell Atlantic (800/638–5215).

DoubleD (703/912–6636).

Radix Net (301/567–9831).

Starpower (877/782–7769).

Sysnet Communications (301/664–6000).

Tidalwave Telephone (888/400–9283).

World Data Network (703/648–0808).

PETS

adoptions

Adoption Hotline (202/529–7634).

D.C. Animal Shelter (1201 New York Ave. NE, 202/576–6664).

Washington Animal Rescue League (71 Oglethorpe St. NW, 202/726–2273).

Washington Humane Society (7319 Georgia Ave. NW, 202/723–5730).

grooming

A Clip Above (1444 Addison Rd., Capitol Heights, MD, 301/350–8888).

The Animal Hut (4620 Wisconsin Ave. NW, 202/363–5891).

sitting

Peace of Mind Pet Sitters (301/613–7487).

Sit-a-Pet (703/243–3311).

training

Merit Puppy Training (3265 S St. NW., 703/461–7387).

Olde Towne School for Dogs (529 Oronoco St., Alexandria, VA, 703/836–7643).

veterinary hospitals

Adams-Morgan Animal Clinic (2112 18th St. NW, 202/638–7470).

Jane's Veterinary Clinic (520 8th St. SE, 202/543–6699).

MacArthur Animal Hospital (4832 MacArthur Blvd. NW, 202/337–0120).

Ross Veterinary Hospital (5138 MacArthur Blvd. NW, 202/363–1316).

PHARMACIES OPEN 24 HOURS

CVS Pharmacy (14th St. and Thomas Circle NW, 202/628–0720; 7 Dupont Circle NW, 202/785–1466).

POLICE

Emergency (911).

Non-Emergency (202/727–1010).

metropolitan (d.c.) police community centers

First District (415 4th St. SW, 202/727–4655; substation: 500 E. St. SE, 202/727–4660).

Second District/Headquarters (3320 Idaho Ave. NW, 202/282–0070).

Third District (1624 V St. NW, 202/673–8615).

Fourth District (6001 Georgia Ave. NW, 202/576–6745).

Fifth District (1805 Bladensburg Ave. NE, 202/727–4510).

Sixth District (100 42nd St. NE, 202/727–4520).

Seventh District (2455 Alabama Ave. SE, 202/698–1500).

Harbor Branch (550 Water St. SW, 202/727–4582).

U.S. Park Police (202/619–7300).

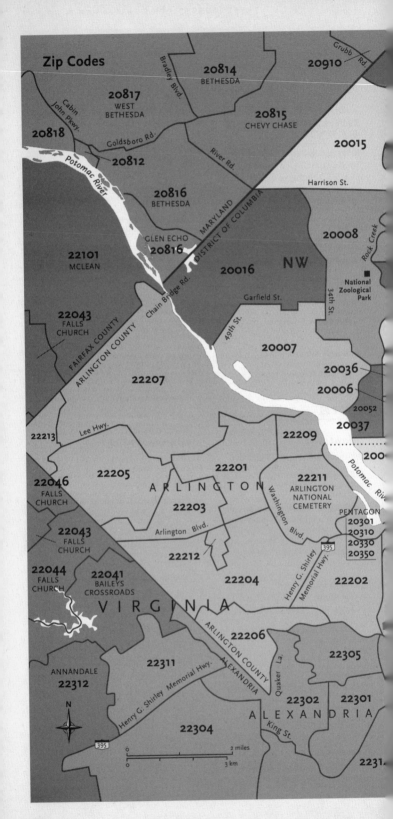

Zip Codes

20910

20814
BETHESDA

20817
WEST
BETHESDA

Bradley Blvd.

Grubb Rd.

20818

Cabin John Pkwy.

Goldsboro Rd.

20812

20815
CHEVY CHASE

20015

River Rd.

Potomac River

20816
BETHESDA

Harrison St.

GLEN ECHO
20816

MARYLAND

DISTRICT OF COLUMBIA

20008

22101
MCLEAN

20016

NW

Rock Creek

National
Zoological
Park

22043
FALLS
CHURCH

Chain Bridge Rd.

Garfield St.

49th St.

34th St.

FAIRFAX COUNTY

ARLINGTON COUNTY

22207

20007

20036

20006

20052

20037

22213

Lee Hwy.

22209

200

Potomac Riv

22046
FALLS
CHURCH

22205

A R L I N G T O N

22201

22211
ARLINGTON
NATIONAL
CEMETERY

PENTAGON
20301
20310
20330
20350

22043
FALLS
CHURCH

22203

Arlington Blvd.

Washington Blvd.

22044
FALLS
CHURCH

22041
BAILEYS
CROSSROADS

22212

22204

395

Henry G. Shirley Memorial Hwy.

22202

V I R G I N I A

22206

Quaker La.

22305

ANNANDALE
22312

22311

ARLINGTON COUNTY

ALEXANDRIA

Henry G. Shirley Memorial Hwy.

N

22302

22301

395

22304

King St.

A L E X A N D R I A

2 miles

3 km

2231.

230

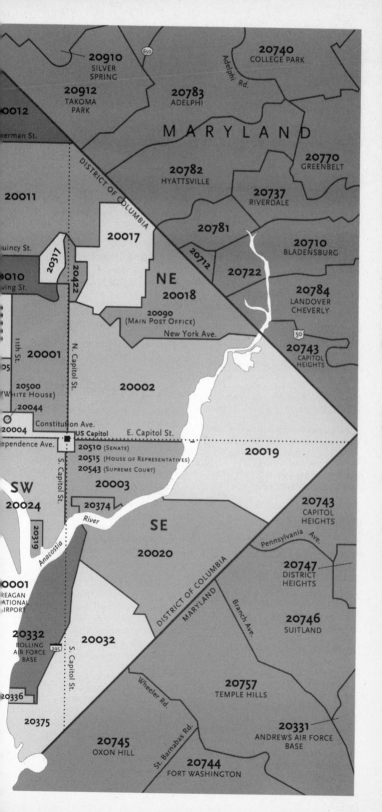

20910 SILVER SPRING

20912 TAKOMA PARK

0012

kerman St.

650

20783 ADELPHI

Adelphi Rd.

20740 COLLEGE PARK

M A R Y L A N D

20011

DISTRICT OF COLUMBIA

uincy St.

20317

0010
ving St.

11th St.

05

20001

N. Capitol St.

20500
(WHITE HOUSE)

20044

20004

Constitution Ave.

ependence Ave.

US Capitol

20510 (SENATE)
20515 (HOUSE OF REPRESENTATIVES)
20543 (SUPREME COURT)

S. Capitol St.

SW

20024

20319

20422

20017

NE

20018

20090
(MAIN POST OFFICE)

New York Ave.

20002

E. Capitol St.

20003

20374

Anacostia River

SE

20020

20782 HYATTSVILLE

20770 GREENBELT

20737 RIVERDALE

20781

20712

20722

20710 BLADENSBURG

20784 LANDOVER CHEVERLY

50

20743 CAPITOL HEIGHTS

20019

20743 CAPITOL HEIGHTS

Pennsylvania Ave.

20747 DISTRICT HEIGHTS

20746 SUITLAND

0001
REAGAN
ATIONAL
IRPORT

20332 BOLLING AIR FORCE BASE

295

20032

S. Capitol St.

DISTRICT OF COLUMBIA

MARYLAND

Branch Ave.

20336

20375

Wheeler Rd.

20757 TEMPLE HILLS

20331 ANDREWS AIR FORCE BASE

20745 OXON HILL

St. Barnabas Rd.

20744 FORT WASHINGTON

POSTAL SERVICES

united states postal service
Main offices:

2 Massachusetts Ave. NE (202/523–2323).

900 Brentwood Rd. NE (202/635–5300).

fedex
To find drop-off locations near you, call 800/463–3339.

ups
Two UPS offices are open weekdays from 8 to 7: 6335 Sweitzer Road, Laurel, Maryland, and 14800 Flint Lee Road, Chantilly, Virginia. The office at 5601 Eisenhower Avenue, in Alexandria, Virginia, is open weekdays from 9 to 7. Call 800/742–5877 for other drop-off locations and estimated charges.

SENIOR CITIZEN SERVICES

Department of Health (202/724–5626): information on nursing-home facilities.

Department of Recreation Senior Services (202/576–8677): information on recreational activities for the elderly.

Elder Abuse Adult Protective Services Hotline (202/727– 2345).

Inheritance and Estate Tax Information (202/727–6080).

TELEVISION– CABLE COMPANIES

District Cablevision (202/635–5100).

Stansbury Decker Satellite System (800/487–9602).

Washington Cable (202/646–5102).

UTILITIES

gas
Washington Gas (703/750–1000): turn-on and turn-off, appliance adjustments, service calls, billing, and general information.

electric
Potomac Electric Power Company (202/833–7500): turn-on and turn-off, billing and credit, and general customer information.

telephone
Bell Atlantic (202/954–6263): customer service.

water
D.C. Public Works Department, Water and Sewer Utility Administration (202/645–6365).

important telephone numbers
Energy Hotline (202/673–6750).

Heating Bill Assistance (202/673–3071).

Sewer Emergency (202/727–6600).

Utility Work Repair (electric 202/833–7500, gas 202/750–1000).

VOLUNTEERING

The Washington area is full of opportunities to help others. Many people wait until the holiday season to pitch in, but folks need help year-round. Following are just a few organizations that always need volunteers:

D.C. Central Kitchen (425 Second St. NW, rear entrance, 202/234–0707): nonprofit organization that recovers safe, leftover food from businesses to feed people at social- service agencies. Volunteers are needed to help in sorting and preparing food.

Food & Friends (58 L St. SE, 202/863–1824): provides nutritious meals and groceries to individuals and families homebound with AIDS and other serious illnesses. Volunteers are needed to pack and deliver groceries and to prepare and deliver meals. Food donations are also welcome.

Mary House (3012 14th St. NW, 202/635–9025): privately funded organization providing shelter and support for immigrant families new to Washington. Volunteers are needed to help with housing renovation and upkeep, and tutoring and mentoring. Knowledge of a foreign language is welcome, but not required.

Pets D.C. (2001 O St. NW, 202/463–7387): offers care for companion animals belonging to people with AIDS, enabling them to keep their pets even if illness prevents them from properly caring for them. Volunteers are needed to care for animals and to visit clients; training sessions are held.

Sasha Bruce YouthWork Inc. (741 8th St. SE, 202/675–9340): Community organization helping at-risk youths, including group housing for teen mothers and their babies. Volunteers are needed for Big Brothers and Sisters mentoring, tutoring, and residential assistance. Food and clothing donations are always appreciated.

ZONING & PLANNING

Office of Zoning, Zoning Adjustment, Zoning Commission (202/727–6311).

learning

ACTING SCHOOLS

Arena Stage (6th St. and Maine Ave. SW, 202/588–8113): workshops and classes lasting from one day to six weeks.

National Conservatory of Dramatic Arts (1556 Wisconsin Ave. NW, 202/333–2202): accredited classes, days and evenings.

Studio Theatre Acting Conservatory (1333 P St. NW, 202/232–7267): introductory and realism classes, voice, and musical theater.

Theatre Lab (202/588–8113): beginning through advanced classes in voice, speech, and more. Class locations vary.

Washington Actors Training Company (4100 Massachusetts Ave. NW, 202/364–8433): variety of classes at different sites.

ADULT EDUCATION IN PUBLIC SCHOOLS

D.C. Public Schools (202/724–4222).

ART & PHOTOGRAPHY SCHOOLS

Capitol Hill Arts Workshop (CHAW; 545 7th St. SE, 202/547–6839): community arts school offering classes in drawing, painting, ceramics, computer graphics, and flower arranging; private instruction is available.

Corcoran College of Art and Design (500 17th St. NW, 202/639–1820): Washington's only accredited school of art and design offers year-round classes in drawing, painting, photography, printmaking, and sculpture. Juried shows are held regularly in attached art museum.

Washington Studio School (3232 P St. NW, 202/333–2663): drawing, painting, printmaking, and sculpture.

Washington Very Special Arts (WVSA; 1100 16th St. NW, 202/296–9100, TTY: 202/261–0201): art gallery and studio offering arts-based vocational training to young people with disabilities (ages 14–25).

BALLROOM DANCING

Capitol Hill Arts Workshop (CHAW; 545 7th St. SE, 202/547–6839): learn to cha-cha, fox-trot, rumba, tango, and waltz.

Chevy Chase Ballroom & DanceSport Center (5207 Wisconsin Ave. NW, 202/363–8344): the gamut of ballroom and Latin dances, right down to the quickstep and jive.

Spanish Ballroom at Glen Echo Park (7300 MacArthur Blvd., Glen Echo, MD, 301/492–6229): a wide range of in-depth dance classes are offered on weekday nights. Evening and Sunday-afternoon dances are often preceded by an introductory lesson for everyone.

COLLEGES

Several nationally recognized colleges and universities throughout the D.C. area offer evening and weekend courses for adults.

American University (4400 Massachusetts Ave. NW, 202/885–1000).

Capitol College (11301 Springfield Rd., Laurel, MD, 301/953–3200): studies in engineering and information technology.

Catholic University (620 Michigan Ave. NE, 202/319–5000).

Gallaudet University (800 Florida Ave. NE, 202/651–5000): largest school in the world for people who are deaf.

George Mason University (4400 University Dr., Fairfax, VA, 703/993–1000).

George Washington University (2121 I St. NW, 202/994–1000).

Georgetown University (37th and O Sts. NW, 202/687–5055).

Howard University (2400 6th St. NW, 202/806–6100).

Marymount University (2807 N. Glebe Rd., Arlington, VA, 703/522–5600).

Prince George's County Community College (301 Largo Rd., Largo, MD, 301/336–6000).

Southeastern University (501 I St. SW, 202/488–8162).

Strayer College (202/722–8100): business courses at several locations.

Trinity College (125 Michigan Ave. NE, 202/884–9000).

University of the District of Columbia (4200 Connecticut Ave. NW, 202/274–5000).

University of Maryland (College Park, MD, 301/405–1000).

COMPUTER TRAINING

Ameritrain (8245 Boone Blvd., Suite 250, Tysons Corner, VA, 888/700–8765): day and evening sessions, long-term programs, 11-day intensive training courses, placement services.

Computer ABC's, "Training for the Terrified" (7001 Hopewood St., Bethesda, MD, 301/320–2595): At-home computer-literacy classes, from the basics to software to the Internet.

Computer Learning Institute (4429 Wisconsin Ave. NW, 202/237–8121).

Computer Institute (1335 Rockville Pike, third floor, Rockville, MD, 301/424–0044 or 703/849–0099).

GS Graduate School USDA (600 Maryland Ave. SW, course information 202/314–3650, registration 202/314–3320): the U.S. Department of Agriculture offers evening and weekend courses in beginning and advanced computer technology, software applications, the Internet, and other subjects. Classes are conducted in various convenient locations, all near Metro stops.

COOKING SCHOOLS

L'Academie de Cuisine (5021 Wilson La., Bethesda, MD, 301/986–9490; 16006 Industrial Dr., Gaithersburg, MD, 301/670–8670): beginning and advanced cooking classes, including accredited professional training in all aspects of the culinary arts. Scholarships are available.

Chinese Cookery Inc. (14209 Sturtevant Rd., Silver Spring, MD, 301/236–5311): five-week courses in Chinese cooking feature demonstration and participation.

École de Cuisine de La Varenne (202/337–0073): two- month program of cooking classes at the Greenbrier Resort in White Sulphur Springs, West Virginia, approximately a four-hour drive from Washington, D.C.

Robyn Webb's "A Pinch of Thyme" (308 S. Payne St., Alexandria, VA, 703/683–5034): year-round classes geared to the home chef stress low-fat cooking.

Thai Cookery (Thai Basil Restaurant, Rte. 50, Chantilly, VA, 703/631–8277): learn to cook with noodles, coconut-milk, Asian basil, lemongrass, and hot peppers.

DANCE

Capitol Hill Arts Workshop (CHAW; 545 7th St. SE, 202/547– 6839): jazz, modern, hip-hop, and more for adults and children; occasional classes in African dance, Irish step dance, and other international styles.

Dance Place (3225 8th St. NE, 202/269–1600): modern, African, jazz, hip-hop, Latin, and stretch.

Erika Thimey Dance & Theater Company, Inc. (730 9th St. SE, 202/543–2081): professional nonprofit arts organization providing instruction in traditional and modern dance for all ages, plus performances.

Washington School of Ballet (3515 Wisconsin Ave. NW, 202/362–1683): graded classes for all levels; adult programs.

LANGUAGE SCHOOLS

Berlitz (1050 Connecticut Ave. NW, 202/331–1160): native speakers conduct private and group classes in dozens of languages.

GS Graduate School USDA (course info 202/314–3650, registration 202/314–3320): evening and weekend courses in 28 foreign languages taught by native speakers are geared to government workers. Classes are conducted in various convenient locations, all close to Metro stops.

International Center for Language Studies (727 15th St. NW, Ste. 400, 202/639–8800): day and evening classes in more than 70 languages; small groups or private instruction.

International Language Institute (4301 Connecticut Ave. NW, 202/362–2505): instruction offered in more than 30 languages, including English.

Professional Speech Associates (2 Wisconsin Circle, Suite 700, Chevy Chase, MD, 202/362–9777): public speaking, accent modification.

esl

International Language Institute (4301 Connecticut Ave. NW, 202/362–2505).

SED Center (1840 Kalorama Rd. NW, 202/462–8848): low-cost "survival" English.

french

Alliance Française de Washington (2142 Wyoming Ave. NW, 202/234–7911): French for all levels, taught by native speakers; private and group lessons, including total immersion sessions.

italian

Casa Italiana (595 ½ 3rd St. NW, 202/638–1348): qualified native speakers teach Italian to adults and children at a cultural center/church; evening, weekend, and immersion courses are offered.

japanese

RICE Japanese Program, (5335 Wisconsin Ave. NW, Suite 900, 202/537–7423): well-established school with evening classes for small groups of 3 to 10 students; private instruction also available.

russian

Specialized Russian Training Center (4 Monroe St., Suite 1304, Rockville, MD, 800/839–7987): individually tailored Russian-language programs and refresher courses.

spanish

SED Center (1840 Kalorama Rd. NW, 202/462–8848): low-cost Spanish classes in Adams-Morgan location.

MUSIC SCHOOLS

Duke Ellington School of the Arts (3500 R St. NW, 202/965–3141): well-known, highly regarded school teaching drama, all kinds of music, and voice.

Levine School of Music (2801 Upton St. NW, 202/686–9772): private lessons and group classes in everything from piano to voice to woodwinds to musical theater.

WINE PROGRAMS

D.C. Tasting Society (202/338–5588): promotes wine knowledge and enjoyment through a series of tastings and seminars held at local restaurants, hotels, and embassies.

The Sommelier Wine & Food Society (3609 9th St., Arlington, VA, 703/685–7970): nine-week courses winter, spring, and fall; one-night classes also available.

vacation & travel information

AIRLINES

For lost items, *see* Lost & Found *in* Resources for Challenges & Crises, *above.*

Aeroflot (800/955–5555).

Aeromexico (800/237–6639).

Air Canada (800/776–3000).

Air France (800/237–2747).

Air Nippon (800/235–9262).

AirTran (800/247–8726).

America West (800/235–9292).

American, American Eagle (800/433–7300).

Austrian (800/843–0002).

British Airways (800/247–9297).

Continental (800/525–0280).

Delta, Connection Carrier, Express, Shuttle (800/221–1212).

Eastwind (888/327–8946).

Frontier (800/432–1359).

Icelandair (800/223–5500).

KLM (800/374–7747).

Korean (800/438–5000).

Lufthansa (800/645–3880).

Midway (800/446–4392).

Midwest Express (800/452–2022).

Northwest (800/225–2525).

Pakistan International (800/221–6024).

Pan American (800/359–7262).

Qantas (800/227–4500).

Sabena (800/955–2000).

SAS (800/221–2350).

Saudia (800/472–8342).

Southwest (800/435–9792).

Spanair (800/545–5757).

Swissair (800/221–4750).

TACA (800/535–8780).

Transbrasil (800/872–3153).

TWA, TWA Express (800/221–2000).

United, Express (800/241–6522).

USAirways, Express, Shuttle (800/428–4322).

Varig (800/468–2744).

Virgin Atlantic (800/862–8621).

Western Pacific (800/930–3030).

airline complaints

U.S. Department of Transportation Aviation Consumer Protection Division (202/366–2220).

FAA Consumer Hotline (800/322–7873).

AIRPORTS

getting there by public transportation

SUBWAY

Unless you have heaps of luggage or live far from a Metro stop, Metrorail is the best way to reach Ronald Reagan National Airport. The Yellow and Blue lines go there directly (with fewer stops, the Yellow is much faster than the Blue line). Metro riders can walk directly from the subway platform to a walkway leading to the airport's main terminal; a free shuttle bus goes to terminal A.

The Washington Flyer express bus line serves Ronald Reagan National, Dulles, and the Washington Convention Center with stops at the West Falls Church (Orange Line) Metrorail station. Hotel pickups can be arranged at the Grand Hyatt, Harrington, J. W. Marriott, Courtyard Marriott, Marriott Wardman Park, Mayflower, Omni Shoreham, Washington Hilton, and Washington Renaissance hotels. Call 703/685–1400 for schedules and fares.

SHUTTLE LIMOUSINE

Shuttle prices to Ronald Reagan National Airport range from about $8 (from Dupont Circle) to about $26 (from Southeast and Brookland). Prices to Dulles International Airport range from about $17 (from Chevy Chase) to about $26 (from D.C.). Prices to Baltimore–Washington International Airport range from about $25 (from parts of Chevy Chase and Brookland) to about $40 (from D.C.).

Airport Express (301/588–0455 or 800/977–2828).

Montgomery Airport Shuttle (301/590–0000).

Royal Airport Shuttle (301/657–0888 or 800/653–0888).

Suburban Shuttle (301/279–2222 or 800/996–9393).

SuperShuttle (800/258–3826).

United Transport Services (800/517–5288).

TRAIN

Baltimore–Washington International Airport is served by Amtrak (800/872–7245) and MARC (Penn line only; 800/325– 7245) trains from Union Station and New Carrollton; a shuttle bus meets each train. The trip from the station to the terminals takes about 15 to 20 minutes, depending on traffic. The MARC fare is $5 one-way, $8.75 round-trip; the Amtrak fare is $15.

getting there by car

Dulles International: take I–66 to Exit 67, the Dulles Access Road. (From D.C., reach 66 via I–395 or Constitution Avenue.) The airport is 26 mi west of Washington.

Ronald Reagan National: take I–395 or I–95 to the George Washington Parkway. Follow signs to the airport.

Baltimore–Washington International: take the Baltimore– Washington Parkway (I–295) to the BWI exit, which puts you on I–195 east, a direct route to the airport. The airport is about 35 mi northeast of Washington.

AIRPORT PARKING

All airport parking lots accept major credit cards.

Ronald Reagan National: there are four parking areas. Lot A has hourly sections near Terminal A and daily and rental-car sections on the Crystal City side. Lot B, across the Metrorail station from Terminal B, in the new building, has multilevel hourly and daily sections. Lot C, a multilevel hourly and daily lot immediately past Lot B (across the Metrorail station from Terminal C in the new building), is farthest north. Remote parking is at the Alexandria end of the terminal, next to the General Aviation entrance. It's often wise to choose your parking lot based on your airline. For USAirways, choose C; Continental, Midway, Northwest, TWA, and TWA Express are closest to A. For other airlines, it's essentially a toss-up, to be decided by traffic and space (as indicated by the signs outside the lots' entrances). The remote lot is served by shuttle bus.

Finding a space is generally no problem, but Fridays and holidays can be difficult. The current hourly rate is $2 each half hour for the first two hours, $4 per hour thereafter, to a maximum of $28 for 24 hours. The daily rate is $2 per hour, to a maximum of $12 for 24 hours. Remote parking is $1 per hour, to a maximum of $8 for 24 hours. Call 703/417–4311 for a recording on rates and parking-space availability, or tune to 530 AM on your radio when approaching the airport.

SunPark, across from the Crystal City Hyatt and minutes away from National, offers hassle-free parking for $7.50 a day, with shuttle service. Call 703/416–5095 or 888/507–0004.

Dulles International: short-term (hourly) parking is available in front of the Main Terminal and is intended for passenger pickup and drop-off. It costs $3 for the first hour, $4 per hour for the second through seventh hour, to a maximum of $27 for 24 hours. Daily (general) Parking Lot 1 is located just beyond the hourly lot in front of the Main Terminal; it's aimed at those who wish to leave their cars for a few days. Rates are $5 per hour, to a maximum of $10 for 24 hours. Daily (general) Parking Lot 2 is located east of the Main Terminal and is also for extended stays. Rates are $5 per hour, to a maximum of $10 for 24 hours. For all three parking areas, there is no charge if you stay less than 20 minutes.

Long-term (economy) parking is available in the Blue, Green, and Red lots located along the North Service Road away from the Main Terminal. Free shuttle service is provided, at 10- to 15-minute intervals, for picking up and discharging passengers 24 hours a day, seven days a week. Rates are $1 per hour, to a maximum of $6 per 24 hours.

Valet parking, available directly in front of the Main Terminal, is geared to the traveler with more money than time. Go to the main parking-lot level through the hourly entrance and follow the signs to the Valet Service Center. Service is provided 24 hours a day, seven days a week. Rates are $20 for the first 24 hours, $12 each additional day or fraction thereof. For more information, call 703/661–5742.

Wheelchair-accessible parking is provided in the hourly lot at daily rates and at economy parking lots in spaces next to the shuttle-bus stops.

As you approach the airport, tune your radio to 530 AM for up-to-the-minute details on parking rates, locations, and availability.

Baltimore–Washington International: the garage in front of the terminal is for passenger pickup and drop-off; the first half hour is free, after which you'll pay $2 per half hour, to a maximum of $12 for 24 hours. The Park N Walk lot is for slightly longer short-term parking, at $2 an hour to a maximum of $9 for 24 hours; there's no shuttle service, but you can make the trek to the terminal on moving walkways.

For long-term parking, the 8,700-space satellite lot is the most economical option: follow the blue highway signs to the lot on Maryland Route 170/Aviation Boulevard. A free shuttle runs to and from the terminal roughly every 10 minutes; allow an additional 45 minutes' travel time for this ride. Satellite parking costs $1 per hour, to a daily maximum of $7. The seventh day is free.

Express Service Parking (ESP) offers personalized parking service for overnight stays, allowing you to park your own car and be whisked to the terminal in a shuttle bus that picks you up *at* your car and takes you back to your car when you return. ESP is $4 per hour, to a maximum of $12 per day.

CAR RENTAL

major agencies
You must be 21 years old to rent a car in D.C., and the rate may be higher if you're under 25. Multiple drivers cost extra, as may child seats. A major credit card is usually required.

Alamo (800/327–9633).

Avis (800/831–2847).

Budget (800/527–0700).

Dollar (800/800–4000).

Hertz (800/654–3131).

National (800/227–7368).

local agencies
These companies don't have airport branches, but do have locations scattered throughout the area.

Standard Leasing Corporation (4720 Baltimore Ave., Hyattsville, MD, 301/699–1030).

Total Car Rental (800/382–2520): one- to three-month rentals at locations in Alexandria, Arlington, Rockville, and D.C.

CURRENCY EXCHANGE

If you're going abroad, you may want to buy some foreign currency before you leave, just in case there's a long line (or terrible rates) at the airport you enter. D.C. has several vendors of foreign currency, but not as many as you might expect; there are a few in the city center, open weekdays, and more in suburban shopping centers, with similar hours. Most exchanges are handled on the spot, but you may have to come back a day or so later for exotic currencies or very large amounts. Phone ahead to confirm that what you want is on hand.

Many banks sell traveler's checks, which you can buy in U.S. dollars and sometimes in any of several foreign currencies. Traveler's checks are issued by American Express, MasterCard, and Visa and are accepted worldwide.

American Express Travel Services (1150 Connecticut Ave. NW, 202/457–1300; Mazza Galleria, 5300 Wisconsin Ave. NW, 202/362–4000; 1864 Galleria, McLean, VA, 703/893–3550; Springfield Mall, Springfield, VA, 703/971–5600; Pentagon City Mall, Arlington, VA, 703/415–5400).

Capital Foreign Exchange (825 14th St. NW, 888/842–0880): highly recommended for the variety and ready availability of foreign currency, and for the congeniality of the staff.

Riggs Bank (800 17th St. NW, 202/835–6767): some branches conduct foreign exchange; hours and services vary. For recorded information on current exchange rates, call 202/835–5119.

Thomas Cook (1800 K St. NW, 202/872–1233; Union Station, across from Amtrak Departures; Dulles Airport, east and west ends of Main Terminal, International Arrivals, Midfield; National Airport, National Hall North, National Hall South, and adjacent to South Pier): for hours and information on currency availability, call 800/622–5058 or 202/872–1233, weekdays 8:30–8.

EMBASSIES

Antigua and Barbuda (3216 New Mexico Ave. NW, 202/362– 5122).

Argentina (1600 New Hampshire Ave. NW, 202/939–6400).

Australia (1601 Massachusetts Ave. NW, 202/797–3000).

Austria (3524 International Ct. NW, 202/895–6700).

Bahamas (2220 Massachusetts Ave. NW, 202/319–2660).

Bahrain (3502 International Dr. NW, 202/342–0741).

Barbados (2144 Wyoming Ave. NW, 202/939–9200).

Belarus (1619 New Hampshire Ave. NW, 202/986–1604).

Belgium (3330 Garfield St. NW, 202/333–6900).

Belize (2535 Massachusetts Ave. NW, 202/332–9636).

Benin (2737 Cathedral Ave. NW, 202/232–6656).

Bolivia (3014 Massachusetts Ave. NW, 202/483–4410).

Bosnia and Herzegovina (2109 E St. NW, 202/337–1500).

Brazil (3006 Massachusetts Ave. NW, 202/238–2700).

Bulgaria (1621 22nd St. NW, 202/387–7969).

Canada (501 Pennsylvania Ave. NW, 202/682–1740).

Chile (1732 Massachusetts Ave. NW, 202/785–1746).

China (2300 Connecticut Ave. NW, 202/328–2500).

Colombia (2118 Leroy Pl. NW, 202/387–8338).

Congo (1800 New Hampshire Ave. NW, 202/234–7690).

Costa Rica (2114 S St. NW, 202/234–2945).

Croatia (2343 Massachusetts Ave. NW, 202/588–5899).

Cyprus (2211 R St. NW, 202/462–5772).

Czech Republic (3900 Spring of Freedom St. NW, 202/274– 9100).

Denmark (3200 Whitehaven St. NW, 202/234–4300).

Dominican Republic (1715 22nd St. NW, 202/332–6280).

Ecuador (2535 15th St. NW, 202/234–7200).

Egypt (2310 Decatur Pl. NW, 202/895–5400).

El Salvador (2308 California St. NW, 202/265–9671).

Estonia (2131 Massachusetts Ave. NW, 202/588–0101).

Ethiopia (2134 Kalorama Rd. NW, 202/234–2281).

Fiji (2233 Wisconsin Ave. NW, 202/337–8320).

Finland (3301 Massachusetts Ave. NW, 202/298–5800).

France (4101 Reservoir Rd. NW, 202/944–6000).

Georgia (1511 K St. NW, 202/393–5959).

Germany (4645 Reservoir Rd. NW, 202/298–4000).

Greece (2221 Massachusetts Ave. NW, 202/939–5800).

Grenada (1701 New Hampshire Ave. NW, 202/265–2561).

Guatemala (2220 R St. NW, 202/745–4952).

Guinea (2112 Leroy Pl. NW, 202/483–9420).

Guyana (2490 Tracy Pl. NW, 202/265–6900).

Haiti (2311 Massachusetts Ave. NW, 202/332–4090).

Honduras (3007 Tilden St. NW, 202/966–7702).

Hungary (3910 Shoemaker St. NW, 202/362–6730).

Iceland (1156 15th St. NW, 202/265–6653).

India (2107 Massachusetts Ave. NW, 202/939–7000).

Indonesia (2020 Massachusetts Ave. NW, 202/775–5200).

Ireland (2234 Massachusetts Ave. NW, 202/462–3939).

Israel (3514 International Dr. NW, 202/364–5500).

Italy (1601 Fuller St. NW, 202/328–5500).

Jamaica (1520 New Hampshire Ave. NW, 202/452–0660).

Japan (2520 Massachusetts Ave. NW, 202/939–6700).

Jordan (3504 International Dr. NW, 202/966–2664).

Kazakhstan (3421 Massachusetts Ave. NW, 202/333–2957).

Kenya (2249 R St. NW, 202/387–6101).

Korea (2450 Massachusetts Ave. NW, 202/939–5600).

Latvia (4325 17th St. NW, 202/726–8213).

Lebanon (2560 28th St. NW, 202/939–6300).

Liberia (5201 16th St. NW, 202/723–0437).

Lithuania (2622 16th St. NW, 202/234–5860).

Luxembourg (2200 Massachusetts Ave. NW, 202/265–4171).

Madagascar (2374 Massachusetts Ave. NW, 202/265–5525).

Mali (2130 R St. NW, 202/332–2249).

Malta (2017 Connecticut Ave. NW, 202/462–3611).

Mexico (1911 Pennsylvania Ave. NW, 202/728–1600).

Moldova (2101 S St. NW, 202/667–1130).

Mongolia (2833 M St. NW, 202/333–7117).

Mozambique (1990 M St. NW, 202/293–7146).

Myanmar (2300 S St. NW, 202/332–9044).

Namibia (1605 New Hampshire Ave. NW, 202/986–0540).

Nepal (2131 Leroy Pl. NW, 202/667–4550).

Netherlands (4200 Linnean Ave. NW, 202/244–5300).

New Zealand (37 Observatory Circle NW, 202/328–4800).

Nicaragua (1627 New Hampshire Ave. NW, 202/939–6570).

Nigeria (1333 16th St. NW, 202/986–8400).

Norway (2720 34th St. NW, 202/333–6000).

Oman (2342 Massachusetts Ave. NW, 202/387–1980).

Pakistan (2315 Massachusetts Ave. NW, 202/939–6200).

Panama (2862 McGill Terr. NW, 202/483–1407).

Papua New Guinea (1615 New Hampshire Ave. NW, 202/745–3680).

Paraguay (2400 Massachusetts Ave. NW, 202/483–6960).

Peru (1700 Massachusetts Ave. NW, 202/833–9860).

Philippines (1600 Massachusetts Ave. NW, 202/467–9300).

Poland (2640 16th St. NW, 202/234–3800).

Portugal (2125 Kalorama Rd. NW, 202/328–8610).

Qatar (4200 Wisconsin Ave. NW, 202/274–1600).

Romania (1607 23rd St. NW, 202/332–4848).

Russia (2650 Wisconsin Ave. NW, 202/298–5700).

St. Kitts and Nevis (2100 M St. NW, 202/833–3550).

St. Lucia (3216 New Mexico Ave. NW, 202/364–6792).

St. Vincent and the Grenadines (3216 New Mexico Ave. NW, 202/364–6730).

Saudi Arabia (601 New Hampshire Ave. NW, 202/337–4076).

Senegal (2112 Wyoming Ave. NW, 202/234–0540).

Sierra Leone (1701 19th St. NW, 202/939–9261).

Singapore (3501 International Pl. NW, 202/537–3100).

Slovak Republic (2201 Wisconsin Ave. NW, 202/965–5160).

Slovenia (1525 New Hampshire Ave. NW, 202/667–5363).

South Africa (3051 Massachusetts Ave. NW, 202/232–4400).

Sudan (2210 Massachusetts Ave. NW, 202/338–8565).

Suriname (4301 Connecticut Ave. NW, 202/244–7488).

Sweden (1501 M St. NW, 202/467–2600).

Switzerland (2900 Cathedral Ave. NW, 202/745–7900).

Syria (2215 Wyoming Ave. NW, 202/232–6313).

Tanzania (2139 R St. NW, 202/939–6125).

Thailand (1024 Wisconsin Ave. NW, 202/944–3600).

Togo (2208 Massachusetts Ave. NW, 202/234–4212).

Trinidad and Tobago (1708 Massachusetts Ave. NW, 202/467–6490).

Tunisia (1515 Massachusetts Ave. NW, 202/862–1850).

Turkey (1714 Massachusetts Ave. NW, 202/659–8200).

Ukraine (3350 M St. NW, 202/333–0606).

United Arab Emirates (1255 22nd St. NW, 202/955–7999).

United Kingdom of Great Britain and Northern Ireland (3100 Massachusetts Ave. NW, 202/588–6500).

Uruguay (2715 M St. NW, 202/331–1313).

Vatican City (3339 Massachusetts Ave. NW, 202/333–7121).

Venezuela (1099 30th St. NW, 202/342–2214).

Vietnam (1233 20th St. NW, 202/861–0737).

Yemen (2600 Virginia Ave. NW, 202/965–4760).

Zambia (2419 Massachusetts Ave. NW, 202/265–9717).

Zimbabwe (1608 New Hampshire Ave. NW, 202/332–7100).

INOCULATIONS, VACCINATIONS, & TRAVEL HEALTH

For general information call 888/232–3228, or visit the detailed Web site of the Centers for Disease Control and Prevention at www.cdc.gov.

PASSPORTS

You must appear in person if this is the first time you're applying for a passport, your last passport was issued more than 12 years ago, or if your passport has been lost or stolen. Children under 13 need not appear in person; a parent or legal guardian may appear to apply on their behalf.

Passport application forms are available from designated post offices, court clerks, county and municipal offices, and travel agencies, or by calling the National Passport Information Center at 900/225–5674 (35¢ per minute). Forms are also available on the State Department's Consular Affairs Web site, www.travel.state.gov, an exhaustive resource. Besides filling out the forms, applicants must submit two identical recent 2″ × 2″ photos; the area around the passport office is full of passport photo shops.

Apply at least three months before your planned departure. If you need visas from foreign embassies, allow even more time. If you know the exact dates of your trip, it's a good idea to include them on your application forms, as these are processed in order of departure dates. If you're in a hurry, you can expedite the process for an additional fee. In a grave emergency after hours (such as the death of a relative abroad), call the passport duty officer at the U.S. State Department at 202/647–4000.

The fee for a new passport is $60 ($40 for travelers 15 and younger); a renewal costs $40. If you need an emergency passport for travel within the next 10 days, add $35 for "expedited service."

Passport *renewal* is best handled through the mail. Simply obtain the forms and photos as outlined above and mail them, or drop them off at the nearest passport acceptance facility.

The following facilities are in the District:

U.S. Post Office–Ben Franklin Station (12th St. and Pennsylvania Ave. NW, 202/523–2386): open weekdays 10–4.

U.S. Post Office–Friendship Heights Station (4005 Wisconsin Ave. NW, 202/635–5305): open weekdays 8–6.

passport photo agency

MotoPhoto (1105 19th St. NW, 202/293–5484).

Woodley Photo (2627 Connecticut Ave. NW, 202/265–0223).

TOURIST INFORMATION

D.C. Chamber of Commerce (202/347–7201).

D.C. Chamber of Commerce Visitors Center (Ronald Reagan Building and International Visitors Center, 1300 Pennsylvania Ave. NW, 202/328–4748): maps, guides, and interactive kiosks point visitors in the right direction. It's open Monday–Saturday 8–6; call for Sunday hours.

D.C. Government Tourist Information (202/724–5644).

U.S. CUSTOMS

General Information (202/927–6724).

VISA INFORMATION & TRAVEL ADVISORIES

International Visas and Passports Services (1312 18th St. NW, 202/293–8334): helps U.S. citizens obtain visas for traveling abroad.

U.S. Department of State Office of American Citizen Services (202/647–5225): advisories for overseas travel.

Visa Information (Department of Justice, 202/633–1225).

DIRECTORIES

alphabetical listing of resources & topics

restaurants by neighborhood

shops by neighborhood

resources & topics

restaurants by neighborhood

ADAMS-MORGAN

Bardia's New Orleans Café (Cajun/Creole), 10–11
Belmont Kitchen (American/casual), 4–5
Bukom Café (African), 3
Cashion's Eat Place (contemporary), 14
Cities (contemporary), 14
Felix (contemporary), 15
Fio's (Italian), 29
Grill From Ipanema (Brazilian), 9
I Matti (Italian), 29
La Fourchette (French), 23
Lauriol Plaza (Latin), 5, 34
Little Fountain Café (American), 4
Mama Ayesha's (Middle Eastern), 36
Meskerem (Ethiopian), 21
Millie & Al's (American/casual), 8
Mixtec (Mexican), 35
Pasta Mia (Italian), 31
Perry's (Japanese), 33
Peyote Café/Roxanne Restaurant/On the Rooftop (contemporary), 18
Red Sea (Ethiopian), 21
Rumba Cafe (Latin), 34
Star of Siam (Thai), 46
Tom Brazil (Brazilian), 9
Tom Tom (contemporary), 20
Tryst (café), 10

ADELPHI, MD

Ledo (pizza), 26, 38

ALEXANDRIA, VA

Austin Grill (Tex-Mex), 45
Blue Point Grill (seafood), 39–40
Bullfeathers (American/casual), 5
East Wind (Vietnamese), 47
Ecco Café (Italian), 28
Elysium (contemporary), 15
Faccia Luna (pizza), 38
Firehook Bakery (American/casual), 6–7
Generous George's (pizza), 38
Geranio (Italian), 29
Hard Times Cafe (American/casual), 7
Hee Been (Korean), 33
La Bergerie (French), 23
Le Gaulois (French), 24
Le Refuge (French), 24
Murphy's (American/casual), 8

shops by neighborhood

259